HERBS FOR HEALTHY LIVING

RECOGNITION, GATHERING, USE AND EFFECT

Dr Ute Künkele   Till R. Lohmeyer

HERBS FOR HEALTHY LIVING

RECOGNITION, GATHERING, USE AND EFFECT

Dr Ute Künkele   Till R. Lohmeyer

PaRragon

Bath New York Singapore Hong Kong Cologne Delhi Melbourne

The authors and the publishers

All the information in this book has been carefully researched by the authors. However, they will accept no liability for any of this information, particularly as medical, naturopathic and homeopathic opinion is often divided on the effects of some herbs in their various applications, and many of the constituents of the herbs have been insufficiently researched or not researched at all.

Plants or parts of plants may be poisonous or cause allergies in individuals. Side effects in combination with prescribed medicines also cannot be excluded. Self-treatment with herbs cannot replace medical therapies and, if improperly used, can cause considerable damage to health. The warnings given in the text for various species should be carefully noted; consult your doctor or a pharmacist.

Where there is the slightest doubt about correct identification, plants or parts of plants (leaves, berries, roots, etc.) should not be ingested or used in any other way.

The abbreviations following the scientific names of plants refer to those who first described the plant and those who first classified the plant according to the most recently applicable criteria. The frequent abbreviation 'L.' indicates that the plant has been described and named by the founder of modern plant classification, the Swedish doctor and natural historian Carolus Linnaeus (1707–1778) – for instance, marigold, *Calendula officinalis L.* If a species name has been moved to another category, the original classifier or the abbreviation of the original classifier's name will appear in brackets, e.g. the blessed milkthistle, *Silybum marianum* (Linnaeus) Gaertner or (L.) Gaertn.

Preface

This book is for all those who have kept their curiosity about things that grow and thrive in field and forest and garden and want to get to know the plants that underlie the term 'weed'. It describes old customs, forgotten uses, modern scientific knowledge and ecological matters. It shows the features by which we can recognize the plants, the healing powers they contain, and the diseases and ailments for which they can be used, but also warns against charlatans and superstition. However, it is not a medical textbook, and in the case of serious illness it can in no way replace the doctor.

There can hardly be a single area of science whose origins can be followed further back to the origins of civilization than herbal healing. Seen against the millennia in which diseases and complaints were healed or eased by doctors and healers, 'wise women' and shamans, all using plant extracts in the greatest variety of ways, modern drugs and 'hi-tech' medicine seems like a rather arrogant youth wanting to push aside the experience of his elders as 'totally irrelevant'. However, the 'young doctor' himself probably takes echinacea products and sage tea at the first hint of a cold and, when things get worse, inhales steam with chamomile.

That plants can heal and ease is hardly doubted any longer – and yet herbal therapy has a credibility problem, or two, if you prefer. One is that the effect of a herbal healing agent may be obvious due to the recovery of the patient or the easing of the symptoms, but it cannot always be demonstrated by measurable factors. This is particularly true of homeopathy, which uses greatly diluted plant extracts and – in much the same way as traditional Chinese medicine – places far greater importance on the individual condition of each patient than conventional medicine.

And yet while the decoding of the active constituents and the way in which they work has made great progress, thanks to ever more sophisticated methods of research, the second credibility problem is more stubbornly resistant to scientific analysis. This problem involves the close links between herbal therapies on the one hand and religious custom, faith healing and ritual on the other. It can be demonstrated that a root can calm a nervous stomach or help a sore throat, but scientific methods cannot explain why it should be dug up in the night before the first of May or at the full moon while reciting strictly prescribed invocations. You can believe it – or not. Many of these practices are of pre-Christian origin. Yet since the Middle Ages at the latest – due to the monasteries, which passed on the herbal knowledge of antiquity, and also encouraged by the dominant figure of Hildegard of Bingen, knowledgeable in the properties of herbs – the Church held herbal healing in its hand. Seeing the healing properties of herbs as a gift of God still fascinates many people even today. Unfortunately, this often involves repressing or forgetting that the Church's taking over of herbal healing in past centuries also had its victims. 'Wise women' who kept the folk traditions of medicine and applied them were persecuted, tortured and murdered out of ignorance, superstition and bigotry.

Faith may move mountains – but can it heal? The reports from Africa, Latin America and Asia by experts in ethnobotany and ethnomedicine, describing medicine men and shamans achieving surprising results with plant extracts and elaborate rituals, must provide food for thought for even the most sober scientist. There is no doubt that much ancient knowledge has been lost in technology-oriented Western societies with their belief in progress. Estrangement from nature has in part reached alarming proportions, and in a parallel development the knowledge of species has decreased rapidly. In a digital world, where communication with chatroom partners on other continents is an everyday occurrence, fewer and fewer people, due to media-supported fears of rabies, echinococcus infection or avian flu, will go into their home forests. They suffer allergies and hygiene obsessions, and use pesticides in their gardens to battle

against the edible, healing common daisy and the ancient salad vegetable bishop's goutweed, rich in vitamin C.

It's time for a little reflection. A first step would be to reach out again to nature in our home countryside, with its threatened but still rich flora and fauna. With this book, we would like to invite you to get to know the manifold variety of herbs and their uses and to rediscover forgotten treasures.

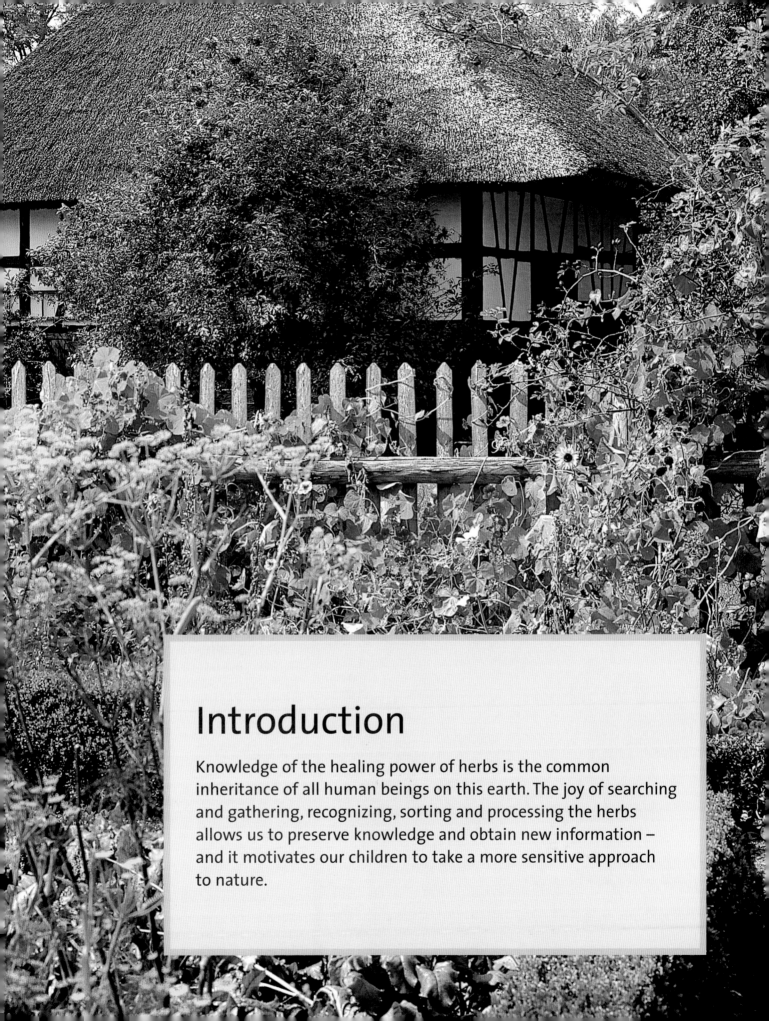

Introduction

Knowledge of the healing power of herbs is the common inheritance of all human beings on this earth. The joy of searching and gathering, recognizing, sorting and processing the herbs allows us to preserve knowledge and obtain new information – and it motivates our children to take a more sensitive approach to nature.

History

Knowledge of the healing power of plants is older than humanity itself. That may seem a paradox and unbelievable, but modern zoology shows us its truth. Michael Huffman, researching primate behaviour with associates from the University of Kyoto, has observed chimpanzees in the wild curing themselves of digestive tract ailments by consuming the bitter marrow of a plant of the aster family, *Vernonia amygdalina*. They also swallowed, unchewed, the hairy leaves of *Aspilia mossambicensis*, a type of wild sunflower, in order to brush tiresome parasitic worms from the intestinal wall in a mechanical action. Being creatures that cannot rely on a doctor when they are sick, they have to rely on whatever nature offers.

According to the theories of the American Terence McKenna, when our animal ancestors came down from the trees and took on an upright posture in the African savannah, it was hallucinogenic fungi that enabled or at least speeded up the development of articulate speech. Many fungi (*Psylocybe* varieties) that today are the object of anti-drugs squad searches grow in the dung of herbivores on open grassland. At first, they probably ended in primate stomachs by accident via the food chain. However, the effect these had inside their heads was, according to McKenna, the origin of those flashes of consciousness that had considerable influence on the development of 'human' nature.

Over millennia, on the long road of evolution, human beings via an endless chain of trial and error gathered bad and good experiences of the agents contained in herbs, trees, mosses, lichens and fungi, knowledge that they integrated into the ever-expanding growth of their survival strategies.

It was easiest – and had the most severe consequences otherwise – to recognize those plants that had an adverse effect on health or even led to death. Accidents and negligence pointed the way for murderers. Plant-based poisons, especially those with a delayed effect, giving the murderer time to get away, have been a feature of human history at least from the beginning of the process that today we call politics. The beaker of hemlock that Socrates was forced to drink is the most famous example from ancient history, and Snow White is the prototype for the devastating consequences jealousy and resentment can have even within the family. Plants have also been used to poison arrows – by no means a privilege reserved for exotic cultures. Poisons and poisoning, toxin and antitoxin are inextricably linked with the science of healing herbs. They are two sides of the same coin, and often, as Paracelsus was not the first to discover, the difference is only a matter of dosage.

Both the healing and fatal effects of plants were known and accepted thankfully or with fear, but how they worked remained unknown. In times when no one had any idea what vitamins

For thousands of years, herbal healing was the domain of priests, shamans and 'wise women'.

were or how the biochemistry of antiviral and bacterial agents functioned, people searched for other explanations. The universe was full of spirits and magic. The Egyptians, the Greeks, the Romans, the Celts and the Teutons each had their pantheon, where responsibilities were delegated as if in a government cabinet. Trade, art and warfare, the hunt, the elements of water, fire, air and earth – all had their own divinity, divinities who, especially for the Greeks, were no strangers to any human failing. Healing, mysticism and magic were inextricably linked; diagnosis, prescription, method of use and ritual were blended together. If you recovered after taking a herbal drink, you thanked the gods of healing and the wise men and women whose knowledge had made divine healing possible.

The wise, however, grew in power. Secret rituals surrounded the digging of particular roots, the collection of fruit, and the making of salves and tinctures. These prescriptions, reserved for the initiate, blending tried and tested knowledge with elaborate hocus-pocus, prevented the erosion of power. Exclusivity was good for business. Not everyone who knew about a few plants and their powers could become a healer. The scent of a flower, the colour, shape or quality of a leaf, stalk or root, the sap of a plant, the changes it underwent during the seasons, or the conditions under which they had to be harvested to unfold their full powers – each and every aspect was, rightly or wrongly, given its specific meaning. Stimulating, intoxicant or consciousness-expanding plants and plant extracts, handed out by shamans and medicine men, put the senses in turmoil or delighted the soul; some created an insuppressible longing for more and more.

Faith, prayer, magic, charisma, birth, life and death – and probably also the human striving for power, influence and wealth – are to this day linked in many forms to herbal healing. It is not always an easy task to separate the mystical chaff from the wholesome wheat, and all who deal with this material have to solve

this problem for themselves. The readers of this book will also not be able to avoid this question.

Found in the Ötztal Alps in 1991, believed to be around 5,400 years old, the 'Ice Man' is probably the first human being in Europe for whom we have evidence, if not of actual use, then at least of actual handling of a healing plant. On his last journey into the mountains, he carried broken pieces of a razor-strop fungus (*Piptoporus betulinus*). The blood-staunching and in certain circumstances digestive effects of this fungus – it is found primarily on dying birch trees in wetland environments – are well known, and have evidently been so, as the 'Ötzis' example shows, for far longer that was previously assumed.

A sophisticated science of herbal treatments developed in Egypt in the Pharaonic era. Egyptian doctors were famed beyond the borders of their country; their renown is emphasized, for example, in the writings of the Greek historian Herodotus. An important source is the 'Ebers Papyrus', dating from the time of

In earlier ages, those skilled in healing were often seen also as magicians and mystics.

The 'Ice Man' from the Öztal Alps already knew of the blood-staunching effect of the razor-strop fungus

Odysseus and the Sirens,
Roman mosaic (Dougga,
Tunisia, AD 300).

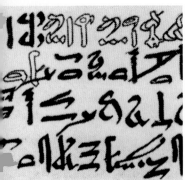

The Egyptian 'Ebers
Papyrus' from around
3550 BC (detail).

the Pharaoh Amenhotep I (around 3550 BC), which, along with numerous magical formulae and invocations, also contains practical notes on the use of herbs in medical treatments. The Egyptologist and biologist Renate Germer, in her book *Die Heilpflanzen der Ägypter* (The Healing Herbs of the Egyptians), has collected a wealth of historical evidence for the herbal knowledge of those times.

The herbal knowledge of the Greeks and Romans

The healing and indeed magical powers of herbs are mentioned as early as Homer's *Odyssey*, dating from the eighth century BC. The far-travelled Odysseus, on his journeys through the Mediterranean, lands with his comrades on the island of Aeaea and is threatened with great danger. For this is the home of Circe, not merely 'fair-hair'd, dreadful, eloquent', but an experienced sorceress who turns half of Odysseus' crew into swine. The hero only escapes this fate because Hermes, messenger of the gods, warns him in good time and arms him:

This said, he gave his antidote to me,
Which from the earth he pluck'd, and told
* me all*
The virtue of it, with what deities call
The name it bears, and moly *they impose*
For name to it.

The plant *moly* protects Odysseus against Circe's magic – an early kind of immunization, if you like. Odysseus escapes the fate of being turned into a pig, and has better fortune. Instead of the pig-sty, he ends up in Circe's bed and is promoted to being her lover. He also succeeds in persuading this charming but dangerous lady to release his companions from the spell and turn them back into men. We will return to the herb *moly* at another time.

The lines quoted are among the earliest references in European literature on the topic of the healing power of plants. Among the Greeks, the knowledge of herbs was highly esteemed – and with it, the value of the herbs themselves. There is no other way of explaining why, as Jacob Burkhardt stated in his *Griechische Kulturgeschichte* (The Cultural

History of the Greeks) that the Draconian Laws set the death penalty on the theft of herbs, just as they did for murder and robbing temples. Among the authorities of ancient Greece, three names stand out whose works have, till the start of modern times, left their mark on medical practice and the beginnings of botany: Theophrastus Eresius, Hippocrates and Dioscurides. These three are considered the founders of scientific botany, medicine and pharmacy. Theophrastus, born around 371 BC on the island of Lesbos, was a pupil and trusted friend of the philosopher Aristotle and inherited his library, probably the most extensive collection of the day. The ninth book of his *History of Plants* is dedicated to their healing powers. Here we learn about root diggers (*rhizotomes*) and 'dealers in medicines' (*pharmacopoles*), both equal founding fathers of Greek natural healing, which has origins far back in archaic times. But even in those days we come across the phenomenon of the tried and tested being enlivened with the fantastical to improve marketing. 'As to what the *pharmacopoles* and *rhizotomes* say,' Theophrastus writes, 'some seems to the point, and other things seem mere noise to attract attention.' This remains a problem today for herbal healing and alternative medicine in general: where does the serious therapy end and the work of quacks and charlatans, out to exploit their 'believers' psychologically and economically, begin? Selling expensive, exotic 'wonder drugs' to the terminally ill, who can no longer be helped by conventional medicine, is a trade that can obviously look back on a long tradition.

It is clear from the writings of Hippocrates, who lived from around 460 to 370 BC on the island of Kos, that the knowledge of healing plants was an integral part of medicine in ancient Greece. However, the most influential work is the *Materia Medica* (Science of Healing Drugs) of Pelanius Dioscurides (from around AD 40 to 90), in which numerous practical healing treatments and prescriptions are noted. Dioscurides, right up until the post-Renaissance

early modern times, was one of the great authorities, whose word was medical law. His work was translated into several languages at an early stage, and later in Renaissance times there were scholars such as Pierandrea Mattioli (1501–1577) who dedicated a great part of their working lives to the translation, research and interpretation of his works.

The Romans adopted and augmented the methods recommended by the Greeks and added to them. Pliny the Elder, the great Roman encyclopaedist, who lost his life in the eruption of Vesuvius (AD 79), paid detailed attention to plants and their effects in Books 20–27 of his *Natural History*, and Claudius Galenus (Galen) from Pergamon (AD 129–199), who among other positions was personal physician to the Roman Emperor Marcus Aurelius, had a decisive influence on the further development of medicine.

A type of chamomile: illustration from Pelanius Dioscurides' Materia Medica, *Latin edition (15th century).*

The Christian tradition and the beginnings of the science of botany

In the Bible there are already scattered references to healing plants. In the Revelation of St John, for example, it says: '… and on either side of the river was there the tree of life, which bare twelve manner of fruits, and yielded her fruit every month; and the leaves of the tree were for the healing of nations'. Sources are scanty for the early Christian period, the Dark Ages and the early medieval period. We know that in Charlemagne's *Capitulary* (*Capitulare de villis vel curtis imperialibus*), dating from 812, just under a hundred fruit, vegetable and medicinal plants are listed to be cultivated on the royal estates. The plants listed in the *Capitulary* can be seen in the Karlsgarten in Aachen-Meltaten, Germany, a memorial of this ancient law. This valuable document shows that, despite centuries of stagnation in scientific research on plants, there can be no doubt that the knowledge of herbal healing was tended even in the 'Dark' Ages, where there are so few sources. It also shows that the knowledge gained by experience – increasingly enriched by fantastic legends, partly of pagan, partly of Christian, and partly most likely of Christianized pagan origin – were passed on, regionally and locally, from one generation to the next. Here and there we come across references to the healing powers of plants in old fairy tales, for instance, in the strange tale collected by the Brothers Grimm, *The Three Snake-Leaves*. In this story, a snake restores its dead mate to life by covering it with the leaves of a magic herb. A grieving man, having watched the snake, does the same for his dead wife and meets with success.

Along with 'herb-women', who not infrequently ended up as 'witches' at the stake, with alchemists, quack doctors and all who gathered around them, it was mainly monks and nuns who, in the medieval and early modern period, concerned themselves with the use and cultivation of plants. The siting of monasteries in sparsely populated places, often on the edges of as yet unexploited forests, required a good measure of self-sufficiency. No plant was too lowly to be despised, whether for eating or because it could help heal wounds and cure diseases. Experiments must have been carried out in the monasteries – with bark and juices, root extracts, leaves and flowers, teas and fruit, in the same way we know they experimented with hops and malt. Vegetables and herbs were grown in separate parts of monastery gardens, and travelling monks spread the knowledge to other regions. Today there are still abbeys where the monastic horticultural tradition continues to be maintained with great care and expertise.

The nun Hildegard of Bingen (1098–1179), later abbess of the monastery of Disibodenberg, situated at the confluence of the rivers Nahe and Glan in Germany, holds a pre-eminent position in the practical application and further development of medieval herbal medicine. The first book of her major work on medicine, the *Physica*, is entitled *Of Plants*. Hildegard – who is considered a saint, though there has been no formal beatification by the Vatican as yet –

Left: A classic monastery garden with a rich store of medicinal herbs.

Below: In 'Hildegard Gardens' – such as this one in Kirchberg near Mattighofen (Upper Austria) – herbs mentioned in the Physica *are cultivated.*

Right: Hildegard of Bingen. For her time, the nun possessed an extraordinary knowledge of healing herbs.

Far right: Albertus Magnus. He was one of the first not just to show interest in the effects of herbs, but also to carry out botanical studies.

divides herbs into 'warm' and 'cold' types and recommends them for the treatment of all kinds of illnesses, ailments and spiritual conditions. Some of her advice is still current today and was deliberately taken up again by famous doctors and natural healers such as Paracelsus and Sebastian Kneipp. Some sounds rather strange. For instance, of the whortleberry (*Vaccinium myrtillus*), whose value today as rich in vitamin C and a remedy against diarrhoea is not in dispute, she writes, 'However, the fruit is harmful to those that eat it, as it arouses the gout.' Of the burnet saxifrage (*Pimpinella saxifraga*), a proven treatment for bronchitis and infections of the urinary tract, she writes, 'It is of little use for man… But yet wear it always about your neck, for then you will not be deceived by the call of demons, by magic words or by sorcery…' In Hildegard's works, Christian visions and medieval demonology mingle with elements of folk medicine that cannot be proven today, or at least require a good deal of interpretation. However, the charismatic abbess from Germany's Rhineland is a presence for us today, stronger than almost any other woman of the Middle Ages. There are 'Hildegard Gardens', lovingly designed with great care – e.g. in Kirchberg, in Upper Austria

(see page 15) – in which the herbs mentioned in the *Physica* are cultivated, and in many countries groups of 'Friends of Hildegard' have taken on the task of preserving not only the medical but also the spiritual legacy of Hildegard of Bingen and passing it on to future generations.

The invention of the movable type printing press by Johannes Gutenberg meant that the works of the classical period, stored in monastery archives, discovered, read, excerpted or copied by monks over periods of time, translated, if they were Greek texts, into Latin and later into the vernacular, were also made available to the literate public. The teachings of Dioscurides, Theophrastus, Galen and other classical authors, as good as forgotten over the centuries, not only came back to life as part of the movement to restore classical values, but were largely received uncritically. The thought that many of the plant names contained in the ancient texts required interpretation seemed never to have occurred to most authors of the herbals that now appeared all over the place. The authors of classical times had gathered their experience – and their plants – in the Mediterranean regions and profited from cultural and mercantile links with North Africa and the Middle East. The attempt to transfer their knowledge, gained from Mediterranean flora, to the climatic conditions and geographic spread of central and northern Europe proved to be a mistake of the first order. Expert botanical knowledge was required for critical definition and interpretation of the ancient plant names, and for most doctors and healers this was lacking, because the scientific study of plants, their morphology, agents and natural relationships, was still in its infancy. For centuries, healers and scholars, with a few exceptions such as the genius Albertus Magnus (1193–1280), had been interested almost exclusively in the *effects* of herbs and had taken little note of basic botanical research, which appeared to have no direct use. Indeed it can be assumed that the dominance of the healing sciences hampered or even blocked the development of modern botany for many years. Johann Wolfgang von Goethe, in one of his botanical studies, writes, 'Rousseau writes that it has been the ill-luck of botany to have become linked with medicine. One can

forgive him such a statement when one considers that in his time it was still disputed as to whether botany could claim to be a separate science, that those of a teleological disposition would not allow weeds to be counted as plants, and that those in need have a greater interest in salvation than in learning.' This situation, unsatisfactory from a scientific point of view, changed only slowly. In his *Geschichte der Botanik* (History of Botany, 1854–1857), Ernst F.H. Meyer described the process as follows: 'The science of plants… did not free itself from its long servitude to the science of healing all at once, but the bonds were gradually loosened; a plant not mentioned by the ancients and to which no healing powers could be ascribed no longer remained unnoticed, as had been the case, and the quantity of such plants increased from year to year.'

A great name in the history of medicine is Aureolus Philippus Theophrastus Bombastus von Hohenheim, known as Paracelsus (1493–1541). His extensive work contained, along with

Johnannes Gutenberg (1400–1468). The golden age of illustrated herbals began with the invention of movable type.

Johann Wolfgang von Goethe (1749–1832). The great poet and thinker also wrote extensively on botany.

The 'Fuchs Garden' is a memorial to Professor Leonhart Fuchs, author of the 'New Kreüterbuch' of 1543.

scientific discoveries that were revolutionary for his times, sarcastic pamphlets aimed at colleagues and rivals in the medical profession. He accused them – as in this example from a broadsheet that appeared in Basle in 1527 – of 'having remained too slavishly attached to the words of Hippocrates, Galen and Avicenna, and others', to the detriment of the sick. Paracelsus, enthusiastically honoured by his supporters, died a poor man in Salzburg, but his medical and chemical discoveries, his writings and his brilliant biography have not lost their fascination even today. From him, herbal healing received the so-called Doctrine of Signatures, with its peculiar system of symbols which, despite science having long since packed it off to the realms of fantasy, is still quoted today in all herbal books and is mentioned on every herb-finding guided tour. The Doctrine of Signatures, with its origins reaching far back into Egyptian antiquity, decides on a plant's or part of a plant's medicinal and therapeutic value on the basis of its shape, colour and structure. The perforated leaves of St John's wort (*Hypericum perforatum*), which look as if they had been punctured by fine needles, teach us, according to the above doctrine, that the plant is good for treating stab wounds. Golden saxifrage (*Chrysoplenum*) has spleen-shaped flowers, hepaticas (*Hepatica nobilis*) have blooms shaped like liver lobes, and the English walnut (*Juglans regia*) is convoluted like a brain, all of which supposedly shows us where and when they can help. Plants with yellow flowers such as common dandelion (*Taraxacum officinalis*) are used to treat gall bladder and liver ailments which, given the bitter substances they contain, is actually plausible. The occasional match between 'signature' and effect may be due to the followers of this doctrine examining well-known healing plants for 'signatures' and then

of course finding them – after all, their own theory put them under a kind of pressure to succeed. For example, common lungwort (*Pulmonaria officinalis*), which has a leaf surface that is supposedly reminiscent of a lung with its little aveoli, was used to treat lung disorders long before this theory was developed. After Paracelsus, the Doctrine of Signatures was taken up and developed further by the Italian naturalist Giambattista Porta (c. 1538–1615) in his work *Physiognomica*.

Paracelsus, the most famous doctor of the Middle Ages, was also a spokesman for astrology in herbal healing. He saw plants as creatures with souls, with qualities determined by the course of the stars. These teachings were, and are even today, paid extravagant homage by followers of the occult and the esoteric.

Five important botanical authors of the early modern age lived only a little later than Paracelsus: Otto Brunfels (around 1500–1534), Hieronymus Bock (1498–1554), Leonhart Fuchs (1501–1566), Konrad Gesner (1516–1565) and Adamus Lonicerus (1528–1586). Like Paracelsus, all were doctors. Brunfels published his work *Herbarum vivae eicones* in 1530. It is famed more for its outstanding illustrations than for its text, which is still strongly oriented towards Dioscurides. The work is seen as a milestone in the history of botanical illustration, which is not surprising considering that the artist, Hans Weiditz, was a pupil of Albrecht Dürer. Hieronymus Bock's *New Kreutterbuch* (New Book of Herbs, 1539) demonstrates the gradual emancipation from classical models. It gives plenty of space to describing the sites of plants, and its very personal style and language is evidence of an excellent gift for observation. Similar things can be said of the *New Kreüterbuch* (New Book of Herbs, 1543) by the professor Leonhart Fuchs, who came from Wemding on the River Danube. This work portrays 500 species of plants in carefully crafted woodcuts by the artists Heinrich Füllmaurer, Albert Meyer and Veit Rudolf Speckle. Each section of text ends with a

Portrait of Paracelsus, from his work Astronomica et Astrologica *(1567)*.

paragraph on the 'power and actions' of the plant in question.

Konrad Gesner from Zurich, son of a furrier, studied in France and in Basle and in the end became city doctor and professor of philosophy in his home town. The widely educated scholar, famous even in his own lifetime, did not live to see the publication of his extensive major work on botany, with the plant illustrations he himself had made. It was not published until 200 years after his death. Better fortune and rapid success, in contrast, accompanied the *Kreuterbuch* of Adamus Lonicerus of Marburg. First published in 1551, it went through six editions before the author's death. Partly unchanged, partly corrected and supplemented by later authors, 'Lonicerus' was offered in new editions right up until the 18th century, and for generations of students it remained the most important botanical text.

In other European countries important illustrated books were also published between 1500 and 1800, among these the two-volume *A Curious Herbal* (1737–1739) by the English plant illustrator Elizabeth Blackwell, with 500 copper engraved and coloured plates, without

Right: Elecampane inula (Inula helenium), an illustration from A Curious Herbal (1737–1739) by Elizabeth Blackwell.

Far right: Carolus Linnaeus. The Swedish naturalist is considered the founder of modern scientific classification.

exception depicting healing plants. The German version, revised and supplemented by the artist Nicolaus Friedrich Eisenberger, was an early work that took Linnaeus classification into account, and is one of the most beautiful plant reference books of its time.

The Swedish naturalist Carl von Linné, often known by his Latinized name Carolus Linnaeus (1707–1778), whose ground-breaking work had the aim of giving every living thing a family and a species name based on its natural relationships, provided appropriate tools for the growing demands for a serious approach to plant naming. New, objective criteria of classification – such as the detailed structure of flowers and fruit – showed the weakness of the older descriptions more clearly than before.

The naturalists of the 18th and 19th centuries had had a humanist education for the most part, but they were now familiar with Linnaeus' system of classification. Thus equipped, they examined the interpretation of classical texts

and descriptions intensively, but by no means all the puzzles that the ancient authors have left us have been solved. New methods of examination are constantly offering us new insights. There had, for example, long been some sort of unity of opinion that the plant 'moly', appearing in the *Odyssey* and often reappearing in classical literature as a magical plant, was probably black garlic (*Allium nigrum*). But then A. Plaitakis and R.C. Duvoisin put up the theory, based on agents contained in the plant, that moly may have been the snowdrop (*Galanthus nivalis*). They suspected that Circe's magic drink, which confused the senses of the crew and against which Hermes immunized Odysseus with *moly*, contained an extract of thorn-apple (*Datura stramonium*). Galanthamin, which is obtained from the snowdrop, is nowadays used in the treatment of Alzheimer's patients.

Homeopathy

The term 'homeopathy' is derived from Greek and means something like 'healing like with like', while conventional medicine, an 'allopathic' system, heals 'with unlike'. This contains a core principle of the medical theory based on knowledge of herbs and developed in his practice by the doctor Samuel Hahnemann (1755–1843), born in Meissen in Saxony, Germany. The doctor explained his theories in his extensive work *Organon of Medicine*. In some respects, his work turned conventional medicine upside down. Starting from the premise that an agent that causes certain diseases is also suited, in low doses, to healing them, Hahnemann tested hundreds of plants on himself and on volunteers. The agents, diluted ('potentiated') according to precise rules, also help with psychological problems, which in the holistic view of homeopathy are closely linked to physical symptoms. The polyglot Samuel Hahnemann, who worked in England and France as well as other countries, was indubitably a great, creative thinker, being in many respects in advance of his time. Although no one has succeeded even today in using scientific methods to demonstrate the way in which the potentiated plant extracts work, homeopathic medicines are now used by many conventional doctors to accompany treatment. Hahnemann's successors have tested countless other plants and natural products according to the principles of their founder and thereby developed his theories further.

Samuel Hahnemann, the founder of homeopathy.

The herb father, healers with a 'vocation' and the 'astonished doctor'

Influenced by Linnaeus' theories, the 19th century saw on the one hand the emancipation of botany from medicine – for a long time, it had led a sorry existence as a dependent of the healing arts. On the other hand, with progress in chemistry and pharmaceutics, the old herbal knowledge gradually lost its dominant position in the medical sciences. And yet – or perhaps even because of this – there were intensive moves in the 19th and 20th centuries not to allow the old knowledge and procedures of herbal medicine, practised and tried for centuries, to be forgotten.

A great preserver and innovator of such traditions was the famous 'Kräuterpfarrer' (herb father), the priest Sebastian Kneipp (1821–1897), who not only made hydrotherapy a folk movement but, with persistence, knowledge and charisma, developed a complete view of the world. Like many other naturopaths, Kneipp was self-taught – that is to say, he had not studied medicine but had acquired a wide range of knowledge by his own efforts, supplementing it by his outstanding gift of observation and testing many of its applications on himself. Kneipp – basing his teaching on Paracelsus in this matter – preached a life close to nature and a return to the healing powers of nature, in particular of fresh water and plants.

Sebastian Kneipp had many adherents and followers, who were inspired by faith as he was and imitated his style, which was rather authoritarian to modern ears. The simple language of many successful herbals is directed to a religious public not given to questioning those in authority. Kneipp's disciples soon took on the authoritarian tone that promised success. 'You must chew dried sweetflag root to cure bleeding gums,' another 'herb father', Hermann Wagner (1907–2003), sternly instructs readers of his little book, which bears the Kneippian title *Gegen jede Krankheit ist ein Kraut gewachsen* (There is a Herb for Every Ailment). The reader is addressed in familiar fashion and commanded to pray, pick herbs and live in a manner both natural and agreeable to God. Johann Künzle (1857–1945) on the other hand, one of the best-known representatives of this folksy herbal medicine with its roots in religious faith, became a best-selling author far beyond the borders of his native land. His 'little book of healing herbs', entitled *Chrut und Uchrut* (Herbs and Weeds), sold over a million copies worldwide, according to information from the publishers. The entertainingly written text combines cheerful

The Kneipp fountain in Bad Wörishofen, Germany.

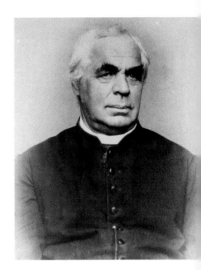

Sebastian Kneipp. Herbal healing is one of the five pillars of his holistic therapy.

Above left: There is a grey area between herbal healing, homeopathy and religious-esoteric healing.

praise of God and recipes for herbal remedies with advertising for teas, elixirs and embrocations from the *Kräuterpfarrer Künzle AG* company. It is said that Künzle, just as Kneipp did, sent many of those seeking his aid to confession before treating them.

Not a cleric, but according to her own words inspired by the Mother of God, the Austrian Maria Treben (1907–1991) wrote the pamphlet *Health Through God's Pharmacy*, which, translated into many languages, also achieved a print run of millions, just like Künzle's *Chrut und Uchrut*. She recommends herbal teas and treatments for almost every complaint and ailment, including serious cases of cancer where conventional medicine is no longer able to help. Conventional doctors, or rather their professional qualifications and social prestige, are especially accepted in her publications (and similar works) if they – to their own utter astonishment – witness a sensational healing by herbs '... then the Professor, an authority in this field, **could find no further evidence of the tumour**'. Or, 'Her own doctor, on receiving the report from the hospital, had never experienced the like.' The 'astonished doctor' is something

of a trademark feature of this entire genre. Treben's critics point out, among other matters, that she at times recommends high dosages without pointing out possible side effects.

There is, therefore, a grey area between traditional herbal medicine, the effectiveness of which can be confirmed in many cases by scientific analyses, homeopathy, where success can be seen but is difficult to measure, and the religious and esoteric healers, who treat disease on behalf of or with the aid of divine or supernatural partners and happen to use herbs among other methods in the process. Those who have been rudely pushed aside by overworked doctors who have forgotten how to listen, those who have been dismissed as hypochondriacs who have been demonstrably wrongly treated, or already given up as incurable, are of course particularly susceptible to such alternatives, especially as faith is known to move mountains and there are certainly individual cases of recovery that cannot, despite all progress in medicine and biology, be scientifically explained. However, these are rare exceptions.

Dr Bach's Flowers

The so-called Bach Flower Remedies, developed by the Englishman Dr Edward Bach (1886–1936), form a special variation on herbal healing. For Bach, who was neither a priest nor a layman in medical matters, but a qualified doctor and homeopath, diseases and ailments are expressions of a spiritual imbalance that cannot be satisfactorily treated by superficial remedies for its symptoms, but require consideration of the whole psychosomatic condition of the patient. Healing powers arise from the energies of wild flowers, each ascribed to the spiritual condition of the patient. Bach divides the disharmony between a human being's personality and the person's 'higher self' into seven basic categories: *fearfulness, uncertainty, lack of interest in present circumstances, loneliness, over-sensitivity to influences and ideas, despair and despondency* and *over-concern for the welfare of others*. For nervous,

*Jewelweed (*Impatiens glandulifera*) has recently spread considerably. It plays a part in the Bach Flower Remedies.*

hectic persons, more in danger of accidents than most, he therefore recommends jewelweed (*Impatiens glanulifera*). Case studies that he uses to illustrate the effects of his flower remedies are reminiscent of the reports of cures that are found in contemporary or later works by the herb priests or Maria Treben. We also meet the legitimizing figure of the 'astonished doctor'. 'When she returned to hospital for a second examination, the doctor was surprised to find hardly a trace remaining of the wound,' the case study for *Impatiens* states. As well as the thirty-eight flower essences discovered and sanctioned by Bach, there are now a number of others, the discoverers or inventors of which invoke Bach without Bach himself being able to express a view on the matter.

Whatever one may think of him and his doctrine in detail, Bach must have been an impressive and extremely sensitive man. He could divide his patients into certain emotional categories simply from their outward appearance, and there are reports of numerous cures attributed only to his presence or his touch. If his biographers and followers can be believed, he also had clairvoyant abilities.

The split between alternative and academic medicine remains today, but there are encour-

aging signs that the trenches dug between the two camps may perhaps one day be bridged, to the advantage of the end user – the patient. Not all doctors, by any means, see their homeopath or healer neighbour as an unloved rival and charlatan, who makes foolish promises to lure away paying patients. Some have added training as a healer to their medical studies and attempt to complement the 'drugs and hi-tech' school of medicine with alternative treatments, or to combine the two. A further important stimulus has been given by the growing influence of holistically oriented Asian healing methods, in particular, traditional Chinese medicine. On the other hand, no serious naturopath free of a sense of religious vocation and occult fanaticism will dismiss conventional medicine so radically as to stop those who come seeking his or her aid from consulting a specialist doctor.

Herbal healing in non-European cultures

In China, herbal healing has always occupied a position within traditional Chinese medicine (TCM) higher than that it enjoys in Europe, and can look back on a correspondingly rich tradition. Its origins go back to the legendary Emperor Shen-nong (around 2900 BC), who is supposed to have experimented on himself to test the effects of many herbs. His name is also invoked by many early Chinese herbals dating from the Qin and Han dynasties (225 BC to AD 220). During the Ming dynasty, in the early 16th century, the opulently illustrated codex on the healing power of herbs (the *Ben Cao*) was created at the command of the Emperor Xiao Zong. The work summarizes the collected knowledge of its time. A glimpse of this astonishing compendium is provided by a selection with thirty-six colour plates, edited by the Italian Sinologist Edoardo Fazzioli, published in German in 1989, and offering not only a treasure trove for botanists, pharmacologists and cultural historians, but also considered a masterpiece of the Chinese bookmaker's art. The number of herbs used in traditional Chinese medicine runs into the thousands (some examples of their uses are given in the book mentioned above). The use of fungi in healing is also widespread in China and other Asian countries; some species, such as *rei-shi* (varnished polypore, *Ganoderma lucidum*), are now exported to Europe.

The Middle East also has a long tradition of botany and herbal healing. In the Middle Ages, Arab scholars in Spain and other countries translated the works of ancient Greek authors and supplemented them with information from other parts of the world such as India, for example, where the so-called Ayurvedic art of healing, still widely used today, had developed thousands of years before. Europe owes its first acquaintance with innumerable spices and healing herbs from Asian regions to the Arabs. Among the numerous works, we will here mention only the *Canon of Medicine*. Ibn Sina (980–1037) came from Bokhara, in modern Uzbekistan. The widely educated scholar, who became known in Western Europe by the name

Avicenna, is one of the most important doctors and naturalists of the Middle Ages.

Two research disciplines, both still young, ethnobotany and ethnomedicine, are concerned with old traditions of phytotherapy among northern, central and southern Native Americans, the peoples of Siberia and Africa, and the original inhabitants of the fifth continent. There are detailed descriptions of the amazing natural medical knowledge of Native Americans, and Australian researchers have discovered that the Aborigines use at least thirty species of the tree family *Acacia* for medicinal purposes. According to diagnosis, leaves, bark, twigs or buds are used in various forms (externally, in watery extracts, by inhaling steam, etc.). Wood-growing fungi of the *Phellinus* (fire bracket) family are used, for example, to fight colds. Another fungus, the dyemaker's puffball (*Pisolithus tinctorius*), a species of the puffball family also found in Europe, is used to treat bleeding wounds and swellings.

Weighing out herbs in a Chinese pharmacy.

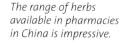

The range of herbs available in pharmacies in China is impressive.

Similar reports have come from Africa. A traditional healer in South Africa's Natal province needs to study for five years with an *Inyanga* master, learning to recognize and use the healing plants of the country. In many cases, laboratory analyses have been able to identify the healing constituents of the plant agents. Healing herbs are so much in demand in South Africa that many species have become rare in the wild or even threatened with extinction; they are now beginning to be cultivated in plantations. In other parts of Africa, too, traditional healers, who often combine herbal medicine with magical rites such as the invocation of spirits or ancestors, are highly esteemed, especially in places where modern medicine is not available, too expensive, or simply has no idea how to help.

In recent years, the worldwide ecological crisis has had its effect on research and led to some unusual alliances. Because, due to the destruction of their environment and climate change, many plants are in danger of extinction before we can even acquaint ourselves with them, never mind analyse their agents for possible therapeutic effects, pharmaceutical companies are sending botanists and environmental experts to the most distant regions of the world. They are supporting nature protection projects to preserve the genetic diversity of the tropical rainforests, not only for purely altruistic reasons but also out of plain self-interest.

In Europe, too, at a time when the conventional health protection systems are threatened with collapse due to the burden of ever-rising costs, interest in phytotherapy and traditional folk medicine is growing. There is an almost unmanageable wealth of information offered about healing and culinary herbs, their cultivation and use, by bodies such as the German *Gesellschaft für Arzneimittelforschung* (Society for Pharmaceutical Research), the French *Institut technique interprofessionel des*

Below left: Ibn Sina (Avicenna) in discussion with apothecaries.

Below right: The stall of a medicine man in Africa has a remedy for almost every complaint.

Healing herbs cultivated in Cuba.

plantes médicinales, aromatiques et industrielles (iteipmai), or the development association *Artemisia e.V.*, by pharmaceutical and cosmetic companies, pharmacists' associations, health insurers, growers' associations and specialized plant nurseries. Traditional, partly forgotten medicinal plants flourish in herb, wild and museum gardens, and new research is constantly being presented at conventions, symposia and further training courses. However, the foundation for all those interested in herbs and their manifold uses is solid basic knowledge of the variety of species outside their front doors, in parks, in the close and not so close vicinity of where they live. This book would like to make a contribution towards such knowledge.

Tips for gathering

Six questions: Where? – What? – When? – How? – How much? – Why?

At the start of every practical herbal are the answers to the six questions on the gathering of herbs.

Where can you gather herbs?

Herbs, of course, should only be gathered in unpolluted spots (particularly good places are the edges of woodland, extensively used meadows – e.g. woodland or mountain meadows – dry sites such as gravel pits, and above all your own garden. In national parks and protected areas, take note of the regulations that apply. It is useful, during the course of a year, to write down the places where the desired herbs appear, so that you can collect them again and again at the right moment.

What can be collected?

The same principle applies as for mushroom gathering – only collect herbs that you recognize for certain. Many plants have lookalikes that are not particularly good for you, or are even poisonous. Others, such as many orchids, are protected and therefore taboo.

A herb guide with pictures is only helpful if you study the pictures and texts with great care. Simply comparing the photograph or drawing with the plant in question is not enough! It is a good idea to expand 'book knowledge' by going on guided herb tours; these will provide you with new information and confidence for your own expeditions into the natural world.

Only gather plants or parts of plants that show no sign of disease and have not been attacked by insects.

Above: Protected plants such as early purple orchid (Orchis mascula) and other orchid species are out of bounds for the herb gatherer.

Right: Many healing herbs, long extinct in intensively used agricultural areas, have found a refuge In fertilizer-free mountain meadows, such as this one in the Dolomite range in Italy.

When is it best to collect?

The early and later months of spring, when young tender leaves and needles are sprouting, is the best time to collect them for salads, soups, herb butter, and teas (e.g. common dandelion, common daisy, bishop's goutweed, pine needles). Flowers are best gathered in spring (e.g. primrose, sweet violet) and summer (St John's wort, marigold), when they are fresh and fully in bloom. Bark (birch, willow) and sap (e.g. for maple syrup) are also best collected in spring, when the sap is rising. Autumn, however, is best for gathering berries and roots, when the agents and the strength have gone back into the roots. The roots of biennials are harvested at the end of the vegetation period, those of perennials in autumn or spring from the second year onwards. Fine weather is essential for gathering, so that the plants are not subject to attacks by mould due to high humidity. The harvesting period can vary by a month, more or less, according to region, altitude and climate.

There are no rules without exceptions: the bright yellow fig buttercup, *Ficaria verna,* which flowers from March to April in shady spots in the garden and in humus-rich, moist woodland borders, is a good example of how vital it is to take careful note of collecting times. The spicy, club-shaped, light brown root bulbs must not be harvested until after flowering in May or June. The young leaves and buds, to be picked before flowering, have a pleasant, mild flavour and are very rich in vitamin C (in earlier years, this 'scurvy-herb' was used to cure vitamin C deficiency). During and after flowering, on the other hand, protoanemonin builds up, which has a hot taste and is poisonous for human beings. The fig buttercup is a member of the buttercup family, which contains many poisonous plants, including the highly toxic aconite (*Aconitum*).

How best to gather?

The literature always advises gathering herbs into a basket. However, linen or plastic bags are better. In an open basket or in a hot car, the herbs will dry out very quickly on warm spring days. They soon look unappetizing and end up on the compost heap – shame about all the effort, shame about the enjoyment… It is

*Above left: Lesser celandine (*Ranunculus ficaria*) with its tubers.*

Above right: Drying herbs.

Build a 'herb spiral', with culinary and medicinal herbs, not too far from your kitchen door.

*In phytotherapy, the word **'drug'** means plants or parts of plants (such as dried leaves, flowers or roots) prepared for use, or the active constituents of those plants (such as essential oils or fats).*

digging up the roots is prohibited – for instance, with gentians (*Gentiana*).

Why gather?

An old proverb claims that the way to the heart is through the stomach. Our ancestors gathered herbs, grasses, flowers, roots, berries and bark, and these formed an important part of their diet.

The use of plants extends from tasty spring salads and soups, to herb butter and spinach-like vegetables, to baked dishes and pizzas. Culinary herbs and herb salts improve the flavour of meat, fish, egg, cheese and pasta dishes. The flavours range from mild (daisy, *Bellis perennis*) to sour (garden sorrel, *Rumex acetosa*), from hot (cuckoo flower, *Cardamine*) to slightly bitter (common dandelion, *Taraxacum*), from aromatic (ground ivy, *Glechoma hederacea*) to resinous and lemony (spruce needle tips, *Picea abies*).

Knowledge of the healing effects of various plant-based drugs has come down to us over the years. However, please do remember that taking plant medicines can have side effects. The same infusion, for example, should not be drunk or applied over a long period of time. After four or five weeks, you should change the tea or the tea blend. The ever-popular mint tea, for example, can lead to irritation of the stomach. Chamomile tea should be drunk only 'medicinally' – for inflammation, for example – and not as an ordinary tea. It is essential to contact a doctor for ailments that last for several days.

sensible to use a separate bag for each species. This will make sorting and cleaning at home easier, as well as the final check to make absolutely certain nothing unhealthy or even poisonous is in with your day's collection. This final check is particularly vital if children have been helping to gather herbs; however, adults make mistakes too.

How much to gather?

There is a rough rule that says you should not pick more herbs than you can actually use. With herbs for teas, do not gather more than you and your family can use in a year, as the agents of dried herbs gradually lose their effect over time. For some species, only the plant above ground may be harvested. In many cases,

The active constituents of healing herbs include, among others, essential oils, alkaloids, bitter principles, tannins and glycosides that affect the heart, which may in the wrong dosage cause strong side effects and, in certain circumstances, even death.

Herbs can be used as teas or infusions, baths, poultices, salves or tinctures.

For a spring detoxification, a course of drinks – for instance, with nettle tea – is highly recommended. Other plants with a blood cleansing, purifying effect are bishop's goutweed (*Aegopodium podagria*), field horsetail (*Equisetum arvense*) and birch leaves (*Betula*).

ONLY GATHER

- Herbs you know well
- Only as much as you and your family will be able to use in one year
- In the mornings, once the dew has dried, or in the evenings – not in the midday heat
- **Whole herbs:** At the start of the flowering season. When harvesting, cut your herbs an inch or two above the ground
- **Leaves:** Very young, but fully unfolded. Before flowering, during the whole growing season
- **Buds:** Before flowering
- **Flowers and flower heads:** Before these have fully opened
- **Flowers and flowering shoot tips:** Early in the flowering period, before the seeds develop
- **Fruits, seeds:** When these are quite ripe
- **Roots:** When these are sturdy and fully developed (mainly in autumn or early in spring, when the agents are concentrated in the roots)
- **Bulbs:** After flowering
- **Tubers:** During flowering
- **Bark:** In spring, from young twigs (three to four years old) or in autumn after the leaves have fallen, in damp weather
- **Sap:** In spring and summer, when the sap is rising

Processing, drying, storing

When harvest time has come, cut off the flower heads or flowering tips or, if required, the whole plants with gardening or pruning scissors. Dig up roots, root stocks, bulbs and tubers in dry weather and, before taking them home, remove the worst of the dirt and any wormed or rotten patches.

It is important to transport your plants carefully (do not squeeze or press them) and to continue to process them quickly, in order to keep their original colour as much as possible. Collected herbs, the species divided up in separate linen bags, are easily transported in a basket. Poisonous plants must be separated and processed away from others. When collecting, you should have no open wounds on your hands, nor should you eat anything. Afterwards, your hands and the implements used for gathering must be washed thoroughly with soap and water. Eating unfamiliar plants can be fatal.

Drying herbs in bunches.

You can also bunch your harvest ready for drying on site, or sort it into plastic or cloth bags for immediate processing. Roots, rhizomes, bulbs and tubers must be thoroughly cleaned before drying.

The herbs, cleaned, with all extraneous matter, and rotted or wilted parts removed, can be dried in an airy, shady spot, on drying racks or in a dryer. Plants harvested whole – for example, mint (*Mentha*), sweet balm (*Melissa officinalis*), and twigs of trees and shrubs – are bunched according to species and hung upside down on a laundry line to dry. Tie about fifteen to twenty stalks together at the base with twine, with one piece of the string protruding by about 8 in. (20 cm). Use this to hang up the bunches, in full sunlight, for a short time, to allow the plants to dry out quickly. After that, however, they must be dried as quickly as possible in an airy, shady place with no unpleasant smells (e.g. an attic or barn) at a natural temperature, in order – among other things – to preserve the essential oils, which volatilize at temperatures above 104°F (40°C).

Herbs are spread out to dry in boxes.

After washing, cut roots and tubers into ½–1 inch (1–2 cm) sized pieces. Thick, fleshy roots should be halved. Bulbs, however, should not be washed but simply freed of fibrous roots and the dry plant.

Spread out shoot tips, flowers, leaves and pieces of root in a single layer on drying racks or sieves. The drying racks should consist of simple wooden frames with a loose-woven cloth or non-rusting wire mesh.

Berries – such as hawthorn (*Crategeus*) or bilberry (*Vaccinium myrtillus*) – and seeds can easily be dried in a flat cardboard box or small box if the fruits or seeds are turned by daily shaking. Any leaves or bits of twig collected with the berries can be easily separated by holding the box at a sloping angle. The fruits or seeds will roll downwards, and the unwanted bits of plant will remain and can be removed.

Drying is the simplest way to preserve herbs. Other possibilities are freezing or the preparation of tinctures, wines, syrups and salves (see page 37 ff.). Some leaves – e.g. parsley (*Petroselinum crispum*), wild garlic (*Allium ursinum*) or water mint (*Mentha aquatica*) – lose much of their scent and flavour when dried and should only be used fresh or frozen. The right climate is important for optimum drying of the leaves, in order to preserve the agents and avoid mould (mouldy herbs can damage health). Some parts of plants, particularly the flowers, should when dried keep their original colour, scent and appearance.

The end of the drying period (one to two weeks for air drying, three weeks at the longest) is reached when the stems snap when broken, the leaves break easily along the ribs and veins, and rustle, and when berries and the small pieces of root have become hard. The drying time depends on the water content of the plant in question and the drying temperature. Flowers and leaves dry more quickly than the whole herb; roots, tubers, and bulbs need the longest drying times. The drying temperature for drugs containing essential oils must not rise above

95°F (35°C), and for plants with glycosides that affect the heart it must not exceed 120°F (50°C).

The loss of weight of freshly gathered herbs compared to their dried form is given in the table below.

Storage

Drugs should be stored according to type, protected from air, light, dust, and moisture, in tightly closed glass jars, metal or plastic containers, or airtight plastic bags. It is important to label them exactly according to species, year of harvest and origin.

The storage space should be cool, dark, and dry. The storage period should, in general, not exceed a year, as the agents lose their effect over a period of time. Any herbs

Herbs	1/4
Leaves	4/5
Flowers	5/6
Bark	1/4
Roots	2/3
Fleshy fruits	6/7
Seeds	1/5

Poisonous drugs must in all cases be stored separately from others and be identified as such.

remaining after a year should be composted. From time to time, medicinal herbs you have collected or bought must be checked for damage by pests or mould.

The best way to do this is to spread the herbs out on a sheet of white paper—if they gather into lumps or perhaps even draw threads, you can usually discover maggots with the aid of a magnifying glass. If you have doubts about their condition, the herbs should only be used for compost. To use them for treatment could damage your health.

Constituents and active agents

Pharmaceutical research in recent decades has decoded the chemical composition of many well-established healing plants and thereby enabled the pharmaceutical industry to copy many agents in a purely chemical form and to make new combinations – for the good of patients, but also protecting natural resources. However, many questions in phytotherapy remain open, especially in regard to the action of the drugs, which can vary considerably due to location, time of harvesting and processing (drying, storage, etc.). In general, it can be said that because scientific evidence for an action is at present not available, that does not mean such an action should be excluded forthwith; homeopathy is only one therapy that can provide a wealth of examples.

The following summary contains only the most important group of substances these plants contain. Among others, often contained only in very small proportions by weight, are vitamins, minerals (e.g. silicic acid) and trace elements. Of great importance for human nutrition, both in quantity and quality, are oils obtained from the seeds of various plants and proteins (e.g. in beans and other members of the pea family).

In the laboratory, herbs are tested to discover their agents.

Oregano,
Origanum

Mint,
Mentha

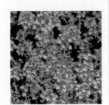

Thyme,
Thymus vulgaris

Barberry,
Berberis

Hawthorn,
Cratageus

Arnica,
Arnica montana

ESSENTIAL OILS

... are a mixture of liquid, volatile (i.e. evaporating at room temperature), oil-soluble substances with a characteristic scent. Ingredients are terpenes and phenylpropenes (e.g. camphene, pinene, thymol, menthol, etc.).

In the carrot and aster families, and in plants of the cypress, mint, laurel, pine and madder families, the essential oils are responsible for the specific and often very intense scent and flavour of the plant in question, whether it be spicy, aromatic, bitter or peppery, and are also the source of the healing effect. They are antibacterial (e.g. oregano, Origanum), anticonvulsant and stimulating to the circulation (e.g. mint, Mentha), irritating to skin or mucus membrane and thereby stimulating secretions (e.g. thyme, Thymus) or stimulating to the appetite and digestion (e.g. angelica, Angelica), either as a tea, embrocation or inhalation.

Essential oils are obtained by distilling with water, whether by extraction or with steam, by cold-pressing or other methods of extraction. They also have many applications in the cosmetics and food industries (e.g. oil of fennel, bitter almond oil, peppermint oil).

FLAVONOIDS

... are a common group of natural substances responsible among other things for the colouring of leaves, flowers, fruits and other parts of plants. There are three main groups: flavonols (e.g. rutin, querictrin), flavanones (e.g. hesperidin), and flavones (e.g. apiin).

The flavonoids are of great importance for pharmacology, as because of their different chemical structures and combinations, e.g. with glycosides (= flavonoid glycosides) they affect a wide range of different organs. Rutin and hesperidin (e.g. in horse chestnuts, Aesculus hippocastanum) have a sealing effect on capillaries and are used in venous diseases. Flavonoids are also effective as antioxidants, antiexudatives, antiphlogistics and radioprotectives, and can therefore be used in many illnesses. For example, they strengthen the immune system, block allergic reactions and relax the smooth muscle of the heart. This results in expansion of the blood vessels, leading to improved circulation, greater urine production, and an antispasmodic action on the stomach and intestine. The increase in bile production also improves digestion. They are found, for example, in buckwheat (Fagopyrum esculentum), hawthorn (Cratageus), barberry (Berberis) and arnica (Arnica).

Belladonna,
Atropa belladonna

Aconite,
Aconitum

Opium poppy,
Papaver somniferum

Whortleberry,
Vaccinium myrtillus

Erect cinquefoil,
Potentilla erecta

Blackberry,
Rubus

ALKALOIDS

... are nitrogen-containing natural substances, mostly reacting as bases, derived from amino acids. They often bear the name of the plant in which they form the main alkaloid. Atropine, for example, is named after belladonna (Atropa belladonna), ranunculin after plants in the buttercup family (Ranunculaceae). Alkaloids have a powerful effect on organs. There are many dangerous poisons in this group, e.g. aconitine, derived from the deadly aconite. There are also important medical drugs, some of which lower and some of which increase blood pressure, some which have anesthetic, antispasmodic, sedative or anti-parasitic qualities.

TANNINS

... have an astringent effect and are used for tanning leather. They are cytotoxins, but their astringent properties protect the uppermost layers of tissues from penetration by bacteria, fungi, chemicals and mechanical irritants. They have an anti-inflammatory effect, act as an antibiotic and local anaesthetic on the mucus membranes in the mouth and throat, throughout the entire gastrointestinal tract, and on haemorrhoids and bleeding wounds. Plants containing tannins are, for example, oak (Quercus), European chestnut (Castanea sativa), English walnut (Juglans regia) and bilberry (Vaccinium myrtillus). Tannins are also found in members of the rose family such as erect cinquefoil (Potentilla erecta), silverweed (P. anserina), and raspberries and blackberries (Rubus).

Gentian,
Gentiana lutea

Sage,
Salvia officinalis

Angelica, Angelica

BITTER PRINCIPLES

Drugs containing bitter principles stimulate saliva and stomach secretions through the vagus nerve, have a stimulating effect on the appetite and subsequently ensure better digestion of the food. The amara work best if taken about fifteen minutes before eating. They also help combat bloating and wind, and encourage the flow of bile. Bitter principles are found primarily in plants of the gentian family (yellow gentian, Gentiana lutea) and in members of the aster (absinthe, Artemisia absinthum), mint (sage, Salvia officinalis) and carrot (angelica, Angelica) families.

Lily of the valley,
Convallaria majalis

Foxglove,
Digitalis purpurea

Boucingbet,
Saponaria officinalis

GLYCOSIDES

... are widely occurring chemical compounds that are contained in a large number of pharmaceutically effective preparations. Apart from sugars (both simple and compound), other glycosides include those that act on the heart (European lily of the valley, Convallaria majalis, foxglove, Digitalis purpurea), saponins (bouncingbet, Saponaria officinalis, common chickweed, Stellaria media), anthraglycosides that act on the stomach (common buckthorn, Frangula alnus) and glucosinates (mustard oil in mustard and related species, Sinapis).

Pine, Pinus   *Spruce*, Picea   *Fir*, Abies

RESINS

... are hard substances, softening and melting when heated, produced by woody plants (e.g. pine, Pinus) and insoluble in water. Resins that occur dissolved in essential oils are known as balsams. Resins are not susceptible to rot and can, as is proved by amber, last for millennia. They have a disinfectant and anti-inflammatory action and are primarily present in the secretions of conifers.

Horseradish,   *Black mustard,*
Armoracia rusticana   Brassica nigra

HOT SUBSTANCES

... are widely varying compounds found in different plant families, all with a hot flavour and irritating to the heat and pain receptors in the skin. Internally, they increase the production of saliva and stomach acids, thereby helping to control bloating and stomach problems. Externally, the 'irritants' act to control muscular pains and rheumatic ailments.

STARCH

... is the most common energy storage substance in the plant kingdom and to a large extent covers the human requirement for carbohydrates. Particularly high in starch are the grasses, especially the grain varieties, together with potatoes (Solanum). Starch is also widely used in the pharmaceutical industry, whether as a carrier in tablet manufacture or as a base for powders or salves.

Plantain, Plantago   *Marshmallow*, Altheae *Flax*, Linum

PLANT MUCILAGE

... in combination with water, produces viscous, colloidal solutions which suppress irritation in (for example) coughs and bronchitis (plantain, Plantago), are mildly laxative (flax, Linum), and also provide protection against stomach acid and increase smoothness and slipperiness. Mucilaginous plants such as marshmallow (Althaea), flax and African plantain are used in inflammatory gastroenteric diseases such as peptic ulcers, but also as a mild laxative, to soothe irritants and to stimulate the immune defences.

APPROVAL AS A MEDICINE

Up until 1995, the so-called Kommission E in Germany had examined and evaluated 330 medical plants (see Bisset and Wichtl) for their effective action. These examinations laid the foundation for their approval as medical drugs in Germany. Since then, at European level, ESCOP (European Scientific Cooperative on Phytotherapy) has been concerned with the drawing up of criteria on the quality, safety and effectiveness of the plant in question. To be approved, a plant must have undergone clinical studies and those medicines sold as ready-made preparations (capsules, pills, drops, elixirs) must be distributed through pharmacies. To get around the strict legal regulations, many traditional medicinal herbs are marketed as food supplements and can be bought in ordinary drug stores and healthfood stores. These are subject to food legislation.

At European level, the law of pharmaceutical drugs is now by and large uniform.

Use and preparation

The most common method of use for herbs is as a tea. But they can also perform their healing and beneficial actions used as syrup, electuary, juice, tincture, wine, bath, compress, poultice, salve, inhalation preparation and gargle. Medicinal and culinary plants are used fresh or dried, internally or externally, unprocessed or prepared according to certain (often very old) recipes, individually or in blends. It is generally – though not always – best to use fresh herbs, whether as a tea or juice. To unlock the beneficial effects, the herbs are chopped, grated or crushed. Some herbs contain only one or two relevant active constituents; others have many. In Germany, finished medicinal plant products for sale in pharmacies are subject to legal drug restrictions based on the 1976 Medicines Act. In approving medicines for use, the quality, effectiveness and safety of medicines on the market within the European Union is documented.

Tea

Teas often consist of mixtures of various herbs blended according to certain rules.

Rules for blending teas
- Basic medicine = *remedium cardinale* (maximum of two to three basic medicines)
- Supporting medicine = *adjuvans* (generally something that strengthens or lessens the effect of the basic medicine)
- Supplement = *constituens* (substance with a positive effect on appearance and colour) and flavour enhancer = *corrigens*, e.g. mint, aniseed, primrose, rosehip, mallow, vanilla, untreated lemon or orange peel

For preparation, use non-corroding vessels such as china or glass. Iron, steel or other objects containing metal can lead to a loss of active constituents. Teas to be drunk over the course of a day should always be kept covered so that they cannot collect impurities and the agents cannot degenerate through contact with oxygen. Thermos flasks are very useful.

Note:

Herbal teas are drunk as a cure, but should be used thus for no longer than four to five weeks. The body must not be allowed to become accustomed to a particular blend, for even in the case of herbal teas, side effects must be taken into account. So-called general drinking teas are an exception. For example, a mixture of blackberry and raspberry leaves, perhaps with dried apple peel or currant leaves added, can be drunk daily.

Syrups and electuaries

To make a syrup, an extract of the drug (either as extract or tincture) is mixed with cooled sugar syrup (slowly dissolve 5–7 oz [150–200 g] of sugar in 3–4 fl oz [100 ml] of water over a low heat), or mixed with sugar in a 1:1 ratio and heated, stirring constantly with a wooden spoon until it forms a thick liquid.

Syrup can only be stored for a limited period.

The following **measures** *are in general use:*

	Average weight of dried herbs	
	Liquid content fl oz/ml	Dry content oz/g
1 small pinch		0.035/1
1 large pinch		0.07–0.12/3
1 handful		1.5–1.8/45–50
1 large handful		2.5/70
1 level teaspoon	0.17/5	0.1/3
1 level dessertspoon	0.32/10	0.035–0.07/1–2
1 level tablespoon	0.5/15	0.35/10
1 liqueur glass	1/30	
1 wine glass	2.4/70	
1 cup	5/150	
1 small bowl	6.8/200	

Above: Drops of some essential oils, e.g. lavender oil, can be added to bath water.

Above right: To make creams or salves, the flowers of St John's wort are ground into oil or fat in a mortar.

Preparation:

- **Tea or infusion:** The leaves, flowers and seeds are put in a strainer insert in a cup and boiling water is poured on. After five to ten minutes, remove the strainer insert. Teas are best drunk in small sips, unsweetened, though you can add honey or brown sugar or lemon juice. Most teas should be drunk hot. Sweetened teas often have a calming effect. Bitter teas are drunk cool or lukewarm.
- **Quantity:** As a rough rule, one to three teaspoons per cup, which equates to 0.05 oz (1.5 g) to a maximum of 0.2 oz (6 g) of the drug. Fresh herbs require correspondingly greater quantities.
- **For children** the dose should be reduced by half or a third, according to age and doctor's instructions (see page 272).
- **Decoction:** Hard, coarse parts of plants such as bark, wood, stems or fruit husks should be put into cold water and boiled for ten to thirty minutes according to the hardness of the material. The tea can be drunk at once, hot.
- **Quantity:** One tablespoon = 0.2–0.35 oz (6–10 g) roots or fruits.
- **Cold water extraction or maceration:** Roots and sometimes other parts of plants (e.g. bearberry leaves) should be soaked in cold water for six to twelve hours at room temperature and then heated, according to the type of herb, and should be left to stand for several days.
- Some recipes also require removal of an **extract** using alcoholic spirit, wine (red or white) or oil.
- **Hot water extraction or digestion:** Hard parts of plants such as bark or wood are soaked in hot water (86–104°F, 30–40°C) for several hours.

Electuaries are made from ripe, juicy fruit, cooked until soft or forming a thick liquid and are intended for immediate use.

Fresh juice

Fresh plants are mixed with a little water, sometimes blanched, pressed and then filtered or squeezed through a linen cloth. The juice must be used at once or mixed with alcohol or syrup.

Tinctures

Fresh, dried, grated or pulverized parts of plants are mixed with 70 per cent per volume alcohol in a 1:5 ratio, allowed to stand for one to six weeks in a closed container at room temperature, and thoroughly shaken every now and then. Afterwards, the extract is filtered and kept in dark containers. It is usual to differentiate between thin liquid (*extracta fluida*), thick, honey-like liquid (*extracta spissa*) and dry extracts (*extracta sicca*).

Rinses, clysters, gargles

The cooled herb infusion or extract is inserted either directly or with a syringe into the natural bodily orifices (e.g. nose, ears, vagina) to rinse.

Clysters or enemas are administered to the rectum with a clyster bulb or syringe to rinse out the colon, for instance, in cases of chronic constipation or to combat intestinal parasites.

Gargles have a disinfectant and soothing action on the mouth, pharynx, throat, tonsils and mucus membranes. Application takes place several times a day. Gargles should never be swallowed.

Aromatic waters
Essential oils are mixed with distilled water by shaking thoroughly. Steam distillation is another possibility.

Inhalations
The steam from an infusion of herbs with essential oils (e.g. dwarf mountain pine, chamomile) is inhaled. The patient inhales the steam directly for ten to fifteen minutes, holding his or her head, covered with a cloth, over the bowl. Inhalations are used especially to combat diseases of the respiratory tract.

Powders
The herbs are either finely crushed or ground in a mortar and then sieved. (When on a journey or in the office, powder is easier to take, with a little liquid in a teaspoon, than tea.)

Baths
There are several kinds – partial or localized baths for parts of the body (e.g. foot or arm baths), hip baths (sitz baths) and full baths, and also steam baths. The herb extract or infusion is added to the bath water according to the desired effect. The herbs required are put into a gauze or cloth bag, hot water is poured on, and the bag and extract are added to the bath water. In spa treatments, health and comfort are further increased by the addition of essential oils. For steam baths, the herbal vapour has to work on the affected part of the body (e.g. for haemorrhoids) for ten to twenty minutes.

Wraps and compresses
Wraps and compresses are old, well-tried healing treatments. Wraps involve wrapping individual parts of the body, such as the throat, chest or calves, or wrapping the whole body.

There are cold and hot, wet and dry wraps. Cold wraps are generally used for inflammation, bruises and fever. To ease cramp (e.g. abdominal or menstruation pains), for some rheumatic complaints and to speed the healing process, warm or hot wraps are used. Another kind of wrap are herb pillows, which are warmed and then used to combat colds, excessive wind, diarrhoea in young children or insomnia. Compresses are smaller (e.g. compresses for the forehead to treat headaches).

These and the following methods are also used in spa treatments.

Poultices (cataplasm)
The finely (e.g. mustard powder) or coarsely (e.g. flax seed) ground herb is boiled with water or milk to make a thick paste, spread onto a thin (e.g. muslin) cloth, placed hot (104°F, 40°C maximum) onto the affected part of the body and covered with a cloth. Poultices are used to treat skin diseases, exhaustion and excess weight.

Creams, salves and embrocations
Creams, salves and embrocations are used primarily for skin diseases, for the care, cleansing and protection of the skin and also for problems with the musculoskeletal system (e.g. comfrey salve, St John's wort oil).

Herb extraction (maceration).

PLANT RECOGNITION TABLE

*Scientific descriptions of plants
contain specialist botanical
expressions which are often difficult
for non-botanists to understand.
On this and the following pages
we have listed and illustrated the
most important.*

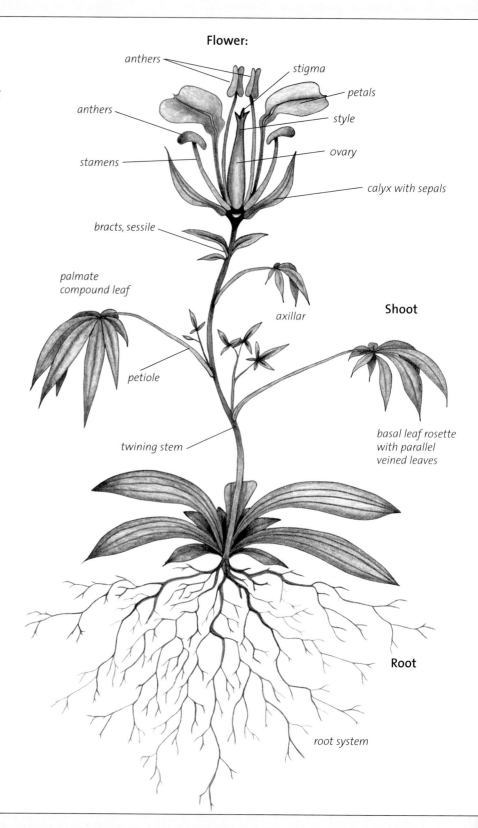

Flower:

anthers

stigma

petals

anthers

style

stamens

ovary

calyx with sepals

bracts, sessile

palmate
compound leaf

axillar

Shoot

petiole

basal leaf rosette
with parallel
veined leaves

twining stem

Root

root system

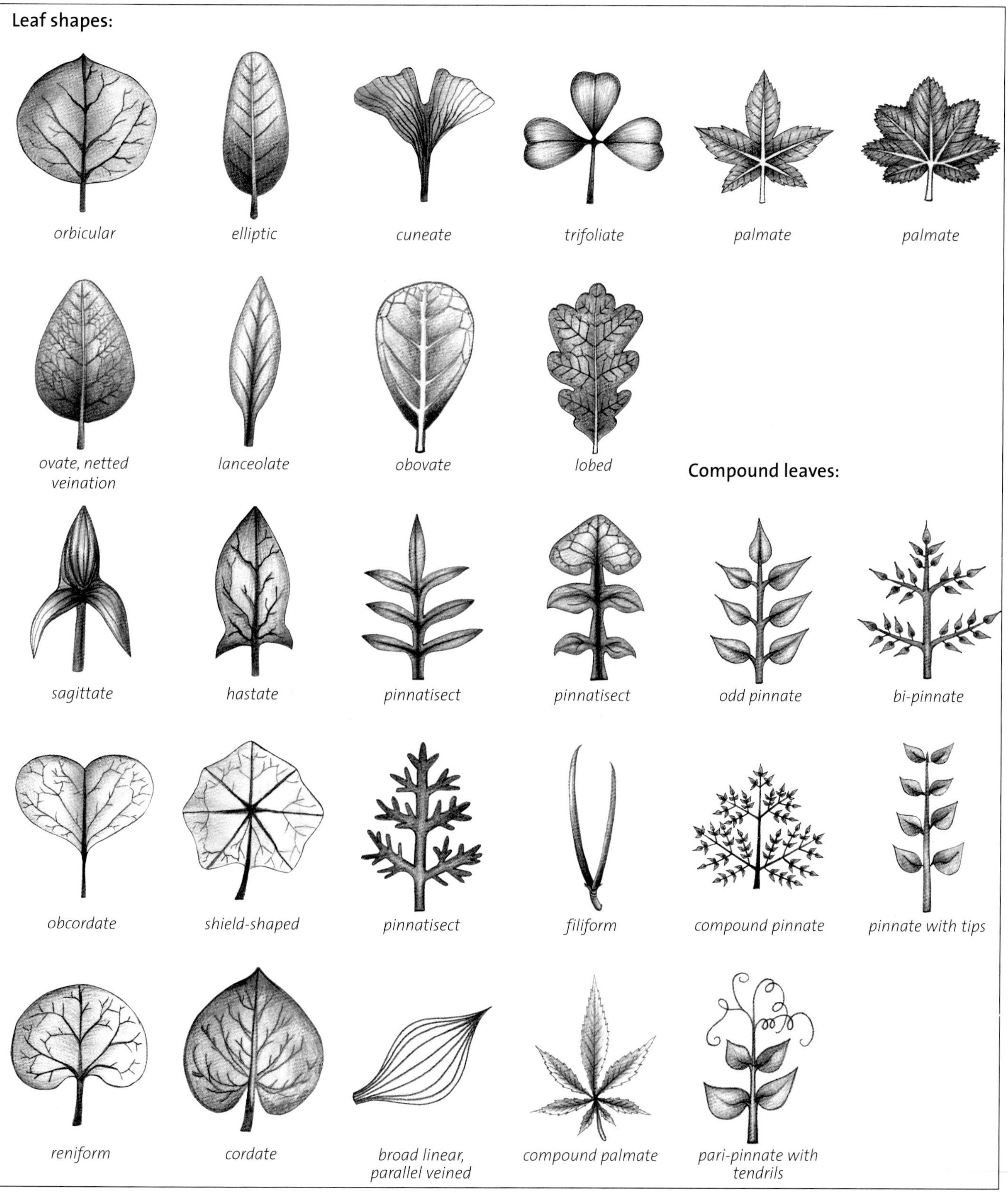

Leaf shapes:

orbicular

elliptic

cuneate

trifoliate

palmate

palmate

ovate, netted
veination

lanceolate

obovate

lobed

Compound leaves:

sagittate

hastate

pinnatisect

pinnatisect

odd pinnate

bi-pinnate

obcordate

shield-shaped

pinnatisect

filiform

compound pinnate

pinnate with tips

reniform

cordate

broad linear,
parallel veined

compound palmate

pari-pinnate with
tendrils

Leaf edges:

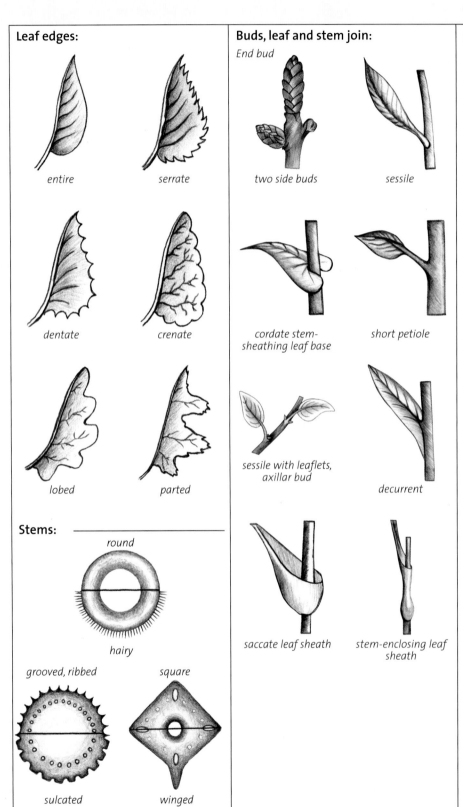

entire

serrate

dentate

crenate

lobed

parted

Stems:

round

hairy

grooved, ribbed

square

sulcated

winged

Buds, leaf and stem join:

End bud

two side buds

sessile

cordate stem-sheathing leaf base

short petiole

sessile with leaflets, axillar bud

decurrent

saccate leaf sheath

stem-enclosing leaf sheath

Shoot, axil and leaf arrangement:

rosalate, basal leaf rosette

basal

erect, decussate

erect, alternate

rising, opposite

twining

climbing, with tendrils

prostrate, creeping

creeping with runners

whorled

Flower shapes, symmetric:

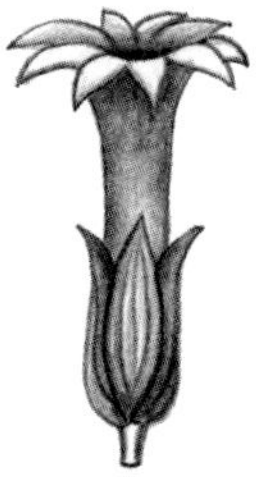

tubular

club-shaped

campanulate

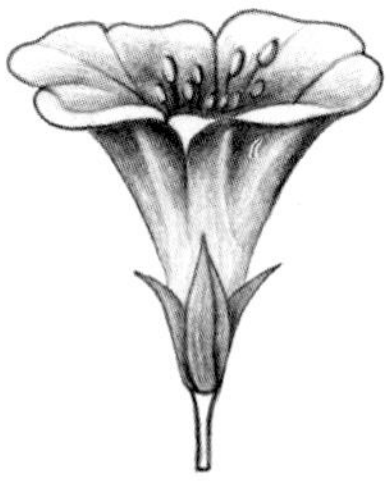

funnelform with calyx

funnelform, fused

urceolate

four-petalled, cruciform, free

five-petalled, free

five-petalled, fused with sepals

pink, rayed a

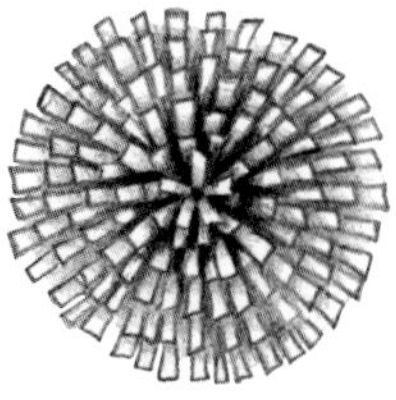

rayed b

tubular rayed c

ligulate rayed d

Flower shapes, asymmetric:

violet

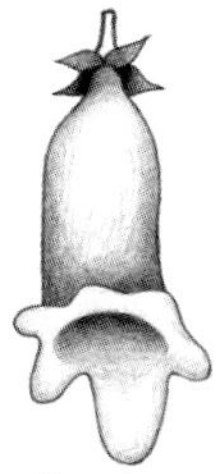

foxglove

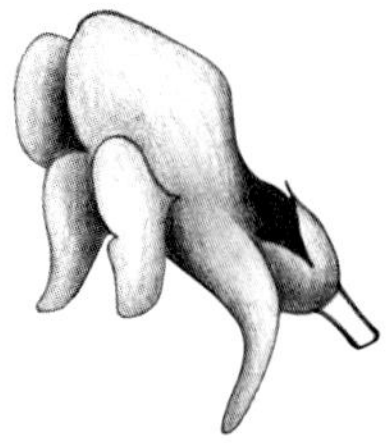

scrophulariaceous flower with spur

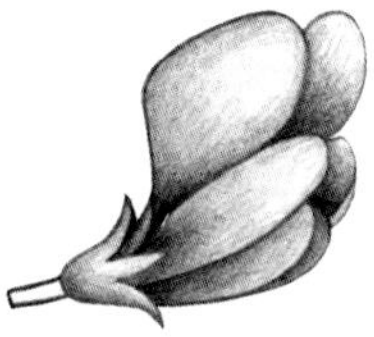

papillonaceous flower, side view

labiate flower

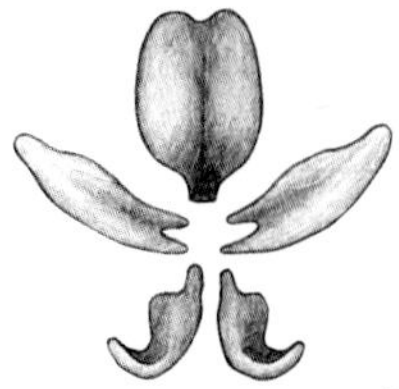

a

b

zygomorphic flower dissected

a

b

Flower shapes (inflorescence):

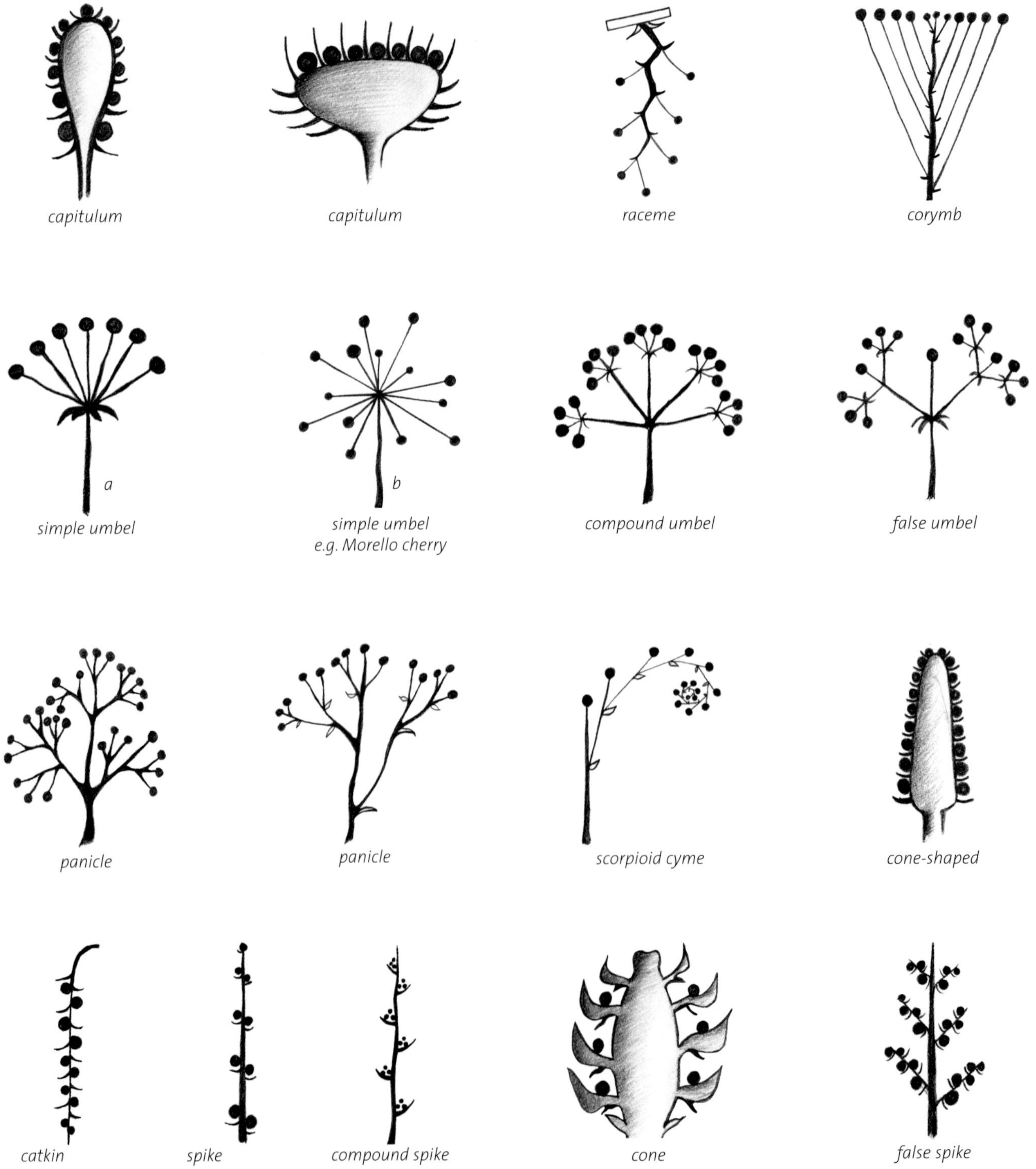

capitulum

capitulum

raceme

corymb

simple umbel
a

simple umbel
e.g. Morello cherry
b

compound umbel

false umbel

panicle

panicle

scorpioid cyme

cone-shaped

catkin

spike

compound spike

cone

false spike

Fruit: Drupe (stone fruit)

*pome with leathery,
tough wall*

with thick wall

Indehiscent (closed) fruit:

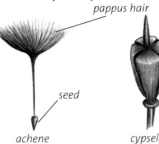

pappus hair

seed

achene   *cypsela*

Dry fruit:

capsule

silicle

silique

legume

loculicidal capsule

follicle

Aggregate fruit:

*strawberry with
numerous nutlets*

*raspberry with
numerous drupes*

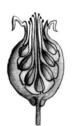

*false fruit
e.g. rosehip*

*nut
e.g. acorn*

cone

Root:

root system

*tap root with underground
runners*

root tubers

rhizome

Healing herbs

A colourful meadow of flowers is more than a feast for the eye. It forms a harmonious community of living things, composed of hundreds of species and thousands of individual plants, and if you count the smallest and tiniest organisms at ground level, the number of different species soon becomes astronomical. The confusing variety of leaves, flowers, fruits, stems and rhizomes hide healing powers that human beings have been using for thousands of years.

The plants portrayed are arranged in alphabetical order, taking their natural relationships into account, in sub-classes (ending '...-idae' e.g. 'Rosidae'). Within the sub-classes they are arranged according to family (ending '...aceae'

e.g. 'Rosaceae'), genus (e.g. 'Rosa') and species (e.g. 'Rosa canina'). In the 'Other Angiosperms...' section (page 262), various families have been placed together for organizational reasons.

Asteridae

ASTERIDS

The **Asterids** are the most extensive group not only in botanical classification but also in this book, as the aster (Asteraceae), borage (Boraginaceae) and mint (Lamiaceae) families alone contain many medicinal and culinary herbs.

*Summer meadow with German chamomile (*Chamomilla recutita*) and corn poppies (*Papaver rhoeas*).*

Asterids
Asteraceae and Cichoriaceae

The family of the asterids is rich in species and comprises shrubs and tall plants as well as herbs. The flower heads, usually surrounded by bracts, are composed of numerous little individual florets. The fruit is a closed (indehiscent) fruit (achene), often equipped with an aid to flight (pappus hairs). There are tubular and ligulate asterids. In the tubular forms (Asteroidae), either all the florets are tube-shaped or only the ones in the central disc, which is then surrounded by a ring of ligulate florets. The larger flowers around the edge of the flower head are often sterile and act as a visual attraction for insects. The ligulate asterids (Cicheroidae) often also contain a milky sap.

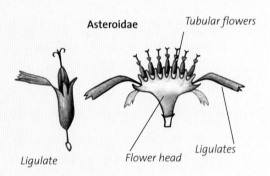

Asteroidae   Tubular flowers

Ligulate   Flower head   Ligulates

Cichoroidae

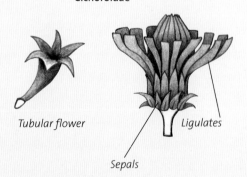

Tubular flower   Ligulates

Sepals

Achillea millefolium L.
COMMON YARROW

Milfoil, Nosebleed, Staunchweed, Bloodwort, Carpenter's Weed, Thousand Seal, Soldier's Woundwort

The finely pinnate leaves of the yarrow have been poetically referred to as 'Venus' eyebrow'.

Yarrow tea is particularly recommended for disorders of the digestive tract (as is shown by its German name *Bauchwehkraut*, 'Belly-Ache Weed'). Nowadays, however, we know that some people are allergic to the aster family and that the innumerable sub-species of yarrow do differ in their constituents. Both are possible causes for unwelcome reactions up to and including allergic shock. On no account should you exceed the recommended dose of yarrow products. If in doubt, fall back on the mantra of pharmaceutical advertising; ask your doctor or pharmacist.

- **Description:** Height up to 2 ft 8 in. (80 cm); leaves are dark green, long, finely bi- or tri-pinnatisect; stems erect, usually hairy, leafed; flowers white or pale lilac, false umbel with few flowers in corymbs, ligulates to the outside, tubular flowers within; many different varieties, usually evergreen.
- **Flowering:** June to October
- **Scent and flavour:** Savoury when young, later bitter and astringent

- **Location:** Dry meadows, pasture land, way-sides, railway embankments
- **Distribution:** Very common
- **Drug:** Herba, Flores Millefolii
- **Constituents:** Essential oils (azulen, cineol), bitter principles, tannins, flavonoids, cumarin, seed oil
- **Treatments:** For stomach ache, digestive tract problems, flatulence, liver and gall bladder complaints, loss of appetite, menstruation problems, bleeding wounds, ulcers, skin diseases, bleeding gums, leucorrhoea, cramp in the female abdominal organs
- **Uses:** Tea, pressed juice, poultices, rinses, baths, culinary (cream cheese, herb butters, salads, soups, sauces); leaves used to dye wool yellow
- **Homeopathic uses:** See above; particularly for haemorrhages
- **What and when to gather:** Young leaves April to June, flowers and flowering shoot tips June to August
- **Lookalikes:** None
- **Other information:** Daily dose about ⅟₇ oz (4.5 g); take care with allergies to other aster family plants and to azulen

The female flowers and bracts of the pussytoes are pinkish-red.

Antennaria dioica
COMMON PUSSYTOES

■ *protected* ■
Cat's foot, Cudweed, Strawflower, Mountain Everlast

It is no longer possible today to continue recommending the collection of some herbs. Some have been found to contain poisons that only become noticeable over a period of time; others – including the common pussytoes – have had their numbers reduced so markedly by industrialization, overuse of fertilizers, land drainage and other factors, that they now need to be classified as endangered. In the past, pussytoes was recommended for liver and gall bladder ailments, bronchitis and diarrhoea, and the flowers are still used today in dried flower arrangements, for which the cultivated dwarf everlast (*Helichrysum arenarium*) or the strawflower from Australia (*H. bracteatum*) are just as suitable. It is necessary, with pussytoes also being known as 'strawflower' and dried flowers of *H. arenarium* being called 'pussytoes', to use the scientific name.

- **Description:** Height up to 1 ft (30 cm); white hairs; leaves entire, sessile, alternate, semi-sheathing, spatulate below, lanceolate at top; stems round, erect; flowers tubular, in multi-flowered raceme; dioecious, effuse, bracts white, female flowers pinkish-red, upright; achene with pappus; perennial.
- **Flowering:** May to August
- **Scent and flavour:** Flowers smell savoury when rubbed; flavour bitter and astringent
- **Location:** Dry, sandy, lime-poor heathland, scanty grassland, mountain meadows, roadside, gardens

The male flowers have white, dry, membranous bracts.

Like pussytoes, the strawflower has woolly to felt-like white down.

- **Distribution:** Scattered
- **Drug:** Flores Antennariae dioicae
- **Component:** Flavonoids, camphor glycosides, bitter principles, essential oils, cumarins
- **Treatments:** For liver and gall bladder complaints, jaundice, bronchitis, diarrhoea
- **Uses:** Tea, improves appearance of bronchial teas
- **What and when to gather:** Flower heads May to September
- **Lookalikes:** Dwarf everlast: bracts gold to orange-yellow, diuretic, improves appearance of tea; strawflower: flowers yellow, red, purple, blue, white; ornamental plant

Below left: The flower heads of great burdock with their curved bracts.

Below centre: It is easy to mistake the leaf rosettes.

Below right: The woolly burdock (Arctium tomentosum) has the undersides of the leaves and flower heads covered with thick white 'wool' as a protection from the sun's rays. It has sticky threads instead of little hooks.

Arctium lappa L.
GREATER BURDOCK

Burdock, Beggar's Buttons, Personata, Clot-bur

Many people who live in cities are more familiar with Velcro than the plant that inspired its inventor. Greater burdock does, however, grow in cities – along railway embankments, on empty ground, in overgrown gardens. Thanks to its hook-like husks, the plant is the origin of a labour-saving means of attachment.

Greater burdock has always been used as a wild vegetable and for healing purposes. According to Bisset and Wichtl, modern analyses confirm the antibiotic qualities of the root extract and its stimulation of liver and gall bladder function, but not, alas, its supposed effect on men who have lost or are losing their hair. The three species of burdock can be used in the same way. The roasted roots can be used as a coffee substitute.

- **Description:** Height up to 6 ft 6 in. (2 m); leaves in basal rosette, large, cordate, long petiole, coarsely dentate, green above, whitish-grey below, finely haired; stems very sturdy, pithy, grooved, often hairy, leaves alternate; flowers large (1–1½ in., 3–4 cm), in false umbels, red to violet-red, flower heads almost round, on long stalks, bracts green, hooked and curved upwards; fruits pale reddish-brown with wreath of hairs; does not flower until second year; root thin, up to 20 in. (50 cm) long, branching; biennial.
- **Flowering:** July to September
- **Scent and flavour:** Root: smell is musty to intensely sharp; flavour slimy, sweetish to bitter
- **Location:** Waysides, railway embankments, gravel pits, fences
- **Distribution:** Common
- **Drug:** Herba, Folia, Radix, Fructus Bardanae

Flowering arnica in a mountain meadow.

- **Constituents:** Essential oils, glycosides, tannins, mucilage, bitter principles, fatty oil
- **Treatments:** For skin diseases, gout, rheumatic complaints, diabetes, wounds, digestive disorders, liver and gall bladder ailments
- **Uses:** Tea, poultices, rinses, culinary vegetable (young sprouts, roots)
- **Homeopathic uses:** See above
- **What and when to gather:** Leaves April to May, roots (September first year, March to April second year), seeds
- **Lookalikes:** Coltsfoot: young leaves with white down on both sides, long petioles, cordate, leathery; pestilence wort: young leaves; lesser burdock *(A. minus)*: height up to 4 ft (120 cm), flowers ½–1 in. (1–2.5 cm) in diameter

Arnica montana L.
ARNICA

■ *slightly poisonous* ■

European Arnica, Leopard's Bane, Mountain Arnica, Mountain Tobacco

The classical authors of Greek and Roman natural history and medicine seem to have been unfamiliar with arnica. In the 12th century, Hildegard of Bingen mentions it, though she warns, 'But if a man or woman burns with desire and if a person touches that man or woman with green arnica, they will burn with love for that person, and when that herb is withered, the man or woman touched with it will be infatuated with that love, so that he or she will from then on become foolish.'

The phenomenal rise of arnica in herbal healing did not come about until the 17th and 18th centuries. Preparations of arnica are recommended for bruises, sprains, hematomas and insect

North American Chamisso arnica (A. chamissonis sub-species foliosa) is cultivated for pharmaceutical purposes.

bites. The crushed leaves are recommended for use in first aid. However, arnica should not be taken by mouth, as it contains the heart toxin helenalin.

Arnica has proved so popular that it can no longer be found in many places. In many countries, the plant is protected. Düll and Kutzelnigg recommend changing to *Calendula*, which has the same active constituents.

- **Description:** Height to 2 ft (60 cm); leaves in basal leaf rosette, ovate, distinctly five-veined stem; leaves opposite, sessile; stems erect, downy hair, usually not branching; flowers yolk to orange-yellow, peripheral flowers up to 1 in. (2.5 cm) long; fruits with long pappus hairs; long, more or less creeping root, perennial
- **Flowering:** June to August
- **Scent and flavour:** Scent aromatic; taste bitter
- **Location:** Acid soils, wetland meadows, mountain meadows, heathland, up to an altitude of 8,200 ft (2,500 m)
- **Distribution:** Rare
- **Drug:** Flores, Herba, Rhizoma Arnicae
- **Constituents:** Flavonoids, essential oils (chinon), choline, cumarin, alkaloids, helenalin, bitter principles, tannins, mucilage, resin; rhizome: starch, inulin
- **Treatments:** For wounds, weak circulation, bruises, sprains, haematomas, rheumatic ailments, insect bites
- **Use:** Tinctures, salves, poultices
- **Homeopathic uses:** See above, and also for haemorrhages, and heart and circulatory diseases
- **What and when to gather:** Flowers June to August, leaves May, roots March, April, September
- **Lookalikes:** Common plantain (see page 106): similar leaf rosettes, but different flowers and locations
- **Other information:** Tincture to be used only in dilution (4- to 5-fold), not on open wounds or internally

Artemisia spec.
WORMWOOD, ABSINTHIUM

Species of Artemisia have been used since earliest times as healing, sacrificial and magical herbs, as aphrodisiacs and as intoxicants. In his chapter on Artemisia, Christian Rätsch reports the presence of wormwood in large quantities near the settlements of the reindeer hunters of the caves of Lascaux, and in Ancient Egypt absinthium was used as a medicine. The intoxicant qualities of wormwood are mentioned in the Bible: 'He hath filled me with bitterness, he hath made me drunken with wormwood' (Lamentations 3:15). The bitter taste of the plant means that the word is also taken to mean 'suffering' in the metaphorical sense.

Artemisia vulgaris L.
COMMON WORMWOOD

■ *may be poisonous* ■
Mugwort, Common Mugwort, St John's Wort

There are many species in the *Artemisia* genus, among them numerous well-known culinary herbs such as common wormwood, absinthium and tarragon (*A. dracunculus*), the lemon-scented southernwood *(A. abrotanum)*, which grows up to 3 ft 3 in. (1 m) high, and also the evergreen santonica *(A. cina)*, native to Central Asia.

In Europe, wormwood is used today almost exclusively as a culinary herb, and those who suffer from allergies fear its aggressive pollen. In earlier centuries, it was different. The ethnobotanist Wolf-Dieter Storl points out numerous treatments in the medieval and early modern ages when the herb was used in gynaecology, for instance, to induce birth, as a hip bath to treat infertility, for amenorrhoea, and to procure abortion.

For more than 2,000 years, wormwood has also been part of 'moxibustion', a treatment in traditional Chinese medicine, described by Edoardo Fozzi as follows: 'Small cones of dried, finely rubbed wormwood are placed on the skin and lit from beneath. Wormwood powder burns without a flame.' According to the Ben Cao herbal codex, dating from the early 16th century (see page 24), patients in a coma were restored to consciousness by filling the navel with cooking salt, placing a fresh slice of ginger on top and on the latter burning a cone of wormwood.

The European belief that wormwood, worn around the foot, will protect against tiredness is unfortunately just a legend.

■ **Description:** Height to 5 ft (1.5 m); leaves pinnate, serrate, auriculate at base, dark green and smooth above, silvery and downy on underside; stems grooved, smooth below,

Santonica has finely pinnate leaves. The unopened buds, so-called 'santonica seeds', were in the past used to combat roundworms.

Common wormwood has dark green leaves, smooth on the upper surface. The tips of flowering shoots provide good seasoning for roast goose or pork.

*'Weather magic is easy to carry out with a plant dedicated to the god of thunder.
Long after their conversion to Christianity, farmers gathered wormwood in season
and placed twigs above the front door or under the roof to ward off lightning strikes.'*

Wolf-Dieter Storl,
Healing herbs and magic plants

*Below left: French
tarragon, found in many
herb gardens. The flavour
of the smooth, entire,
lanceolate leaves refines
vegetable, fish and meat
dishes.*

*Below right: Russian
tarragon; the sturdy
herbs produce an
intensive flavouring for
cucumber.*

often reddish, branching, not becoming woody; flowers inconspicuous, yellowish or reddish brown, in densely leafed panicles, bracts downy, often tinged with brownish or reddish colour; no wreath of hair; rhizome woody, branching.

- **Flowering:** August to September
- **Scent and flavour:** Scent aromatic; taste bitter, aromatic
- **Location:** Clay soils, waysides, scrub, embankments, wasteland
- **Distribution:** Common
- **Drug:** Herba, Radix Artemisiae
- **Constituents:** Essential oils (cineol), bitter principles, tannins, mucilage, inulin, vitamins
- **Treatments:** For loss of appetite, digestive disorders, gall bladder ailments, menstrual problems, to combat fever, worms and insects
- **Use:** Tea, culinary
- **Homeopathic uses:** See above, and also used to treat epilepsy
- **What and when to gather:** Herb March and April, flowering shoot tips July and August, root September, October
- **Lookalikes:** Other *Artemisia* species; their leaves have a different colour
- **Other information:** Those allergic to pollen should not use wormwood as a culinary herb; because it can act as an abortifact, care is required in pregnancy

Absinthium with its yellow, nodding flowers is one of the few asterids with a stem that is woody at the base.

Artemisia absinthium L.
ABSINTHIUM

■ *poisonous* ■

Absinth Wormwood, Absinth Sagewort, Old Man

The absinthe spirit distilled from *Artemisia absinthium*, prohibited in many countries (since 1921 in Germany), has driven many addicts to a miserable death. The nerve poison thujone, contained in the alcoholic extract, causes epileptic fits and lasting psychological damage. Medicines based on absinthium are still prescribed for problems with the digestive tract, but it is essential to avoid overdoses.

- **Description:** Height to 2 ft 8 in. (80 cm); leaves downy, grey, bi- or tri-pinnate, with petiole; stems silky, downy, with many small branches, woody in the lower sections; flowers yellow, spherical, short stalk, nodding, in racemes; wind pollinated; no wreath of hairs; rhizome markedly branched
- **Flowering:** July to September

- **Scent and flavour:** Scent aromatic; taste very bitter
- **Location:** Lime-poor and dry waysides, gravel pits, wasteland
- **Distribution:** Eastern Mediterranean, cultivated elsewhere
- **Drug:** Herba, Flores Absinthii
- **Constituents:** Bitter principles (absinthin), essential oils (thujone, proazulen), vitamins
- **Treatments:** For loss of appetite, digestive disorders, gastro-enteric, liver and gall bladder diseases, intestinal parasites, colds
- **Use:** Tea, tea blends, powder, wine, liqueur
- **Homeopathic uses:** See above, and for nervous cramps
- **What and when to gather:** Flowering herb July to September
- **Lookalikes:** Common wormwood (see page 55): leaves not downy on the upper surface
- **Other information:** Daily dose one cup of tea

Bellis perennis L.
COMMON DAISY

English Daisy, Lawn Daisy, Meadow Daisy,
Dog Daisy, Bruisewort

With their leaf rosettes, daisies form dense carpets, even on frequently mown lawns.

It's amazing where daisies will grow. In meadows and on lawns, in parks and gardens, on sports fields, despite the heavy trampling, and school grounds, on the little strip of green between pavement and roadway. It's a pity that these locations are often polluted, because this modest little plant, which moreover flowers just about the whole year through, is edible from root to flower. And because it looks pretty, it is often used to garnish salads or sandwiches.

In naturopathy, the vitamin C-rich daisy, because of its decongestant qualities, has long been used to treat bronchitis and asthma-related ailments. It is also used for tumours, and kidney and liver complaints, as well as skin eruptions and boils. In a similar way to arnica (see page 53), crushed plants can be used as first aid for sprains and bruises.

The word 'daisy' is believed to come from the Saxon phrase *daeges eage*, meaning 'day's eye',

originally referring to the sun, but then transferred to the plant, perhaps because of the flower, which opens at dawn and closes at dusk. Because it is used to help the healing process in bruises and wounds, the medieval name of 'bruisewort' still persists in some places.

- **Description:** Height to 6 in. (15 cm); leaves in evergreen rosette, leaves downy, crenate, spatulate; stems with short hairs or smooth with single flower; flower heads with yellow tubular flowers, ligulates white, often with a pink tinge; bracts green, elongate, in two rows; fruit small, ovate, no pappus hairs; roots short, thick; perennial
- **Flowering:** Year-round
- **Scent and flavour:** No scent; taste mild, sweetish at first, and then bitter
- **Location:** Meadows, pasture, gardens, parks
- **Distribution:** Very common
- **Drug:** Flores, Herba Bellidis
- **Constituents:** Saponins, essential oils, mucilage, bitter principles, tannins, flavonoids, inulin
- **Treatments:** For bruises, sprains, wounds, skin diseases, coughs, angina, asthma (decongestant), severe menstrual pains, liver ailments, jaundice, blood purifier
- **Use:** Tea, juice, syrup, salads, soups, substitute for capers
- **Homeopathic uses:** See above, and for haemorrhages, rheumatic complaints
- **What and when to gather:** Flowers and leaves year-round
- **Lookalikes:** None

Calendula officinalis L.
POT MARIGOLD

Marigold, English Marigold, Garden Marigold, Mary Gold, Golds, Ruddles

Even in the age of chemical and industrial pharmaceutics, the marigold has successfully defended its niche as an anti-inflammatory and antibacterial herbal medicine. This is due not least to Sebastian Kneipp, the 'herb father', who held it in high esteem. Salves made from the flowers to treat wounds, and marigold extracts for gargling to help sore mouth and throat membranes, are part of the stock inventory for many domestic medicine cabinets. Other practitioners recommend 'Calendulatonicum' with rose water and, if required, three drops of geranium oil as a natural cosmetic 'for large-pored, tired skin with poor circulation'. According to Bisset and Wichtl, however, the internal use to treat liver, gall bladder and stomach complaints only plays a subordinate role these days. Hildegard of Bingen recommended pot marigold to treat poisoning, favus and digestive disorders, though she limited the last to ruminant livestock.

In the wild, these healing herbs, of Mediterranean origin, will be found only as garden fugitives in areas close to human settlements. In some climatically favoured areas, however, it is possible to find scattered examples of the field marigold (*C. arvensis*), with its smaller, pale gold flowers. Due to its scarcity in many countries though, it may not be picked in the wild. As the garden marigold is easy to cultivate – it was frequently grown in country gardens because of its medicinal qualities and also because it could be used to colour butter and cheese – *Calendula* products in the stores are mostly produced from cultivated plants.

- **Description:** Height to 20 in. (50 cm); leaves fleshy, downy, spatulate, sessile, alternate; stems upright, glandular-hairy, branching; flowers 1–2 in. (2–5 cm) in size, yellow to

orange-yellow, bracts green; fruits strongly crenate, curving inwards, root spindle-shaped; annual
- **Flowering:** June to October
- **Scent and flavour:** Scent of flowers aromatic; taste bitter to slightly bitter
- **Location:** Cultivated, gardens
- **Distribution:** Wild in Mediterranean lands
- **Drug:** Flores cum/sine calycibus, Herba Calendulae
- **Constituents:** Essential oils (plus carotin and lycopin), bitter principles (calendulin), mucilage, saponins, glycosides, cumarins
- **Treatments:** For liver and gall bladder disorders, stomach and duodenal ulcers, wounds, ulcers (ulcus cruris), inflammations of the mouth and pharyngeal mucous membranes, fever, cramps
- **Use:** Tea, salve (skin care), tincture, pressed juice, baths, culinary, garnish
- **Homeopathic uses:** See above
- **What and when to gather:** Whole flowers or flowers without bracts June to October
- **Lookalikes:** Field marigold (*C. arvensis*), wild in fields and vineyards, flowers ½–1 in. (1–2.5 cm), pale yellow, rare
- **Other information:** Marigolds were once used as 'false saffron'

Marigolds come from the Mediterranean region; in the wild in Europe they are escapees from gardens.

Chamomilla spec.
Matricaria spec.
Chamaemelum spec.
CHAMOMILE

In most European countries, no other medicinal herb is used as often as chamomile – and there are few plant names that cover so many species. There are many chamomile-like Asteraceae, scented and unscented, not originally native to the lands where they are used but introduced at a later period. In Saxony, Germany, the cultivation of the German chamomile was a considerable factor in the economy. Today, most products come from western and south-eastern Europe or from South America.

German chamomile. The flower head is composed of white ligulates and yellow tubular flowers.

Chamomilla recutita (L.) *Rauschert*
GERMAN CHAMOMILE

German chamomile (*Chamomilla recutita*) can be recognized by the hollow cone-shaped flower head, while the flower heads of disc mayweed (*Matricaria discoidea*) and Roman chamomile (*Chamaemelum nobile*) are filled with pithy matter. The pleasantly scented Roman chamomile or common chamomile is most widely distributed in western and southern Europe.

German and Roman chamomile overlap in the areas of the body where they can be used for treatment. Their efficacy in combating cramps, various stomach disorders, problems of the mouth, throat and bronchial tubes, and for gynaecological and skin problems is well known. Chamomile is also used in treating sick children and in veterinary medicine. In contrast to many other herbs recommended by and used in herb medicine, the antibacterial agents of chamomile have been scientifically tested (see Bisset and Wichtl). However, there are warnings of allergic reactions; also, chamomile tea should not be drunk regularly over a longer period of time. Closely related to the perennial Roman chamomile is the golden chamomile, whose yellow ligulate flowers produce a yellow dye, and the widespread but medicinally useless corn chamomile (*A. arvensis*) with white ligulate flowers, dome-shaped, pithy flower base and no aromatic scent.

- **Description:** Height to 20 in. (50 cm); leaves finely bi- or tri-pinnate, with narrow linear leaflets; stems round, upright, branching, with single or few flower heads (0.2–0.2 in., 5–8 mm wide), tubular flowers yellow-gold, ligulates white, no pallea; base of flower head cone-shaped, hollow; fruit small, five-ribbed achene with no pappus hairs; root spindle shaped; annual
- **Flowering:** May to August
- **Scent and flavour:** Characteristic chamomile scent; flavour savoury, bitter

- **Location:** Lime-poor and dry fields, fallow ground, roadsides, meadows, gravel pits, dumps; this herb loves warmth
- **Distribution:** Widely distributed, often escaped from cultivation
- **Drug:** Flores Chamomillae
- **Constituents:** Essential oils (chamazulen, bisabolol), flavonoids, glycosides, mucilage, cumarin, bitter principles
- **Treatments:** For all kinds of cramps, inflammation of the stomach lining, stomach ulcers, indigestion, sore throats, sinus infections, bleeding gums, gynaecological disorders, in childbirth, skin disorders, haemorrhoids, etc.
- **Use:** Tea, poultices, baths, gargles, inhalation, salve, oil, hair shampoo (cares for and lightens the hair)
- **Homeopathic uses:** See above, and for irritable emotional states
- **What and when to gather:** Flower heads May to August
- **Lookalikes:** Disc mayweed: Height up to 16 in. (40 cm), stems markedly branched, no ligulate flowers, tubular flowers greenish-yellow, strongly scented; scentless false mayweed (*Matricaria inodora*): flower head pithy, very common, contains no proazulen and therefore has no anti-inflammatory action; corn chamomile, see above
- **Other information:** The proazulen (chamazulen) obtained from the flowers is produced by heating (pouring boiling water over) the azulen.

Disc mayweed has no ligulate flowers.

Roman chamomile has a flat-based, pithy flower head, with dry scales.

The purplish-red flowering blessed milkthistle is a native of the Mediterranean region.

Right: The silver thistle's flower only opens in fine weather.

Cirsium spp.
Carduus spp.
Carlina spp.
THISTLES

Browsing through old books about thistles, the picture gained is ambivalent. On the one hand, we have the prickly plant that can scratch painfully and, when it runs riot, transform good pasture or fields into a worthless wilderness. On the other hand, many thistles are edible, including the artichoke (Cynara scolymus), one of the finest and most expensive vegetables in Europe. The bizarre beauty of thistle flowers and leaves has not only aroused the interest of botanists, but also the curiosity of artists, and some species are deep-rooted in religion and myth.

Carlina acaulis L.
SILVER THISTLE

■ *protected* ■

Stemless Carline Thistle, Dwarf Carline Thistle, Hunter's Bread, Carlina Angelica

Once, every traveller in mountainous regions knew that you could eat the flower head base of the silver thistle, like that of the artichoke, which earned the plant the name 'hunter's bread'. In medicine, root extracts were used as gargles for throat inflammations and to treat kidney and stomach ailments; externally, it was used to combat skin rashes (according to Bisset and Wichtl, the presence of antibacterial agents in the drug has indeed been scientifically proven). The parts of the plant used are the long taproots.

- **Description:** Height to 4 in. (10 cm); basal leaf rosette, leaves prickly, pinnatisect, dentate, woolly down on underside; stems short or missing; flowers up to 6 in. (15 cm) across, white to reddish violet, bracts silvery white, shiny; achenes close to the plant, with yellow hairs; root thick, c. 4 in (10 cm) long, yellow-brown with milky sap; perennial
- **Flowering:** July to September
- **Scent and flavour:** Fresh root has an unpleasant sharp scent, dried root pleasantly aromatic; flavour sweetish at first, then bitter and hot
- **Location:** Dry, sunny mountain meadows, waysides; this herb is lime-loving
- **Distribution:** Scattered, cultivated
- **Drug:** Radix Carlinae
- **Constituents:** Essential oils, inulin, tannins, bitter principles, resin
- **Treatments:** For loss of appetite, kidney, liver, and stomach ailments, colds and skin diseases, wounds, as a mouthwash
- **Use:** Tea, tincture, powder, stomach digestive, poultices; veterinary use to encourage fattening or estrus
- **Homeopathic uses:** See above
- **What and when to gather:** Roots, unpeeled, March to April and September to October
- **Lookalikes:** Carline thistles (*C. vulgaris*): height up to 20 in. (50 cm), stems leafy, bracts straw-yellow, biennial
- **Other information:** Use with care: high doses may lead to diarrhoea and vomiting

Cirsium arvense **CANADA THISTLE**

The Canada thistle (Cirsium arvense), with its thorny leaves, is also used medically.

Cirsium oleraceum **CABBAGE THISTLE**

Folk medicine considers the cabbage thistle (C. oleraceum) to be a wound healer and a tonic (digestive bitters), and it can also be used as a vegetable.

Other kinds of thistle

Species of the genus *Carduus* have prickly dentate leaves and fruits with no feathery pappus. The most common of these is the blessed milkthistle (formerly *Carduus marianus*, now *Sylibum marianum*), where the upper surfaces of the leaves are marbled white. According to legend, the pale stripes were made by the Virgin Mary, when she lost some of her milk fleeing the soldiers of King Herod. Blessed milkthistle preparations are used to stabilize the liver, and also in heart, circulatory and digestive disorders. Most effective are the bitter principles, extracted from leaves, roots and seeds.

Cichorium intybus L.
CHICORY

Blue Daisy, Blue Dandelion, Blue Sailors, Coffeeweed, Succory

The 17th-century English apothecary and author of *The Complete Herbal*, Nicholas Culpeper, had a high opinion of chicory, recommending it for 'swooning and passions of the heart, for heat and headache in children, and for the blood and liver', among many other uses. The blue, star-shaped flowers of this impressive plant do not open until high and late summer, when most other wildflowers have already finished blooming. In folk tales, it symbolizes the girl left behind, waiting faithfully and in vain for the return of her lover. It is even credited with magic powers. Detlef Ernet reports that 'If someone touches a person he or she loves with a chicory plant, dug up on Good Friday with a silver coin while invoking the Trinity, that person will passionately return his or her love.'

Chicory – blue flowers by the wayside.

Like many other herbs containing bitter principles, chicory is also used to combat liver and gall bladder ailments and for spring detox treatments. One use, familiar from dandelion (see page 73), is to roast the root and use it as 'chicory coffee'.

In Dr Edward Bach's Flower Remedies, chicory is recommended for people who tend towards self-centredness, a need for control and self-pity, and who cannot deal with the resulting problems. A close relative of chicory is the endive (*C. endivia*), cultivated as a salad plant.

- **Description:** Height to 4 ft (120 cm); basal leaf rosette with obovate leaves, lower leaves pinnate and lobate, upper leaves entire, long, sheathing stem at base; stems rough-haired, hollow, stiff, branching; ligulates pale blue, later whitish to pinkish; achenes with scales on calyx join; tap root yellowish-white with milky sap; perennial
- **Flowering:** July to September
- **Scent and flavour:** Unscented; taste savoury, bitter
- **Location:** Waysides and roadsides, meadows, gravel pits, banks
- **Distribution:** Very common
- **Drug:** Radix, Herba, Flores Cichorii
- **Constituents:** Inulin, bitter principles (intybin), choline, tannins, cichoriin, essential oils, vitamins, anthocyan dye (blue)
- **Treatments:** For liver and gall bladder disorders, poor digestion, nervous exhaustion, diabetes, loss of appetite
- **Uses:** Tea, root, culinary (root roasted as coffee substitute)
- **Homeopathic uses:** See above
- **What and when to gather:** Young leaves in April, May; herb June, July; root September, October
- **Lookalikes:** None
- **Other information:** Soaking the leaves and the root in water before preparation lessens the bitter taste

Cnicus benedictus L.
BLESSED THISTLE

Carduus Benedictus, Holy Thistle, St Benedict's Thistle

'St Benedict's herb' is a name often given to a different plant, avens (*Geum urbanum*), also known as herb bennet or way bennet, so we will refer to *Cnicus benedictus* throughout as the 'blessed thistle'. The plant is native to the Mediterranean region and is mainly found cultivated in herb gardens. It is sometimes confused with the blessed milkthistle (see page 63), also from the Mediterranean, which can however be distinguished by its milky-white marbled leaves and which can grow to twice the size of the blessed thistle.

At the beginning of the early modern period, the blessed thistle was considered almost a kind of universal cure, used to treat digestive tract disorders and liver and gall bladder complaints; indeed, even smallpox. As late as 1962, Oertel and Bauer recommended it for inflammations in the intestinal and gall bladder area and added, 'The action is strengthened by adding centaury, yarrow, some sweetflag and absinthium.'

Although we do not hear much about this herb now, the drug is still produced and sold. It stimulates the production of stomach juices and saliva, but should only be given for brief periods and in small quantities, as overdosing may lead to poisoning.

- **Description:** Height up to 2 ft (60 cm); leaves pale green, pinnate, lobate, thorny, and serrate, thorny tip; stems square, upright, hairy, branching; flower heads hairy, sticky, yellow-white tubular flowers, bracts thorny; achenes with pappus hairs; root reddish-brown; annual
- **Flowering:** May to August
- **Scent and flavour:** Scent strongly aromatic, unscented when dried; taste very bitter
- **Location:** Loves warmth and limy soils

- **Distribution:** In the Mediterranean region and in herb gardens
- **Drug:** Herba Cardui benedicti
- **Ingredients:** Essential oils, bitter principles (cnicin), flavonoids, mineral salts, vitamins
- **Treatments:** For loss of appetite, gastro-enteric disorders, liver and gall bladder ailments, heart function disorders, rheumatic complaints, fever; externally for ulcers, chilblains, menstrual problems
- **Use:** Tea, poultices, bath additive, liqueur, herb extract
- **Homeopathic uses:** For chronic liver diseases
- **What and when to gather:** Leaves and shoots with flowers June to August, stem without rind April
- **Lookalikes:** Blessed milkthistle (*Sylibum marianum*, see page 63): larger, leaves marbled white
- **Other information:** Take care to keep to the recommended dose (two cups per day), as otherwise nausea and irritation of the intestines may occur; do not drink if kidneys are inflamed

The flower of the blessed thistle is reminiscent of an exotic starfish.

The purple coneflower, which can grow to more than 3 ft, is here shown in a garden with a yellow-flowered, closely related species of Rudbeckia.

Narrow-leafed coneflower in the Antheringer herb garden near Salzburg, Austria.

Echinacea angustifolia DC.
NARROWLEAFED CONEFLOWER

Echinacea, Black Samson, Coneflower, Snakeroot

In many old herbals, coneflowers are missing. This is not surprising. On the one hand, the *Echinacea* is a genus not native to Europe and therefore something of a parvenu among the old-established healing herbs known since the days of the Greeks and Romans. In North America, on the other hand, the home of the coneflowers, the healing powers of *Echinacea* have long been known. Native Americans used root extracts as an antiseptic to treat inflammations and also for toothache, colds and snakebite.

Not until the second half of the 20th century did science begin to concern itself intensively with the active constituents and discover interesting antibacterial effects. These then formed the base of various preparations that quickly penetrated the world markets and are now among the best-selling products among the herbal healing pharmaceuticals. Those who suffer from tuberculosis, AIDS, multiple sclerosis or any other disease of the autoimmune system should not, however, take *Echinacea* products.

- **Description:** Height up to 2 ft (60 cm); leaves narrow, hairy, stems rough-haired, branching; the few narrow ligulates are strikingly pink to scarlet, tubular flowers brownish-red, flower head markedly domed, scales on fruit body yellow-orange, base of fruit thorny; root sturdy; perennial
- **Flowering:** July to October
- **Scent and flavour:** Root slightly scented; taste at first slightly sweetish, savoury, then bitter, astringent
- **Location:** Gardens and cultivated, gravelly, rocky, dry limestone soils
- **Distribution:** Cultivated, native to North America
- **Drug:** Radix Echinaceae angustifoliae and E. purpureae, Herba Echnicaceae purpureae
- **Ingredients:** Caffeic acid derivatives (echinacoside, cynarin)
- **Treatments:** Preventative to ward off colds, for injuries, wounds that are slow to heal, burns, insect bites, pain, toothache
- **Use:** Tincture, salves, drops, injections
- **Homeopathic uses:** For serious infections with fever
- **What and when to gather:** Root, herb of E. purpurea
- **Lookalikes:** Purple coneflower (E. purpurea): over 3 ft 3 in. (1 m) high, flowers c. 4 in. (10 cm) diameter, ligulates broader and more numerous, leaves broadly lanceolate, rough-haired
- **Other information:** Purple coneflower and pale purple coneflower (E. pallida) can also be used pharmaceutically

Eupatorium cannabinum L.
HEMP AGRIMONY

*Water Hemp, Water Agrimony, Gravel Root,
Hindheal, Holy Rope*

There are more than 500 species worldwide in the *Eupatorium* genus, including a few trees. There are very few examples in central Europe – with the exception of hemp agrimony, which is widely distributed. The species name *Cannabinum* is owed to the similarity of its leaves to those of hemp, *Cannabis sativa* (see page 163); the genus name *Eupatorum*, however, is derived from the name of Mithridates Eupator, a king of Pontus (in the eastern Mediterranean region) in the first century AD.

Although its healing tradition goes back to ancient times, hemp agrimony is accorded little importance today. Düll & Kutzelnigg indeed call it a 'former healing herb', which is not quite correct, as in homeopathy its three North American relatives – lesser snakeroot (*E. aromaticum*), common boneset (*E. perfoliatum*) and gravel root (*E. purpureum*) – continue to be used. In earlier years, the herb and root were used for medicines to treat liver disorders and ulcers. According to Hieronymous Bock, hemp agrimony also improves virility.

- **Description:** Height to 5 ft (150 cm); leaves hemp-like, short petiole, opposite, stems edged, upright, branching, often reddish, hairy; few, dark pink to reddish-purple tubular flowers per flower head, together forming dense panicles; achenes black, with pappi; root branching; perennial
- **Flowering:** July to September
- **Scent and flavour:** Scent of the root very unpleasantly sharp; taste bitter, biting
- **Location:** Ditches, river banks, water meadows; meadows of tall plants; this herb indicates presence of nitrogen
- **Distribution:** Common
- **Drug:** Herba, Radix, Eupatorii cannabini

- **Constituents:** Essential oils, flavonoids (euparin), alkaloids, tannins, inulin, polysaccharides
- **Treatments:** For liver and gall bladder complaints, externally for swelling, bruises, rheumatic ailments; as an immune system stimulant and gentle laxative
- **Uses:** Tea, poultices, dye (black)
- **Homeopathic uses:** See above and for influenza-related diseases
- **What and when to gather:** Leaves May to June, roots April, May, October, November – use as fresh as possible
- **Lookalikes:** None
- **Other information:** Take care: overdoses can lead to nausea and vomiting. Once used to combat dysentery and snakebite; a use similar to that of *E. perfoliatum*

Attractive hemp agrimony often grows on the edges of meadows and in meadows of tall plants.

Helianthus annuus L.
COMMON SUNFLOWER

Above: The sunflower turns its blooms to face the sun.

Below: The Jerusalem artichoke flowers late in the year and spreads through tubers, which contain lots of inulin, protein, calium and vitamins.

The amazement of Old World gardeners and flower-lovers when the first sunflowers arrived after the European discovery of America was enormous, especially when, as they soon discovered, these could easily be propagated from seed. At first these exotic plants bore names such as 'Indian Sun'. Artists, too, succumbed to the fascination of the sunflower – one need only think of Vincent van Gogh's famous sunflower paintings. Today, in Europe and in America, large fields are covered with cultivated sunflowers, summer after summer. The seeds are used for baking or to feed birds, but primarily for the production of a valuable oil, used in, among other products, margarine. In natural cosmetics, powdered sunflower seeds, mixed with honey and various vegetable oils, are used as face masks to improve circulation and to smooth and refresh the skin.

The Jerusalem artichoke (*Helianthus tuberosus*) from South America looks like the sunflower's little brother. It is widespread in country gardens and occasionally occurs as a garden escape in the wild. Its tubers are rich in minerals and fructose, so it is perhaps best known as the 'diabetic's vegetable'.

- **Description:** Height to 13 ft (4 m); leaves large, cordate, rough-haired; stems sturdy, pithy, branching at top; flower up to 16 in. (40 cm) in diameter, nodding, composed of thousands of brown tubular flowers; ligulates sunshine yellow, sterile; achenes bare, numerous palleae; roots reach a depth of up to 6 ft 6 in. (2 m); annual
- **Flowering:** July to September
- **Scent and flavour:** Unscented; seeds have nutty taste
- **Location:** Gardens, fields, loves light and rich soil
- **Distribution:** Gardens, fields, native to subtropical Central America
- **Drug:** Flores, Folii, Semen, Oleum Helianthi
- **Constituents:** Flavonolglycosides, saponins (helianthus saponin), histidine, tannins; seed: fatty oil, protein, carbohydrates
- **Treatments:** Flowers for fever (mainly for malaria if patient is resistant to quinine), for liver and gall bladder diseases, ascites, haemorrhoids, eye inflammations; oil (lowers cholesterol) to combat hardening of the arteries, decongestant, skin care
- **Uses:** Tea, seeds (bread, muesli, bird food), oil (massage oil, margarine production)
- **Homeopathic uses:** See above and for gastro-enteric diseases, hives, bruises, wounds
- **What and when to gather:** Freshly opened ligulates July to September, leaves July, seeds (seed cores) September
- **Lookalikes:** Jerusalem artichoke, Jerusalem sunflower (*H. tuberosus*): tubular florets yellow, flower head smaller, tubers (diabetic flour, vegetable, animal feed, potato substitute, alcoholic spirit)
- **Other information:** Supplies oil (c. 35 per cent fatty oil and rich in protein): sunflower oil

Inula helenium L.
ELECAMPANE INULA

Elf Dock, Elf Wort, Horseheal, Helenium

If you want to see the elecampane inula, native to western and central Asia, in the wild in central Europe, you'll have to be very lucky. It's more common to see the attractive plant, up to six feet six (2 m) tall, in monastery and herb gardens, where the garden designers are familiar with the 2,000-year tradition of elecampane inula as a healing and magical plant. Hildegard of Bingen recommended it for lung disease. Elecampane root contains antiseptic agents, used to treat dry coughs and whooping cough. Elecampane extracts are employed in homeopathy, too. In Germany, during the Nazi period, the possible advantages of 'mass cultivation' were enthusiastically promoted – for instance by M. Lassel in his book, very popular at the time, *Kräutergold* ('Herb Gold'). Voices calling for caution have since multiplied, warning against taking elecampane products because of allergy (see Bisset and Wichtl).

The second part of the botanical name is derived from Homeric legend – beautiful Helen is supposed to have adorned herself with elecampane flowers before seducing Paris. In later years, elecampane was believed to be a protection against witches' magic and was worn like an amulet on a string about the neck.

- **Description:** Height up to 6 ft 6 in. (2 m); base leaves up to 1 ft (30 cm) long, ovate to elliptic, dentate, hairy, stem leaves narrow, cordate, sessile, semi-leaf-sheathing, white down on the underside; stems sturdy, upright, hairy; flower heads 2–3 in. (6–8 cm) in diameter, numerous large yellow ligulates, bracts vary in length; achene with long reddish pappus hairs; rhizome sturdy, up to 2 in. (5 cm) thick, branching, reddish-brown outside, whitish inside; perennial
- **Flowering:** July to September

- **Scent and flavour:** Scent when fresh pleasant, camphor-like, aromatic, dried like violets; taste savoury, bitter
- **Location:** Damp meadows, streams, woodland borders, hedges, herb gardens
- **Distribution:** Rare. Native to central Asia
- **Drug:** Rhizoma, Folii Helenii
- **Ingredients:** Rhizome: essential oils (helenin, lactones), inulin, bitter principles
- **Treatments:** For dry coughs (smoker's cough), bronchitis, loss of appetite, heart, digestive, or gall bladder complaints, metabolic disorders, menstruation problems, inflammation of the urinary tract, haemorrhoids, parasitic worms
- **Uses:** Tea, tonic, oil, tincture, powder, vegetable, perfume industry, patisserie, diabetic products
- **Homeopathic uses:** For chronic coughs, stomach ulcers, discharge
- **What and when to gather:** Unpeeled rhizome of 3- to 4-year-old plants in March, April, September, October, leaves in June
- **Lookalikes:** British yellowhead (*Inula britannica*) – identical uses
- **Other information:** Take care – touching elecampane root can cause allergies. Oleum Helenii is brown and thick and contains elecampane camphor and azulen. Like santonin, it combats worms, but is less toxic

Elecampane inula in a herb garden.

Butterbur grows in central mountain ranges of Germany and in the Alps and their foothills. It has smaller leaves than pestilence wort.

Below left: The large leaves of pestilence wort often border the banks of streams and rivers, sometimes stretching for miles.

Below right: The flower heads appear in early spring.

Petasites hybridus (L.) P. Gaertn.
PESTILENCE WORT

Bog Rhubarb, Sweet Coltsfoot, Umbrella Plant

People who go on guided herb-finding tours often ask if the heart-shaped leaves, grey on the underside and up to three feet across, that cover riverbanks in such profusion are 'wild rhubarb'. The garden plant, medical rhubarb, is a polygonaceous plant with smooth, grooved stems. Pestilence wort is also often confused with coltsfoot (see page 74), which grows in similar locations but has much smaller leaves and quite different flowers. The large flower heads, which break out of the moist ground in early spring even before the leaves, also attract attention.

In earlier times, people placed great trust in pestilence wort. Because it stimulated perspiration and was a decongestant, it was believed to be a cure for the plague, a disease which in the Middle Ages and in early modern times depopulated whole swathes of Europe. However, recent studies have proved that all parts of pestilence wort contain toxic pyrrolizidine alkaloids, which can alter the genetic material and are considered carcinogenic. For this reason, the advice today is to avoid using medicines based on pestilence wort.

- **Description:** Height up to flower 16 in. (40 cm), up to seed ripening 3 ft 3 in. (1 m); leaves with long, ribbed stem 1–3 ft 3 in. (30–100 cm) wide, cordate to reniform, irregularly dentate, thick grey down on underside; stems upright, hollow, with cobwebby hairs, reddish, elongated scale leaves; numerous flowers, with stems, fleshy red to reddish-white, in cylindrical raceme, no ligulates; achenes with silky white pappus hairs; roots bulbous, horizontal shoots, hollow, long, creeping runners
- **Flowering:** March to May
- **Scent and flavour:** Flowers almost unscented, roots have sweetish smell, stem smells unpleasant; slimy, somewhat bitter flavour
- **Location:** Banks of streams and rivers, embankments, damp meadows, wet woodlands
- **Distribution:** Common
- **Drug:** Radix, Folia, Flores Pestatitis
- **Constituents:** Leaves – mucilage, essential oils, bitter principles, alkaloids (pyrrolizidine alkaloids), flavonoids (astragalin); root – also contains petasin, tannins, inulin
- **Treatments:** For gout, menstruation problems, coughs, colds, wounds, joint pains, nervous stomach complaints, liver and gall bladder disorders, worms
- **Uses:** Tea (leaves and flowers, root), poultices (freshly crushed leaves), tincture (root)
- **Homeopathic uses:** See above and for neck pain and headaches, urinary tract inflammations, diseases of the pancreas
- **What and when to gather:** Flowers March to May, leaves April to May, root September to October
- **Lookalikes:** Butterbur (*Petasites albus*): flowers yellowish-white, leaves rounder, even thicker down on underside; coltsfoot (see page 74): leaves hand-sized, edges finely serrate, single flowers, yellow

Solidago virgaurea L.
EUROPEAN GOLDENROD

Goldenrod, Woundwort, Aaron's Rod

Goldenrod is one of those healing plants where the healing practices of past centuries have been confirmed by modern analyses of the ingredients, animal experiments and clinical experience. The Swiss doctor Martin Furlenmeier writes: '*Solidago* is an organ-specific treatment for kidney disorders of the first rank, and has excellent effects on chronic kidney disease, but also on acute inflammatory kidney and bladder diseases when… improvement is slower than was hoped.' However, dosage of the medicine should be left to the doctor in all cases. In the past, goldenrod was also highly esteemed as a cure for wounds.

European goldenrod has a few close relatives native to North America. These were cultivated in Europe as garden plants or food for pheasants and have spread widely through large parts of the continent. According to research quoted by Bisset and Wichtl, Canadian goldenrod (*S. canadensis*) and giant goldenrod (*S. gigantea*) contain other agents. However, both species have no doubt been mistaken for the common goldenrod and mixed with it.

In the garden, it can happen that goldenrod spreads very quickly, usually to the detriment of other plants. It is therefore recommended that the flowering panicles be cut off before seeds form.

- **Description:** Height up to 3 ft 3 in. (1 m); leaves elongate, lanceolate, serrate; stems rod-like, erect, branching at top, densely leafed, flower head erect, dense panicle, tubular flowers hermaphrodite, yellow-gold, 8–12 large, yellow, female ligulates; fruit with pappus hairs; root up to 3 ft 3 in. (1 m) deep, no runners; perennial
- **Flowering:** July to September
- **Scent and flavour:** Flowers have spicy scent, herb unscented; taste bitter, astringent

- **Location:** Open woodland, woodland clearings, heathland
- **Distribution:** Common
- **Drug:** Herba Solidaginis virgaureae
- **Ingredients:** Caoutchouc, essential oils, flavonoids, saponins, glycosides, tannins
- **Treatments:** For kidney and bladder diseases, bedwetting, diarrhoea, badly healing wounds, coughs, sore throats, rheumatic complaints, gout, diseases of the prostate, insect stings (crushed leaves), for purifying the blood
- **Uses:** Tea, tincture, fresh leaves
- **Homeopathic uses:** See above and for diseases of the liver, gall bladder, and pancreas
- **What and when to gather:** Flowering herb July to September
- **Lookalikes:** Canadian goldenrod – flower heads are smaller

Above left: European goldenrod – here a garden variety – flowers in dense panicles.

Above right: Canadian goldenrod was used by native Americans to treat snakebite.

The leaves of common tansy are fern-like; the button-like flowers are still glowing in September.

Tanacetum vulgare L. *(Syn. Chrysanthemum vulgare)* COMMON TANSY

■ *poisonous* ■
Bachelor's Buttons, Bitter Buttons, Golden Button, Cow Bitter

Before using any part of tansy for healing purposes, you should be warned that all parts of this plant contain the nerve toxin thujone, which causes damage to kidneys and the liver and can in the worst cases lead via the central nervous system to paralysis of the respiratory system. What looks like an insoluble contradiction at first glance is a principle known since Paracelsus' day; the dose is the deciding factor. Hildegard of Bingen recommended hip baths of tansy and other herbs to treat retention of urine and amenorrhoea. For a long time, tansy preparations were considered a tried and tested vermifuge – hence the names, in some countries, meaning 'worm herb' or 'worm's death' – and have also been used to combat head lice. These days, the advice is, if you must use it, to do so only under medical supervision and never during pregnancy.

Tansy plays a certain role in biological pest control. As a spray to combat turnip maggots and codling moths, a mixture of 18 oz (500 g) tansy and wormwood (see page 57) to 2½ gallons (10 l) water is used. Combined with alum, tansy is also used as a dye plant.

The related costmary (*Tanacetum balsamita*) is a cultivated plant.

- **Description:** Height up to 4 ft (1.2 m); evergreen, leaves alternate, dark green, pinnate, markedly dentate; stems erect, hardly branching, ridged, hollow; numerous flower heads in flat-topped panicles with yellow-gold tubular flowers, no ligulates, fruits without pappus, but with crown-shaped, skin-like seam; root very branched, perennial
- **Flowering:** July to September
- **Scent and flavour:** Intensive, unpleasant, camphor-like scent; flavour savoury to bitter
- **Location:** Waysides, railway embankments, slopes, stony river banks, gardens
- **Distribution:** Common
- **Drug:** Flores, Herba Tanceti
- **Constituents:** Essential oils (thujone, camphor, borneol), bitter principles (tanacetin), glycosides, flavonoids, tannins, cumarins, inulin
- **Treatments:** For combating worms, insects (moths), for digestive and urinary problems, metabolic disorders, rheumatism
- **Uses:** Tea, oil, baths, washes, herb pillows, herb bouquets, culinary
- **Homeopathic uses:** See above and for nervous exhaustion, muscle cramps
- **What and when to gather:** Blossoming herb, flowers July to September
- **Lookalikes:** Costmary: leaves sturdier, ovate, finely dentate, scent like balm, balm oil as a treatment for wounds, cultivated
- **Other information:** Take care: use only under medical supervision and not during pregnancy

Taraxacum officinale Wiggers
COMMON DANDELION

Blowball, Dandelion, Faceclock, Bitterwort, Fortune-teller

In April, dandelion flowers cover lawns and meadows in glowing yellow. The plant grows on roadsides and in gardens, forces its way up through joins in paving slabs in the middle of the city, colonizes railway embankments, strips of grass and gravel pits. Always astonishing is the swift metamorphosis of its flower to the 'dandelion clock', with its parachute-like seeds, flying away when you blow on them. No wonder that the flower was once seen as a symbol for the spread of the Christian faith. It may be simple to recognize a dandelion as a dandelion, but the wealth of sub-species and varieties already described makes it hard even for qualified botanists to determine the individual species.

Young dandelion leaves should be in the first wild herb salad of the season; the buds can be used as capers, and the roasted roots can be used, like chicory (see page 64), to brew a coffee substitute. In addition, a dandelion meadow is a good food source for bees and a popular feeding spot for pet rabbits. Tea made from dandelion leaves purifies the blood and is also recommended for colds. Extracts of the herb and root are contained in many medicines to support liver and gall bladder function and to increase the appetite. Delicious jellies, honey and dandelion wine can be made from the flowers.

- **Description:** Height up to 16 in. (40 cm); basal leaf rosette, leaves deeply dentate with marked main rib; stems smooth, hollow, with milky sap; single flower heads with c. 200 yellow-gold ligulates, bracts green; achene with parachute-like pappi; root spindle-shaped, fleshy, up to 6 ft 6 in. (2 m) deep; perennial
- **Flowering:** April to July
- **Scent and flavour:** Unscented; bitter flavour

- **Location:** Meadows, fields, roadsides, gardens
- **Distribution:** Very common
- **Drug:** Herba, Folium, Radix, Succus Taraxaci
- **Ingredients:** Bitter principles (taraxacin), flavonoids, inulin, tannins, essential oils, vitamins, caoutchouc (milky sap), fatty oil (achenes), xanthophylls
- **Treatments:** For loss of appetite, bloating, flatulence, liver and gall bladder diseases, cirrhosis of the liver, ascites, jaundice, gall stones, haemorrhoids, purifying the blood, rheumatic complaints
- **Uses:** Tea, juice, salad, vegetable, wine, jelly, caper substitute, coffee substitute
- **Homeopathic uses:** See above
- **What and when to gather:** Leaves March and April, buds April and May, flowers April to June, root September and October
- **Lookalikes:** Odorous pig-salad (*Aposeris foetida*): leaves evenly dentate, smell of crushed leaves unpleasant

Ripe dandelion seeds shortly before 'take-off'.

Few wild flowers are as widespread and well-known as the dandelion.

Above left: When coltsfoot flowers, spring can't be far away.

Above right: A few weeks later the leaves appear, with white down on the underside.

Tussilago farfara L.
COLTSFOOT

Asses Foot, Bullsfoot, Clayweed, Coughwort

When the snow begins to melt, coltsfoot is, so to speak, already on the starting block. Along with the snowdrop (*Galanthus nivalis*) and paradise plant (*Daphne mezereum*) it is one of the early arrivals of the year – and one of the first in choosing its location. A 'pioneer plant', it colonizes bare ground such as wasteland, embankments, freshly constructed road embankments, backyards, and pathways. As with pestilence wort (see page 70), sometimes known as 'large-leafed coltsfoot', the leaves appear after flowering.

Coltsfoot preparations are among the classic natural medicines for colds, chronic bronchitis, and asthma. Old herbals often recommend inhaling the smoke of dried leaves or roasted roots (see opposite). Today, sweetened teas made from coltsfoot flowers or leaves are preferred. However, it is known that coltsfoot contains small amounts of pyrrolizide alkaloids which can damage the liver or the

chromosomes. When out hiking, crushed coltsfoot leaves can act as first aid for insect bites.

- **Description:** Height up to flowering 6 in. (15 cm), up to seed ripening 1 ft (30 cm); leaves with long stems, hand-sized, cordate, edges roughly notched, finely dentate, whitish-green at first, then green; white down on underside; stems with leafy scales, brownish, with white down; single yellow flower head at top of stem, 30–40 male tubular flowers, about 300 female ligulate flowers around the edge, nodding once flower has opened; achene with pappus; root scaly, creeping, with runners; perennial
- **Flowering:** February to April
- **Scent and flavour:** Unscented; flavour mild, slightly savoury, astringent
- **Location:** Waysides, gravel pits, landfill sites, banks, railway embankments
- **Distribution:** Very common
- **Drug:** Folia, Flores Farfarae
- **Constituents:** Mucilage, essential oils, bitter principles, tannins, tussilagin, flavonoids, saltpeter, inulin, yellow dye (xanthophyll)
- **Treatments:** For colds, chronic bronchitis, asthma, poor healing of wounds, diarrhoea, swellings; first aid for insect bites, tobacco substitute
- **Uses:** Tea, juice, extract, inhalation, poultices (fresh crushed leaves)
- **Homeopathic uses:** See above
- **What and when to gather:** Flowers (not fully opened) March and April, leaves April to June
- **Lookalikes:** Pestilence wort (*Petasites* spec., see page 70): the leaves are much bigger, grows on stream and river banks
- **Other information:** Take care: according to location, the flowers may contain poisonous pyrrolizide alkaloids (damaging to liver and chromosomes, carcinogenic); if used long-term, there is a danger of poisoning from the leaves; the recommended daily allowance amounts to 1/7–1/5 oz (4.5–6 g).

Dogbane family
Apocynaceae

Most members of the dogbane family are tropical or subtropical species. The leaves are generally evergreen, undivided, entire and opposite. The dark green, glossy evergreen leaves and the shape of the flowers are reminiscent of the oleander (Nerium oleander) native to the Mediterranean.

Vinca minor L.
LESSER PERIWINKLE

■ *poisonous* ■
Small Periwinkle, Running Myrtle

The persistence with which periwinkle gradually covers ever greater areas and opens its beautiful sky-blue flowers year after year shows why the plant symbolizes faithfulness and loyalty in popular belief. Wreaths of periwinkle are symbols of eternal life and were therefore often placed in graves. Even today, you still frequently see the plant in cemeteries.

Periwinkle has been known as a healing herb for a long time; its applications, however, vary according to source. Its most widespread use was evidently as a treatment for loss of appetite and anaemia. Delaveau and colleagues report on research which shows that the alkaloid vincamin, isolated from the periwinkle, dilates the blood vessels and lowers blood pressure. In homeopathy, periwinkle products are used to treat scalp eczema and painful itching.

- **Description:** Height up to 8 in. (20 cm), evergreen semi-shrub; leaves dark green, glossy, leathery, elongate and lanceolate, short petiole, opposite; flowers pale blue to blue-violet, long stems, five outspread petals with pointed tips, five funnel shaped sepals and five stamens; fruit follicular; runners up to 3 ft 3 in. (1 m) long, prostrate and rooting
- **Flowering:** March to May
- **Scent and flavour:** Scent aromatic, fresh; flavour bitter
- **Location:** Deciduous woodland, beech woods, ground cover in shady gardens
- **Distribution:** Rare in the north, often colonizing and invasive in the south
- **Drug:** Foliae Vincae pervincae
- **Constituents:** Alkaloids (vincamin), flavonoids, phenoles, tannins, pectin, mineral salts
- **Treatments:** For loss of appetite, anaemia, diabetes, bruises, haematomas, heart and circulatory disease, kidney and bladder complaints, lowering blood pressure, weaning
- **Uses:** Tonic, gargle
- **Homeopathic uses:** See above and for skin diseases, blood clotting disorders
- **What and when to gather:** Leaves all the year round, in March for drying
- **Lookalikes:** Garden varieties, e.g. *Vinca major*: large flowers, leaves often with white patches

Flowering periwinkle in a shady deciduous forest. The flowers resemble those of the hepatica (Hepatica nobilis), another plant that flowers early in the year.

Borage family
Boraginaceae

The members of the borage family not only have rough-haired leaves, but also hairs on the stems and flowers. These bristly hairs can cause skin reactions in sensitive people. The fruits often have oil-rich attachments (elaiosomes) which provide nourishment for ants and thereby ensure the distribution of this herb's species.

Borago officialis L.
COMMON BORAGE

Beebread, Star-flower

Borage, introduced from the Mediterranean region, is one of the best-known culinary herbs and also esteemed as food for bees. Furthermore, it belongs in every herb garden. In places close to human settlements it can be found as an escape in the wild. In the kitchen, borage is mainly used for salads (in particular, cucumber salads) and herb soups, but you can cook the leaves like spinach. The pretty blue flowers are used to garnish salads and also to dye vinegar blue.

The doctor-botanists of the early modern period recommend borage for memory problems, dizziness, and melancholy. (Leonhart Fuchs: 'The little flowers of borage laid in wine and then drunk thereof, make a man happy… and drive away sorrow and all melancholy.')

- **Description:** Height up to 2 ft (60 cm); leaves large, oval, alternate, wrinkled; stems hollow, erect, branching; flowers star-shaped, sky-blue, more rarely white, nodding in loose scorpioid cymes, white scales in the centre protruding from the flower, anthers purplish-black; fruit with elaiosomes, annual

- **Flowering:** May to September
- **Scent and flavour:** Cucumber-like
- **Location:** Soils rich in nutrients and lime, cultivated in gardens, escaped plants in the wild (vineyards, derelict land)
- **Distribution:** Native to the Mediterranean
- **Drug:** Flores Herba, Oleum Boraginis
- **Constituents:** Mucilage, allantoin, resin, essential oils, tannins, blue anthocyan dye, silicic acid, vitamin C, calium salts
- **Treatments:** For diseases of the urinary and respiratory tracts, constipation, fever, wounds, ulcers, menopause problems, skin eruptions (oil)
- **Uses:** Tea, medicinal wine, poultices, culinary (salads, spinach-type vegetable, soup), animal fodder
- **Homeopathic uses:** For diseases of the respiratory tract

Flowering borage; flowers, stems and leaves have bristly hairs.

- **What and when to gather:** Flowers and herb at start of flowering, young leaves fresh for flavouring, juice of leaves and stalk June to August
- **Lookalikes:** None
- **Other information:** Take care: the herb contains pyrrolizine, which has carcinogenic and mutagenic qualities; use sparingly

Lithospermum officinale L.
EUROPEAN STONESEED

Gromwell, Common Gromwell, Pearl Gromwell

The common name of this plant directly translates the Latin of the genus name, which for its part goes back to the Greek words *lithos* meaning stone and *sperma* meaning seed. The little nuts of stoneseed, white and looking like little polished porcelain hearts, are indeed very hard. The species name *officinale*, as with many other herbs, indicates medicinal use, though it plays a small part today and is not even mentioned in the comprehensive *Materia Medica* of homeopathy. In past centuries it was believed that bladder stones could be treated with stoneseed. The leaves have been used as substitutes for black tea, in a form known as 'Bohemian' or 'Croatian' tea. Purple Gromwell (*L. purpurocaeruleum*) is a popular, attractive garden plant.

- **Description:** Height up to 3 ft 3 in. (1 m); leaves alternate, lanceolate, sessile, dark green above, glossy, lighter on underside, veins easily visible; stems erect, markedly branched; flowers small, greenish-yellow or white; fruit smooth, white, with porcelain-like gleam; rhizome thick, hard; perennial
- **Flowering:** May to July
- **Scent and flavour:** Unscented; taste astringent, fruits sweetish
- **Location:** Lowland forest, sunny hillsides; this herb loves lime
- **Distribution:** Scattered
- **Drug:** Herba, Fructis Lithospermi

- **Constituents:** Calcium, silicium, lithospermic acid, pyrrolizide alkaloids
- **Treatments:** Folk medicine: for diseases of the urinary tract, bladder stones, as a contraceptive
- **Uses:** Tea
- **What and when to gather:** Fruits, leaves, flowering shoots July, August
- **Lookalikes:** Field gromwell, field stoneseed (*L. arvense*): flowers white (April to June), seeds brown, almost matt
- **Other information:** Take care not to exceed dose: pyrrolizide alkaloids are mutagenic and carcinogenic, and can damage the liver

Typical of European stoneseed are the alternate, sessile leaves.

Pulmonaria officinalis L.
COMMON LUNGWORT

Lungwort, Jerusalem Cowslip, Jerusalem Sage, Bethlehem Sage

The common names of this plant show something of the reverence in which it was held for its healing powers. There are several reasons for the fame of common lungwort. On the one hand, it appears and flowers fairly early in the year, when the observer's attention is still keen after the long winter; on the other hand, even non-botanists will notice at once that there are flowers of different colours on one and the same stem. These are not different types of flower, but flowers of differing ages: they start life pink and gradually turn blue.

Last but not least, lungwort has a long folk tradition as a healing herb. The medieval doctrine of signatures (see page 18 ff.) accorded the plant special powers in the curing of lung diseases because of the spotted leaves, reminiscent of the human lung with its bronchial tubes. As so often happens, modern analysis of the ingredients of the plant gave a rather sobering result, making it difficult to see

anything in the doctrine of signatures other than an erroneous belief full of fantasy. However, teas made from lungwort leaves or flowers are still recommended for decongestant purposes in colds. A powder of crushed leaves has proved itself as a treatment for diarrhoea.

- **Description:** Height up to 1 ft (30 cm); base leaves with petiole, broadly ovate, with clearly visible white spots; stem leaves alternate, sessile, elongate to ovate; flowers funnelform in scorpioid cymes at the end of the stem, first reddish-pink, then blue; fruits with elaiosomes; thin, creeping rhizomes; perennial
- **Flowering:** March to May
- **Scent and flavour:** Unscented; taste slimy, astringent, musty
- **Location:** Deciduous and mixed forests, banks of streams, scrub
- **Distribution:** Widespread, common, protected in certain regions
- **Drug:** Herba Pulmonariae maculosae
- **Constituents:** Mucilage, silicic acid, flavonoids, tannins, saponins, calcium, allantoin, vitamin C
- **Treatments:** For colds, sore throats, coughs, lung ailments, urinary organ diseases, diseases of the digestive tract, haemorrhoids, wounds, skin impurities
- **Uses:** Tea, culinary (soup, spinach-type vegetable, salad)
- **Homeopathic uses:** See above
- **What and when to gather:** Flowering herb and young leaves March to May, rosette leaves July, August
- **Lookalikes:** Common bugloss (*Anchusa officinalis*) and nonea (*Nonea pulla*): no white spots on leaves, dry locations
- **Other information:** The summer leaves, appearing after flowering, have long petioles, are ovate, pointed, and cordate or rounded at the base

Flowering common lungwort in a lowland forest.

Symphytum officinale L.
COMMON COMFREY

Knitbone, Boneset, Bruisewort, Healing Herb, Blackwort, Slippery Root

The use of comfrey as a healing herb goes back to ancient times. The botanical genus name refers to its particular qualities: the Greek word *symphein* means 'make grow together'. The alternative common names of knitbone and boneset refer to this characteristic.

While most other herbs act upon problems with the inner organs, or externally on skin diseases, comfrey's 'specialty' is injuries to the musculoskeletal system, such as fractures, bruises, sprains, joint inflammations, and periostitis, dislocations, and strains and arthritic complaints. 'Crush the root and place it on broken limbs, and it will heal,' Adamus Lonicerus says tersely, and basically nothing has changed with this method of healing, though comfrey is now more often applied to the affected parts in salve form.

Modern research has disclosed the active agent allantoin as the bone-healing benefactor in comfrey. Unfortunately the plant also contains pyrrolizidine alkaloids, which in overdose and in long-term use can be carcinogenic and mutagenic. External use of comfrey products is therefore recommended.

- **Description:** Height up to 3 ft 3 in. (1 m); leaves large, broadly ovate, elongated, entire, base of leaf wing-like, decurrent to the branching point, sturdy, thorny and rough stem; flowers campanulate, bluish-red, pinkish-purple, dark blue, or yellowish-white with scales, nodding scorpioid cymes; fruits with elaiosomes; sturdy taproot, more than 3 ft 3 in. (1 m) long, black outside and white within, darkening quickly when exposed to the air
- **Flowering:** May to July
- **Scent and flavour:** Almost unscented; taste faintly savoury, sweetish, slimy

Left: The pink-flowered standard variety of comfrey.

Below: The sub-species bohemicum has yellow-white flowers and narrower leaves, but its uses are identical.

- **Location:** Lowland forest, banks of streams, ditches, damp meadows, roadsides
- **Distribution:** Common, widespread
- **Drug:** Radix, Herba Consolidae
- **Constituents:** Allantoin, glucosides, pyrrolizidine alkaloids, inulin, mucilage, tannins
- **Treatments:** Externally for bruises, sprains, strains, fractures, chronic inflammation
- **Uses:** Tincture, poultices, packs, salves, powder, gargle
- **Homeopathic uses:** For fractures and contusions
- **What and when to gather:** Young shoots and leaves April to August, root March, April, September, October
- **Lookalikes:** None
- **Other information:** High doses of pyrrolizidine alkaloids can damage the liver and cause cancer; do not use during pregnancy and do not apply to open wounds

Gentian family

Gentianaceae and
Bogbean

Menyanthaceae

*Members of the gentian family mainly
have opposite leaves and five-tipped
flowers; their roots contain bitter principles.
All gentians are protected plants. The
medical and luxury products obtained from
the roots are from cultivated plants,
licensed gentian harvesters or imported.
The bogbean (Menyanthes trifoliata) was,
in the past, considered as part of the
gentian family but has recently been
reclassified in the Menyanthaceae.*

*An attractive patch of
yellow gentian.*

Gentiana lutea L.
YELLOW GENTIAN

■ *protected* ■
*Bitter Root, Bitterwort, Gentian, Great Yellow
Gentian*

The impressive yellow gentian, which can grow
up to 5 ft tall (150 cm) and live for about 60
years, is mainly found at higher altitudes in the
Alps and in the Black Forest in Germany. It was
much sought after in the past, due to the bitter
principles in its roots. Even today, demand
outstrips the yield from cultivation, which means
the plant is endangered in Europe because of
poaching, despite various protective measures.
If you are buying gentian root for medicinal
purposes, check its exact origin; it is only
possible to recommend, with a clear conscience,
products from cultivated sources. If you buy
gentian spirits, it won't hurt to ask the distillers
where their raw materials come from.

Inexperienced herb-spotters sometimes mistake
the white false hellebore (*Veratrum album*), one
of the lily family, for yellow gentian. This
poisonous plant is instinctively avoided by cows
in Alpine meadows. In homeopathy, white false
hellebore is used, according to Furlenmeier
among others, for those with weak circulation
and with a tendency to collapse and also for
manic-depressive conditions. Several other
species of gentian were, in earlier years, also
considered healing herbs, among them the marsh
gentian with its dark-blue flowers, although it is
arguable whether it actually helps in lung
disease. In the Bach Flower Remedies,
Gentianella amarella, the autumn dwarf gentian,
is used to treat certain types of depression.

■ **Description:** Height up to 5 ft (150 cm),
leaves cordate-ovate, with 5 to 7 arched ribs,
opposite, the lower leaves with petioles,
the upper sessile, up to 1 ft (30 cm) long
and 6 in. (15 cm) wide; stems thick, smooth,
round, hollow; cup-shaped, yellow flowers
with red anthers in 3- to 10-flowered false
umbels, positioned in the leaf axils; root
fleshy, brown outside, brownish-yellow
inside, somewhat woody

- **Flowering:** June to August
- **Scent and flavour:** Scent intense; taste very bitter
- **Location:** Lime-rich soils, mountain meadows, Alpine meadows, pasture, cultivated
- **Distribution:** Mountains, rare; Switzerland, Tyrol (Austria), Bavaria, Black Forest (Germany)
- **Drug:** Radix Gentianae
- **Constituents:** Glycoside bitter principles (amarogentin, gentiopicrin, gentianin, gentianose), fatty oil, mucilage, pectin, sugar, rubber
- **Treatments:** For loss of appetite, poor digestion, weak stomach, flatulence, to heal wounds
- **Uses:** Tea, distillation of alcoholic spirits, poultice for badly healing wounds
- **Homeopathic uses:** For digestive ailments
- **What and when to gather:** Roots and rhizomes in spring, also in autumn
- **Lookalikes:** White false hellebore: leaves alternate, hairy on underside, flowers white, poisonous

Spotted gentian is occasionally used to distil spirits.

- **Other information:** Slight headache, flushed face or nosebleeds may occur after long-term use or overdose; take care with dosage in pregnancy

Below left: The sturdy rhizome of yellow gentian.

Below right: Serious cases of poisoning have in the past been caused by the white false hellebore being mistaken for yellow gentian.

Centaurium erythraea Rafn.
EUROPEAN CENTAURY

■ *protected* ■

Common Centaury, Centaury, Century, Centre of the Sun

It's best to study the pretty pink flowers of this plant around midday, for it opens in the morning and then starts to close soon after the sun has passed the zenith. Intensive agriculture has meant that centaury has become rare in many places. It does not thrive in nitrogen-polluted soils. It is primarily found in protected areas and in special locations – for example, grassed-over anti-flooding dykes – which are not used in agriculture.

Its healing powers have been praised for centuries. Hildegard of Bingen recommends centaury for the healing of broken bones. Lonicerus writes: 'The herb, drunk each day morning and evening, kills and drives out the worm.' The bitter principles in centaury have been demonstrated to improve appetite, which explains their use in stomach, liver, and gall bladder ailments. Dr Bach's Flower Remedies recommend centaury for persons whose weakness of will leads them be there only for others and always places their own interests well behind.

The common name of the plant has led to some misunderstandings. Originally, the genus name *Centaurium* came from the Greek, *Kentauroi* (centaurs). These were mythical beings with a human head and torso and the lower body of a horse. A prominent member of this race, the wise Chiron, was, legend says, healed by this herb. As, even in the Middle Ages, a good foundation in classical Greek studies was the privilege of a minority, this etymology was forgotten, and attempts were made to explain the word from Latin. People concentrated on *centum* meaning a hundred, and linked the plant with the word, as in the spelling 'century'.

- **Description:** Height up to 20 in. (50 cm); basal leaf rosette, leaves obovate, five-veined, stems rectangular, with forked branching only in the upper section, stem leaves opposite, ovate-lanceolate, three-veined; flowers ½–1 in. (1–2.5 cm) long, rose-red, funnelform, short stems, in bushy umbel-like corymb, five-tipped, calyx shorter than the calyx tube, five anthers; fruit capsule narrow, cylindrical, with many seeds; root short; annual or biennial
- **Flowering:** June to September
- **Scent and flavour:** Unscented; long-lasting, extremely bitter taste
- **Location:** Poor clay soils, dry roadsides; dry slopes, in forest clearings, up to 5,000 ft (1,400 m)
- **Distribution:** Scattered in Europe
- **Drug:** Herba Centaurii
- **Constituents:** Bitter principles (gentiopicrin, swertiamarin, sweroside, gentiopicroside), alkaloids, flavones, xanthone derivatives, triterpenes, resin, a little essential oil
- **Treatments:** For loss of appetite, liver and gall bladder diseases, heartburn, weak stomach, intestinal parasites
- **Uses:** Tea, powder, liqueur
- **Homeopathic uses:** For stomach, liver and gall bladder complaints

The five-tipped flowers of European centaury show its relationship to the gentians.

- **What and when to gather:** Flowering herb and shoots (top 8 in., 20 cm), June to August; dry in bunches and keep in paper bags (to preserve colour)
- **Lookalikes:** None
- **Other information:** Take care not to exceed dose; do not use if suffering from stomach or duodenal ulcers

Menyanthes trifoliata L.
BOGBEAN

■ *protected* ■

Bog Buckbean, Bogbean, Marsh Clover, Marsh Trefoil

'Trefoil' and 'clover' in the alternative common names for this plant are as incorrect as the German name '*Fieberklee*'. The elegant, white-flowering plant only superficially resembles clover, in that it has tripartite leaves. And *Menyanthes* contains bitter principles which, in contrast to the belief expounded in folk medicine, are unsuited to treating fever, according to Bisset and Wichtl.

If you spot bogbean, you are likely to be in a wetland area on lime-poor soil, and will probably be looking at not just one plant, but at least a group of them, if not a large spread covering many square yards. Bogbean displays the very best adaptation to its wet habitat. At the base, the stem merges into a creeping rhizome, well able to find a hold on muddy ground.

- **Description:** Height up to 1 ft (30 cm); leaves large, trifoliate as for clover, long petioles, with sheath-like widening at base; stems smooth, leafless; flowers 5–15, white to pinkish, funnelform, with beard-like fringes, in upright raceme, anthers violet; fruit capsule divided in half, with many seeds; rhizome thick, creeping (3 ft 3 in.–10 ft, 1–3 m), with scale-like cataphylls
- **Flowering:** Late April to June
- **Scent and flavour:** Almost unscented; long-lasting, intensive, bitter taste
- **Location:** Lowland marsh, marshy ditches, wet, peaty meadows
- **Distribution:** Rare
- **Drug:** Folia Menyanthis, Folia Trifolia fibrini
- **Ingredients:** Bitter principles (foliamenthin, menthiafolin, loganin, gentianin), tannins, flavonol glycosides, saponins, resins
- **Treatments:** For loss of appetite, poor digestions, weak stomach, gall bladder, liver, and lung ailments
- **Uses:** Tea, liqueur
- **Homeopathic uses:** For diseases of the central nervous system, fever attacks
- **What and when to gather:** Leaves during or after flowering, April to June
- **Lookalikes:** None
- **Other information:** Do not use in pregnancy; higher doses may cause sickness

The characteristic flowers of buckbean with their beard-like fringes.

Mint family
Labiatae (Lamiaceae)

Among the members of the mint family are many scented and culinary herbs, rich in essential oils. They originated in the Mediterranean region and were cultivated in Europe, north of the Alps, in monastery and country gardens. The stems are rectangular. The individual flowers, mostly without stalks, are set close together in whorls in the axils of the bracts. The asymmetrical flowers have a lower lip consisting of three petals and an upper lip, more or less arched, composed of two fused petals. The calyx, which is tube- or bell-shaped, is usually five-tipped. The fruits consist of four nutlets, each containing one seed (cypsela). See drawings.

Labiate flower Lamiaceae

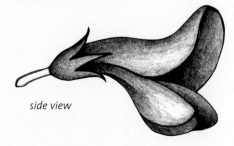

side view

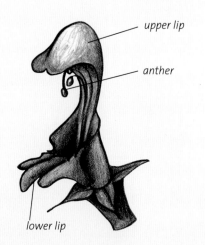

upper lip

anther

lower lip

Ajuga reptans L.
COMMON BUGLE

Bugleweed, Carpet Bugle

The evergreen common bugle is present in almost every garden or park and every meadow. It spreads rapidly through its runners and can completely cover many square yards of ground. It is often confused by the inexperienced with other herbs such as self-heal and ground ivy (see page 85).

- **Description:** Height up to 1 ft (30 cm); evergreen, leaves with tapering base sessile on stem, spatulate, crenate, in basal rosette; flowers blue, upper lip very short, lower lip three-petalled, flower head pyramid-shaped, in spikes; fruits with elaiosomes; sprouting runners up to 8 in. (20cm) long, with leaves, perennial
- **Flowering:** April to June

The leaves of self-heal are ovate, entire, and have petioles.

It is easy to recognize common bugle by its pyramid-shaped flower head and blue labiate flowers.

'An herb for all inward wounds, exulcerated lungs, or other parts, either by itself, or boiled with other similar herbs… It speedily helps green wounds, if bruised and bound thereto.'

Nicholas Culpeper,
A Complete Herbal

- **Scent and flavour:** Unscented; taste intensely savoury, bitter
- **Location:** Meadows, waysides, woodland, gardens
- **Distribution:** Very common
- **Drug:** Herba Ajugae
- **Ingredients:** Tannins, glycosides, essential oils, saponins, mineral salts
- **Treatments:** For mouth and pharyngeal inflammations, gall bladder complaints, wounds, haemorrhages, diarrhoea
- **Uses:** Tea, poultices, baths, gargles, culinary
- **Homeopathic uses:** See above and for metabolic disorders, rheumatic ailments
- **What and when to gather:** Whole herb at start of flowering, April, June
- **Lookalikes:** Blue bugle (*A. genevensis*): no runners, several flowering stems per plant; ground ivy (*Glechoma hederaceum*): leaves cordate, decussate, two to six flowers, purple; dense false spike, June to October, effective for sore throats, edible
- **Other information:** Seeds spread by ants

Glechoma hederaceum L.
GROUND IVY

■ *mildly poisonous* ■
Alehoof, Gill-over-the-Ground, Gill-Go-by-Ground, Turn-Hoof, Hay-Maids

In their work on 'Magic Plants', Wolf-Dieter Storl and Christian Rätsch refer to the famous Purity Law, passed in Bavaria, Germany, in 1516, as 'one of the earliest drug laws'. This decision to allow only hops (see page 164), barley malt and water to be used in the brewing industry spelled the end for other, older 'beer herbs'. Ground ivy was one of the best known of these. Our forebears also ascribed other amazing powers to the plant, whether as a magical defence against witchcraft or as a healing herb. Hildegard of Bingen devotes one of her longest chapters to ground ivy and recommends it primarily for lung and throat diseases as well as to stop ringing in the ears. For sore throats, folk medicine advises gargling with ground ivy;

Ground ivy spreads everywhere. The similar common bugle has a pyramid-shaped flower head and spade-shaped leaves.

occasionally, ground ivy simmered in milk is also recommended. Ground ivy leaves were also laid on infected wounds, or a ground ivy tincture applied. Ground ivy was used as a culinary herb for soups, cream cheese, herb butter and vegetables.

- **Description:** Height up to 20 in. (50 cm); evergreen, leaves with petiole, opposite, decussate, cordate, glossy above, matte green below; stems thin, hairy, creeping, only the flowering shoot rising; two to six purple/blue flowers in false whorls, the lower lip larger than the flat upper lip, short calyx; numerous runners, rooting at nodes
- **Flowering:** March to July
- **Scent and flavour:** Scent faintly aromatic, flavour savoury, somewhat bitter
- **Location:** Moist, rich sites, meadows, paths, fences, mixed and lowland forest, gardens
- **Distribution:** Very common
- **Drug:** Herba Hederae, Glechomae
- **Ingredients:** Tannins, bitter principles (glechomin), essential oils, flavonoids, vitamin C, calium
- **Treatments:** For coughs, asthma, gastro-enteric diseases, diarrhoea, bedwetting, bladder inflammations, menstruation problems; externally: small, infected injuries, inflammations of the mouth, rheumatic complaints, gout
- **Uses:** Tea, juice, gargle, poultices, culinary (soup, cream cheese, butter, vegetables, meat dishes, punch)
- **Homeopathic uses:** See above and for haemorrhoids
- **What and when to gather:** Young leaves and shoots of the flowering herb (without roots), April to June
- **Lookalikes:** Common bugle (*Ajuga reptans*, see page 84), leaves spatulate, flowers blue, in pyramid-shaped flower head
- **Other information:** The large, unpleasant-smelling sub-species *hirsuta* is not harvested. Fatal poisoning has been reported of horses that have eaten too much of this weed

Hyssopus officinalis L.
HYSSOP

Hyssop

This herb, harvested in the Mediterranean region since ancient times, is only rarely found in the wild in Europe north of the Alps. Cultivated, the half-shrub thrives well in sunny rockeries and herb gardens and is excellent food for bees. The deep, dark blue of its flower is reminiscent of meadow clary (see illustration page 96). In the past, as Marianne Beuchert reports, hyssop – the common name is derived directly from Greek *hyssopos* – 'was used as rods by priests for asperging and consecration'. In pre-Christian times, it was already accounted a plant of purification and atonement. In the *Macer floridus*, by the monk Odo Magdunensis, a work predating even Hildegard of Bingen's writings, it is accorded almost universal importance as a medicine to treat catarrh, constipation, roundworms, toothache, and even consumption. Many of these uses have, however, now been forgotten or did not pass modern pharmacological tests.

- **Description:** Height up to 2 ft (60 cm), semi-shrub, leaves opposite, sessile, narrow, and lanceolate, coarse, glossy; stems thickly branched; flowers blue-violet to reddish, more rarely yellowish-white, in one-sided, leafed, false spike some 4 in. (10 cm) long, calyx and corolla almost equal in length, upper lip short, lower lip twice the size, three-petalled; root woody
- **Flowering:** July to September
- **Scent and flavour:** Scent aromatic, spicy; taste savoury, bitter
- **Location:** Rocky slopes, walls; this herb loves warmth and nourishment
- **Distribution:** Native to the Mediterranean, cultivated
- **Drug:** Herba, Oleum Hyssopi
- **Constituents:** Essential oils (pinocamphone, pinene, thujone), tannins, flavonoids, bitter principles, dye

Hyssop is an aromatically scented healing and culinary herb, an ornament to any herb garden. It grows in the wild in the Mediterranean region.

- **Treatments:** For inflammations of the urinary tract, gastro-enteric diseases, chronic bronchial catarrh, angina, asthma, coughs, menstruation problems, weak circulation, heart complaints, excessive sweating, night sweats, worms
- **Uses:** Tea, oil, washes, gargles, culinary (meat, salads, soup), pharmaceutical industry, perfume and liqueur production (Benedictine, Chartreuse)
- **What and when to gather:** Soft, well-leafed shoots; first cut in June, second cut in August
- **Lookalikes:** Rosemary (*Rosmarinus officinalis*, see page 95): flowers pink, not one-sided, different scent: thyme (*Thymus vulgaris*, see page 99): leaves smaller, flowers pink, different scent

- **Other information:** Take care: if suffering from nervous complaints, only use low doses due to its strong stimulative effect. The healing action is comparable to that of sage (*Salvia officinalis*, see page 96)

'Hyssop… gives out a strong, aromatic scent. For this reason, older women in some regions place it in their prayer books, so that the sharp smell prevents them from nodding off in church.'

Pierre Delaveau et al.,
Secrets and Healing Powers of Plants

Lamium album L.
WHITE DEADNETTLE

White Deadnettle, White-Nettle, Archangel

Even more widespread than the white is the red-flowering spotted deadnettle, which is edible but not a healing herb.

The nectar-rich flowers of the white deadnettle taste sweet as honey when sucked.

The white deadnettle is one of the most common herbs native to western and central Europe and has also been introduced to North America. As a nitrogen-loving plant, it is often found near human habitation, and is widespread in gardens, parks, scrub and meadows where fertilizers are used. The leaves resemble those of the stinging nettle, often found in the same locations, but have no stinging hairs. The astringent tannins of the white deadnettle are suitable for wound-healing. In folk medicine, the tea was used as a decongestant. In gynaecological matters, the white deadnettle, in combination with the lady's mantle (see page 234) has been used for all kinds of abdominal problems. According to Bisset and Wichtl, animal experiments have demonstrated the presence of inflammation-controlling triterpenes; many other constituents have not been sufficiently researched. Deadnettle flowers form part of various herb tea blends with a calming effect. The young leaves of the white deadnettle and its close relative, the spotted henbit (*Lamium maculatum*) can be added to salads.

- **Description:** Height up to 2 ft (60 cm); leaves with petiole, resembling stinging nettle, opposite, with fine hairs, no stinging hairs; stems hollow; flowers white, five to eight in false whorls, upper lip helmet-shaped, lower lip two-petalled; rhizome creeping, with runners; perennial
- **Flowering:** April to September
- **Scent and flavour:** Faint honey scent; flavour mildly savoury, aromatic, mildly bitter
- **Location:** Paths, forest edges, scrub, meadows, fences, rubble; this herb loves nitrogen
- **Distribution:** Very common
- **Drug:** Herba, Flores Lamii albi
- **Constituents:** Saponins, flavonoids (isoquercitrin, camphor oil), glycosides, mucilage, essential oils, amino acids
- **Treatments:** For diseases of the respiratory tract, dry coughs, congestion, diarrhoea, gastro-enteric disorders, flatulence, gynaecological problems, leucorrhoea, menstruation disorders, menopause and prostate problems, purifying the blood, treating varicose veins, skin diseases, burns
- **Uses:** Tea, powder, poultices, gargles, vegetable, soup; roots boiled for salad
- **Homeopathic uses:** See above, and for tuberculosis
- **What and when to gather:** Young leaves and shoots before flowering, March to April; flowers (without calyx) or flowering herb April to August, roots September
- **Lookalikes:** Stinging nettle (*Urtica dioica*, see page 170): stinging hairs on the underside of the leaves, catkin-shaped, inconspicuous flowers, dioecious
- **Other information:** Take care: daily dose of two to three cups should not be exceeded; root extract provides a yellow dye

Lavandula angustifolia Mill.
ENGLISH LAVENDER

True Lavender

The are numerous species and cultivated forms of lavender, all rich in scented oils. Apart from English lavender, broad-leaved lavender (*L. latifolia*) and the purple-flowered French lavender (*L. stoechas*) are important. The highly desirable lavender oils are obtained from fresh flowers or flower heads by steam distillation.

Apart from its uses in the perfume, cosmetic, and food industries, lavender also has medicinal qualities. The calming effects of lavender extracts have been known for centuries. Bunches of lavender were laid in the cradles of fretting babies. On the other hand, the scent of lavender is believed to be enlivening and refreshing, which is why the oil is used in the production of bath essences and freshen-up wipes.

- **Description:** Height up to 2 ft (60 cm), semi-shrub, leaves opposite, 1½–2 in. (2–5 cm) long, linear-lanceolate, edge rolled inwards, young leaves grey and downy, later green; stems erect, distinctly branching; flowers bluish-violet, in spikes with flower at end; root woody
- **Flowering:** June to August
- **Scent and flavour:** Scent very aromatic; flavour bitter
- **Location:** Dry, sandy soils, gardens; this herb is sensitive to frost
- **Distribution:** Native to the Mediterranean, cultivated
- **Drug:** Aetheroleum, Flores, Herba Lavandulae
- **Constituents:** Essential oils (linanyl acetate), cumarin, tannins, bitter principles
- **Treatments:** For insomnia, nervous restlessness, nervous stomach pains, gastroenteric and circulatory problems, flatulence, rheumatic complaints, gout, neuralgia, headaches, migraines, fainting
- **Uses:** Tea, embrocation, baths, poultices, culinary, food and perfume industries

- **Homeopathic uses:** See above
- **What and when to gather:** Flowers and flower heads shortly before flowers open, June to August
- **Lookalikes:** None
- **Other information:** Take care: exceeding the dose and prolonged use can lead to headaches

Above left: What hops are to Bavaria, lavender is to Provence; a plant of great economic importance, shaping the landscape and identified with the region by visitors from all over the world. The south of France is still responsible for more than half the world's lavender production.

Above right: Broad-leafed lavender is used primarily to treat acute and chronic bronchial diseases and rheumatic complaints.

'If Louis XIV desired a lady, he would send her lavender flower spikes dipped in ambergris. If she was inclined to agree to his wishes, she would, in the King's sight, put one of these flower spikes into her mouth.'

Marianne Beuchert,
Symbolism of Plants

Gypsywort is often confused with motherwort. It has deeply dentate and serrate leaves and white flowers. As a healing herb, it is used to treat slight overactivity of the thyroid gland.

Motherwort has maple-like leaves, deeply palmate and reddish flowers.

Leonurus cardiaca L.
COMMON MOTHERWORT

Lion's Ear, Lion's Tail, Throw-Wort

In many industrialized nations, common motherwort is becoming rare; in some areas, for example, the number of known locations has decreased by around 50 per cent since 1950. It would be a pity if this ancient healing herb – often even destroyed as a 'weed' where it does grow – were to disappear from the wild. In medical herb gardens, those living museums of medical history, this impressive plant can regularly be seen. In the past, it was very highly regarded. 'Motherwort is excellent for the beating of the heart,' Leonhart Fuchs wrote in 1543, and Adamus Lonicerus, in 1582, added to this, 'With its root crushed and laid upon the chest, it removes constraint of the heart. And used thus, it makes the breast roomy.' The 'cardiaca' element of the botanical name is a reference to this quality. The herb was often used to combat heart problems, such as palpitations, 'heart cramps', and 'oppression of the heart'. Analysis of the ingredients has in fact discovered 'three glycosidal bitter principles which have an action similar to digitalis' (Aichele and Schwegeler). Modern research appears to confirm the traditional treatments.

- **Description:** Height up to 5 ft (150 cm), leaves petiolate, dark green above, grey on underside, downy, decussate, opposite, palmate, cordate, upper three- to five-lobed; stems erect, often tinged with red, hollow-leafed right up to the tip; flowers pinkish-red or pale violet in long, dense, 'bushy' false spikes, perennial
- **Flowering:** June to September
- **Scent and flavour:** Scent unpleasant, intensive; taste bitter, hot
- **Location:** Hedges, fences, paths, ruins, landfill sites, herb gardens
- **Distribution:** Rare
- **Drug:** Herba Leonuri cardiacae
- **Constituents:** Bitter principles (leonurine), tannins, essential oils, alkaloids (leonucardin), glycosides
- **Treatments:** For weak hearts, nervous heart complaints, angina pectoris, overactive thyroid gland, migraine, panic attacks, menopausal and prostate gland problems, haemorrhoids, anaemia, flatulence, diarrhoea
- **Uses:** Tea, powder
- **Homeopathic uses:** See above
- **What and when to gather:** Flowering, soft shoots, June to September
- **Lookalikes:** Gypsywort (*Lycopus europaeus*); leaves narrower, pale green, flowers white, red spots inside, with two anthers, damp locations, common
- **Other information:** Take care: tea should only be drunk after consulting your doctor, and never during pregnancy

Melissa officinalis L.
COMMON BALM

*Sweet Balm, Lemon Balm, Bee Balm,
Balm Mint*

Common balm enriches human life with an extraordinary variety of uses. This is why the pleasantly lemon-scented plant, originally native to the Mediterranean region, is present in almost every herb garden. If you suffer from insomnia and exhaustion with no organic cause, try balm tea before resorting to more radical pharmaceutical methods. It is also recommended for loss of appetite and nervous disorders of the digestive tract. In addition, common balm can be used as a culinary herb in a variety of ways.

- **Description:** Height up to 2 ft 8 in. (80 cm); leaves yellowish-green, short petiole, ovate, pointed, edge roughly serrate, soft down; stems sturdy, woody, branching, hairy; flowers very small, partly tinged with pink, blue or yellow, flat upper lip, three-petalled lower lip, three to six flowers in a semi-whorl; rhizome strongly branching; perennial
- **Flowering:** June to September
- **Scent and flavour:** Scent intensively lemony when rubbed; flavour savoury, slightly bitter

- **Location:** Well-nourished soils, sunny sites, vineyards, gardens
- **Distribution:** Native to the Mediterranean, cultivated
- **Drug:** Folia, Herba, Oleum Melissae = Folia Citronellae
- **Constituents:** Essential oils (citral, citronellal, neral, geranial), tannins, flavonoids, bitter principles, cumarins
- **Treatments:** For exhaustion, depressive moods, hysteria, nervous palpitations, loss of appetite, digestive disorders, insomnia, colic-like diarrhoea, painful menstruation, cramps, nausea, headache, toothache, rheumatism
- **Uses:** Tea, juice, baths, poultices, herb pillows, culinary (sauces, soups, meat dishes, desserts, drinks), perfume and liqueur production
- **What and when to gather:** Herb and leaves shortly before flowering, June to August once or twice up to September
- **Lookalikes:** Horehound (*Marrubium vulgare*): whole plant with woolly down, leaves whitish-green, wrinkled, no lemon aroma
- **Other information:** Daily dose three cups

Above left: Common balm helps with stress and is a versatile culinary herb.

Above centre: The aromatic, minty scent of the rare catnip, Nepeta cataria, attracts cats. As a healing herb, it is used to treat diarrhoea and chronic bronchitis, but is also reputed to be a sedative and a painkiller.

Above right: Horehound is distinguished from common balm by its hairy, whitish-green leaves. It also has no scent.

Mentha spec.
MINT

The genus *Mentha* (mint) is not only very rich in species. The different species tend, as botanists say, to 'hybridize', meaning that they cross over in reproduction and are then harder to determine than they were before. The flowers are mostly violet and are either arranged in dense whorls in levels up the plant stem or, in the taller species, in false spikes with a flower at the tip. One of the best-known hybrids – these are usually sterile, but reproduce rapidly through runners – is the intensively scented peppermint (*M. piperita* var. *piperita* 'Mitcham').

One of the sturdiest and most widespread is horsemint (*M. longifolia*), with dense grey down on the stem and elongated, lanceolate, sharply serrate leaves. It is used to treat headaches and gastro-enteric diseases.

- **Description:** Height up to 20 in. (50 cm), leaves opposite, decussate, broad ovate to lanceolate, edge usually serrate or crenate; stems generally erect, branching above, often hairy and reddish-tinged; flowers pale violet, pink to whitish, calyx five-pointed, corolla tubular, lower and upper lip almost even, in dense false whorl in the leaf axil or elongated, cylindrical, end or side false spikes; forms runners, perennial
- **Flowering:** July to September
- **Scent and flavour:** Scent of peppermint taste; burning, aromatic, cooling
- **Location:** Wet to moist locations, soils rich in nutrients
- **Distribution:** Widespread, cultivated
- **Drug:** Herba, Folia, Oleum Menthae piperitae; M. crispae
- **Constituents:** Essential oils (menthol, menthone – in *M. piperita*), tannins, bitter principles
- **Treatments:** For loss of appetite, gastro-enteric disorders, nausea, nervous vomiting, colic, flatulence, abdominal cramps, nerve pains, nervousness, insomnia, dizziness, bronchial catarrh, colds
- **Uses:** Tea, mouthwash, inhalation, baths, compresses, herb pillows, salve, culinary (cream cheese, sauces, drinks, desserts), perfume and food industries
- **Homeopathic uses:** See above and for colds
- **What and when to gather:** Leaves and flowering shoots July to September; dry and store separately from other herbs
- **Lookalikes:** More than 200 species and various hybrids, all more or less aromatic
- **Other information:** Take care: do not use if you suffer from serious liver or gall bladder diseases, also do not use for children and

Below left: The intensely scented, spicy-savoury 'Mitcham peppermint', a cross between green and water mint, is sterile and spreads only by runners. Peppermint oil is obtained by steam distillation.

Below centre: The flowers of the pleasantly aromatic water mint (M. aquatica) are arranged in almost spherical false whorls at the end of the leafy stem. Water mint contains no menthol and can therefore be given to babies and small children.

Below right: The leaves of curled spearmint (Mentha spicata var. crispata) are curly, broadly ovate, with a deeply serrate edge; the flowers are in long, pink-to-violet false spikes.

babies (menthol can cause cramp in the larynx and breathing difficulties); pennyroyal (*M. pulegium*) should not be taken in pregnancy. Japanese menthol is obtained from *M. japonica*

Ocimum basilicum L.
SWEET BASIL

Basil, Garden Basil

Culinary trends can determine how familiar a plant becomes. A few years ago, slices of mozzarella with tomatoes, pepper and a basil leaf became a very popular *antipasto*, and vinegar with basil ('aceto basilico') has long since made its way into supermarkets. It's easy to forget that the 'king of herbs' – the name derives from the Greek word *basileus*, king – is also a healing herb. Basil tea is particularly recommended for flatulence and bloating, as a sedative and anti-spasmodic. In folk medicine, salves made from basil extracts were used to treat skin inflammations.

Christian Rätsch reports that the plant had already reached Egypt from India in Pharaonic times, and Pliny attributes aphrodisiac qualities to it. In central Europe, it had arrived by the early Middle Ages at the latest. Most gourmets agree that fresh leaves are essential because vital ingredients are lost in drying.

- **Description:** Height up to 20 in. (50 cm); bushy; leaves dark green, opposite, decussate, ovate to lanceolate; stems easy to snap; flowers white, yellowish-white or red; annual

- **Flowering:** June to September
- **Scent and flavour:** Scent aromatic, musty; flavour savoury
- **Location:** This herb loves warmth, soils rich in nutrients, gardens
- **Distribution:** Cultivated
- **Drug:** Herba, Oleum Basilici (= Ocimi)
- **Ingredients:** Essential oils (methyl chavicol, eugenol, estragol, thymol), tannins
- **Treatments:** For digestive problems, flatulence, nausea, vomiting, skin inflammations (Wolf), hysteria, headaches, coughs, fever
- **Uses:** Tea, salve, culinary (salads, soups, meat), perfume industry, incense
- **Homeopathic uses:** See above
- **What and when to gather:** Herb at the start of flowering, several times a year, best to use fresh
- **Lookalikes:** None
- **Other information:** Oil for external use only, as there is a suspicion that it may have a mutagenic action, damaging the chromosomes

Basil is very sensitive to cold and is therefore most often grown as a potted plant.

Origanum vulgare L.
OREGANO

Knotted Marjoram, Wild Marjoram,
Perennial Marjoram

Below: Oregano does not demand much from its location – it can be grown in almost any garden.

Bottom: Marjoram (Majorana hortensis) is often confused with oregano; it is used to flavour meat and sausage, meatballs and liver sausage. In homeopathy, marjoram is used as an anaphrodisiac to calm excessive sexual excitement.

In contrast to haemp agrimony (see page 67), which this herb resembles in the colour of its flowers, oregano grows in dry meadows and in other places exposed to the sun.

This plant and the smaller marjoram (*Majorana hortensis* = *Origanum majorana*) have been used since ancient times to heal and ease a great variety of physical ailments. In the Middle Ages, when belief in demons was widespread, oregano was considered helpful in combating witchcraft and evil spirits, although Hildegard of Bingen advised those suffering from leprosy to take a sweat bath and then rub themselves with a mixture of horehound, oregano, and henbane. Today, oregano is found in herb pillows, and teas and gargles made from (or blended with) oregano are produced; the oil, obtained by steam distillation, is recommended for toothache. However, it is most widely used as a culinary herb – on pizzas, for example.

- **Description:** Height up to 2ft (60 cm); leaves opposite, decussate, short petiole, ovate, entire edges, soft down; stems branching at top, reddish tinge, hairy; flowers numerous, pink to violet in long stemmed, more or less spherical, dense panicles, upper lip flat, lower lip three-petalled, hairy; root thin, branching, woody; perennial
- **Flowering:** July to September
- **Scent and flavour:** Scent strongly aromatic; flavour bitter, savoury
- **Location:** Dry lawns, scrub, woodland and waysides
- **Distribution:** Common in southern Europe, rare in northern Europe, introduced to US
- **Drug:** Herba, Oleum Origani
- **Constituents:** Essential oils (thymol, carvacrol, origanene), flavonoids, rosmarinic acid, tannins, bitter principles, resins
- **Treatments:** For pain, loss of appetite, digestive disorders, liver and gall bladder disorders, flatulence, menstruation problems, coughs, whooping cough, sore throats, skin diseases, toothache, rheumatic complaints, parasite infestations
- **Uses:** Tea, gargle, baths, herb pillows, culinary (butter, cream cheese, pizza), food and perfume production
- **Homeopathic uses:** See above and for excessive sexual excitability, disease of the male reproductive organs
- **What and when to gather:** Flowering herb, flowering shoot tips, July to September
- **Lookalikes:** Marjoram; more savoury taste, leaves grey-green, flowers very small, whitish-pink, annual; used as incense and added to baths

Rosmarinus officinalis L.
ROSEMARY

Dew of the Sea

Thyme, lavender, and rosemary; reminders of summer days in the south! The Mediterranean is a herb garden for much of Europe and beyond. Many of the healing and culinary herbs that we see only in gardens grow wild there, their beguiling scents filling the air. The ancient Greeks and Romans held rosemary in high esteem, and it plays a part in their mythology. It is said to have been brought to central Europe by Benedictine monks in the Middle Ages. Rosemary, as an evergreen plant, is associated with eternal faithfulness and everlasting life (linking it to death and funerary rites).

Rosemary has many varied uses and is cultivated commercially. Chewing rosemary leaves is recommended for people with low blood pressure and depressive moods who find it difficult to get started in the mornings. Rosemary is also supposed to have helped with poor or failing memory. In general, however, care is required in use. Schauenberg and Paris report cases of fatal poisoning after overdose.

- **Description:** Height up to 5 ft (1.5 m); evergreen shrub; leaves dark green, opposite, sessile, narrow, lanceolate, leathery, hard, edge rolled inwards, dark green above, white and downy on underside; twigs markedly branching, rod-like; flowers small, short-stemmed, blue or pale violet, calyx bell-shaped, upper lip two-petalled, lower lip three-petalled
- **Flowering:** April to July
- **Scent and flavour:** Scent intensive, aromatic, camphor-like; taste aromatic, bitter
- **Location:** Heathland with lime-rich, nutrient-rich soils, macchia scrub, gardens, sensitive to frost
- **Distribution:** Native to the Mediterranean region, cultivated
- **Drug:** Folia, Flores, Aetheroleum Rosmarini

Left: Rosemary in flower.

- **Constituents:** Essential oils (camphor, borneol, cineol, pinene), tannins, rosmarinic acid, flavones, glycosides, bitter principles, resin, saponins
- **Treatments:** For loss of appetite, digestive problems, gastro-enteric disorders, liver and gall bladder complaints, menstruation problems, depressive moods, exhaustion, low blood pressure, wounds, haematomas, eczema, oral infections, toothache
- **Uses:** Tea, spirit, gargle, wine, salves, embrocation, baths, herb pillows, culinary (meat, fish, vegetables), perfume and cosmetic industries
- **Homeopathic uses:** See above and for disease of the central nervous system and female reproductive organs
- **What and when to gather:** Herb and flowering shoots all year round
- **Lookalikes:** The drug has in the past been adulterated with leaves of the now rare Labrador or marsh tea (*Ledum palustre*), the mountain germander (*Teucrium montanum*), and bog rosemary (*Andromeda polifolia*)
- **Other information** Take care: kidney damage and fatal poisoning is possible if the dose is exceeded; consult your doctor before use.

Above: The poisonous marsh tea is a rare protected plant. A native of north America, it grows in damp places in the northern US and Canada, northern Europe and Asia.

Meadow clary; pretty, but not as valuable a healing herb as kitchen sage.

Below left: Flowering sage in a country garden.

Below right: The clary sage (Salvia sclarea) was used in the past, among other things, to give Muscatel wine its characteristic aroma.

Salvia officinalis L.
KITCHEN SAGE

Garden Sage, Common Sage, Broadleaf Sage

Salvia, with almost 900 species, is one of the richest flowering plant genera in the world. Only a handful of these species is native to central Europe, among them the attractive meadow clary (*S. pratensis*), its blue to purplish-blue helmet-like flowers adorning meadows and waysides in late spring and early summer. It was chosen as 'Healing Herb of the Year' for 2003. In Europe, north of the Alps, kitchen sage is mainly seen in herb gardens. As the name, deriving from the Latin word *salvare*, leads us to assume, its use is linked to a long tradition of healing uses, going back to the time of the Pharaohs.

Sage extracts are used above all for colds and inflammations of the mouth and pharyngeal region (as gargles and cough sweets). Sage tea is also recommended for night sweats and disease-related perspiration, and it is reputed to help depression. However, prolonged use and high doses can lead to poisoning.

- **Description:** Height up to 2 ft 8 in. (80 cm); evergreen semi-shrub, woody at base; leaves with petioles, opposite, grey-green, elongate, ovate, wrinkled, with white down when young; stems erect, with downy hair, markedly branched; flowers blue-violet or white, in spikes, upper lip almost straight, lower lip three-petalled
- **Flowering:** May to July
- **Scent and flavour:** Scent camphor-like, aromatic; flavour astringent, bitter
- **Location:** Dry soils rich in lime and nutrients, monastery and cottage gardens, cultivated
- **Distribution:** Native to the Mediterranean region, cultivated
- **Drug:** Folia, Oleum Salviae
- **Constituents:** Essential oils (thujone, cineol, salviol, camphor), bitter principles, tannins, saponin, flavonoids, glycoside, resin, vitamins
- **Treatments:** For sore throats, inflammations of the throat and pharyngeal region, diabetes, night sweats, neurological disorders, depression, diarrhoea, flatulence, skin diseases, menstruation problems, dizziness, menopausal problems, for weaning
- **Uses:** Tea, powder, oil, gargle, tincture, washes, baths, disinfectants, cosmetic, food, and liqueur industries, culinary
- **Homeopathic uses:** See above and for diseases of the central nervous system
- **What and when to gather:** Leaves before flowering, tips of flowering shoots May to July, dry separately from other herbs
- **Lookalikes:** Meadow clary (*S. pratensis*): stems not woody, leaves hairless, dentate, flowers large, dark blue, in dry meadows, contains less of the essential oils
- **Other information:** Perspiration reduction sets in about two hours at the latest after taking and can last several days
- **Care needed:** Prolonged use and higher doses can lead to poisoning – consult your doctor before taking.

Satureja hortensis L.
SUMMER SAVORY

Savory

As a digestive addition to rich roasts and to counteract the flatulence resulting from eating legumes, summer savory has an established place in the kitchen. It is a good example of the not infrequent overlap between the culinary and healing properties of herbs. But in this case, the way to the heart is not just through the stomach. In classical times, summer savory, such a modest herb seen from the outside, was praised as an aphrodisiac, and its botanical genus name is duly derived from the 'satyrs', those ever-lusty spirits of fertility who followed Dionysus, the Greek god of wine. The ancients loved then, but in the Middle Ages they were frowned on – at any rate by the higher authorities in the Church, who, as Christian Rätsch reports, forbade the monks not only from eating, but even from growing summer savory.

- **Description:** Height up to 1 ft (30 cm); leaves small, linear, lanceleote, glandular, spotted, hairy at edge; stems erect, bushy, branching, base more or less woody, often tinged with violet; flowers very small, with stems, pale purple or white, green or violet within; root woody; annual to biennial
- **Flowering:** June to September
- **Scent and flavour:** Scent intensively aromatic; taste intensively savoury
- **Location:** Dry, lime-rich soils, herb gardens
- **Distribution:** Native to the Mediterranean region, cultivated
- **Drug:** Herba, Oleum Saturejae
- **Constituents:** Essential oils (carvacrol, cymol)
- **Treatments:** For sore throats, loss of appetite, digestive problems, flatulence, diarrhoea, menstruation problems, troublesome insects and as an aphrodisiac
- **Uses:** Tea, gargle, cosmetic and food industries, culinary (beans, lamb, sausage, soups, stews)

- **Lookalikes:** Winter savory (*S. montana*): taller, stems woody, flowers larger, pink or violet in spikes, leaves broader

Flowering summer savory in a herb bed, with parsley in the background.

Betonica officinalis L.
COMMON HEDGE-NETTLE

Wood Betony, Betony, Spiked Betony, Bishopwort

While many herbs among the mint family prefer dry and rocky locations, the hedge-nettle is found in damper places, in boggy meadows, and heathland. Its historical importance can hardly be exaggerated. It was praised as early as the 9th century by Walahfrid Strabo in his 'Garden Poem' (*Hortulus Sanitatis*), and Odo Magdunensis, in his work *Macer floridus* (11th century), equally strongly influenced by classical authorities, devotes a long chapter to the herb. In this, he claims that all manner of ailments, from consumption to broken skulls and from eye diseases to hernias, gynaecological problems, and even epilepsy can all be cured with betony. It is often difficult to say why it is that plants once highly esteemed gradually lose their importance in folk medicine while others continue to be used to the present day. An interesting note is provided by Delaveau and colleagues: 'Used as a tobacco substitute, betony can make giving up smoking easier.'

Hedge-nettle in flower in a garden.

- **Description:** Height up to 2 ft (60 cm); basal rosette with cordate, crenate leaves with long petioles, stem leaves ovate, elongate, dentate, hairy; stems erect, hairy; flowers purple or pinkish-red in dense spike with flower at end, two-lipped; perennial
- **Flowering:** June to September
- **Scent and flavour:** Flavour bitter, hot
- **Location:** Bog meadows, heathland, meadows with poor soil
- **Distribution:** Widespread
- **Drug:** Herba Betonicae
- **Constituents:** Betonicin, stachydrin, bitter principles, tannins
- **Treatments:** In the past: for colds, asthma, digestive disorders, diarrhoea, heartburn, headaches, giving up smoking, sneezing stimulant
- **Uses:** Tea, powder, poultices (fresh leaves), tobacco substitute
- **Homeopathic uses:** See above and for diseases of the digestive tract, liver, gall bladder, and pancreas
- **What and when to gather:** Flowering herb June to August, (rhizome)
- **Lookalikes:** Whitespot (*Stachys sylvatica*): leaves cordate, smells of bugs, found in woodland; marsh hedge-nettle (*Stachys palustris*): leaves elongate, flowers red, white-spotted, found along ditches – both kinds have anti-spasmodic qualities, the tubers of both betony species provide a nourishing vegetable
- **Other information:** Take care: the fresh rhizome and leaves in high doses have an emetic and laxative action

Thymus vulgaris L.
GARDEN THYME

The genus *Thymus* comprises about 350 species, and their exact classification is not easy even for a botanist. Lemon thyme (*T. pulegioides*) has small, evergreen, leathery leaves, prefers poor, stony soils and even colonizes cracks in rocks or anthills. Creeping thyme (*T. serpyllum*) is a protected species, limited to sandy pine forests and sand dunes, while mother of thyme (*T. praecox*) is largely confined to lime soil regions. The garden thyme (*T. vulgaris*) presented here is native to the Mediterranean region, but has been cultivated in northern Europe since the Middle Ages.

The constituents can vary markedly, depending on species, location, and exposure to sun. Thymol, an effective antiseptic, is the best known. Conventional medicine also acknowledges the curative action of thyme for all kinds of colds and diseases of the digestive tract.

- **Description:** Height up to 16 in. (40 cm); evergreen dwarf shrub; leaves grey-green, elongate, ovate, opposite, thick white down on the underside, edge rolled inwards; stems erect, markedly branched, square, woody; flowers small, purple-pink to delicate lilac in racemes, two-lipped; roots spindle-shaped, some varieties form runners
- **Flowering:** May to October
- **Scent and flavour:** Scent intensely savoury, aromatic; flavour aromatic, slightly bitter
- **Location:** Sandy, stony soils, poor grassland
- **Distribution:** Native to the Mediterranean area, cultivated
- **Drug:** Herba, Oleum Thymi Vulgaris
- **Constituents:** Essential oils (thymol, cymol, carvacrol), bitter principles, tannins
- **Treatments:** For loss of appetite, digestive disorders, gastro-enteric complaints, persistent cough, whooping cough, bronchitis, asthma, bad breath, nervous stomach and heart complaints, insomnia, rheumatic ailments, haematomas, sprains, combating worms – strong antiseptic

- **Uses:** Tea, tincture, oil, gargle, baths, herb pillows, culinary (butter, sauces, rich meat dishes, fish, pizza, fried potatoes, legumes, etc.), pharmaceutical, food and cosmetic industries (toothpaste, mouthwashes, perfume)
- **Homeopathic uses:** See above
- **What and when to gather:** Whole plant (without root) shortly before and during flowering May to October
- **Lookalikes:** Many garden varieties on sale with a very wide range of scents
- **Other information:** Take care: poisonous in overdose. It can irritate the digestive tract and lead to serious metabolic disorders (over-functioning thyroid gland); fatal poisoning is possible

Above left: Garden thyme (Thymus vulgaris) has leaves with a rolled-in edge, with dense soft down underneath. It is generally not hardy through the winter.

Above right: Wall germander (Teucrium chamaedrys), an ancient healing plant rarely used today, is often confused with thyme.

Olive family
Oleaceae

In Europe, the great olive family is mainly represented in the Mediterranean region. The one tree from this group in more northerly European regions is the European ash (Fraxinus). A few ornamental shrubs also belong to the olive family, such as lilac and forsythia (Syringa and Forsythia), as well as the poisonous privet (Ligustrum). The name originates with the famous olive, though north of the Alps the climate is too cold for the tree.

Fraxinus excelsior L.
EUROPEAN ASH

Common Ash, Weeping Ash

The European ash, which grows up to 130 ft (40 m) high, is a stately forest tree. Its natural habitats include flood plains ('hardwood plains'), and mountain and gorge woodlands.

Often, however, the trees are cultivated, as the European ash is an important forestry tree because of its hard, elastic wood. In the past, it was the arms industry that profited: whole armies were equipped with spears, lances and bows made of ash wood. In spring, mushroom collectors seek out ash groves because the highly desirable edible morel (*Morchella esculenta*) grows there. In folk medicine, the bark and the boiled root of the ash were used to treat wounds.

In Scandinavian mythology the ash takes on a central role. Threatened by the serpent Nidhögg, which gnaws constantly on its root, the enormous 'World Ash' known as Yggdrasil links the underworld, earth and heaven. Odin, father of the gods, created the first human beings from an alder and an ash. The woman's name was Embla, the man's Ask – and even today *ask* is the Swedish word for an ash tree.

■ **Description:** Height up to 130 ft (40 m); tree with pale grey, smooth bark, finely cracked in age; buds black, velvety, cap-like; leaves with long petioles, opposite, odd pinnate,

Below left: Dried and ground, the winged seeds of the ash can be used as a spice for baking.

Below right: A sugary sap (mannite sugar) is obtained from the bark of the flowering or manna ash, which grows in southern Europe. Dried, it is eaten as 'manna' and is a mild laxative.

with 7 to 11 lanceolate to ovate, serrate leaflets; flowers in dense bushy panicles, greenish-yellow with reddish-brown anthers, fruit winged, seeds nutlike

- **Flowering:** April, May
- **Scent and flavour:** Flowers slightly scented; seeds taste savoury, bitter, leaves bitter, astringent
- **Location:** Lowland forests, mixed forests, banks of streams and rivers, often cultivated
- **Distribution:** Widespread
- **Drug:** Folia, Cortex Fraxini
- **Constituents:** Glycosides (fraxin), sugar, mannitol, flavonoids (rutin), tannins, mucilage, essential oils, vitamins, dyes, fatty oils (seeds)
- **Treatments:** For rheumatic diseases, kidney and bladder ailments, fever (bark), wounds, worms, as a strengthening tonic
- **Uses:** Tea, extract, embrocation (made from the fruits)
- **Homeopathic uses:** For extra-articular rheumatism
- **What and when to gather:** Young leaves May to June, bark of two- to three-year-old twigs April to June, seeds September to November
- **Lookalikes:** Flowering ash (*F. ornus*): white flowers in dependent panicles; European mountain ash (*Sorbus aucuparia*, see page 249): leaflets sharply serrate, flowers white, red berries, rose family
- **Other information:** As with many wind-pollinated trees and shrubs, the flowers appear before the leaves. As birch trees flower around the same time, those allergic to pollen are subject to extreme stress in April and May.

Olea europaea L.
OLIVE

Olive Tree

What would the Holy Land be – what would the whole Mediterranean region be – without its olive groves! To sit down on a hot summer's day in the shade of a thousand-year-old olive

Old olive tree on the Mount of Olives in Jerusalem.

tree to a picnic of ewe's cheese, salami, white bread, a handful of fresh olives and a drink of dry local wine is to feel you have gone back to an earlier period of human history, before the word 'stress' was invented.

In ancient Greece, the goddess Athene was the patron deity of olive trees. In the Old Testament, it is reported how the dove sent by Noah returned to the Ark with the twig of an olive branch in its beak. Since then, the dove and the olive branch have symbolized peace. For Hildegard of Bingen, the olive was a symbol of mercy. The power of the symbol remains today; a recent political alliance in Italy came together under the sign of the olive tree.

Above left: Branch of an olive tree in flower; the leaves are partly dusted with pollen, which can cause allergies.

Above right: Green olives.

To describe the many different uses of the oil obtained from olives would cover many pages. A healthy food, without which it is impossible to imagine the cuisine of the countries bordering the Mediterranean, it was also used as a lamp oil, pharmaceutically, for skin care and cosmetics, and for natural medicine. Sources document its use by the ancient Egyptians 5,000 years ago. Olive oil, massaged gently into the scalp, is recommended as a home treatment for migraines.

- **Description:** Height up to 50 ft (15 m), can reach an age of more than 1,500 years; markedly branching, gnarled, twisted, evergreen; leaves opposite, elongate to lanceolate, leathery, grey-green above, silvery on the underside; flowers small, whitish-green, in 1–2½ in. (3–6 cm) long panicles; fruits ¾–1 in. (2–3 cm) long, oval, green when unripe, then red, finally black, with hard seed
- **Flowering:** April, May
- **Scent and flavour:** Slightly scented; taste bitter when raw, oil aromatic to nutty according to quality
- **Location:** Loves warmth
- **Distribution:** Mediterranean region, cultivated
- **Drug:** Folia, Oleum Olivae
- **Constituents:** Terpenoids, flavonoids, fatty oil (oleic acids), glycosides, vitamins, mineral salts (calcium)
- **Treatments:** For high blood pressure, diabetes, fever, wounds, gout, rheumatic complaints, loss of appetite, skin ailments
- **Uses:** Cold-pressed oil, pharmaceutical and food industries, skin care, spa treatments
- **Homeopathic uses:** See above
- **What and when to gather:** Leaves and fruit (green), black (for oil), October to March
- **Lookalikes:** None
- **Other information:** Wind pollinated, can cause allergies

'Let's assume that of all the trees that don't grow in our latitudes we could wish for one in our gardens... My choice would not be the coconut palm, or the blue cypress of Kashmir, but the olive tree. The olive tree has grace and dignity...'

Hugh Johnson,
The Big Book of Trees

Broomrape family
Orobanchaceae

In the broomrape family, the leaves are often dentate or deeply lobed, while the flowers, mostly in racemes, are frequently fused to form a tube. The fruits are multi-seeded capsules.

Euphrasia rostkoviana Hayne
EYEBRIGHT

Common Eyebright, Glossy Eyebright

Beautiful eyebright is a semi-parasite, drawing nutrients and mineral salts from the grasses that are its hosts, but it does also have chlorophyll (the substance that makes the leaves green) to turn sunlight into energy. Full parasites such as the related broomrape (*Orobanche*) manage without chlorophyll.

The curative action of eyebright on eye inflammations, conjunctivitis and colds is based on the experience of folk medicine and homeopathy – in other words, it has not yet been possible to verify it by research. This is not to say that such action does not exist – only that scientific proof is lacking. All we have is the suggestive power of the name and the mysterious ways of healing through belief in what doctors in earlier centuries, and charismatic herb women and priests too, recommended to their patients and customers. For hygienic reasons, you are these days advised not to self-treat.

- **Description:** Height up to 10 in. (25 cm), stems glossy green, branching, dense glandular hairs; leaves grey-grey, opposite, decussate, sessile, ovate, elongate, crenate and dentate; flowers white, often with violet veins, upper lip helmet-shaped, two-petalled, lower lip three-petalled, yellow spot in throat, in cyme with flower at tip and leaves; short root, annual
- **Flowering:** June to October
- **Scent and flavour:** Scent balsam-like, taste bitter, hot
- **Location:** Meadows, dry slopes, woodland borders
- **Distribution:** Very common
- **Drug:** Herba Euphrasiae
- **Constituents:** Tannins, essential oils, glycosides (aucubin), bitter principles, resin
- **Treatments:** For eye inflammations, weakness of the eyes, styes, coughs, sore throats, slight stomach problems
- **Uses:** Tea, poultices, eye baths, compresses
- **Homeopathic uses:** See above and for streaming colds
- **What and when to gather:** Flowering herb June to October
- **Lookalikes:** Many sub-species, difficult to distinguish; drug eyebright (*E. stricta*): flowers reddish-violet, probably with the strongest healing action
- **Other information:** Always make fresh tea for eyewashes and filter it – if polluted, there is a danger of blindness. For safety reasons it is always essential to consult a doctor for eye diseases

Great for sore eyes – at least visually; eyebright.

Plantain family
Plantaginaceae

According to the old classification, only the genera plantain (Plantago) and shoreweed (Litorella) were assigned to the plantain family. More recent phytogenetic discoveries have also added genera previously assigned to the figwort family such as foxglove (Digitalis), hedgehyssop (Gratiola), flax (Linaria), and speedwell (Veronica) to the plantain family. These are for the most part herbs with hermaphrodite, often zygomorphic flowers which have fused to form a tube; the fruits are often multi-seeded capsules.

Digitalis purpurea L.
FOXGLOVE

■ *very poisonous* ■

In many areas, the foxglove is *the* summer flower, and when, on a hilly forested ridge, dense patches of it fill the clearings made by logging or wind-fallen trees, these purple-flowered plants, up to five feet

high, become the definitive feature of the landscape.

This species is a classic example of Paracelsus' sentence *Dosis facit venenum* – the dosage makes the poison. On the one hand, as little as 0.02 oz (0.3 g) of dried leaves will poison an adult; on the other, the glycosides obtained from foxglove are effective, frequently prescribed medicines to lower the heart rate. Drugs containing *Digitalis*, though, may only be prescribed by a doctor. Today, they are mostly derived from cultivated plants.

■ **Description:** Height up to 5 ft (1.5 m); leaves very large, lanceolate, with soft down, in basal rosette; stems erect, leaves arranged in spiral pattern; flowers purple-red, spotted and hairy within, c. 2½ in. (6 cm) long, thimble-shaped, bag-like, in one-sided racemes; root spindle-shaped, many side roots; biennial
■ **Flowering:** June to August
■ **Scent and flavour:** Scent rather unpleasant, taste very bitter
■ **Location:** Clearings, open woodland, avoids lime
■ **Distribution:** Widespread in localized patches, cultivated, escaped into the wild
■ **Drug:** Folia Digitalis
■ **Constituents:** Glycosides (digitalin, digitoxin, glucogitaloxin, purpurea glycoside), mucilage, saponins
■ **Treatments:** For heart insufficiency, heart muscle disease
■ **Uses:** Ready-made drugs, only to be taken if prescribed by a doctor
■ **Homeopathic uses:** See above and for migraines
■ **What and when to gather:** In the first year, the leaves of the basal rosette, in the second year the stem leaves on sunny days around midday; always dry and store separately from other herbs
■ **Lookalikes:** Grecian foxglove (*D. lanata*): flowers pale brown, dark brown within, woolly hairs, leaves linear-lanceolate, cultivated

Like foxglove, hedgehyssop (Gratiola officinalis) contains glycosides which act on the heart. It is a strong laxative, diuretic, and emetic, and strengthens the heart. The yellowish-white, reddish veined flowers, about ½ in. (1 cm) long, have long stems. This protected plant is poisonous for grazing animals as well.

Left: Foxglove is often cultivated as a garden plant.

Plantago
PLANTAIN

Plantain

The three species of plantain are among the 'first-aid plants', as they can be found almost anywhere and have such characteristic features that even children can recognize them without difficulty. The crushed leaves bring rapid relief for insect bites and small cuts, or after painful contact with stinging nettles.

In the Mediterranean region, fleawort (*P. afra*) and sand plantain (*P. arenaria*) are used as healing herbs. The seeds of fleawort are rich in mucilage and known to be a good laxative.

Plantago lanceolata L.
NARROWLEAF PLANTIN

English Plantain, Buckhorn Plantain, Lanceleaf Plantain, Ribgrass, Ribwort

As with other species of plantain, the leaves of the narrowleaf are arranged in a basal rosette, but they are far narrower than for the common and hoary plantain. As a culinary herb, narrowleaf plantain has a number of uses; finely chopped in salads or in mixed vegetables; dried as a flavouring, baked in pancakes or batter dough. In addition, it is a recognized healing herb, used above all as a bronchial tea for colds. There are also cough mixtures and cough sweets based on narrowleaf plantain. Narrowleaf plantain seeds, taken with plenty of water, are considered a proven treatment for constipation. Other practitioners recommend narrowleaf plantain in natural cosmetics for dry as well as for 'patchy, nervous, and flaking' skin. 'Put a few drops on a damp piece of cotton wool and gently rub face, neck, and décolleté area with it.'

- **Description:** Height 20 in. (50 cm); leaves three- to seven-veined, narrow, lanceolate, parallel veined; stems leafless, grooved; flowers numerous, inconspicuous, in short, elongated, ovate spike, stamens and anthers white, protruding, capsule fruit, perennial
- **Flowering:** May to September
- **Scent and flavour:** Unscented, slightly bitter, astringent
- **Location:** Meadows, pasture, waysides
- **Distribution:** Very common in Europe
- **Drug:** Herba Plantaginis lanceolatae
- **Constituents:** Glycosides (aucubin, catalpol, iridoid glycoside), mucus polysaccharides, flavonoids, tannins, minerals, silicic acid, phenolcarbon acids, aesculetin (cumarin)
- **Treatments:** For catarrh, coughs, bronchitis, asthma, inflammations of the mouth and pharyngeal region, insect bites, skin diseases, small wounds, constipation, eye inflammations
- **Uses:** Tea, salad, soup (herb and root)
- **Homeopathic uses:** See above
- **What and when to gather:** Young whole plants (before flowering)
- **Lookalikes:** Broad-leafed grasses (Poaceae, see page 179): no stems with flower spike

The commonly occurring narrowleaf plantain with its unmistakable narrow lanceolate leaves.

Plantago major L.
COMMON PLANTAIN

Broadleaf Plantain, Rippleseed Plantain

The common plantain can be recognized by its rosette of broad leaves with long petioles and by the flower head, a spike up to 4 in. (10 cm) long. The green seeds can be chewed raw ('Nature's muesli bars'), fried in butter or enjoyed as a tea. Seeds stick to the soles of shoes and are distributed in this manner.

- **Description:** Height up to 16 in. (40 cm); leaves three- to seven-veined, broadly ovate, mostly smooth, long petioles; spike ½–4 in. (2–10 cm) tall; cylindrical; flowers numerous, inconspicuous, greenish to reddish, stamens yellowish-white, capsule fruit, perennial
- **Flowering:** June to October
- **Scent and flavour:** Unscented, slightly bitter, astringent; green spike nutty
- **Location:** Sandy to clay soils; on paths, landfills, waysides
- **Distribution:** Very common in Europe up to 7,700 ft (2,350 m) altitude
- **Drug:** Herba, Semen Plantaginis majoris
- **Constituents:** See narrowleaf plantain
- **Treatments:** See narrowleaf plantain
- **Uses:** Tea, green seed spikes raw or fried in butter, ripe seed spikes as bird food
- **Homeopathic uses:** For headaches, toothache (root), skin rashes, bedwetting, diarrhoea
- **What and when to gather:** Herb during flowering, seeds when ripe; June to October
- **Lookalikes:** Hoary plantain (*P. media*, see following): spike shorter, flowers pink to purple

Plantago media L.
HOARY PLANTAIN

The broad leaves of hoary plantain are reminiscent of common plantain, but have shorter petioles. The flower head, delicate pink to white, is in shape more like those of narrowleaf plantain.

- **Description:** Height up to 20 in. (50 cm); leaves five- to nine-veined, lightly downed, short petioles, broadly elliptic; stems two to five times as long as the cylindrical flower spike; flowers numerous, delicate pink to purple, scented, with long stamens; capsule fruit; perennial
- **Flowering:** May to July
- **Scent and flavour:** Flowers sweetish, leaves unscented; taste slightly bitter, astringent
- **Location:** Clay soils with lime, semi-arid grassland, meadows, waysides, paths

Right: The common plantain with its typical leaf rosette and long flower spikes.

Far right: The hoary plantain is less common than the two other species. Here it is shown in full flower.

- **Distribution:** Widespread in Europe to 5,900 ft (1,800 m) altitude
- **Drug:** Herba Plantaginis mediae
- **Constituents:** Glycosides (aucubin, catalpol), mucus polysaccharides, flavonoids, tannins, silicic acid
- **Treatments:** For catarrh, coughs, bronchitis, asthma, inflammations of the mouth and pharyngeal regions, insect bites
- **Uses:** Tea
- **Homeopathic uses:** For skin inflammations, insect bites, headaches, toothache, earache, wounds
- **What and when to gather:** Herb May to September (before flowering)
- **Lookalikes:** Common plantain (*P. major*): spike as long as the stem, leaves with long petiole

Veronica officinalis L.
COMMON GYPSYWEED

Common Speedwell, Heath Speedwell, Drug Speedwell, Fluellen

Over the course of time, the popularity of some plants can wax and wane remarkably. It can happen that a herb is highly esteemed for centuries and then almost forgotten in a relatively short period of time. Nicholas Culpeper recommends speedwell 'applied with Barley-meal to watering eyes', to 'stay all manner of bleeding at nose or mouth', and claims that 'it cleanses and heals all foul or old ulcers'. Although modern pharmacology has not been able to demonstrate any active agents in gypsyweed to justify these claims, gypsyweed tea continues to be recommended for bronchitis, and the savoury-to-bitter leaves can be added to wild herb salads.

- **Description:** Height up to 2 ft (60 cm), hairy; leaves with short petioles, opposite, decussate, obovate, edge serrate; stems erect or rising, rooting; flowers pale blue to pale purple, wheel-shaped, with four petals and two stamens in dense, spike-like racemes; capsules heart-shaped; roots spindle-shaped; perennial
- **Flowering:** May to August
- **Scent and flavour:** Scent slightly aromatic, spicy; taste bitter, astringent
- **Location:** Sunny forest borders, dry meadows with poor soils, slopes, scrub
- **Distribution:** Widespread
- **Drug:** Herba Veronicae
- **Constituents:** Bitter principles, glycosides (little aucubin), flavonoids, tannins, essential oils
- **Treatments:** Purifying the blood, diseases of the respiratory tract, digestive tract, liver, kidneys, bladder, skin diseases, itching, inflammations in the mouth and pharyngeal area, rheumatic complaints, gout
- **Uses:** Tea, gargles, salad, pressed juice, poultices, rubbing alcohol
- **Homeopathic uses:** For chronic bronchitis, skin diseases, bladder infections
- **What and when to gather:** Flowering herb, May to August
- **Lookalikes:** There are many similar speedwells, though these are not used medicinally

European speedwell (Veronica beccabunga) with its ovate, serrate, juicy, glossy leaves grows on the banks of streams and in clean, flowing water, like watercress (see page 140). It is good for salads and can also be drunk as a tea for cleansing the blood.

Gypsyweed is often mistaken for ground ivy (see page 85).

Madder family
Rubiaceae

Dyer's plants such as the yellow-flowered madder (Rubia tinctorum), whose root supplies rose madder, are members of the madder family. The coffee plant is another. The leaves are opposite, in whorls, the flowers in loose false umbels; the fruits break into two parts.

Galium odoratum (L.) Scop.
SWEETSCENTED BEDSTRAW

Star Grass, Sweet Grass, Sweet Woodruff, Woodruff

Sweetscented bedstraw grows in neutral humus soils in nutrient-rich beech forests – so reliably that plant sociologists have named a certain type of beech wood *Galio-Fagetum* ('Bedstraw Beechwood') after the plant. Sweetscented bedstraw became popular as a colouring and flavouring for some types of dessert and, in Germany, for Berlin's national drink, '*Weisse mit Schuss*' (wheat beer with a shot of syrup – usually raspberry, sometimes lemon or sweet woodruff-flavoured). However, as the contents are suspected of being carcinogenic, its use in the food industry was prohibited by German law in 1981. This does not mean that lovers of the traditional spring punch have to go without their annual indulgence. A few leaves are enough to give the punch its desired aroma of sweetscented bedstraw. It is important that the leaves are dried a little before use, as the cumarin glycoside is released in wilting.

In natural healing, sweetscented bedstraw tea is used mainly for its sedative effect and has been prescribed for stomach ache, headaches, and migraine (but do not exceed the dose, or it may have the opposite effect!). Furlenmeier also recommends the herb for congestion of the liver and retention of urine. The treatments mentioned in old herbals for kidney stones and liver diseases such as jaundice – Adamus Lonicerus still calls sweetscented bedstraw the 'liver herb' – are of almost no importance today.

- **Description:** Height up to 8 in. (20 cm); leaves sessile, lanceolate, with bristly hairs at edge, in whorls of six to eight; stems square; flowers small, white, star-shaped with short tube; fruit with hooks and bristles; rhizome thin, creeping; perennial
- **Flowering:** April to June
- **Scent and flavour:** Scent of rubbed and dried leaves like hay and meadow flowers (cumarins); flavour aromatic, slightly bitter
- **Location:** Shady beech woods
- **Distribution:** Common
- **Drug:** Herba Asperulae odoratae
- **Constituents:** Cumarins, flavones, glycosides (asperulosid), bitter principles, tannins
- **Treatments:** For headaches, migraines, insomnia, nervousness, circulation problems, liver disease, jaundice, kidney and bladder stones, haemorrhoids
- **Uses:** Tea, crushed herb, punch, desserts, liqueur, perfume manufacture, protection against moths
- **Homeopathic uses:** See above
- **What and when to gather:** Whole herb before and during flowering, May, June

Sweetscented bedstraw in the 'bedstraw beech wood'.

- **Lookalikes:** Other bedstraw species (*Galium* spec.): other locations and flowering times, without the typical scent, taller
- **Other information:** Take care in pregnancy; in high doses, cumarin can cause severe headaches; carcinogenic qualities are suspected

Lady's bedstraw, with its golden honey-scented, small flowers is a very attractive, if not very conspicuous plant.

Galium verum L.
LADY'S BEDSTRAW

Yellow Bedstraw, Maid's Hair, Cheese Rennet

As is often the case, lady's bedstraw has hidden qualities that only reveal themselves if you examine both the experiences gathered over millennia and modern research into plant constituents.

According to legend, the straw on which the infant Jesus was bedded in Bethlehem consisted of the bracken fern (*Pteridium aquilinum*) and lady's bedstraw – hence the English common name, reflected also in other languages such as the German '*Liebfrauenstroh*'. The lady's bedstraw was one of a number of plants sacred to the Virgin Mary, and these were spread onto the beds of women in childbed to keep ill-luck away from pregnant women and their children. Among them were yarrow (see page 50), thyme (see page 99), oregano (see page 94), and of course the 'mother herb', chamomile (see page 60). Lady's bedstraw owes one of its modern names to a very unusual quality; the ferment it contains will make milk proteins curdle. The herb was therefore used in cheese-making before the development of modern fermentation techniques.

Tea made of lady's bedstraw is diuretic and provokes sweating. The herb was also used externally in wound healing and to combat skin diseases, but according to Bisset and Wichtl there is as yet no scientific confirmation of these folk medicine treatments.

- **Description:** Height up to 2 ft 8in. (80 cm); leaves glossy, narrow, lanceolate, pointed, rolled back at the edges, in whorls of eight to twelve; stems erect, square to round, branching; flowers pale yellow, in false umbels with flower at end; fruit smooth; rhizome cylindrical, creeping; perennial
- **Flowering:** June to September
- **Scent and flavour:** Scent strong, sweet, honey-like; taste astringent, sour
- **Location:** Dry meadows, slopes, waysides, open woodland
- **Distribution:** Common
- **Drug:** Herba Galii lutei
- **Constituents:** Ferment, glycosides, essential oils
- **Treatments:** For liver, gall bladder, kidney, and bladder diseases, externally for skin diseases, nosebleeds, wounds, swollen ankles
- **Uses:** Tea, crushed leaves, decoction, dye (for Cheshire cheese)
- **Homeopathic uses:** See above
- **What and when to gather:** Flowering herb June to September
- **Lookalikes:** None
- **Other information:** Lady's bedstraw flowers contain a yellow dye, the root a red one

Stickywilly (G. aparine), with its white flowers, can be used in the same way as lady's bedstraw.

Elder family
Sambucaceae

Members of this family include the elder (Sambucus) and the viburnum (Viburnum). The leaves, entire or pinnate, are opposite; the flower heads are false umbels. In the past, both genera were classified under the related honeysuckle family (Caprifoliaceae), which includes among others the honeysuckle (Lonicera) as well as ornamental shrubs such as snowberry (Symphoricarpus) and weigela (Weigela).

Dwarf elder with reddish-white flowers.

Sambucus ebulus L.
DWARF ELDERBERRY

Dwarf Elder, Elderberry

Compared to the European black elderberry, which can reach tree height, the dwarf elderberry is rather an inconspicuous plant with herb-like stems, distinguished by its reddish-white, disagreeably sweet-smelling flowers with reddish-violet anthers. In contrast to the European black elderberry, the fruit heads are erect, and the leaves also smell fairly disgusting when rubbed. Dwarf elderberry grows on woodland borders and waysides, railway embankments, in clearings and comparable sites.

In the past, dwarf elderberry was accorded the same curative powers as common elder. The black berries are poisonous and can, in extreme cases, be fatal. As late as the first half of the 20th century, a mush of the berries was recommended as a laxative. However, as it can also cause nausea, vomiting and dizziness, its use is not advised. The root was used to make a strongly diuretic tea, used in kidney diseases.

■ **Description:** Height up to 6 ft (2 m); herb-like, not woody, stems grooved with white pith; leaves odd pinnate, leaflets lanceolate, serrate; flowers reddish-white in thick false umbel, anthers violet; fruit small, black, glossy berry with three seeds, juice intensively staining; rhizome fibrous, white, creeping

The ripe fruit heads are erect, unlike those of the European black elder.

- **Flowering:** June to August
- **Scent and flavour:** Scent of flowers and leaves unpleasant, distasteful when rubbed, flavour hot and bitter, fruit bitter-sweet
- **Location:** Woodland clearings, woodland borders, stony slopes
- **Distribution:** Common
- **Drug:** Radix, Folia, Fructus Ebuli
- **Constituents:** Bitter principles, glycosides (sambunigrin), flavonoids, tannins, saponins, essential oils
- **Treatments:** For kidney and bladder ailments, sore throats, rheumatic complaints, purifying the blood and as a laxative
- **Uses:** Tea, gargle, dye (berries)
- **Homeopathic uses:** See above
- **What and when to gather:** Fruits in August and September, root March to May, September to October
- **Lookalikes:** European black elderberry (*S. nigra*, see following): tall shrub, flowers creamy white; red elderberry (*S. racemosus*): flowers greenish-yellow, in oval or conical panicles, berries red, seeds poisonous
- **Other information:** The mush of berries has a laxative action, but due to the slight toxicity (nausea, vomiting, dizziness) they should not be used

---

Sambucus nigra L.
EUROPEAN BLACK ELDERBERRY

Elder, Black Elder, Common Elder, Bore Tree, Pipe Tree

Elderberry bushes will find a niche in which to survive almost anywhere: behind the house, in moist, shady, far corners of the garden, on the banks of streams, in gorge woodlands and in small woods. As they will tolerate large quantities of nitrogen, they thrive near dunghills and compost heaps. Even slurry, which sprayed on to fields has moved dozens of more sensitive plants to red status on the lists of endangered species, will not ruffle the elderberry's composure. It will happily continue to thrive at the stinking border of the woodlands next to the cornfield. Neither flowers nor berries make a particularly inviting harvest in such locations.

Elderflower tea is a successful febrifuge for treating feverish colds. It stimulates perspiration and lowers fever. You can also fry the flowers in pancakes or in batter and serve them sprinkled with cinnamon and sugar. The juice of the berries is also very popular, and not just the home-made variety – it has found a place on the shelves of health food stores. Coming home from a long winter walk, there is nothing like a glass of hot elderberry juice. In large quantities, it acts as a laxative and, according to Eva Aschenbrunner, helps to combat shingles. There are warnings nowadays about the use of bark, leaf and root extracts as recommended by old herbals, since parts of the black elderberry, such as the unripe berries, are poisonous.

- **Description:** Height up to 23 ft (7 m); shrub, grey bark, warty (= lenticellular), young twig green, pith white, soft; leaves with five to seven leaflets; odd pinnate, dentate; flowers

The spherical, glossy black berries of the privet are often mistaken for elderberries. They are extremely poisonous and have even proved fatal for children. Adults usually escape with a serious gastro-enteric inflammation, cramp and diarrhoea.

The hanging ripe false umbels of the European black elderberry.

Elderflowers – a sweet-smelling treat in June.

- **Location:** Lowland forest, hedges, scrub, gardens; this herb loves nitrogen
- **Distribution:** Very common
- **Drug:** Flores, Fructus, Folia, Cortex Sambuci
- **Constituents:** Essential oils, glycosides (sambunigrin, rutin), flavonoids, saponin, mucilage, alkaloids (leaves and bark), bitter principles, tannins, vitamins (berries)
- **Treatments:** For loss of appetite, fever, colds, purifying the blood, rheumatic ailments, neuralgic pains
- **Uses:** Tea, gargle, liqueur, syrup, juice, soup, wine, pancakes, preserves, food industry, dyes
- **Homeopathic uses:** For diseases of the respiratory tract
- **What and when to gather:** Flowers June and July in dry weather, berries September and October (only when fully ripe), bark (only the green layer between outer bark and wood) February to April, root bark September to November
- **Lookalikes:** Dwarf elderberry (*S. ebulus*, see page 110): leaves a little narrower, flowers reddish; young leaves of bishop's goutweed (*Aegopodium podagria*, see page 198): herb, umbelliferous, edible; privet (*Ligustrum vulgare*): black berries in panicles, leaves elongate, lanceolate, evergreen, poisonous
- **Other information:** The flowers produce plenty of pollen, although they are insect-pollinated. The pith is used for microscopic dissection. Take care: unripe and raw berries, together with high doses, can lead to nausea, stomach pains and vomiting

creamy white, in spread-out false umbels; fruit blackish-purple, glossy berries with purple-red juice

- **Flowering:** June, July
- **Scent and flavour:** Scent of flowers intensely sweet, of leaves and bark intensive, rather unpleasant; taste of leaves and bark hot, bitter, flowers sweetish, berries aromatic, slightly sour, very characteristic

> *'As far as elderberry is concerned, there are three sorts of people: those gripped by nausea as soon as they smell elder, even from a distance; those who don't mind elder soup; and those who are not only capable of eating raw elderberries with milk and sugar but actually look forward to doing so.'*
>
> *Jürgen Dahl*

Viburnum opulus L.
EUROPEAN CRANBERRY BUSH

Guelder Rose, Viburnum

During the flowering period between the end of April and June it is easy to recognize the European cranberry bush. A ring of large, sterile, snow-white false flowers, visible from quite a distance, is grouped around the small fertile flowers in the middle. In the winter, the glossy red, single-seed berries bring points of colour into snowy woodlands or gardens – birds avoid them even in the coldest of weather. They are unsuitable for human consumption as well, although there is some argument among experts about exactly how poisonous they actually are and to what degree the toxins contained in them can be destroyed by heating. For healing purposes, bark extracts are mainly used. They are used in gynaecology – also homeopathically – for instance, if there is danger of miscarriage or for menstruation problems.

- **Description:** Height up to 13 ft (4 m); shrub, twigs smooth, glossy, flexible; leaves with petioles, three to five lobes, dentate; flowers white with large, sterile, 'radiant' five-petalled false flowers along the outside, inner flowers small, fertile, in false umbels; berries red, spherical, with a single seed
- **Flowering:** June, July
- **Scent and flavour:** Taste astringent, bitter
- **Location:** Moist scrub, forest borders, deciduous and lowland forest, gardens
- **Distribution:** Common
- **Drug:** Cortex Viburni opuli
- **Constituents:** Bitter principle (viburnin), tannins, glycosides
- **Treatments:** For gynaecological problems such as menstruation difficulties, the threat of miscarriage, false contractions
- **Uses:** Liquid extracts
- **Homeopathic uses:** For diseases of the female reproductive organs, the threat of miscarriage, painful menstruation

- **What and when to gather:** Bark February to April
- **Lookalikes:** Wayfaringtree (*V. lantana*): downy, entire leaves, flowers white, no radiating false flowers, green, red and ripe black fruits all at the same time; garden variety (*V. opulus* var. *roseum*) with spherical flower head, flowers sterile
- **Other information:** The unripe fruit causes inflammations of the digestive tract; however, cooked, they can be used as stewed fruit or jelly

The wayfaringtree, which has no false flowers, is a popular garden plant. Its fruits ripen one after the other, so that green, red and black berries can be seen on the bush at the same time. The leaves are used as a gargle to treat diseases of the mouth and pharyngeal region.

Autumn moods: the berries of the European cranberry bush are ripe; the leaves have already turned.

Figwort family
Scrophulariaceae

The members of the figwort family, scrophulariaceous plants, comprise more than 200 genera. The species native to central Europe are all herbs. The flowers, often in a raceme flower head, are more or less asymmetric. Of the petals – usually five, fused – the front one 'masks' the entrance to the tube of the corolla either with a nectar spur or a dome shape. The fruit is generally a multi-seeded capsule.

Scrophularia nodosa L.
WOODLAND FIGWORT

■ *poisonous* ■
Throatwort

Among the great variety of plants growing on the banks of streams, ponds, and rivers or in moist woodland, figwort is one that is easily overlooked at first glance. Not until you look more closely do you notice the colour of the little flowers. They are purplish-brown! The plants owe their botanical species name to the knotty 'nodes', the thickened bumps, on its rhizome. Whether this was the reason it was recommended for the treatment of swellings and tumours, even of cancers (see the Doctrine of Signatures, page 18ff.) is doubtful, as not the root, but the crushed and salted leaves were laid on the tumour (Leonhart Fuchs). Constituents that lower the blood sugar and can be used to treat diabetes have now been discovered in the root extracts.

- **Description:** Height up to 3 ft 3 in. (1 m); leaves opposite, decussate, ovate or cordate-ovate, edge biserrate, underside with netted veination; stems erect, sharply rectangular, smooth, not winged, thickened nodes at the leaf bases, not branching below the flower head; flowers maximum ½ in. (1 cm), roundish, purple-brown, olive green at base, sepals rounded, membraneous edge, in panicle with flower at the tip; capsule ovate, seeds small; roots with nodular thickening, perennial
- **Flowering:** June to August
- **Scent and flavour:** Smell when rubbed unpleasant; taste bitter
- **Location:** Moist woodlands, woodland borders, river banks
- **Distribution:** Common
- **Drug:** Herba, Radix Scrophulariae
- **Constituents:** Glycosides (small quantities of glycosides with action on the heart), saponins, flavonoids, iridoids, alkaloids
- **Treatments:** For swelling of the lymph glands, sore throats, wounds, skin diseases (rashes), tumours and swellings, haemorrhoids, mild heart disease, rheumatic complaints, gout, eye diseases, diabetes (root), purifying the blood
- **Uses:** Tea, tincture, poultices, gargle, salve
- **Homeopathic uses:** See above
- **What and when to gather:** Herb June to July, root October
- **Lookalikes:** Water betony (*Scrophularia alata*): winged stem

The leaves of the woodland figwort are small and inconspicuous.

Verbascum densiflorum Bertol.
DENSEFLOWER MULLEIN

Dense Mullein, Wool Mullein

The denseflower mullein was known to Hildegard of Bingen as a herb for treating bronchial diseases and since then this type of treatment has remained remarkably constant through all the ages of herbal healing. 'Seethed in water and drunk, it will ease the long-standing cough' (Leonhart Fuchs, 1543): '... for the soreness of the throat' (Adamus Lonicerus, 1679). The 'herb father', Künzle (1922), makes the dense mullein part of a syrup for lung disease and influenza, and Bisset and Wichtl attribute the effect on colds to the saponins contained in the plant.

The impressive plant, up to 10 ft (3 m) tall, often found at the edge of gravel pits, overgrown landfill sites and railway embankments, has tall flower heads that were once used as torches. In many Catholic countries, it forms the centerpiece of the herb bunches that are dedicated on August 15 (Assumption of the Virgin Mary).

- **Description:** Height up to 10 ft (3 m); basal leaf rosette, leaves large, sturdy, wrinkled, obovate, with woolly, felted down, stem leaves broadly lanceolate, decurrent, distinctly crenate; stems erect, candle-shaped, hairy; flowers up to 2 in. (5 cm) in size, yellow, almost wheel-shaped with five white, woolly anthers, calyx hairy, in a dense, almost spike-shaped raceme; biennial
- **Flowering:** July to September
- **Scent and flavour:** Flowers with faint honey scent; flavour sweetish, slimy, slightly scratchy in the throat
- **Location:** Sunny slopes, waysides, landfill sites, dry locations
- **Distribution:** Scattered
- **Drug:** Herba, Flores Verbasci
- **Constituents:** Mucilage saponins (verbasco-saponin), essential oils, flavonoids, glycosides, aucubin, sugar, xanthophylls

The flowers of the denseflower mullein are gathered at the same time as seeds are ripening.

- **Treatments:** For colds, dry coughs, smoker's cough, breathing difficulties, asthma, pneumonia, leaves externally for burns, chilblains, ulcers, itching, rheumatic complaints
- **Uses:** Tea, gargle, poultices, baths, visual improver for teas, aroma additive in liqueurs
- **Homeopathic uses:** See above
- **What and when to gather:** Leaves in August, September, flowers in full bloom, always in the mornings once the dew has dried, July to September
- **Lookalikes:** Orange mullein (*V. phlomoides*): stem leaves barely decurrent, indistinctly crenate, diameter of flowers up to 1½ in. (3 cm); common mullein (*V. thapsus*): height up to 5 ft (1.5 m), flowers up to ¾ in. (2 cm); black mullein (*V. nigrum*): filaments violet, wooly, leaves with thin felted hair on the underside only
- **Other information:** Do not boil the tea, as too-high temperatures will destroy the mucilage. All species can be used in the same way. The seeds, poisonous due to the saponins they contain, were in the past used as fish bait

Potato family
Solanaceae

Alongside the family of nightshade plants belong agricultural crops such as potato (Solanum tuberosum) and tomato (Lycopersicum esculentum) as well as some well-known poisonous plants such as belladonna, jimsonweed and henbane, which from time immemorial have been used in intoxication, magic and witchcraft They are mostly herbs or shrubs with alternate, undivided, or feathered leaves. As a general rule, the stellar flowers are curled. The fruits are either fleshy berries like belladonna, capsules like the jimsonweed, or a berry enclosed in a membranous calyx like ground cherries (Physalis spec.).

Atropa belladonna L.
BELLADONNA

■ *highly poisonous* ■
Deadly Nightshade, Nightshade, Devil's Cherries, Black Nightshade, Sleeping Nightshade

This plant is native to Europe and widespread. A warning of its poisons ought to precede any praise of its valuable medicinal qualities. As few as two or three berries can be fatal for a child, with a slightly higher dose required for adults. Poisoning initially leads to cheerfulness and euphoria, but this quickly turns to confusion, hallucinations and raving. The final stage, in the worst cases, is paralysis and death.

Children should be informed of the dangers of the attractive black berries, which are often taken for genuine cherries or indeed for bilberries.

Not only the berries, but also the leaves, flowers and roots of belladonna are toxic. The leaves provide alkaloids such as atropine, which has established itself in ophthalmology because of its ability to dilate the pupils. As atropine also limits saliva production, it is used in operations.

- **Description:** Height up to 5 ft (1.5 m); shrub, leaves uneven in size, pale green; stems erect, branching; flowers c. ¾ in. (2 cm), bell-shaped, brownish-violet, yellowish inside, single or in three-flowered scorpioid cymes; berries green at first, when ripe glossy black with numerous purplish seeds; tap root up to 3 ft 3 in. (1 m) in length, brownish-yellow outside, whitish inside; perennial
- **Flowering:** June to August
- **Scent and flavour:** Slightly scented; taste sweetish, aromatic
- **Location:** Deciduous and mixed woodland, clearings
- **Distribution:** Scattered
- **Drug:** Folium, Radix Belladonnae
- **Constituents:** Alkaloids (hyoscyamine, atropine, scopolamine)
- **Treatments:** For eye complaints and to relax the eye musculature, fungal poisoning, opium and morphine overdose, Parkinson's disease
- **Uses:** Medical diagnosis and therapy
- **Homeopathic uses:** For fever cramps and diseases of the nervous system

Belladonna flowers.

Ripe belladonna berries at the edge of a field.

- **What and when to gather:** Herb before flowering May, June, root February and March, September and October. The drug must be stored separately from other herbs, due to its toxicity
- **Lookalikes:** Fruit: cherries have a stone, bilberries are smaller
- **Other information:** Take care: all parts of the plant, but in particular the fruits, contain potentially fatal poison

Datura stramonium L.
JIMSONWEED

- *poisonous* -

Thornapple, Madapple, Moonflower, Stinkwort

Most species of the genus *Datura*, which includes the angel's tears (*D. suaveolens*), originate in Central and South America. Jimsonweed, all parts of which are poisonous, has spread to Europe, where it is now found in the wild. Botanists describe it as a naturalized 'neophyte'. It needs soil containing nitrogen and therefore favors rubble, overgrown landfill sites, wasteland, and sometimes gardens that have been allowed to run wild. On no account must it be confused with the edible vegetable plants spinach (*Spinacia oleracea*) or Swiss chard (*Beta vulgaris*). The characteristic feature is the thorny fruit, to which the plant owes one of its names.

In the past, smoking dried jimsonweed leaves was recommended to combat asthma ('asthma cigarette'). In homeopathy, *Datura* extracts are used to treat Parkinson's disease and various neurological diseases. However, handling this plant is not a job for amateurs. Only a doctor should decide under what circumstances *Datura* extracts should be taken. Overdoses can be fatal.

- **Description:** Height up to 4 ft (1.2 m); shrub, leaves with long petiole, large, distinct veination; stems smooth, forking, branched; flower up to 3 in. (8 cm) long, funnelform,

with folds, white or violet, flower tips pointed; fruit thorny, four-compartmented capsule that springs open; root spindle-shaped, annual
- **Flowering:** June to September
- **Scent and flavour:** Scent unpleasant
- **Location:** Gardens, rubble, land with nitrogen indicator plants
- **Distribution:** Mediterranean; escaped to the wild
- **Drug:** Folium, Semen Stramonii (= Daturae)
- **Constituents:** Alkaloids (hyoscyamine, scopolamine), tannins, seeds have fatty oil
- **Treatments:** In the past, to combat asthma and persistent coughs
- **Uses:** Tincture, asthma cigarettes, incense powder, veterinary uses
- **Homeopathic uses:** To combat Parkinson's disease, brain and neurological diseases, whooping cough, diseases with high-temperature fevers
- **What and when to gather:** Leaves in June, July, seeds before fruit ripens. Because of its toxic nature, the drug must be store separately from other herbs
- **Lookalikes:** Spinach (*Spinacia oleracea*): upper leaves sagittate, dark green, different flowers; Swiss chard (*Beta vulgaris*): leaves large, pale green, in rosette, not branching
- **Other information:** After eating the seeds, symptoms of poisoning are similar to those that occur after eating belladonna

The large, white funnelform flowers of jimsonweed.

The prickly four-compartmented fruits (capsules) of jimsonweed.

Valerian family
Valerianaceae

The leaves of plants of the valerian family are opposite; the usually elongated, tubular individual flowers grow in panicle-like false umbels. There are plants with male, with female and with hermaphrodite flowers.

Valeriana officinalis L.
GARDEN VALERIAN

Garden Heliotrope, Allheal, Common Valerian, European Valerian

It is generally well known that the root of the Garden Valerian provides one of the most effective plant-based sedatives. However, despite intensive research, scientists are still not of one opinion as to which of the numerous constituents or combinations of constituents is, in the end, responsible for the sedative effect. Right up until the first half of the 20th century, valerian water was recommended as an eye tonic. In the past, people found the ecstasy that overcame tomcats when they smelled valerian uncanny. It is possible that the magical powers ascribed to this plant were linked to this observation.

The vitamin A-rich Lewiston cornsalad, well known as a winter salad vegetable, is one of the valerian family.

- **Description:** Height up to 5 ft (1.5 m); leaves opposite, odd pinnate; stems hollow, ribbed, unbranched; flowers small, whitish to pale pink, five-pointed, slightly asymmetrical in spread-out false umbel; fruits single-seeded with feathery wreath of hairs, later dropping off; rhizome short, with numerous thin, pale brown roots; forms runners
- **Flowering:** July to August

- **Scent and flavour:** Flowers pleasantly scented, root with intensive, characteristic, sweaty smell and flavour
- **Location:** Damp meadows, ditches, river banks, scrub, mixed forest
- **Distribution:** Widespread and common
- **Drug:** Radix Valerianae
- **Constituents:** Essential oils (borneol), iso-valerianic acid, alkaloids (valerin, chatinin and similar = valepotriates), tannins, polysaccharides
- **Treatments:** For insomnia, nervousness, restlessness, exhaustion, stress, hysteria, migraines
- **Uses:** Tea, oil
- **Homeopathic uses:** See above and for diseases of the central nervous system, the heart, the digestive tract, and the musculoskeletal structure
- **What and when to gather:** Rhizome with rootlets in the second or third year, August to October
- **Lookalikes:** Marsh valerian (*V. dioica*); basal leaves not pinnate, smaller, male flowers reddish, female ones white; Alpine valerian (*V. celtica*): all leaves entire, flowers yellow, mountain plant
- **Other information:** Take care: prolonged use and overdose can lead to habituation and dependency; paralysis and sight and hearing disorders are possible

The leaf rosettes of cornsalad, growing wild or planted in August/September, can be dug out of the snow in the winter.

Rhizome of garden valerian.

Garden valerian in bloom, with small, white to pale pink flowers.

Verbena family
Verbenaceae

The most famous species of the verbena family are the sun-loving ones with colourful flowers, frequently adorning balconies and south-facing window boxes. The opposite leaves and the zygomorphic, two-lobed flowers are characteristic of the family. The fruits divide up into four single-seeded nuts (clypsela).

Verbena officinalis L.
HERB OF THE CROSS

Vervain, European Vervain, Holywort

Herb of the Cross is one of the oldest-known healing herbs and is surrounded by more legends than almost any other. The Roman natural historian Pliny wrote that the druids used Herb of the Cross for soothsaying. Often, too, you can read in old manuscripts that the mood in rooms sprayed with vervain water is more lively and cheerful. Worn as an amulet, Herb of the Cross was supposed to protect against ghosts, evil magic and bad weather; as a healing herb, *Verbena* was particularly recommended for the treatment of wounds made by iron weapons. 'Hardly anything remains today,' Delaveau and colleagues write, 'of all this tradition and renown.' They point out that even the infusion of vervain, well-known in Europe, is made from a non-native species (*V. odorata*).

In Dr Edward Bach's Flower Remedies, *Vervain* is intended to help those with fixed opinions and a missionary-like sense of vocation who are unable to relax.

- **Description:** pinnate; stems long, thin, stiff, erect, branching, edged, grooved on two sides, roughened by short, bristly hairs; flowers small, pale violet, in long, non-glandular, switch-like, axillar spikes; thin roots; perennial
- **Flowering:** June to September
- **Scent and flavour:** Unscented, flavour bitter
- **Location:** Gravelly river banks, waysides, walls, rubble; this herb loves nitrogen
- **Distribution:** Widespread
- **Drug:** Herba Verbenae
- **Constituents:** Glycosides (verbenalin, verbenin), flavones, mucilage, essential oils, tannins and bitter principles
- **Treatments:** For diseases of the respiratory tract, the urinary tract, the digestive organs, oral and pharyngeal mucous membranes, menstruation problems, slow-healing wounds
- **Uses:** Tea, powder, gargles, tincture, medicinal wine
- **Homeopathic uses:** See above and for haematomas
- **What and when to gather:** Herb and shoots during flowering, June to August
- **Lookalikes:** None
- **Other information:** Only used homeopathically these days. The garden varieties are not harvested. Verbenalin is considered mildly poisonous

Herb of the Cross – a good deal of stiff, hard herb and small, pretty flowers.

The tips of the corolla vary in length, making the pale violet flower appear two-lipped.

Caryophyllidae

CARYOPHYLLIDS

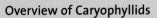

The **Caryophyllids** are mainly herb-like plants with radiating flowers that have five petals, sepals and stamens each. They contain saponins, silicic acid and the sour-tasting oxalic acid. Saponins have a decongestant effect and are diuretic.

Bouncingbet likes gravelly, sunny sites, but is also cultivated in herb gardens.

Pink family
Caryophyllaceae

The pink family are for the most part herb-like, forking, branching plants with decussate, opposite, entire, sessile leaves. The flowers, often very attractive, are radial, the petals contracted in linear section into a claw-like base (unguis). The seeds mainly ripen in capsules, more rarely – as for instance with rupturewort (Herniaria) – in nut form. The stems often display thickened nodes.

Pink family
Flowers five-petalled, radiant, petals deeply notched.

Herniaria glabra
SMOOTH RUPTUREWORT

Rupturewort, Herniaria

Smooth rupturewort loves sandy soils.

In some older herbals rupturewort is referred to as 'sanicle', though this is confusing, as the plant has nothing to do with the wood sanicle (*Sanicula europaea*, see page 211).

Smooth rupturewort was, in the past, used to cure ruptures (hernias) and owes its name to this injury. It has a diuretic action and for a long time was considered a proven means of easing bladder and kidney complaints. The so-called 'hernia tea' recommended by Adolf Dinand in his *Handbuch der Heilpflanzenkunde* (Manual of Herbal Healing) was composed 45:55 of rupturewort and bearberry leaves (see page 146). As with many other herbs used to treat inflammatory diseases, smooth rupturewort also faded from memory with the victory of antibiotics. It is, however, still on sale in the form of teas and pills for kidney complaints. Most authors recommend the fresh herb, as dried rupturewort soon loses its efficacy. Rupturewort is primarily found in areas with a warm summer climate in dry sandy and gravelly soils, and it looks fairly unassuming – neither the leaves nor the little greenish-yellow flowers of this creeping plant are particularly

A botanical curiosity: hairy rupturewort.

conspicuous. The related hairy rupturewort (*H. hirsuta*) is much rarer and should not be picked.

- **Description:** Height up to 6 in. (15 cm); leaves very small; stems yellowish-green, delicate, prostrate, markedly branched; flowers small, yellowish-green; roots thin; annual to perennial
- **Flowering:** July to September
- **Scent and flavour:** Unscented; taste slightly bitter
- **Location:** Heathland and dry, sandy places
- **Distribution:** Scattered
- **Drug:** Herba Herniariae
- **Constituents:** Saponins, flavonoids, cumarins (herniarin, umbelliferon), essential oils, alkaloids
- **Treatments:** For kidney and bladder ailments, chronic bladder and urethra infections, purifying the blood
- **Uses:** Tea, tea blends
- **Homeopathic uses:** See above
- **What and when to gather:** Flowering herb July to September
- **Lookalikes:** Hairy rupturewort (*Herniaria hirsuta*): leaves and stem with grey-green hair, smell of cumin; protected; prostrate knotweed (*Polygonum aviculare*, see page 127): larger, nodes on stem

Saponaria officinalis L.
BOUNCINGBET

Soapwort, Sweet Betty

If when looking for herbs you find bouncingbet on riverbanks or on sparsely covered gravelly soils, you can carry out a little experiment. Pick a few leaves, moisten them and rub them. You will soon see little bubbles of foam between your fingers, as if you had dipped your hand in green soapsuds (only do this if you have no open cuts or grazes on your hands, as it may irritate the skin). It is the saponins, present in every part of the plant, that are responsible for this surprising effect. They only appear in such

Bouncingbet, with flowers and elongated seed capsules.

quantities in a few species native to Europe (e.g. in primrose root, see page 153). Hippocrates (around 460 to 370 BC) recommended soapwort as an aid to washing. For those who are allergic to ordinary soap, *Saponaria* is an alternative. The root of bouncingbet is used to treat bronchial diseases.

- **Description:** Height up to 2 ft 4 in. (70 cm); leaves large, lanceolate to elliptic, five-veined, almost smooth, sessile; stems erect, ridged, with soft down, tinged red to violet; sometimes branching at top; flowers large, white to pale pink, long corolla tubus, in bushy cymes; capsules elongated, many seeds; root brown, lemon yellow within, markedly branched; perennial
- **Flowering:** June to September
- **Scent and flavour:** Flowers slightly scented, root unscented; taste bitter, savoury
- **Location:** Waysides, river banks, wasteland, gardens, loves lime
- **Distribution:** Scattered, often cultivated
- **Drug:** Radix, Herba Saponariae
- **Constituents:** Glycosides, saponins, flavonoids, resins, vitamin C
- **Treatments:** For liver and gall bladder ailments, jaundice, coughs (decongestant, expectorant), skin diseases (eczema, acne, boils), rheumatic complaints, purifying the blood

- **Uses:** Tea, washes, hair shampoo, stain remover
- **Homeopathic uses:** See **Treatments**, and for headaches and painful eyes
- **What and when to gather:** Leaves April to June, root March and April, September and October
- **Lookalikes:** Rock soapwort (*S. ocymoides*): smaller, red flowers, cushion-forming garden plant; phlox (*Phlox* spec.): leaves petiolate, does not foam when rubbed
- **Other information:** Take care: cytotoxic effect has been noted with high doses

Stellaria media (L.) Vill.
COMMON CHICKWEED

Chickweed, Starflower, Starwort

In an extensive gardening encyclopaedia dating from 1961 (Meyer and Andresen), chickweed appears under the heading 'Particularly troublesome garden weeds'. Düll and Kutzelnigg (1992), on the other hand, say: 'Chickweed is generally classed as a weed, but it is quite useful especially on cultivated ground such as vineyards and gardens, as it keeps the soil moist, prevents erosion, and covers the ground in winter as well.' If you do want to remove chickweed, because it is taking over your garden, you should use it (without the tough stems) as a vegetable and for salads, as it not only tastes good but is also rich in vitamin C, potassium and mineral salts. Any remaining plants should be composted, as the silicic acid in the chickweed will improve the compost's quality. The botanical genus name and the picturesque common name 'starflower' or 'starwort', refer to the pretty, star-shaped white flowers.

- **Description:** Height up to 20 in. (50 cm); leaves ovate, lower leaves petiolate, upper sessile; stems soft, sappy, with single rows of hairs, prostrate, occasionally rising, much branched; flowers white, small, star-shaped, at the ends of shoots, with five deeply indented petals; six-toothed capsule fruit; annual to biennial
- **Flowering:** March to November
- **Scent and flavour:** Flavour mild, slightly astringent
- **Location:** Waysides, fields, vineyards, gardens, landfill sites, nutrient-rich soils
- **Distribution:** Common
- **Drug:** Herba Stellaria media
- **Constituents:** Saponins, mineral salts, silicic acid, calium, vitamin C, rutin
- **Treatments:** For colds, lung disease, rheumatic complaints, pain on being touched, haemorrhoids, small wounds, rashes, ulcers, haematomas, for weaning
- **Uses:** Tea, juice, poultice, vegetable, salad
- **Homeopathic uses:** See above
- **What and when to gather:** Flowering herb April to September
- **Lookalikes:** Other chickweeds, stitchworts, and starworts (*Stellaria* spec.): larger flowers, erect

Common chickweed is a pioneer plant on nutrient-rich ground.

Goosefoot family
Chenopodiaceae

Most members of the goosefoot family are herb-like plants with inconspicuous small flowers. When the perianth (the outer part of the flower) falls, the seeds surrounded by it fall too. Vegetable and livestock fodder plants such as the common beet (Beta vulgaris), chard, beet, sugar and white beet belong to this family, as does goosefoot (Chenopodium), used as a healing herb, and orache (Atriplex). Some species in this family are now classified as part of the amaranth family (Amaranthaceae).

Chenopodium album L.
LAMBSQUARTERS

Fat Hen, White Goosefoot

As human beings moved further and further away from nature, knowledge of the uses of numerous local plants was forgotten. Occasionally it was replaced by new information, but there were errors. Generations of children were made to eat spinach, supposedly so rich in iron, before it was discovered that this was based on a mistake in the calculations. And yet lambsquarters, which provide a tasty, spinach-like vegetable, are seen by many gardeners as a nuisance weed, to be exterminated as quickly as possible. This one-sided view also obscured the fact that the plant had once been a healing herb used to treat kidney and bladder complaints as well as lung disease. A similar fate has befallen two more plants in the goosefoot family, Good King Henry (*C. bonus-henricus*) and garden orache (*Atriplex hortensis*), characterized by its bluish-green leaves and rich in vitamin C.

- **Description:** Height up to 5 ft (1.5 m); leaves with short petioles, rhomboid to three-lobed, bluish-grey, with floury bloom; stems markedly branched; flowers inconspicuous, greenish-white, at end of shoot or axillar, pyramid-shaped false spike; annual
- **Flowering:** July to September
- **Scent and flavour:** Unscented; taste mild, savoury
- **Location:** Fields, fallow and wasteland
- **Distribution:** Common
- **Drug:** Herba Chenopodii
- **Constituents:** Saponins, betalain, flavonoids, oxalic acid, proteins, minerals
- **Treatments:** Purifying the blood, for kidney and bladder ailments, lung disease, bleeding wounds
- **Uses:** Tea, vegetable, soup, salad
- **Homeopathic uses:** See above
- **What and when to gather:** Young leaves May to August
- **Lookalikes:** Good King Henry (*C. bonus-henricus*): lower, a little sticky, leaves with long petioles, hastate, pleasantly scented

Above: Garden orache (Atriplex hortensis) is, like lambsquarters and Good King Henry, a healing herb now known only to folk medicine, but it is cultivated as a vegetable.

Below left: Eat your enemies! Lambsquarters, unloved in agriculture, makes a tasty vegetable...

Below right: ... as does Good King Henry, used in the past to treat inflammations and ulcers.

Knotweed family
Polygonaceae

Characteristic features of the knotweed family are the knotted stems and the bag-like tube ('ochrea') by the fused leaflets at base of the petioles. The leaves are alternate, the flowers small. The three-sided fruits often fall off with the surrounding perianth.

Fagopyrum esculentum Moench
BUCKWHEAT

Garden Buckwheat, Beechwheat, French Wheat

Buckwheat is nothing to do with wheat – the well-known grain is, botanically speaking, a grass, and buckwheat is a member of the knotweed family. It received its common name (from the German, *Buchweizen*) because the fruits resemble beechnuts (cf. the alternative common name, 'beechwheat'). The seeds can be cooked like rice, but can also be ground and used like flour.

Buckwheat had its heyday in the Middle Ages and early modern period, when it was discovered that the plant could be cultivated even on nutrient-poor, sandy soils. But the introduction of potato and maize meant that it lost much of its importance, until it was rediscovered in the fashion for all things 'organic', and its constituents were analysed. Buckwheat is particularly suitable for those who cannot tolerate grain products because of a gluten allergy. In Russia, popular medicine would be unthinkable without buckwheat. As Dr Karine Markarian (a doctor specializing in naturopathy) reports, a porridge made of buckwheat is an essential part of slimming diets. For various treatments, buckwheat is heated, wrapped in a linen cloth and applied to the diseased body part. A tea of buckwheat flowering shoot tips and nettle leaves is considered a general strengthening tonic.

- **Description:** Height up to 20 in. (50 cm); leaves sagittate-cordate, pointed; stems with nodes, erect; flowers white or red, at ends of shoots or in axillar racemes; nut black, glossy, sharply triple-edged; annual
- **Flowering:** June to August
- **Scent and flavour:** Unscented; taste floury
- **Location:** Wild meadows, cultivated and escaped to the wild
- **Distribution:** Native to Russia
- **Drug:** Herba Fagopyri
- **Constituents:** Albumin, tannins, minerals (phosphate, calcium, iron, copper), vitamins, rutin
- **Treatments:** For gastro-enteric problems (gluten allergy, other allergies), during convalescence, preventing varicose veins, blockages in veins, preventing hardening of the arteries, high blood pressure
- **Uses:** Tea, tonic, poultices, gruel, diet food, porridge
- **Homeopathic uses:** For headaches, skin and liver diseases accompanied by itching
- **What and when to gather:** Flowering herb June to August, seeds August and September
- **Lookalikes:** None

Flowering buckwheat in a wild meadow.

Polygonum aviculare L.
PROSTRATE KNOTWEED

Knotweed, Knotgrass, Box Knotweed, Yard Knotweed, Knowgrass

Prostrate knotweed is one of the 'wholesome weeds' that annoy gardeners but can be used in many ways for therapeutic and culinary purposes. As a plant that survives trampling, it sometimes grows directly on pathways, is a pioneer plant on fallow land and doesn't despise landfills or the banks of gravel pits either.

Its preference for settled land is obvious, so it came to human attention early on. In times before supermarkets or health insurance, people enriched their menus with native or imported herbs and, if possible, used them to cure their illnesses as well.

In the past, prostrate knotweed was mainly used for blood stanching. It was also known as a diuretic and fever-reducing agent. Today it is used in bronchial and cough teas because of its decongestant effect and, according to Delaveau and colleagues, is 'used in the treatment of diabetes to combat thirst'.

- **Description:** Height up to 20 in. (50 cm); leaves small, lanceolate to ovate, membranous ochrea, silvery, with pale brown veins; stems dark green, prostrate and creeping to erect, markedly branched, nodes reddish-brown; flowers small, greenish-white or pink, two to five in axillar position; roots fibrous; annual
- **Flowering:** May to November
- **Scent and flavour:** Unscented; taste astringent, dry, savoury
- **Location:** Paths, fields, wasteland
- **Distribution:** Common
- **Drug:** Herba Polygoni avicularis
- **Constituents:** Silicic acid, tannins, flavonoids, mucilage, essential oils
- **Treatments:** For slight catarrh, inflammations of the oral mucus membranes, thirst quencher for diabetes, in the past used to treat lung disease, tuberculosis, coughs, kidney and gastro-enteric diseases, renal gravel, haemorrhoids, diarrhoea, bleeding wounds
- **Uses:** Tea, tea blends, juice, vegetable, bird food
- **Homeopathic uses:** For rheumatism in the fingers
- **What and when to gather:** Young stems and leaves May to September
- **Lookalikes:** Many small species, spotted lady's-thumb (*P. persicaria*) on moist sites
- **Other information:** Other knotweed species such as marshpepper knotweed (*P. hydropiper*) were also used as a pepper substitute

Far left: The widespread common knotweed.

Left: Meadow bistort (Polygonum bistorta) often covers large patches of damp meadows. Besides its healing use in treating diarrhoea and bleeding wounds, it can be cooked and eaten as a spinach-like vegetable.

Rheum palmatum L.
CHINESE RHUBARB

Chinese Rhubarb, Turkey Rhubarb

Chinese rhubarb, which originated in the Far East, is often planted in parks and gardens, where its 3 ft 3 in. (1 m) broad, palmate lobed leaves and its total height of up to 10 ft (3 m) ensure it cannot be overlooked. In herbal medicine, its root extracts are in demand. They provide a good treatment for constipation, especially in cases involving painful anal fissures and/or haemorrhoids, where only soft stools will help. Care is needed, however, as overdose has a constipating effect. The drug should not be taken regularly (habituation is a danger) or in pregnancy. Those suffering from rheumatism, gout and kidney disease are generally advised not to take rhubarb products because of the high oxalic acid content. This also applies to the well-known garden rhubarb (*R. rhabarbarum*), whose red leaf stems make excellent stewed fruit. This and a few other related species have the same active constituents as Chinese rhubarb, though they are considerably less concentrated. The large leaves can, if eaten, even prove poisonous.

- **Description:** Height up to 10 ft (3 m); large, palmate lobed leaves (up to 3ft 3 in. [1 m] across) with long, fleshy petioles; stems hollow, striped reddish-brown, erect; flowers small, dark red, on erect, leafy, panicle-like flower heads; fruit broadly winged; thick, fleshy rhizome, blackish-brown on the outside, yellow within; perennial
- **Flowering:** May to July
- **Scent and flavour:** Root has a characteristic scent; taste of the root bitter
- **Location:** Gardens, cultivated
- **Distribution:** Native to northern China and Tibet
- **Drug:** Rhizoma Rhei
- **Constituents:** Glycosides (antrachinon), tannins
- **Treatments:** For constipation, diarrhoea, loss of appetite, misuse of alcohol, worms
- **Uses:** Powder, tincture, syrup, ready-made products
- **Homeopathic uses:** For diarrhoea, behavioural problems in children, teething difficulties
- **What and when to gather:** Root September and October, petioles May and June
- **Lookalikes:** Garden rhubarb (*R. rhabarbarum*): height up to 6 ft (2 m), leaves entire, edges curled, flowers whitish-pink; other species of rhubarb
- **Other information:** Urine may turn a yellow-brown colour

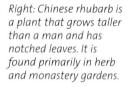

Right: Chinese rhubarb is a plant that grows taller than a man and has notched leaves. It is found primarily in herb and monastery gardens.

Far right: Only the stalks of garden rhubarb are used. The large, attractive leaves are poisonous.

Far left: Garden sorrel with its stem-sheathing leaves.

Left: Curly dock has leaves with distinctive curled edges.

Rumex actosa L.
GARDEN SORREL

■ *slightly poisonous* ■
Sorrel, Sour Dock

There is hardly a meadow where this plant is missing – it even occurs on miserable strips of green in the city's asphalt jungle. It is one of the most common northern European herbs. Sorrel soup was once a meal for the poor, but is now on the menus of gourmet restaurants. Common, well-known, containing vitamin C, and tasty – what could go wrong?

But don't be deceived. Garden sorrel can be devious. The same conditions apply to using it as to using the related rhubarb species: the oxalic acid it contains – responsible for the characteristic tart flavour – can in high doses lead to violent diarrhoea, indeed even to life-threatening kidney damage.

A few leaves can be nibbled raw or added to salads at home, but it is definitely not advisable to eat large quantities, unless the sorrel has been cooked beforehand. So there's no need to worry when ordering sorrel soup in a three-star restaurant!

- **Description:** Height up to 2 ft 8 in.(80 cm); evergreen; leaves sagittate, fleshy, lower leaves with long petioles, upper leaves sessile; stems erect, branching, often tinged with red; flowers inconspicuous, reddish-green, in large loose panicle; triangular nut-like fruits; root dark brown to almost black; perennial
- **Flowering:** May, June
- **Scent and flavour:** Unscented; taste sour
- **Location:** Moist meadows, waysides
- **Distribution:** Widespread
- **Drug:** Herba Rumicis acetosae
- **Constituents:** Potassium hydrogen oxalate (= salt of sorrel), oxalic acid, vitamin C
- **Treatments:** Purifying the blood, mildly laxative
- **Uses:** Tea, soup, herb butter
- **Homeopathic uses:** For dry coughs, skin complaints, cramps
- **What and when to gather:** Young leaves and stems April to September
- **Lookalikes:** Curly dock (*R. crispus*): leaf edges curled, used for digestive problems; bitter dock (*R. obtusifolius*): leaves not saggitate, not sour, roots up to 6ft (2 m) deep
- **Other information:** Due to its high pollen production the wind-pollinated sorrel is not for hay fever sufferers

Dilleniidae

DILLENIIDS

The **Dilleniids**, whose name derives from the tropical *Dillenia* species, include spicy plants such as horseradish and mustard from the mustard family (Brassicaceae), vitamin sources such as bilberries (Ericaceae), spring blooms such as the primrose (Primulaceae) and trees such as the linden (Tiliaceae).

Common St John's wort (Hypericum perforatum, see page 149) in bloom. It grows on stony slopes and dry waysides.

Mustard family
Brassicaceae (Cruciferae)

In the mustard family we often find plants with a basal leaf rosette. The upper stem leaves are often a different shape from the generally alternate base leaves. The white, yellow or red to violet flowers are nearly always in racemes. Species are distinguished as bearing either siliques (fruit at least three times as long as broad) or silicles (fruit at most three times as long as broad).

Many members of the mustard family are of economic importance as condiments (e.g. cress, mustard), as salad or vegetable plants (e.g. lettuce, horseradish, all the cabbages – white cabbage, red cabbage – and kohlrabi), or provide oil (e.g. rape), but there are also 'field weeds' (e.g. shepherd's purse) and other culinary and healing herbs.

The mustard oil glycosides (glycosinulates) which contain sulphur are responsible for the intense, peppery, cress-like, horseradish-like or garlicky flavour and smell.

Mustard family
Petals four in number, cruciferous (cross-shaped).

Alliaria petiolata (M. Bieb.) Cavara and Grande
GARLIC MUSTARD

Hedge Garlic, Jack-by-the-Hedge, Sauce-Alone

This rather inconspicuous little herb, with its small white flowers, loves shady places in

The leaves of garlic mustard are shaped like those of a nettle (see page 170). When rubbed, they smell strongly of garlic.

forests, parks, and gardens that have run wild. Its leaves, when rubbed, smell and taste strongly of garlic. The only plant that could be mistaken for it is the broadleaf enchanter's nightshade (*Circaea lutetiana*), which has smaller flowers and blooms later.

Garlic mustard makes a very good, aromatic flavouring for herbed cream cheeses, soups and various salads. As a healing herb, garlic mustard can, according to Delaveau et al., be used for healing wounds, as it has antiseptic qualities; it should, however, only be used fresh.

■ **Description:** Height up to 3 ft 3 in. (1 m); basal leaves with long petiole, large, reniform, crenate with large indentations, stem leaves triangular to cordate at base, crenate with large indentations; stems ridged, hairy below; flowers white; siliques 1–2 in. (3–6 cm) long, rectangular, erect; seeds brown, striped; biennial

- **Flowering:** April to June
- **Scent and flavour:** Intense garlic smell and flavour when rubbed
- **Location:** Forest borders, fences, deciduous woodland, loves shade
- **Distribution:** Common
- **Drug:** Herba Alliariae officinalis, only to be used fresh
- **Constituents:** Mustard oil glycosides, vitamins (mainly vitamins A and C)
- **Treatments:** For colds, rheumatic complaints, gout, treating badly healing wounds
- **Uses:** Juice, tea, freshly crushed herb as a poultice for wounds, alcoholic extract; flavouring for cream cheese, salad, soup, sauce
- **What and when to gather:** Leaves, fresh flowering herb with root April to June
- **Lookalikes:** Broadleaf enchanter's nightshade (*Circaea lutetiana*); smaller, different flowers, no smell of garlic
- **Other information:** Use as wild garlic, garlic or mustard, though the effect is weaker; seeds (spicy flavour) can be used as a substitute for black mustard (*Brassica nigra*, see page 136)

Armoracia rusticana Ph. Gärtn.
HORSERADISH

Wild Horseradish, Mountain Radish

The mustard oil glycosides in horseradish don't agree with everyone. If you suffer from stomach or duodenal ulcers or kidney disease, you will have to do without horseradish. Pregnant women, too, are advised not to eat it. On the other hand, because of its antibiotic qualities, horseradish is recommended as a healing herb, particularly for colds, and also for gout and rheumatism. Its vitamin C content is higher than that of lemons. It was not introduced to Europe from western Asia until the early modern period, but horseradish has long since found itself a small but stable market garden niche. Now and then individual horseradish plants break out of gardens and fields and establish themselves in the wild. If you know a place where they have settled, you can harvest them for years.

- **Description:** Height up to 4 ft (125 cm); base leaves up to 3 ft 3 in. (1 m) long, cordate, crenate, lower stem leaves ovate-lanceolate, crenate to serrate, upper leaves elongate; stems ridged, grooved, hairless; flowers white, silicle fruits spherical, $\frac{1}{5}$–$\frac{2}{5}$ in. (4–6 mm) long; root long, yellowish-grey, fleshy, perennial
- **Flowering:** May to July
- **Scent and flavour:** Scent and flavour hot, spicy, making eyes water
- **Location:** Moist, shady sites in gardens, meadows, along paths, forest borders, ditches
- **Distribution:** Widespread in south-eastern Europe, often escaped into the wild in Europe
- **Drug:** Radix Armoraciae
- **Constituents:** Mustard oil glycosides (gluconasturtin and sinigrin, constituents of mustard oils)
- **Treatments:** Combating anaemia, for coughs, sore throats, bronchitis, loss of appetite, flatulence, gout, rheumatic complaints (skin irritating poultice), chilblains (bath), scurvy, infections of the urinary tract
- **Uses:** Fresh root for poultices, baths, as a condiment
- **Homeopathic uses:** For eye inflammations, bronchitis, stomach colic

The highly desirable long root is sometimes not easy to harvest, but it is worth the trouble.

Flowering horseradish in a field.

- **What and when to gather:** Fresh root July, August
- **Lookalikes:** Curly dock (*Rumex crispus*) and bitter dock (*Rumex obtusifolius*): leaves smaller, no smell of mustard oil, grows in meadows
- **Other information:** Daily dose ¾ oz (20 g) fresh root. Take care: do not use if you have stomach or duodenal ulcers and kidney disease, or in pregnancy

Barbarea vulgaris R. Br.
GARDEN YELLOWROCKET

Yellowrocket, Winter Cress

Winter is a rather quiet time even for herb-lovers, but with some good luck and a knowledge of species you can get a fresh wild salad between November and February. The evergreen yellowrocket, also known as winter cress, is frequently found on wasteland such as railway embankments, landfill sites, and fallow fields, and appears as a pioneer plant on bare soil disturbed by excavation. Our forebears primarily used yellowrocket to treat wounds. There are several theories as to how yellowrocket came by its botanical name. The more widespread theory, supported by E. & K. Hollerbach among others, assumes a connection with St Barbara's Day, December 4, 'on which it is still possible to gather the leaves to make a salad'. The other theory, put out by Leonhart Fuchs as early as the 16th century, is that *Barbarea* and the German common name 'Barbarakraut' derive from the Latin *Carpentarium herba*. The 'carpenter's herb' was, according to this theory, a popular cure for wounds among joiners, carpenters and wagoners.

- **Description:** Height up to just under 3 ft (90 cm); base leaves in basal rosette, glossy, a little fleshy, with deep lyre-shaped notches, end lobes rounded, upper stem leaves stem-sheathing, almost entire, dentate; stems ribbed, often multiple, twiggy, branched; flowers golden yellow in branching, conspicuous racemes at the end of the shoot; siliques ½–1 in. (1.5 to 2.5 cm) long, splitting into two sections, biennial
- **Flowering:** April to July
- **Scent and flavour:** Faint scent; taste cress-like, savoury, slightly sour, spicy
- **Location:** Sand and gravel soils, moist fields, waysides, railway embankments, river banks
- **Distribution:** Widespread in Europe
- **Drug:** Herba Barbarea
- **Constituents:** Mustard oil glycosides, Vitamin C
- **Treatments:** For loss of appetite, treating gout, skin diseases, scurvy
- **Uses:** Tea, fresh for salads, vegetable
- **What and when to gather:** Leaf rosettes September to March
- **Lookalikes:** Oilseed rape (*Brassica napus*): Leaves with bluish-grey bloom, stems individual

The bright yellow flowers of garden yellowrocket in lively contrast with the green of the leaves.

Brassica napus L. emend. Metzg.
OILSEED RAPE

Rape, Mustard

Rape or oilseed rape is primarily cultivated as a livestock fodder plant but, given worldwide energy shortages, it is gaining in importance as a supplier of energy and motor fuel. The oil-rich seeds are also in demand in the food industry, where they are used in the production of margarine and chocolate, among other processes.

- **Description:** Height up to 4 ft 8 in. (140 cm); leaves with blue-green bloom; upper stem leaves sessile or stem-sheathing, smooth, underside slightly downy; flowers yellow-gold, in racemes, calyx and stamens protruding, the unopened flowers above the opened flowers; siliques 1½–4 in. (4–10 cm) long; seeds spherical; root thin, spindly
- **Flowering:** April to September
- **Scent and flavour:** Spicy, hot, seeds mild, oily
- **Location:** Nutrient-rich soil
- **Distribution:** Cultivated, escaped into the wild
- **Drug:** Oleum rapae
- **Constituents:** Mustard oil glycosides, enzymes, fatty oil, linolenic acid, sterols
- **Treatments:** For chilblains, irritation of the upper respiratory tract
- **Uses:** Edible oil, base for salves, food industry, energy and lubricant production
- **What and when to gather:** Ripe seed according to cultivation time
- **Lookalikes:** Rutabaga (*B. napus* ssp. *rapifera*): root with beet-like thickening, with bunched leaves on top; charlock mustard (*Sinapis arvensis*): diffuse, very distinctly multiple-branched; leaves juicy green, hairy, upper leaves generally entire
- **Other information:** Oilseed rape is closely related to field mustard (rape mustard, turnip rape, *Brassica rapa*).

Brassica napus L. ssp. *rapifera* Metzg.
RUTABAGA

The fleshy rutabaga is a sub-species of rape with a beet-like thickened root. It gained historic importance in Europe during World War I, when supplies of food for the population became critically low due to the war, the long winter of 1916/1917 and a wretchedly poor potato harvest. The rutabaga alone was available in larger quantities and helped to prevent the worst. In Germany, the term '*Steckrübenwinter*' (rutabaga winter) is still used in memory of a time characterized by hunger and misery.

Above: Oilseed rape flowers with the four petals typical of the mustard family.

A flowering field of oilseed rape – a lovely sight, but not without problems for those allergic to pollen.

Brassica nigra (L.) Koch
BLACK MUSTARD

Mustard, Shortpod Mustard

Black mustard with its spicy-tasting leaves is found, escaped to the wild, in river valleys among other places. Together with the closely related species *Sinapis alba* (white mustard) and *Sinapis juncea* (India mustard), the ripe seeds form the base for that 'mustard yellow' to brown paste without which the meat and sausage industry would surely have far fewer satisfied customers. Nutritionists confirm that mustard, which stimulates the production of stomach juices, makes it easier for the body to accept and digest fatty meat dishes. The French city of Dijon became famous as the 'Mustard Metropolis', and other cities – in Germany e.g. it is Düsseldorf – have laid claim to the title.

As a healing herb, mustard is used among other treatments for loss of appetite, rheumatic complaints and inflammation of the joints. Soaked mustard powder is used for wraps and poultices. Too much mustard oil, however, causes health problems in the digestive tract; those who suffer from kidney and stomach diseases are generally advised to abstain. External application can also lead to skin inflammation and blisters.

- **Description:** Height up to 5 ft (1.5 m); leaves with blue-green bloom, lower leaves lyre-shaped and pinnate, upper leaves serrate, very top leaves entire, linear; stems markedly branched, with protruding hairs in the lower part; flowers yellow-gold in racemes at the end of shoots; siliques $1/2–3/4$ in. (15–20 mm) long, rectangular, clinging at fruiting time; annual
- **Flowering:** June to September
- **Scent and flavour:** Unscented, leaves with hot spicy flavour
- **Location:** Fields, paths, landfill sites, river banks
- **Distribution:** Cultivated, escaped into the wild in some places
- **Drug:** Oleum, Semen Sinapis
- **Constituents:** Fatty oil, linolenic acid; mustard oil glycosides (sinigrin), mucilage
- **Treatments:** For loss of appetite, digestive problems, mild skin irritation in rheumatism, inflammation of the joints
- **Uses:** Edible oil, skin therapy; mustard powder for wraps, baths, poultices (cataplasma), plasters; hot, spicy mustard
- **Homeopathic uses:** For irritation of the upper respiratory tract and the digestive tract
- **What and when to gather:** Ripe seeds August and September, according to cultivation
- **Lookalikes:** Oilseed rape (*B. napus*): upper stem leaves sessile, flowers yellow-gold; white mustard (*Sinapis alba*): upper leaves lyre-shaped, flowers lemon yellow, dense
- **Other information:** Take care to avoid high doses and prolonged use. Poisoning is possible if the stomach and intestinal membranes are irritated, if the kidneys are inflamed, and in particular in small children. Mustard oil causes strong sensations of heat and burning, and if applied for a prolonged period may lead to blisters and pus formation

Black mustard in flower.

Cabbage ready for harvesting.

Brassica oleracea L.
CABBAGE

■ *wild variety protected* ■
Wild Kale, Wild Cabbage

The Atlantic wild cabbage is the parent form of all known cabbage species such as cauliflower, white cabbage, red cabbage, brussel sprouts, red cabbage and broccoli. It is found in the wild on sparsely vegetated slopes of rocky scree by the cliff coasts of western and southern Europe.

Cabbage in its many forms is not just one of the most important vegetables in the world. Sauerkraut, prepared by fermentation of lactic acid, was originally used as a means to prevent scurvy, and from its original home in Germany it conquered the world (earning the Germans the rather unflattering nickname of *krauts*).

- **Description:** Height up to 4 ft (1.2 m); lower leaves wrinkled, fleshy, upper stem leaves sessile or stem sheathing; stems branching, smooth; flowers sulphur yellow, in racemes, sepals and stamens erect; siliques 2³/₄–4 in. (7–10 cm) long, erect, protruding, seeds spherical
- **Flowering:** May to September
- **Scent and flavour:** Taste mild to aromatic, savoury
- **Location:** Nutrient-rich, deep soils, gardens; this herb is tolerant of salt
- **Distribution:** Wild in Heligoland, off the coast of Germany; cultivated elsewhere throughout Europe
- **Drug:** White cabbage, sauerkraut
- **Constituents:** Mustard oil glycosides, amino acids, vitamins (above all vitamin C), oils, mineral salts
- **Treatments:** Internal: for indigestion, after alcohol misuse, combating stomach and duodenal ulcers, diarrhoea, intestinal parasites, gout, irritation of the respiratory tract, bronchitis; externally for ulcers, badly healing wounds, burns, boils, insect bites
- **Uses:** Internal: juice; external: crushed, fresh leaves
- **Homeopathic uses:** For an under-functioning thyroid gland
- **What and when to gather:** Fresh, firm cabbage heads, according to time of cultivation

Cardamine spec.
CUCKOO FLOWER and
Nasturtium officinale
WATERCRESS

The name 'cuckoo flower' probably came about because the foam produced by the larvae of the frog-hopper or spittlebug (Philaenus spumarius) is often found on the stems of these plants. The foam is often popularly known as 'cuckoo spit'.

Cardamine amara L.
LARGE BITTERCRESS

■ *poisonous* ■
Bittercress

Large bittercress prefers very moist to wet locations in boggy meadows or forests, or on the banks of ditches or ponds, and is often confused with watercress (see page 140), which grows in streams with flowing, clean water. Bittercress is distinguished by violet anthers and pithy stems; in watercress, the anthers are yellow and the stems hollow. Because of its extremely bitter taste, it is unpleasant to eat bittercress.

- **Description:** Height up to 2 ft (60 cm); five to ten leaves, pinnatisect, no leaf rosette; stems prostrate at ground level, with runners, pithy, ridged; flowers white, up to $^1/_5$ in. (10 mm) long, anthers violet, siliques $^3/_4$–1 in. (20–30 mm) long, seeds in single row
- **Flowering:** April to July
- **Scent and flavour:** Flavour cress-like, spicy, very bitter
- **Location:** Streams and marshy sites, marshy woodland
- **Distribution:** Common
- **Lookalikes:** Watercress (*Nasturtium officinale*): stems hollow, creeping, anthers yellow; cuckoo flower (*C. pratensis*): basal leaf rosette, stems hollow, anthers yellow, in meadows

Large bittercress with its typical pinnatisect leaves.

The petals of cuckoo flower are criss-crossed with violet veins.

Cardamine pratensis L.
CUCKOO FLOWER

Lady's Smock

In contrast to bittercress, cuckoo flower is frequently added to salads, and its peppery, cress-like flavour adds a spicy touch to herbed cream cheeses and herb butters. It is gathered in flower, in spring and early summer. The white to pink flowers, often criss-crossed by violet veins, make it easy to recognize the cuckoo flower out in the countryside. Unfortunately this flower, once so widespread, thrives only in nutrient-rich moist meadows, and its numbers are now markedly diminishing.

- **Description:** Height up to 2 ft (60 cm); base leaves in rosette, often evergreen, pinnate with three to eight leaflets, end leaflet three-lobed, rounded; lower stem leaves sessile; stems hollow, mainly round; petals white, pink, often violet veined, anthers yellow; siliques 1–1½ in. (25–40 mm) long; roots thin, creeping
- **Flowering:** April to July
- **Scent and flavour:** Flavour cress-like, spicy

- **Location:** Moist meadows where fertilizer is not used, gardens, parks
- **Distribution:** Common
- **Drug:** Herba Cardaminae
- **Constituents:** Mustard oil glycosides (glycocochlearin, butyl mustard oil), vitamin C, bitter principles
- **Treatments:** For encouraging digestion and the flow of gall, purifying the blood, stimulating the metabolism, diuretic, vermifuge, prevents scurvy, treating rheumatic complaints
- **Uses:** Fresh herb with flowers and seeds in salad, cream cheese, herb butter, as a spring tonic
- **Homeopathic uses:** As a supplement for diabetics
- **What and when to gather:** Fresh herb in flowering period April to July
- **Other information:** The siliques expel the seed explosively, and the seed can fly for over 6 ft (2 m).

Nasturtium officinale R. Br.
WATERCRESS

Cress, Brown Cress, Nasturtium

Freshly gathered watercress on the banks of a spring.

Watercress is a much-praised healing and culinary herb – and truly a water plant. For the sake of your health, Father Kneipp (the 'herb priest' and hydrotherapist) would recommend combining harvesting watercress with a session of wading in the cold, unpolluted springs and streams. However, it is better to limit yourself to the plants growing near the banks – paddling about in the stream, whether barefoot or in boots, stirs up the bed and means unnecessary pollution of a sensitive ecology. For the same reason, the plants should be picked carefully and not uprooted.

Watercress is very rich in vitamins (vitamins A, B_2, C and E) and therefore makes an especially good spring tonic: fresh in salads or with other herbs sprinkled over pasta or potatoes. However, it should not be eaten for prolonged periods or in large quantities, as the mustard oil glycosides it contains do not agree with everyone. In folk medicine, watercress is recommended for treating gallstones and jaundice. If the leaves are placed on the forehead 'it doth ease the head-ache,' Lonicerus writes. But he also adds a warning: 'Yet women with child should be wary of it and not eat of the herb.' He recommends the spirit of watercress, distilled 'in the midst of May', for a very particular purpose. 'The mouth that doth stink evilly because the teeth do rot, washed out often and richly with the water, doth make the mouth to smell pleasant.'

- **Description:** Height up to 8 in. (20 cm), length up to 2 ft 8 in. (80 cm); leaves dark green, juicy, smooth, glossy, odd pinnate, end lobes almost cordate; stems ridged, hollow, fleshy, markedly branched, creeping along the stream bed to erect; flowers white, small, $1/10–1/5$ in. (3–4 mm), in racemes, anthers yellow; siliques $2/5–3/4$ in. (10–18 mm) long, thick; seeds in two rows; roots white, root-like water leaves whitish, rounded; perennial, evergreen; vegetative reproduction through torn-off shoots or leaf buds
- **Flowering:** June to September
- **Scent and flavour:** Scent spicy, cress-like; flavour peppery, a little bitter (not as bitter as bittercress)
- **Location:** Springs; clean, slow-flowing, cool streams; ditches
- **Distribution:** Common in favoured locations
- **Drug:** Herba Nasturtii
- **Constituents:** Mustard oil glycosides (phenylethyl isothiocyanate), essential oils (glyconasturtiin); vitamins A, B_2, C, E, minerals, wax, tannins
- **Treatments:** For encouraging digestion and the flow of gall, purifying the blood, stimulating the metabolism, diuretic, vermifuge, for rheumatic complaints, bronchitis
- **Uses:** Juice, tea, salad, vegetable, spice, spring tonic
- **Homeopathic uses:** For kidney and bladder complaints
- **What and when to gather:** Fresh herb, without roots, February to September
- **Lookalikes:** Bittercress (*Cardamine amara*); stems pithy, anthers purple; cuckoo flower

(*C. pratensis*): basal leaf rosette, stems generally round, in damp meadows
- **Other information:** Take care in pregnancy: this herb has an irritant effect on the bladder

Cochlearia officinalis L.
SPOONWORT

■ *protected* ■

Scurvygrass, Common Scurvygrass

Like many other members of the mustard family, in the past spoonwort was used as a healing herb. Seafarers used to take the vitamin C-rich herb with its 'spoon-like' leaves, widespread only in coastal regions, to help prevent the vitamin deficiency disease of scurvy on long journeys, giving it the appropriate name of 'scurvygrass'. Today, spoonwort is protected and should not be harvested.

- **Description:** Height up to 20 in. (50 cm); leaves dark green, fleshy, glossy, base leaves with long petioles, broadly ovate to cordate; stem leaves ovate, roughly dentate, upper stem leaves cordate, stem sheathing; stems ridged, branching; flowers white or pink, in corymbs at the end of shoots, scented, sepals green; silicles spherical to oval with dark green central vein; root thin, spindle-shaped; biennial to perennial
- **Flowering:** April to June
- **Scent and flavour:** Scent mustard-like, cress-like; flavour spicy, hot
- **Location:** Salty soils in coastal areas, salty slopes near springs
- **Distribution:** Central Europe, North Sea and Baltic; cultivated
- **Drug:** Herba Cochleariae
- **Constituents:** Mustard oil glycosides (butyl mustard oil glucoside), vitamin C, bitter principles, mineral salts
- **Treatments:** For loss of appetite, stomach complaints, purifying the blood, for gout, rheumatism, scurvy, badly healing wounds, gum diseases

- **Uses:** Juice, crushed leaves as a poultice, tea, salad, as a sandwich filling
- **Homeopathic uses:** For stomach problems, eye inflammations
- **What and when to gather:** Fresh flowering herb April, July
- **Lookalikes:** Other members of the mustard family: no 'spoon-shaped' leaves
- **Other information:** The rare sub-species ssp. *alpina* grows on boggy slopes near springs in the mountains and foothills of the Alps

A dense patch of spoonwort.

Lepidium sativum L.
GARDENCRESS PEPPERWEED

Right: Shoots of gardencress pepperweed, ready for harvesting.

Gardencress pepperweed is a native of the Mediterranean region, where it is occasionally found as an escape in the wild. It was supposedly introduced to central Europe by Roman soldiers. There it quickly established itself as both a healthy and tasty salad and culinary herb. As a healing herb, it was used to treat anaemia, bladder ailments and loss of appetite. If you know only the sprouting shoots from the supermarket, to be harvested with scissors and sprinkled on your sandwich, you will hardly be able to combine that image with a full-grown gardencress plant in flower. It can grow to over 20 in. (50 cm) tall and bears small white flowers in early summer.

Gardeners and soil specialists know the 'cress test'. As the plant germinates after only a few days, it is possible, sowing a few sample seeds, to check relatively quickly whether compost soil, for example, is ready. Sowing gardencress also allows a judgement to be made regarding the nutrient and salt content of the soil.

- **Description:** Height up to 1 ft (30 cm); bluish bloom, smooth; base leaves pinnatisect, upper leaves sessile; flowers white; silicles compressed, round to oval, broadly winged at tip, ½ in. (5 mm) in length; annual
- **Flowering:** May to July
- **Scent and flavour:** Cress-like, spicy, savoury
- **Location:** Meadows, gardens
- **Distribution:** Mediterranean region, cultivated and escaped to the wild
- **Drug:** Herba Lepidii sativi recens
- **Constituents:** Essential oils (benzyl cyanide), mustard oil glycosides (glucotropaeolin), vitamins (carotin, B, C, E, nicotinamide) minerals (potassium, natrium)
- **Treatments:** For purifying the blood, constipation, bladder complaints, coughs, scurvy, stimulant, used in the past as an abortifact
- **Uses:** Salad, seasoning

- **What and when to gather:** Whole plant in flowering period or shortly afterwards, May to July
- **Lookalikes:** Other white-flowering members of the mustard family
- **Other information:** Take care: high doses can lead to skin irritation

Capsella bursa-pastoris (L.) Med.
SHEPHERD'S PURSE

Mother's Heart, Shepherd's Scrip, Lady's Purse, Pick-purse, Pick-pocket, Pepper-and-Salt

Pinching off and snacking on the pleasantly nutty, triangular silicles of shepherd's purse was a pleasure known to the co-author of this book in the 1950s, learned from his grandmother, who was knowledgeable about plants. It is no longer possible quite so casually to stick those delicious little healthy treats, gathered from the wayside, into your mouth. After all, one hears and reads so much about overuse of fertilizers and pollution, and a good general knowledge of edible herbs and their less agreeable lookalikes is also no longer widespread. Shepherd's purse – which owes its name to the shape of its siliques, resembling

Far left: The heart-shaped fruits of shepherd's purse make an inviting snack.

Left: Shepherd's purse often grows on waysides and in fallow fields.

an old-fashioned shepherd's scrip (bag or wallet) – is, however, something of an exception. 'Pinch and snack' appears, oddly enough, to have been passed on in many families from one generation to another and remains largely unaffected by the growing human estrangement from nature.

In the past, shepherd's purse was prescribed for internal and external bleeding, especially for gynaecological complaints linked to haemorrhages. It continues to play a part in homeopathy.

Düll and Kutzelnigg point out that in damp locations the herb is often attacked by the fungus *Albugo candida*, making it unsuitable for consumption.

- **Description:** Height up to 20 in. (50 cm); basal leaf rosette, leaves entire, lobed to pinnatisect, stem leaves entire, with broad auricle, stem sheathing; stems with fine down; generally branching; petals white, longer than the green sepals, flowers in raceme; silicles rounded, triangular to obcordate, multi-seeded; root spindle-shaped; annual to biennial
- **Flowering:** February to October

- **Scent and flavour:** Leaves cress-like, spicy, slightly bitter; seeds mild, nutty to slightly bitter
- **Location:** Meadows, pasture, fields, gardens, paths, wasteland and landfill sites
- **Distribution:** Worldwide, very common, at altitudes up to 7,500 ft (2,300 m)
- **Drug:** Herba Bursae pastoris
- **Constituents:** Proteins, amino acids, flavonoids, choline, acetylcholine, mineral salts, vitamin C
- **Treatments:** In the past, for external and internal haemorrhages, bleeding skin wounds, nosebleeds, haemorrhages from the womb, regulating menstruation
- **Uses:** Tea, poultice for skin rashes, eczema
- **Homeopathic uses:** See above and for bleeding of the mucus membranes
- **What and when to gather:** Plant without roots March to September; seeds
- **Lookalikes:** Other silicle-bearing members of the mustard family, above all pennycress (*Thlaspi* spec.), as it is very variable; the pocket-shaped, wingless fruits are unmistakable

Raphanus sativus L.
CULTIVATED RADISH

Radish, Wild Radish, Garden Radish, Common Garden Radish

There are many cultivated varieties of radish, and at first glance you would hardly believe that they belong to the same species. They differ in the colour and shape of their root – the very part of the plant of most interest to the consumer. Along with the white radish, which in Bavaria, Germany, has reached cult status as an accompaniment to beer and been named '*Bier-Radi*' (beer radish), these include the less common black radish, popular as a winter vegetable, and the famed red radish – but not the true wild radish (*R. raphanistrum*), which is distinguished by, among other features, longer siliques.

The radish is one of humanity's oldest cultivated plants. The ancient Egyptians grew it. It was presumably spread through Europe by the Romans. Hildegard of Bingen knew and recommended it because it 'purified the brain' and reduced 'the damaging juices of the intestines'. Radish juice, dissolved by adding sugar to freshly cut chunks or slices, is still a popular home treatment today for coughs or other cold symptoms. In homeopathy, radish products are used to treat gastro-enteric diseases and certain skin diseases; however, fresh radish should be avoided by those suffering from stomach problems, as it is difficult to digest.

- **Description:** Height up to 3 ft 3 in. (1 m); leaves lyre-shaped, deeply notched, basal leaves rosalate; stems round, branching, with bristly hairs; flowers white with violet veins, in short spikes; siliques short (in the wild radish (*R. rhaphanistrum*) they are long, the seeds lined up like a string of pearls, flowers pale yellow); roots depending on variety long, rounded or fat, bulbous, red, black, or white outside, white inside
- **Flowering:** May to June
- **Scent and flavour:** Smell radish-like; flavour hot
- **Location:** Humus, nutrient-rich garden soils
- **Distribution:** Common, cultivated, presumably descended from Mediterranean varieties

Below left: The purple flowers of cultivated radish with the 'cross-shaped' arrangement of petals.

Below right: Radish seeds and roots.

- **Drug:** Radix Raphani
- **Constituents:** Mustard oil glycosides (gluco-sinulates, glucoraphanin, sulforaphen), vitamin C, methylamine
- **Treatments:** Cough suppressant, for treating catarrh, gall bladder complaints (primarily gallstones), appetite stimulant, for treating scurvy, insomnia and headaches, can remove flatulence, but may also encourage it
- **Uses:** Juice, vegetable, salad
- **Homeopathic uses:** For diseases of the digestive tract and greasy skin
- **What and when to gather:** Root June to September
- **Lookalikes:** Other silique-bearing members of the mustard family

Thlaspi arvense L.
FIELD PENNYCRESS

Pennycress, Frenchweed, Fanweed

Like many other plants in the mustard family, field pennycress contains both mustard oil glycosides and vitamin C. It is not surprising that it was used successfully in the past to help prevent the vitamin C deficiency disease of scurvy. Seafarers above all suffered from scurvy, as they had to subsist for months without fruit and fresh vegetables. The taste, reminiscent of cress – the plant is sometimes known as 'winter cress' – gives a special touch to salads and herbed cream cheeses. As field pennycress is still widespread on wasteland, the borders of fields, railway embankments, river banks and waysides, there are no problems for the environmentally conscious gatherer. The common name of the herb derives from the attractive rounded silicles, each with a broad seam, with a shape reminiscent of coins. Inexpert herb-gatherers sometimes confuse field pennycress with shepherd's purse, which grows in similar locations (see page 142 f.), but its silicles are heart-shaped.

- **Description:** Height up to 20 in. (50 cm); basal leaves pale green, petiolate, obovate; stem leaves sagittate, stem sheathing; stems ridged, grooved, smooth; flowers white, in racemes at the end of shoots; silicles rounded, compressed, up to ½ in. (1.5 cm) long, $^{1}/_{10}$–$^{1}/_{5}$ in.(3–5 mm) winged all around, deep U-shaped notch at tip; root up to 20 in. (50 cm) long; annual
- **Flowering:** May to June
- **Scent and flavour:** Scent like leeks
- **Location:** Clay soil fields, gravel pits, landfill sites
- **Distribution:** Common, worldwide
- **Drug:** Herba Thlaspi
- **Constituents:** Mustard oil glycosides (sinigrin, glycocaparin), oil, vitamin C
- **Treatments:** For treating wounds, haemorrhages, scurvy
- **Uses:** Salad, soup, edible oil
- **What and when to gather:** Leaves, seeds, May to July
- **Lookalikes:** Shepherd's purse (*Capsella bursa-pastoris*): siliques heart-shaped
- **Other information:** Being deep-rooted, the plant is relatively immune to herbicides

Flowering field pennycress with its broad-winged seeds.

Heath family
Ericaceae

The heath family comprises numerous shrubs and dwarf shrubs, usually with small, often hard, evergreen leaves. Symbiosis with various fungi (Mycorrhiza) enables plants in the heath family to colonize acid, mineral-poor soils. The glycosides (arbutin, hydrochinon) in the leaves of some species do not develop their antiseptic action until they reach the alkaline environment of the urinary tract and are particularly efficacious as medicines in this field.

Arctostaphylos uva-ursi (L.) Spr.
BEARBERRY

■ *protected* ■
Kinnikinnick, Mountain Box, Mountain Cranberry, Sandberry

Bearberry is an ancient healing plant whose active constituents have been identified by modern biochemical research methods. The extract of the leaves is used in human and veterinary medicine and serves to disinfect the urinary tract. The glycoside hydrochinon, which has a bactericidal action, only works if the urine is alkali, which is why it is recommended to take sodium bicarbonate at the same time. There is no need to worry if the urine changes colour during a bearberry treatment.

The evergreen plant with its scarlet berries forms extensive carpets on the sites where it grows. In some countries, such as Germany, where it is rare, it is protected. In Europe, it is mainly found in Scandinavia and in the north-east, as well as in the mountains. The leaves can also be used to dye wool and leather.

- **Description:** Height up to 16 in. (40 cm); dwarf shrub; leaves obovate, evergreen, thick, leathery, with netted veination on the underside; stem woody with generally creeping branches; flowers small, white or reddish, bell-shaped, in racemes; berries scarlet, root up to 3 ft 3 in. (1 m) deep
- **Flowering:** March to July
- **Scent and flavour:** Unscented; leaves: flavour astringent, very dry; berries: sour, dry, aromatic, floury
- **Location:** Pine forests, heathland; humus, shallow soils
- **Distribution:** Alps, Scandinavia, rare
- **Drug:** Folia Uvae-ursi
- **Constituents:** Glycosides (hydrochinon, arbutin, methylarbutin), tannins, flavones
- **Treatments:** For kidney and bladder inflammations
- **Uses:** Tea, dye

Flowering bearberry.

- **Homeopathic uses:** See above
- **What and when to gather:** Berries June to September, leaves from flowering in March to May
- **Lookalikes:** Lingonberry (*Vaccinium vitis-idaea*): leaves rolled inwards at the edges, spotted on the undersides; Alpine bearberry (*A. alpina*): leaves sharply dentate, red in autumn, ripe berries blue-black; box (*Buxus sempervirens*): leaves rolled inwards at the edges, tall shrub, poisonous
- **Other information:** Take care: prolonged use or too high a dose can lead to nausea and vomiting

Vaccinium myrtillus L.
BILBERRY

Blueberry, Whortleberry, Hurtleberry, Whinberry

Bilberries are found in bogs and forests on acid soils; indeed, when classifying forests and forest soils, they are *the* indicators for acid soils. They are often found in the company of other *Ericaceae* such as heather (*Calluna vulgaris*) and the lingonberry (*V. vitis-idaea*). In bogs, it is also joined by the bog blueberry (*V. uliginosum*), distinguished from the bilberry by brown twigs and berries with blue bloom.

In herbal healing, the leaves of the bilberry were and are used as well as the fruits. The use of the leaves in treating inflammations of the urinary tract and diabetes is traditional in alternative medicine, but this tradition has not received any confirmation by recent research (quoted in Bisset and Wichtl). Indeed, patients are cautioned against too high a dosage or prolonged use because of possible side effects. However, the dark blue fruits have long been popular and recognized as vitamin-rich healthy nourishment and a delicacy. Dried, they are also a suitable treatment for diarrhoea in children.

- **Description:** Height up to 2 ft (60 cm), maximum 3 ft 3 in. (1 m); leaves pale green,

Above left: The fruits of the bearberry. The undersides of the leaves show netted veination.

Above right: The lingonberry, also known as the mountain cranberry, closely resembles the bearberry, but the undersides of the leaves have glandular spots.

ovate, finely dentate; base woody, twigs evergreen, ridged; flowers greenish-red, campanulate, hanging; berries round, black, wax coating giving them blue bloom; juice red; root creeping, forming runners; perennial

- **Flowering:** May to July
- **Scent and flavour:** Unscented; flavour of leaves astringent, of berries aromatic, acid
- **Location:** Bogs, heathland, acid-soil deciduous and coniferous forests
- **Distribution:** Widespread
- **Drug:** Folium, Fructus Myrtilli
- **Constituents:** Berries: pectins, vitamins, sugar, minerals, dyes; leaves: arbutin, glycosides (hydrochinon), myrtillin, glucokinins
- **Treatments:** Berries: (fresh) for treating constipation, (dried) diarrhoea, digestive problems (flatulence, belching), gum inflammations, over-strained eyes, rheumatic complaints; leaves (in folk medicine): for

bladder and urinary tract infections, light cases of diabetes – take care, see above!
- **Uses:** Tea, dried berries, juice, wine, liqueur, jelly, conserve
- **Homeopathic uses:** For diarrhoea
- **What and when to gather:** Young leaves May and June; berries July and August
- **Lookalikes:** Bog blueberry (*V. uliginosum*): twigs woody, brown, leaves with blue-grey bloom, no dye in berries; lingonberry (*V. vitis-idaea*): leaves evergreen, leathery, rolled inwards at edge, underside with glandular spots, berries red in racemes
- **Other information:** Take care: leaves are slightly poisonous – prolonged use or too high a dose can lead to chronic poisoning

Below left: Ripe bilberry fruits on their typical green twigs. In contrast to cultivated blueberries, the berries stain an intense purplish-red.

Below right: Bog blueberries have a blue-grey bloom, no staining juice, and grow on brown twigs.

Hypericum family
Hypericaceae

Leaves spotted with translucent oil glands are the characteristic feature of the hypericum family. Its only representatives in northern Europe are the St John's wort species. The number five dominates the flowers: they have five petals and five sepals and numerous stamens in little bunches of three to five.

Hypericum perforatum L.
HYPERICACEAE

St John's Wort, Klamathweed, Perforate St John's Wort

If there was ever an attempt to identify a 'typical healing herb', St John's wort would be a good candidate. It has an ancient unbroken tradition as a healing herb, its efficacy has been conformed by biochemical studies, and it is also common enough for its use not to conflict with the conservation of species.

In the countryside, it is easy to recognize the plant, up to 2 ft 8 in. (80 cm) tall, by the flowers; golden yellow and giving off a blood-red juice when rubbed, and by the leaves, spotted with translucent oil glands. It was believed, for example, that because it looked as if it had been punctured by needles, the plant was suited to treating stab wounds. This is not as wrong-headed as it seems, as oil of common St John's wort is recommended for insect bites and in general for healing wounds. Extracts of St John's wort are widespread as medicines to treat mental exhaustion. However, for all applications, it is advisable to avoid sunbathing and using sunbeds, as hypericin has a photo-sensitizing action – that is to say, it increases the skin's sensitivity to light and thereby also the danger of sunburn.

- **Description:** Height up to 2 ft 8 in. (80 cm), leaves opposite, elongate to ovate, entire, 'spotted'; stems erect, hard, round, with two 'wings', branching in the upper part; flowers golden-yellow, black spots, in many-flowered false umbels; capsule fruits; root spindle-shaped; perennial
- **Flowering:** June to August
- **Scent and flavour:** Unscented, flavour dry, slightly bitter
- **Location:** Waysides, meadows, heathland, sparse meadows, woodland clearings, wasteland
- **Distribution:** Common
- **Drug:** Herba, Flores, Oleum Hyperici
- **Constituents:** Flavonoids (hypericin, hyperoside, quercetin), bitter principles, tannins
- **Treatments:** For depression, nervousness, fear, insomnia, lung and urinary tract disease; oil for bruises, haematomas, neuralgia, rheumatic pain, sunburn, small burns, insect bites
- **Uses:** Tea, oil
- **Homeopathic uses:** See above
- **What and when to gather:** Flowers (for oil) June, July; flowering herb (for tea) June to August
- **Lookalikes:** Garden yellow loosestrife (see page 153): flowers do not stain when rubbed, leaves in threes in a whorl

St John's wort flowers.

Mallow family
Malvaceae

The main active constituent of the healing herbs in the mallow family is mucilage, which develops a soothing action, coating the mucus membranes, in colds. The typical mallow fruit, which splits into numerous little fruit segments, is round with a slight depression in the middle and enclosed by the calyx. In shape, they resemble small notched cheeses, hence the common name 'cheeseflower' for the high mallow (see page 151).

Althaea officinalis L.
MARSHMALLOW

■ *protected* ■

Sweet Weed, Mallards, Mortification Root, Wymote

Marshmallow is a healing herb known to the ancients. It is rarely seen in the wild – salty soils along the Baltic coast are one location – and is therefore protected. As an ornamental plant, it is available in garden centers.

As early as the 9th century, Charlemagne commanded the cultivation of the marshmallow. In the 10th century, the monk Odo Magduensis, from the Loire Valley in France, praised the healing powers of marshmallow, as did Hildegard of Bingen some years later, though she did not accord it quite so much importance. It was a stock plant in monastery gardens for centuries and it is still cultivated today for medicinal purposes, especially in eastern Europe. The 'mallow' part of the common name links it to other members of the *Malvaceae* such as the high mallow and common mallow.

- **Description:** Height up to 5 ft (1.5 m); shrub; leaves large, faintly lobed, grey-green; leaves and stems with thick felted hair; flowers 1 in. (2.5 cm) in diameter, white or pink, individual, in racemes; perennial
- **Flowering:** July to August
- **Scent and flavour:** Unscented; slimy taste
- **Location:** Reed beds, saltgrass pasture, loves salt
- **Distribution:** Very rare
- **Drug:** Flores, Folia, Radix Althaeae, Hibisci
- **Constituents:** Mucilage (galactose, arabinose), pectin, sugar
- **Treatments:** Diseases of the respiratory tract, dry coughs, inflammations in the mouth and pharyngeal area and in the digestive tract
- **Uses:** Tea, gargle, clyster, syrup, juice, poultice, baths, dye (wine)
- **Homeopathic uses:** See above
- **What and when to gather:** Flowers July to August; leaves May and June; root March and April, September to November
- **Lookalikes:** Hollyhock (*Althaea rosea*): up to 6 ft (2 m) tall, leaves rounded-cordate, flowers c. 2 in. (5 cm) in diameter, many different colours, country garden plant
- **Other information:** When taking marshmallow preparations, diabetics need to take account of the sugar content

The colourful large flowers of the hollyhock.

Marshmallow.

Malva sylvestris L.
HIGH MALLOW

Mallow, Blue Mallow, Cheeseflower,
Wild Mallow

Mallow flower tea is so popular that you could describe it as a medicine that has long since crossed over to being a beverage. Many people drink it because they like the taste or the colour and not because they hope that it will help to cure a particular ailment. This was not always the case. Odo Magdunensis claims that *Malva* means something like 'that which softens the belly' (Greek *malakos* = 'soft' and Latin *alvus* = 'belly'). Although this definition is by no means proven, disorders of the digestive tract are even today still among those that high mallow and some of its related species are used to treat. It is more commonly used, however, to treat bronchial diseases. The leaves can also be used as a spinach-like vegetable, and the flowers are used as a food colouring.

The high mallow follows cultivation. It likes to grow on nitrogen-rich soils close to areas used for agriculture. Some types of mallow are also recommended as garden plants. Mauretanian mallow (*M. sylvestris* ssp. *mauritiana*) is widely cultivated because of its dark violet flowers.

The large, striped flowers of high mallow.

The leaves of the smaller white or pink-flowered common mallow are rounded to cordate.

- **Description:** Height up to 3 ft 3 in. (1 m); leaves with long petioles, five-lobed, serrate, rounded, with woolly hair; stems erect; flowers single, pale red, c. 1¾ in. (4.5 cm) in diameter; root spindle-shaped; biennial to perennial
- **Flowering:** June to September
- **Scent and flavour:** Unscented, taste slightly slimy
- **Location:** Meadows, waysides, landfill sites
- **Distribution:** Rare
- **Drug:** Flores, Folia, Herba Malvae
- **Constituents:** Mucilage, flavonoids, anthocyan dye (malvin), tannins
- **Treatments:** For irritation of the mouth, throat, stomach and intestinal membranes, dry coughs, inflammations, ulcers, swollen glands, skin rashes, boils

- **Uses:** Tea, gargles, poultices, spinach-type vegetable, pickles, dye, food colouring
- **Homeopathic uses:** See above
- **What and when to gather:** Young leaves April to June; flowers without stems May to September; fruits August to October
- **Lookalikes:** Common mallow (*M. neglecta*): Height to 16 in. (40 cm), stems rising, small pink to white flowers in bunches, same applications and constituents

Primrose family
Primulaceae

The best-known Primulaceae *are the attractive spring blooms such as the different primrose varieties, of which there are numerous garden varieties. The leaves of the* Primulaceae *are usually in rosettes; five petals and stamens are radially arranged and the fruit is a so-called capsule fruit with five flaps. The name* Primula *refers to the primrose being among the earliest flowers of the spring (Latin* primus = first*).*

Lysimachia nummularia L.
CREEPING JENNY

Moneywort, Creeping Joan, Wandering Jenny, Wandering Sailor

Creeping jenny '… creepeth and crawleth on the earth as doth a serpent or adder…The little leaves which are set on both sides of the stem appear rounded and… no broader than a penny.' This vivid description of creeping jenny dates from the 16th century and is by Leonhart Fuchs. In his day, it was sometimes referred to as '*egelkraut*' (leech weed) or '*natterkraut*' (adder weed). An old English name for it is herb twopence. The close relationship of this creeping plant to the upright yellow loosetrife (see page 153), which grows in moist places such as the banks of streams and lakes, is shown by the stalked yellow flower with its five-tipped corolla. Both species, because of the tannins and saponins they contain, are used therapeutically – for instance, to treat coughs and diarrhoea and to stop bleeding – but are nowadays no longer among the first rank of wild herbs considered to be medically effective.

- **Description:** Height up to 20 in. (50 cm), long runners, rooting at nodes; leaves about the size of a cent, almost orbicular, opposite, short petioles; flowers c. ¾ in. (2 cm) across, bright yellow, with stems; reproduces through runners and shoots, fruits are rare
- **Flowering:** June to August
- **Scent and flavour:** Nondescript
- **Location:** Moist, nutrient-rich meadows, waysides, woodland borders
- **Distribution:** Common, patches covering large areas
- **Drug:** Herba Lysimachiae, H. Nummulariae
- **Constituents:** Flavonol glycosides, silicic acids, tannins, mucilage, saponins, potassium
- **Treatments:** Coughs, diarrhoea, haemorrhages, badly healing wounds
- **Uses:** Tea
- **Homeopathic uses:** See above
- **What and when to gather:** Whole plant June to August
- **Lookalikes:** Common bugle (*Ajuga reptans*, see page 84): leaves elongated, pyramid-shaped, erect flower heads; runners root in rosettes

The opposite round leaves distinguish creeping jenny from other prostrate creeping plants.

Lysimachia vulgaris L.
YELLOW LOOSESTRIFE

Yellow loosestrife is still occasionally used as a dye plant; its flowers were once also used to bleach hair. It is occasionally confused with common St John's wort (*Hypericum perforatum*, see page 149), although the latter has opposite leaves with translucent spots and prefers drier locations.

- **Description:** Height up to 5 ft (1.5 m); stems erect with numerous leaves in whorls of three, elongate, entire; flowers gold to dark yellow in long-stemmed racemes at the ends of shoots, perennial
- **Flowering:** June to August
- **Location:** Clay soils, ditches, marshy forests and meadows, ponds, meadows with tall plants
- **Distribution:** Scattered
- **Drug:** Herba Lysimachiae
- **Constituents:** Tannins, glycosides, saponins, vitamin C, sugar
- **Treatments:** For coughs, fever, scurvy, diarrhoea
- **Uses:** Dye for cloth, wool; leaves to bleach hair
- **Homeopathic uses:** See above

- **What and when to gather:** Leaves and flowers June to August
- **Lookalikes:** St John's wort (*Hypericum perforatum*): hard, winged stem, flowers stain reddish-violet when rubbed
- **Other information:** The leaves and stem provide a yellow dye, the root a brown dye

Primula
PRIMROSES

Every child knows what a primrose looks like, but even most adults cannot distinguish between other *Primula* species: for example, they cannot tell an oxlip (*Primula elatior*) from a cowslip (*P. veris*). In fact, the cowslip is in many areas much rarer than the oxlip. Its yellow-gold flowers have little red dots, which are missing in the pale yellow oxlip. And while the cowslip has a pleasant scent, the oxlip is unscented. Both species flower early in the year; the oxlip often as early as March, the cowslip mostly in July.

It is the primrose root that is most often used in herbal healing. Because of its saponin content, it has a decongestant action in bronchial catarrhs and colds. The flower (including the calyx) is also used in teas to treat coughs, although there is disagreement as to whether the oxlip flower is as valuable and effective as the cowslip.

Salads can be garnished with primroses, though they should not be served to those who are allergic. With some people, contact with *primula* species can lead to health problems (such as skin rashes).

In folk medicine, various primrose flowers are also used to treat a number of other diseases and ailments, including neurological problems, heart, kidney and skin diseases. And if, being of a melancholy bent, you are subject to the 'whisperings' of tiresome spirits of the air, you can follow Hildegard of Bingen's advice and place a primrose flower over your heart. Spirits

Yellow loosestrife on the banks of a ditch.

Oxlips, one of our more common spring flowers. It is disputed whether they are just as effective as cowslips in treating coughs and colds.

Below: It is the primrose root that is used most, but in many places it is protected and may not be dug up.

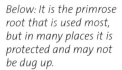

were also involved when the golden key of legend was made, with which, as Günter Dörner tells us, the impudent youth wanted to unlock the door to heaven. But the insolent deed was unsuccessful. The young man fell back to earth, and when he woke from his long sleep he held a flower, just as golden as the key had been, in his hand – the origin of the primrose. The 'key to heaven' is also used to tell the future in folk custom; Friedrich Jantzen writes that in some regions people believed that a girl who found a primrose in Holy Week would marry in the same year and have as many children as there were flowers on the stem.

The cowslip has a bag-like calyx and red spots on the inside of the petals.

Primula veris L.
COWSLIP

■ *protected* ■

Cowslip Primrose, Key of Heaven, St. Peter's Wort, Palsywort

- **Description:** Height up to 1 ft (30 cm); leaf rosette with petiolate, wrinkled, ovate leaves with fine down on the underside; flower stem straight, downy, flower calyx saccate, pale yellow-green, five to fifteen campanulate flower umbels with five reddish spots, root short, very branching
- **Flowering:** April to May
- **Scent and flavour:** Flowers have sweetish scent and taste; root smells of aniseed and has a bitter flavour
- **Location:** Dry meadows, waysides, woods with widely spaced trees, vineyards
- **Distribution:** Rare, loves warmth
- **Drug:** Herba, Flores cum calycibus, Radix Primulae
- **Constituents:** Essential oils, bitter principles, saponins (root, calyx), flavonoids, glycosides
- **Treatments:** For joint pains, fever, colds, coughs (flowers), kidney and bladder ailments
- **Uses:** Tea, flowers in cough sweets
- **Homeopathic uses:** For kidney ailments, neuralgia, skin rashes
- **What and when to gather:** Flowers April and May, roots (from cultivated sources) November and December
- **Lookalikes:** Oxlip (*P. elatior*): calyx close to stem, corolla pale yellow without red spots, flowers March to May; more common
- **Other information:** Some people have allergic reactions from contact with primroses, especially the common primrose (*P. vulgaris*) or the garden variety (*P. acaulis*)

Willow family
Salicaceae

With a few exceptions, plants in the willow family are dioecious – that is to say, the male and female flowers are on different plants. The individual flowers are very small and inconspicuous, the male flowers often catkin-shaped, the females compressed. The leaves do not appear until after flowering.

Populus nigra L.
BLACK POPLAR

■ *protected* ■

In contrast to the streamlined pyramid-shaped poplars (*P. nigra 'italica'*) and the Canadian or hybrid black poplar (*P. nigra x canadensis*), a quick-growing timber supplier often planted on the sites of previous species-rich flood plain woodland, the wild form of the black poplar is a gnarled tree with a broad crown. They can be seen as old remnants of some lowland forests, easily distinguished from other poplar species by the horizontal cork ridges of their deeply cracked bark.

In herbal healing, it is mainly the closed, sticky leaf buds of the black poplar that are used, and have been for a long time. Oertel and Bauer describe the preparation of a salve for treating haemorrhoids and slight burns: 'One part crushed buds and three parts water to boil for three hours. Then two parts pork fat to be added and the mixture heated on a low flame until all water has evaporated; then to be strained through a linen cloth.' The bark of the black poplar, rich in tannins, is also still used at times.

■ **Description:** Height up to c. 100 ft (30 m); tree with broad crown; bark with vertical cracks, blackish; leaves alternate, with long petioles, triangular, smooth; young twigs yellowish-brown; olive-grey in the second year; buds with sticky scales; catkins hanging, female greenish, male with red anthers, wind pollinated; seeds with woolly white hairs (= poplar down)
■ **Flowering:** March, April
■ **Scent and flavour:** Sweetish to bitter
■ **Location:** River banks, lowland forest
■ **Distribution:** Rare to scattered, cultivated
■ **Drug:** Gemmae, Cortex Populi
■ **Constituents:** Tannins, essential oils, glycosides (populin, salicin), flavonoids, wax, resin, sugar
■ **Treatments:** For fever, bronchitis, flatulence, kidney and bladder ailments, kidney and bladder stones, rheumatic complaints, polyarthritis, gout, bruising, sprains, as skin care
■ **Uses:** Powder, tincture, salve, dye (green, yellow)
■ **Homeopathic uses:** See above
■ **What and when to gather:** Bark of twigs in the second to third year, buds March and April
■ **Lookalikes:** European aspen (*P. tremula*): lower, grey bark, petioles compressed sideways, leaves quiver in the slightest breeze, same treatments as black poplar

Top: The hybrid poplar, frequently planted, is a sub-species of the black poplar.

Centre: Black poplars are still found wild in some flood plain forests where there is less cultivation.

Left: The long-petiolate, triangular, smooth leaves of the black poplar.

Fruiting purple osier willow (Salix purpurea) with the cottonwool-like seed hairs.

The leaves of white willow, with silvery-white down on the undersides.

Salix spec.
WILLOW

The branches of the various species of willow – in Germany, for instance, there are around twenty-five and a number of hybrids – are very flexible, tough and fairly undivided. The leaves are generally narrow, lanceolate, and with short petioles; the leaflets at the join are often stem-sheathing. In herbal healing, the treatments and effects for all willow species are the same.

Salix alba L.
WHITE WILLOW

■ *protected* ■
European Willow

It's easy to spot the white willow on walks or when cycling along rivers that flood their banks from time to time. There you can often see impressive old specimens of this typical flood plain forest tree, which in late spring are often covered from top to bottom with the orange-yellow, fleshy-fruiting bodies of sulphur shelf (*Laetiporus sulphureus*).

As a medicine to reduce fever, the willow (or to be more exact, its bark) was known in the ancient world. Its healing powers have been praised by many, from Theophrastus of Ephesus in the 4th century BC to the authors of herbals in the 16th century. The anti-inflammatory and fever-reducing action is due to the tannins and the glycoside salicin, present in the bark and in smaller amounts in the leaves of the willow. Salicin in pure form was first isolated in 1830 by the French pharmacist Pierre Leroux. Bisset and Wichtl describe willow bark as the 'phytotherapeutic forerunner' of acetylsalicylic acid, contained in many painkillers, especially aspirin.

■ **Description:** Height up to 80 ft (25 m); fast-growing tree with vertical cracks in the bark; leaves narrow, finely dentate, silver-white down on the underside; male catkins with dense white hair and long yellow anthers, female green, compressed; seeds very small with long hairs
■ **Flowering:** April to May
■ **Scent and flavour:** Unscented; leaves and bark taste bitter, astringent, sweetish at first then irritating to the mouth and throat
■ **Location:** Flood plain woodland, river banks
■ **Distribution:** Scattered
■ **Drug:** Cortex, Folia Salicis
■ **Constituents:** Glycosides (salicin), tannins
■ **Treatments:** For fever, pain, rheumatic complaints, polyarthritis, gout, diarrhoea, skin impurities, eczema
■ **Uses:** Decoction, powder, poultices
■ **Homeopathic uses:** For gout and rheumatism
■ **What and when to gather:** Bark of twigs (several years old) in April, May or October
■ **Lookalikes:** Other species of willow (*Salix* spec.); no white hair on the undersides of leaves, other locations, often hybridizing
■ **Other information:** In the body, salicin is converted to salicylic acid, well-known under the name 'aspirin' as a medicine and painkiller

Linden family
Tiliaceae

There are about fifty genera in the linden family worldwide, but most of them grow only in the tropics. At our latitudes, the only ones we come across growing in the wild are members of the genus Tilia (linden) with its characteristic cordate leaves. The flowers of the linden grow in little bunches; their stems are fused with a narrow, wing-like bract.

Tilia platyphyllos Scop.
LARGELEAF LINDEN

There are few other trees rhapsodized by poets with quite such enthusiasm as the linden. Many factors have contributed: the considerable age of some trees – they can live for over 1,000 years – the enchanting scent of their flowers in early summer, and their closeness to human settlement. For centuries, in many places, the village linden was the meeting-place for gossip, celebrations, dancing and flirting.

The doctors and natural healers of the past made use of many linden products, from the bark to the leaves. All that is left, in essence, is linden blossom tea as a treatment for and to prevent colds. In folk medicine, linden flower extracts are also used as sedatives and antispasmodics. In natural cosmetics, other practitioners recommend an infusion of linden flowers 'in the form of warm steam inhalations, compresses and to be rubbed into the skin' to treat 'slack, dry, and chapped skin with poor circulation'.

- **Description:** Height about 80 ft (25 m); tree with broad, heart-shaped crown, can grow to over 1,000 years old; leaves alternate, cordate, pointed, petiolate, hairy, small white hairs in the angles of the veins; two to three flowers per flower head, flower yellowish-white, fruit woody, thick-walled, ridged
- **Flowering:** May, June
- **Scent and flavour:** Flowers have an intensely sweet scent; taste slimy
- **Location:** Deciduous forest, parks, avenues, individual trees
- **Distribution:** Common
- **Drug:** Flores Tiliae
- **Constituents:** Essential oils (linalool), flavonoids, glycosides, tannins, mucilage
- **Treatments:** For colds, coughs, rheumatic complaints, cramps, restlessness, insomnia
- **Uses:** Tea, bath additives, perfume
- **Homeopathic uses:** See above, and for inflammation of the female reproductive organs
- **What and when to gather:** Linden flowers with bracts May and June
- **Lookalikes:** Littleleaf linden (*T. cordata*): leaves smooth, brown hairs on the underside in the angles of the veins, flowers June to July, fruit with thin rind, same treatments

Linden trees – here a littleleaf linden – can live for many years.

The scented blossoms of the largeleaf linden.

Violet family
Violaceae

There are neither trees nor shrubs in the violet family, only herbs. The long-stemmed flowers are individual and zygomorphic, i.e. asymmetrical, with five sepals and five petals, with a spur on the lowest petal. The fruit, a capsule, has three flaps that open and scatter a large number of seeds.

Viola odorata L.
SWEET VIOLET

Green Violet, English Violet

The sweet violet is one of the earliest flowering plants of the year. Because it likes to grow close to human habitation, some botanists support the idea that it must be an ornamental plant escaped to the wild. The plant, with its hidden, delicately scented flowers, is often linked in legend and folklore with secret, innocent love – a flower to press in your poetry book!

In herbal healing, the leaves and flowers and also the roots of sweet violet and other violet species are used. The active constituents more or less predestined the plant to be used to treat colds, but violet extracts have been used in treating rheumatic complaints in the joints. The 'rediscovery' of this ancient healing plant evidently goes back to Sebastian Kneipp.

- **Description:** Height up to 4 in. (10 cm); leaf rosette with long petiolate, cordate to reniform, crenate leaves; stems smooth; flowers dark to reddish-violet or white, two petals pointing upwards, three downwards, thick, straight spur; spherical fruit capsule with three opening flaps; root short, forms runners; perennial

- **Flowering:** March to May
- **Scent and flavour:** Pleasant scent; sweetish flavour
- **Location:** Woodland borders, waysides, scrub, gardens
- **Distribution:** Scattered
- **Drug:** Flores, Folia, Radix, Oleum Violae odoratae
- **Constituents:** Saponins, salicylic acid glycosides (gaultherin), essential oils, mucilage, alkaloids (odoratin, violin), dye (blue)
- **Treatments:** For bronchitis, lung diseases, coughs, influenza, skin diseases (ulcers, rashes, pimples), wounds, rheumatic complaints
- **Uses:** Tea blends, syrup (in the past, made into a 'blue' cough mixture for children), poultices, washes, cosmetic industry, perfumes, shampoos
- **Homeopathic uses:** For earache, eye diseases, whooping cough
- **What and when to gather:** Flowers and leaves March to May, root September and October
- **Lookalikes:** Other violets (*Viola* spec.): unscented, no healing action
- **Other information:** Take care: this herb is emetic and strongly laxative in high doses; the oil is also used to protect against ticks

*German iris (*Iris germanica*): its rhizome, given to teething infants to chew, is in some places sold under the incorrect name of 'violet root'.*

Heart-shaped leaves and scented, bluish-purple flowers are characteristic of the sweet violet.

Viola tricolor L.
JOHNNY JUMPUP

Wild Pansy, Heartsease, Stepmothers,
Trinity Violet

This herb has a wealth of common names, and 'stepmothers' is perhaps one of the more unusual. Many theories have been put forward. Not even Jacob and Wilhelm Grimm, the two scholarly brothers who compiled the first German dictionary, could agree. Wilhelm based his theory on the morphology of the flower. The yellow lower petals each have a narrow green leaf beneath them and are supported by it. The upper ones are standing and have no support – those are the stepchildren. However, Jacob Grimm claims that 'the cause for the transfer of the names of step-relatives and in-laws is that colourful clothing was used in folk custom to signify a non-blood relationship, and the most conspicuous feature of the viola tricolour is the colourful appearance of the flower'.

The wild pansy and certain close relations such as the European field pansy (*V. arvensis*) were crossed to create the garden pansy, available today in a great variety of colours and sizes and one of the world's favourite garden flowers. In folk medicine, the constituents of johnny jumpup are used in particular to treat skin diseases such as infantile eczema and cradle cap, but the daily dose of two cups of tea should not be exceeded. Oertel and Bauer recommend accompanying the internal treatment with the placing of pansy compresses on the affected areas of skin.

- **Description:** Height up to 16 in. (40 cm); leaves alternate, lower leaves cordate to ovate, upper lanceolate, crenate, leaflets large, pinnatisect; stems triangular, rising, branching; flowers with long stems, single coloured, yellow-white, yellow-violet or blue-white, each with five unequal sepals and petals, lowest petal with spur; capsule fruit with three flaps; annual
- **Flowering:** April to October

Johnny jumpup. The flowers may be of different colours.

- **Scent and flavour:** Unscented; flowers taste slimy, a little sweetish, bitter
- **Location:** Fields, waysides, meadows
- **Distribution:** Widespread, common
- **Drug:** Herba, Flores Violae tricoloris
- **Constituents:** Saponins, flavonoids, salicylic acid glycosides (gaultherin), alkaloids (violin), dyes, tannins, mucilage
- **Treatments:** For skin diseases (rashes, eczema, ulcers, cradle cap), diseases of the respiratory tract, coughs, rheumatic complaints, indigestion, diarrhoea, diseases of the urinary tract, purifying the blood
- **Uses:** Tea blends, juice, poultices, compresses
- **Homeopathic uses:** For diseases of the skin, kidneys, and bladder
- **What and when to gather:** Flowering herb May to September
- **Lookalikes:** None
- **Other information:** Take care: ensure a daily dose of no more than two cups of tea; larger quantities may lead to nausea and vomiting. Methyl salicylate is obtained by chemical separation from gaultherin. The large-flowered garden pansy is not used

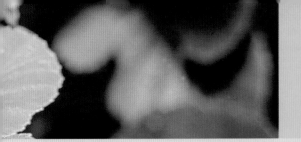

HAMAMELIDS

Many monoecious plants are trees of corresponding significance both ecologically and economically, although hops, hemp and stinging nettles also belong to this family group. As they are borne by the wind – the wind does not have to be attracted by large, colourful or scented flowers – they can survive without a decorative display. The male, catkin-shaped flowers produce large quantities of pollen; the female flowers are usually unassuming in appearance. The plant usually flowers before the leaf is formed so the wind has unhindered access to the aglets. The fruits either have a firm, woody shell (hazelnut), a cup-shaped or prickly shell (acorn, chestnut), are cones (hops) or are tiny single-seeded nutlets (birch, stinging nettle).

Female catkin blossoms of the common alder (Alnus glutinosa). A decoction of the rind used to be a popular remedy for treating colds.

Birch family
Betulaceae

Birch trees dominate vast expanses of the landscapes of north and northeast Europe. They are a pioneer species that conquers fallow terrain and is able to resist icy winters. The dwarf birch (Betula nana) is only found at the far north of Norway and in North Iceland. All birch trees form symbiotic associations (mycorrhizae) with higher fungi, including brown birch boletus, scaberstalk, milk caps and russula.

Betula pendula Roth
SILVER BIRCH

European White Birch, Warty Birch, Weeping Birch

For man, birch has always been much more than just a source of wood. The most famous use is as a tea, made from the dried leaves, which produces a strong diuretic that is recommended for treating kidney and bladder

disease. 'Birch tea', which is made from the rind, is used as 'Lithuanian' or 'Russian Balsam' to treat eczema. The warty buds are used to make a hair tonic and, crisply fried, they and the young leaves are a culinary treat. In Russia, the juice is fermented to make an intoxicating liquor.

However, despite its many blessings, there is also an associated risk: because it produces a massive amount of pollen that can cause a severe allergic reaction in many people, birch trees should not be planted in gardens, schools or public areas.

- **Description:** Tree, height to 100 ft (30 m); rind white, bark brown to black; branches overhanging, warty; leaves with long stalks, triangular, toothed, male catkins, female flowers stand proud; nutlet very small, broad spreading
- **Flowering:** April, May
- **Scent and flavour:** Slightly aromatic smell; taste quite acerbic, bitter
- **Location:** Heathland, light woods and forests, alleys, gardens
- **Distribution:** Common, pioneer species
- **Drug:** Folia, Gemmae, Cortex, Pix, Carbo vegetabilis Betulae
- **Constituents:** Birch camphor, tannins, triterpene (Betulin), flavonoids, saponines, essential oils, mineral salts (calcium oxalate), vitamin C, aromatic hydrocarbons
- **Treatments:** For kidney and bladder complaints, kidney stones, gout, rheumatism, arthritis, varicose veins, respiratory infections, poor digestion and cardiovascular weakness, skin disease, sweaty feet, abscesses, as a tonic to aid hair growth and 'cleansing the blood'
- **Uses:** Tea, juice, hair tonic, birch tar, active coal, baths, compresses
- **Homeopathic uses:** See above
- **What and when to gather:** Leaf buds in March; young leaves May and June; white rind, juice March and April
- **Lookalikes:** Moor birch (*B. pubescens*): young leaves hairy, same uses

Two female (top) and one male hanging catkin.

Left: A birch group on the edge of a wood.

Hemp family
Cannabaceae

The hemp family consists of herbs or bushes with fingered or lobated leaves, whose male and female flowers are dioecious, i.e. they grow on different plants.

Cannabis sativa L.
CULTIVATED HEMP

■ *toxic* ■

Roll Hemp (male), Hemp Seed, Seeds (female)

As the basic ingredient for psychoactive drugs, hemp has developed such a poor reputation that its positive properties are at serious risk of being forgotten. Jack Herer and Martin Brückers have made an impassioned plea to save its reputation and reassess this old cultivated and healing plant, the benefits of which are in grave danger of being lost to us for industrial and political reasons. Farmed crops, whose content of psychoactive tetrahydrocannabinol (THC) is far lower than that required for the production of narcotic drugs, can be used to produce ropes and nets, textiles, oil products, paper, animal feed and much more. Synthetic THC has been reapproved for medical purposes in many states of the USA and in Germany; it is also used to counter the side effects of chemotherapies. In animal trials, hemp oil has been shown to reduce cholesterol, is valuable as a food oil, and is used to make creams for the treatment of cradle cap and dandruff.

- **Description:** Height to 16 ft (5 m); leaves have long stalks, with five to nine narrow, finger-shaped toothed leaves; stalks green, angular, glandular hairs like the leaves, strong fibers; female plant stronger with more branches; male flower yellow-green, loose, panicular; females green, in the axilla, with resin glands; single-seeded nut; spindle-shaped, branched taproot; annual
- **Flowering:** July, August
- **Scent and flavour:** Slightly sweet, hay-like; seeds spicy
- **Location:** Cultivated
- **Distribution:** Home central Asia, cultivated
- **Drug:** Fructus, Herba Cannabis
- **Constituents:** Resin (cannabinoid), essential oils, vitamin K; seeds: fatty oil
- **Treatments:** For pain, anaemia, soothing the nerves, for rheumatic pain, gout, problems with the gastrointestinal tract, kidney and bladder complaints, sleeplessness, as a stimulant
- **Uses:** Gruel made of seeds, tincture, textiles industry, bird seed, oil production
- **Homeopathic uses:** See above; only allowed in high potencies
- **What and when to gather:** Seeds, oil cake August to October
- **Lookalikes:** None
- **Other information:** Hashish, the well-known drug, is obtained from the flowering tops of Indian hemp (*C. sativa var. indica*). The consumption of hashish and marijuana has been decriminalized in some countries and US states. However, its possession and consumption is still illegal in many places. Misuse can cause psychological dependency and damage the nerves.

Flowering hemp. The pretty plant, the growth of which is not permitted in many countries, is occasionally found in forests and on farmland. This is not always the fault of marijuana consumers: the seeds can be found in bird seed mixes.

Humulus lupulus L.
COMMON HOPS

Nettle Hops (male), Strobiles (female)

One would normally only expect to find lianas in the jungle. However, a walk through any central European alluvial forest will reveal a plant 'whose stalks are caused to gain height by the wind, and thereby moves itself into the light' (Aichele and Schwegler). Hop gardens with high stalks and wires are the growers' response to this climber's lifestyle.

Hops provide lupulin, the bitter constituent that gives beer its aroma. It has a calming effect, helps to provide a good night's sleep and calm fears, and has also been used to dampen an over-ardent sexual drive (anaphrodisiac). The young shoots are picked in spring and can be used like asparagus.

- **Description:** Height to 22 ft (7 m), climber; three- to seven-lobed palmate leaves, toothed edge; stalks and leaves rough, bristly, with fine hooks, male flowers small, green, on panicles; females greeny-yellow, approx. ½–1 in. (1.5–2.5 cm) long, in hanging, spherical spadices; cones have yellow-orange resin glands, fruit nutlets, creeping root stock; perennial
- **Flowering:** July, August
- **Scent and flavour:** Intense smell, narcotic, similar to valerian; spicy flavour, butter; young shoots juicy, crispy, aromatic
- **Location:** Forest edges, alluvial forests, banks of rivers and streams, climbs up trees and bushes, cultivated
- **Distribution:** Widespread
- **Drug:** Strobuli, Glandulae Lupuli
- **Constituents:** Resinous bitter constituent (humulone, lupulone), essential oils, tannins, flavonoids
- **Treatments:** For disturbed sleep, restlessness, fear, migraines, nervous heart disturbances, loss of appetite, eczema, slow-healing wounds, problems with the menopause

Left: Female hops, hazel family.

- **Uses:** tea, compresses, young shoots as vegetables, beer production, fibres for ropes
- **Homeopathic uses:** see above and as a tranquillizer and anaesthetic, and anaphrodisiac
- **What and when to gather:** young shoots March to May, cones September, hop flour (gland hairs that are obtained from the mature cones) September
- **Lookalikes:** vine (*Vitis vinifera*): leaf node has more marked indentations, fruits in bunches
- **Other information:** Take care: toxic in high doses, contact with fresh cones may cause an allergic reaction, rash and nausea

Hop leaves with young shoots ('hop asparagus').

'It is good for treating shattered conditions of the nervous system accompanied by nausea, dizziness, headache after a strenuous night.'

William Boericke,
Handbook of homeopathic *Materia medica*

Hazel family
Corylaceae

Corylus avellana L.
HAZELNUT

In nature, the hazelnut, which flowers during the first three months of the year, is an important source of food for bees and other early flying insects. For allergy-sufferers, the 'hazelnut season' is far from pleasant because of its extremely high pollen production of approx. 2.5 million pollen per catkin. It is not advisable to plant hazelnut trees near schools.

The hazel is ascribed magical and medicinal powers; there was little distinction between the two in bygone centuries. Hildegard of Bingen advised men whose sperm was inadequate for reproductive purposes to consume an extraordinary stew consisting of young hazel shoots, stonecrop, the liver of a sexually mature goat and fatty pork – 'and if he does so frequently he will come to children, unless the Will of God decrees otherwise'. Water diviners still use hazelnut rods today, although modern science has not yet fully researched their suitability for this purpose. Extracts of the hazelnut's leaf and bark are used to treat varicose veins and phlebitis, and are supposed to be soothing.

- **Description:** Bush, rarely a tree, height to 30 ft (9 m); leaves short stalked, round to heart-shaped, pointed, double sawn, soft hairs; young branches hairy, very flexible; male flowers in long yellow catkins, females unobtrusive, several together, bud-shaped with red scars; nut fruit with a broad-lobed shell
- **Flowering:** January to March
- **Scent and flavour:** No smell; seed aromatic, nutty
- **Location:** Bushes, hedges, deciduous woods, along streams, gardens
- **Distribution:** Very common
- **Drug:** Folia, Cortex, Fructus Coryli avellanae
- **Constituents:** Leaves, rind essential oils, tannins, flavonoids; fruits fatty oil
- **Treatments:** Leaves, rind for varicose veins, phlebitis, ulcers, soothing
- **Uses:** Tea, nuts for oil, baked goods, food and soap industries
- **What and when to gather:** Catkin, rind February and March; leaves April and May; fruit September and October
- **Lookalikes:** Various breeds, including red-leafed cultivations; lambert nut (*C. maxima*): very large fruits; tree hazel (*C. columa*): tree-shaped, small fruits
- **Other information:** Leaves and bark are used as a substitute for witch hazel (*Hamamelis virginiana*) in tea blends

Flowering hazelnut with unassuming female flowers and striking male catkins.

The leaves of the hazelnut soothe diseases of the veins and ulcers.

Beech family
Fagaceae (Cupuliferae)

Apart from the red beech (Fagus), the central European beech family includes the oak (Quercus) and the sweet chestnut (Castanea) – all important forestry and park trees, much appreciated for their wood. The leaves are either entire (beech), lobed (oak) or toothed (sweet chestnut).

Castanea sativa Mill.
EDIBLE CHESTNUT, SWEET CHESTNUT

Sweet Chestnut, Chestnut, Tame Chestnut, Chestnut Tree

In herbal medicine, a tea brewed from chestnut leaves is believed to help to cure a cold. Similar products are obtained from the bark and the nut shells although, according to Bisset and Wichtl, there is as yet no evidence of the efficacy of the ingredients. Since they have a high carbohydrate content, the fruits are not suitable for consumption by diabetics. Sweet chestnut is a Bach Flower Remedy for people who are in despair and see no chance of an improvement in their condition.

Chestnuts – the fruit of the sweet chestnut and its prickly cover.

- **Description:** Tree, height to 100 ft (30 m); age to over 1,000 years, trunk relatively short and broadly domed; young branches black-brown, angular; leaves dark green and shiny, underside matt, stalked, lance-like, prickly toothed, up to 7 in. (18 cm) long; bark smooth, olive-brown; female flowers white, headed, three flowers at the base of the male hanging, approx. 4 in. (10 cm) long bush-like spikes, on leafed tree, insect and wind pollination; bud scales of side leaves, usually two to three nuts in a round, four-lobed, very prickly cupule
- **Flowering:** June to July
- **Scent and flavour:** No smell; leaves taste acerbic, bitter, fruits floury, sweet
- **Location:** Base rich, chalk-poor soils, mixed oak forests, mild winters
- **Distribution:** Southern Europe, south-west Germany, Styria, cultivated and wild
- **Drug:** Folium, Cortex, Fructus Castaneae
- **Constituents:** Leaves, bark: tannins (ellagi-tannin), flavonoids (quercetin, myricetin), vitamins (B1, B2, C), fruit: starch, fat, protein, mucous, vitamins, minerals
- **Treatments:** For respiratory disease, coughs, throat infections, circulatory problems, diarrhoea, convalescence
- **Uses:** Leaves, bark, shells: tea, cough medicine; fruits: flour, bread, desserts, vegetables (basic staple in southern Europe)
- **Homeopathic uses:** Coughing attacks, rectal infections
- **What and when to gather:** Leaves September and October; fruits September to November
- **Lookalikes:** None

Left: Flowering sweet chestnut.

Fagus sylvatica L.
RED BEECH

Common Beech

Beech-nuts have a high oil content, which is why the laconic sentence at the end of Hildegard of Bingen's long, otherwise mystical-fantastical chapter is probably not without justification: 'And anyone who eats of the beech-nut will not be harmed, but they will become fat.' The young, fresh, light green leaves taste tart, stimulate the metabolism, and are excellent in salads. In the Bach Flower Remedies, beech is recommended for people who always only see the negative in others, who have no understanding for their weaknesses, who are picky to the point of pedantry and who find it hard to relax.

Young beech leaves have silky haired edges.

Bottom: The hornbeam or white beech is more closely related to the birch than the red beech, from which it differs in the finely sawn leaves. The picture also shows the winged seeds.

- **Description:** tree, height to 130 ft (40 m), age to over 300 years, slender trunk, diameter to 6 ft 6 in. (2 m); leaves light green and shiny, oval, wavy, young silky-haired bark and stalk, alternating; bud long, pointed; top third of trunk branches out, bark smooth, dark green when young, later silver grey; female flowers stalked, two to three upright, encased in a shell, male flowers in long stalked, hanging, bushy catkins, burs prickly, bursting open in four lobes, two nuts, brown, shiny shell, triangular
- **Flowering:** April to May
- **Scent and flavour:** No smell; leaves taste tart, resinous
- **Location:** Fresh, nutritious soils, mixed forests, parks, in cool, rainy regions
- **Distribution:** Central Europe, common
- **Drug:** Folium, Fructus, Lignum, Cortex Fagi
- **Constituents:** Leaves: flavonolglycosides, tannins, vitamin C, essential oils; fruits: globulines, fatty oil, hydrocyanic acid glycosides, waxes, etc.; bark: tannins, suberin, glucivanillin, resins; wood: fatty acids, sterols, phenolic compounds, creosote, guaiacol
- **Treatments:** Leaves: for stimulating the metabolism; bark: for bronchial diseases, intestinal parasites, diarrhoea, skin diseases, rheumatic complaints; beech tar: for tuberculosis, bronchial complaints
- **Uses:** young leaves: salad, liqueur, cosmetics industry; fruits: oil, baking, confectionery; bark, wood: beech tar, potash, charcoal against poisoning, wood vinegar, smoking
- **What and when to gather:** young leaves April and May; fruits September and October; wood, bark of the two- to three-year-old branches February
- **Lookalikes:** Hornbeam (*Carpinus betulus*): leaves finely sawn, ribs more protruding, silvery-grey trunk
- **Other information:** Take care: red beech-nuts should only be consumed in small quantities because they contain poisonous hydrocyanic acid glycosides and should not be fed to animals (risk of damage to intestinal membranes); beech rind has been used for tanning, leaves have been smoked. Beech wood dust is believed to be carcinogenic after long periods of exposure

Top: The leaves of the English or common oak have either no stalks, or only short ones, and stalked fruits.

Above: In Germany, the maidenhair oak is only found in warm habitats in the south-west.

Right: Stalked leaves, unstalked fruits – key features of the grape oak.

Quercus spec.
OAKS

Throughout the world there are some 300 different species of oak, most of which are to be found in the moderate to sub-tropical zones of the northern hemisphere. The red or summer oak (*Q. robur*) is the most widely found variety in central Europe, followed by the sessile or durmast oak (*Q. petraea*). Both have smooth leaves and cupules. The undersides of the leaves of the downy oak (*Q. pubescens*) are felty; the acorns of the Turkey oak (*Q. cerris*), which occurs in south-east Europe (to eastern Austria), curve outwards and are scaled. The red oak (*Q. rubra*), which was imported from North America, has large pointed leaves, and already grows wild in many regions. Cork oak (*Q. suber*) and holm oak (*Q. ilex*) are common around the Mediterranean.

The leaves of all oak varieties are, to a greater or lesser extent, lobed along the edges. The male flowers hang in bushy, greeny-yellow catkins; the acorns sit singly in slightly differently shaped cupules, depending on the variety. In the Bach Flower Remedies, oak is used for people who will not be beaten but who are occasionally overwhelmed by this demanding lifestyle.

Quercus robur L.
ENGLISH OR COMMON OAK

Summer Oak

- **Description:** Tree, height 130–160 ft (40–50 m), age 400 to 1,000 years, circumference to approx. 30 ft (10 m); leaves unstalked, inverse ovoid, matt, lobed; trunk scaled with warty branches, male flowers in hanging, yellowy-green catkins, female flowers unassuming, single; fruits with long stalks, ovoid, single seed
- **Flowering:** April, May
- **Scent and flavour:** Taste bitter, acerbic; acorn coffee taste is dry

- **Location:** Deciduous and mixed forests, parks
- **Distribution:** In central Europe, English oaks to 3,940 ft (1,200 m); the holm oak is more sensitive to frost
- **Drug:** Cortex, Folia, Semen (shelled core), Quercus
- **Constituents:** Tannins, tanning acids, minerals
- **Treatments:** For inflammatory skin disease, chilblains, sweaty feet; leaves internally for diarrhoea, bleeding, coughing blood, incontinence, vaginal discharge; acorns for stomach and intestinal complaints, poisoning
- **Uses:** Bark and leaves: externally for bathing, compresses, internally for tea, fruits: coffee, flour substitutes, animal feed
- **Homeopathic uses:** See above
- **What and when to gather:** Rind of the young branches and offshoots (tan bark: smooth and silvery) April and May; young leaves June; fruits (acorns) October until early November
- **Lookalikes:** Sessile oak (*Q. petraea*): stalked, shiny leaves, unstalked, almost seated fruits
- **Other information:** Not to be used if there is extensive inflammatory skin disease, feverish and infectious diseases, heart failure, and high blood pressure. Treatments should not be given for more than 2–3 weeks. Tea: maximum two cups a day. Tanners used to need large quantities of the rind for tanning leather.

Walnut family
Juglandaceae

The true walnut and the black walnut (Juglans nigra) are the two most common varieties of this family, which is widespread in the USA. The flowers develop along with the leaves. The fruits are extremely nutritious.

Juglans regia L.
TRUE WALNUT

The walnut tree, which comes originally from the eastern Mediterranean, has been cultivated to the north of the Alps for centuries and also grows wild, especially in wine-growing regions. The walnuts, so like the human brain in appearance, are much loved (botanically, they are a stone fruit rather than a nut). They are highly nutritious (fat content approx. 55 per cent), and are used in traditional medicine as a tonic for convalescents and to treat anemia.

The name 'walnut' comes from the Old English *walh-hnutu*, meaning 'foreign nut'.

- **Description:** Tree, height to 100 ft (30 m); rind grey; leaves imparipinnate; male flowers in thick cylindrical catkins; females spherical, between three and seven, with three yellow scars; brown brain-like stone fruit encased in a green fibre shell
- **Flowering:** May
- **Scent and flavour:** Leaves smell dry and aromatic; unripe fruits bitter, acerbic, later nutty
- **Location:** Woods and forests, gardens, parks, house tree, sensitive to frost
- **Distribution:** Widespread, cultivated, frequently found in wine regions
- **Drug:** Folia, Nuces, Oleum Juglandis, Cortex Juglandis fructus

- **Constituents:** Tannins, flavonoids, essential oils, vitamin C, bitter constituent; fruit shells also contain glycosides, fatty oils
- **Treatments:** For skin problems (acne, eczema), excessive perspiration, gastro-intestinal diseases
- **Uses:** Tea, baths, liqueur, baked goods, food industry, hair and wool dye, paints, edible oil, sun protection
- **Homeopathic uses:** Wet skin rashes, liver problems, headache, diseases of the central nervous system, vermicide
- **What and when to gather:** Fresh leaves June to September; fresh green fruit shells August and September; ripe nuts September and October
- **Lookalikes:** Black walnut: leaves more strongly feathered, fruit shell uneven, turns black

Green nut shells are an excellent hair dye.

Bottom: Female flowers (centre) and cylindrical male catkins of the walnut.

Nettle family
Urticaceae

The nettle family includes almost fifty species throughout the world – although there are only two in central Europe: the stinging nettle (Urtica) with its well-known stinging hairs and opposing leaves, and pellitory (Parietania) with alternate leaves that do not sting.

Urtica dioica L.
COMMON NETTLE

Bull Nettle, Big String Nettle

The common stinging nettle is loved and hated more than almost any other native plant. Most people know it as a large weed that threatens to take over in areas – and causes an extremely unpleasant burning sensation on the skin when touched. Only a few people understand that the 'nettling' of our landscape is the logical consequence of decades of man's consistent and unremitting poisoning of the earth with liquid manure, which contains large amounts of nitrogen and encourages dramatic growth in some plants (such as the stinging nettle) while robbing others of their life source. However, the stinging nettle does have its friends. It is an extremely versatile healing plant and vegetable that can be used from root to unassuming fruit.

The first tender leaves already appear early in the year; they are perfect for making healthy, tasty soups and spreads, and can also be used like spinach. Nettle tea is a well-known remedy for infectious diseases of the uro-genital tract; nettle root tea can help in the early stages of prostate adenoma to ease problems when passing water.

■ **Description:** Height to 5 ft (1.5 m); leaves with long stalks, decussate, elongated to pointed ovoid, coarsely sawn; stalks upright, no branches, square, stalks and leaves with stinging hairs; dioecious, small flowers,

Bottom left: The rare annual nettle has more noticeably toothed leaves that are also a little wider.

Bottom right: Flowering common nettle.

unassuming, green tinged, in long stalked panicles; roots yellow, spreading, creeping; perennial

- **Flowering:** May to October
- **Scent and flavour:** Virtually no scent; taste aromatic, spicy, tart
- **Location:** Woods and forests, alluvial forests, river banks, under shrubs and bushes, wasteland. This herb thrives in nitrogen-rich soil
- **Distribution:** Common
- **Drug:** Folium, Radix, Fructus Urticae
- **Constituents:** Histamine, acetylcholine, antacid (stinging hairs), flavonoids, (ruton), tannins, vitamin C, chlorophyll, mineral salts
- **Treatments:** For rheumatic complaints, gout, kidney and bladder infections and stones, prostate problems, gastrointestinal problems, skin diseases, anaemia, purifying the blood
- **Uses:** Tea, extract, tincture, unction, baths, shampoo, soup, spinach, salad, gratins, used to be an important source of fiber, dye and forage in poultry farming

- **Homeopathic uses:** See above and for bleeding, ulcers
- **What and when to gather:** Young leaves and shoots from March, several times a year, seeds July to October, roots September to October
- **Lookalikes:** Pellitory (*Parietaria officinalis*): no stinging hairs, leaves are opposite; annual nettle (*U. urens*): leaves rounded at the tip, panicles longer than the leaf stalk, same uses; dead nettle (*Lamium spec.*): no stinging hairs, pretty lipped flower
- **Other information:** Undiluted stinging nettle manure ($2^{1}/_{5}$ lb/1 kg plants to $2^{1}/_{2}$ gallons/10 l water) is an excellent remedy for aphids, and when diluted is used to strengthen and feed houseplants.

Top left: Young stinging nettles in the spring; at the front the strong yellow rhizome.

Top right: At first sight, the spotted dead nettle (Lamium maculatum) looks like the stinging nettle, but its flowers are completely different and it has no hairs. The red buds seen in the picture are about to flower.

Liliidae

LILIIDS

Overview of Liliidae:

Liliaceous plants are monocotyledons: their seeds contain only a single cotyledon (seed leaf). They are mainly herbaceous, usually with parallel-veined leaves; the stalk is not branched. Liliidae include such pretty varieties as orchids, lilies and tulips as well as important sources of nutrition such as bulbous plants and grasses.

The autumn crocus flowers from the end of August until the beginning of October; the leaves and fruits appear in spring.

Lily family
Liliaceae

All lily varieties are geophytes, which means the storage organ is below the ground, and are either onions (allium), tubers (colchicum, autumn crocus) or rhizomes (convallaria, lily-of-the-valley). The leaves are parallel-veined and smooth-edged. The flowers have three petals, the sepals three-chambered capsules or berries. Aloe, which comes from tropical and subtropical regions, uses its fleshy leaves for storage.

Allium spec.
ONION, SHALLOT, GARLIC

The allium includes many well-known vegetable varieties, especially the cooking onion in all its varieties, as well as the leek (*A. porrum*), garlic (*A. sativum*), the shallot (*A. ascalonicum*) and chives (*A. schoenoprasum*). They all help to reduce blood pressure and have diuretic properties. As well as being a valuable culinary ingredient, the onion is also a popular healing plant. The juice of finely chopped onions that

have been steeped in sugar is an excellent cold remedy. Tiny bags of onions are placed on sore ears, insect bites and stings, and chilblains.

Allium cepa L.
ONION

Garden Onion, Shallot

- **Description:** Height to 4 ft (1.2 m); tubular leaves; round-bellied and thickened in the lower 'onion' section, outermost layer turns brown when dry, membranous; flower in mock umbel with abundant flowers, membranous top leaf around the flower; capsule fruits; roots white
- **Flowering:** June, July
- **Scent and flavour:** Onion-like smell, causes the eyes to water; biting taste, spicy
- **Location:** Originally from the steppes of central Asia; gardens
- **Distribution:** Common, cultivated
- **Drug:** Bulbus Allii cepae
- **Constituents:** Essential oils (allylpropyl-disulphide, allicin), sugar, inulin, flavonoids, vitamins including C
- **Treatments:** For loss of appetite, constipation, high blood pressure, atherosclerosis, coughs, throat infections and tonsillitis, asthma, against bacteria, low-grade diabetes,

Onions in a vegetable garden.

Left: Freshly harvested garlic. It is as famous for its blood pressure-reducing abilities as for its intense aroma.

Right: The chive is a naturalized cultivated plant with a high vitamin content.

rheumatic complaints, alcohol and nicotine abuse, corns, warts, bruises, insect stings, worms
- **Uses:** Fresh onions, juice, syrup, decoction, cold extract, vegetable, spice
- **Homeopathic uses:** See above and for gastrointestinal problems, a runny nose, facial neuralgia, phantom pains
- **What and when to gather:** Onion August to October
- **Lookalikes:** None
- **Other information:** Take care: onions should be avoided where there is nervousness, gastrointestinal inflammation, bleeding and skin complaints because it can irritate the skin

Allium ursinum L.
RAMSON

Wild Garlic, Forest Garlic, Gypsy Garlic, Bear's Garlic

In the regions where it occurs, ramson is a much-prized and very early wild vegetable. Some people yearn for 'ramson' time in March and April as much as others do for the morel season (which occurs at almost the same time), and love little more than to devour ramson raw, in salads, or cooked, with pasta. Ramson soup is popular in Austria and Germany. However, others may find it difficult to digest; they are advised to steep leaves and bulbs in milk and then drink the milk in order to benefit from its valuable constituents. Ramson grows in woods and forests on fresh, calciferous soils. Once it has found a home that appeals, it can soon cover large areas – often without competition in the first spring, but often also together with the highly toxic autumn crocus (see page 176), another lily plant.

- **Description:** height to 1 ft 4 in. (40 cm); leaves with long stalks, lanceolate, in pairs; flowers white, star-shaped in a round inflorescence, triangular stalk, no leaves
- **Flowering:** May, June

- **Scent and flavour:** Smells and tastes very strongly of garlic
- **Location:** Alluvial forests, lowland forests
- **Distribution:** Common in southern Germany, otherwise rare
- **Drug:** Herba, Bulbus Allii ursini
- **Constituents:** Essential oil, vitamins, minerals, sugar, mucilage
- **Treatments:** For loss of appetite, clogged arteries, cramps, high blood pressure, infectious diseases, fever, alcohol and nicotine abuse, purifying the blood, against worms
- **Uses:** Salad, juice, herb
- **Homeopathic uses:** See above and to aid the digestion
- **What and when to gather:** Leaves before flowering March to May, flowers May and June, onions July to September
- **Lookalikes:** autumn crocus (*Colchicum autumnale*, see page 176): tulip-shaped leaves, unscented, seed vessel in the middle, flowers in September, toxic; lily-of-the-valley (*Convallaria majalis*, see page 177): leaves rolled up when new, unscented, leaf broad and oval, toxic

Flowering ramson

Warning, toxic doppelganger! Ramson (above) and autumn crocuses (centre) growing side by side in an alluvial forest. The appearance of the autumn crocus in a tulip-shaped rosette is typical.

Colchicum autumnale L.
AUTUMN CROCUS

■ *highly toxic* ■
Autumn Lily, Meadow Saffron, Autumn Crocus

Early in the year the dark green leaves of the autumn crocus break through the forest or meadow floor in a tulip-shaped rosette. Fruit and seeds grow under their protection, then the leaves die. Totally without leaves – and therefore also called 'naked virgins' – the elegant lilac flower appears in September and October.

The fall crocus is one of our most dangerous native plants. In spring, it is easily mistaken for the ramson (see page 175), which grows close by. Every part of the autumn crocus is toxic, with the bulbs and seeds the most dangerous: $1/20$–$1/5$ oz (1–5 g) of the latter is enough to kill a human. On the other hand, used and taken correctly, the toxic constituent (the alkaloid colchicine) is used in various medical products for the treatment of gout and rheumatism, and it is also extremely successful for treating skin diseases. It has long been known that it is a successful treatment for gout, but it should only ever be handled by experts. However, even they are not infallible: Gregory, the Bishop of Antioch, suffered terribly from gout and died

at the end of the 6th century, apparently of the effects of a potion made from the autumn crocus that had been prescribed by a doctor. Gardeners and botanists treat the seeds with a dilute solution of colchicine, thereby increasing the number of chromosomes, and are able to create plant mutations this way.

- **Description:** Height to 1 ft 4 in. (40 cm); leaves a rich dark green, lanceolate in a tulip-shaped rosette in March and April; flowers a pinky violet, six petals, floral tube up to 8 in. (20 cm); stalked capsules with numerous sticky seeds; tuber 1–2½ in. (3–7 cm) long, pear shaped; perennial
- **Flowering:** August to October
- **Scent and flavour:** No smell
- **Location:** Damp fields, meadows, alluvial forests
- **Distribution:** Widespread
- **Drug:** Fructus, Semen, Bulbus, Flores Colchici
- **Constituents:** Alkaloids (colchicine), fatty oil
- **Treatment:** For gout, leukaemia, skin diseases
- **Uses:** Pharmaceutical industry, plant breeding
- **Homeopathic uses:** See above, and for severe rheumatic pain, tendency towards collapse
- **What and when to gather:** Tuber August and September, seeds June and July
- **Lookalikes:** Ramson (*Allium ursinum*, see page 175): leaves with long stalks, in pairs; saffron crocus (*Crocus sativus*): autumn flowering, red thread-like stigma, only cultivated here; other crocus varieties flower in spring
- **Other information:** The various parts of the plant need to be collected, dried, and stored separately

Top: The saffron crocus also flowers in autumn. The flowers have red stigmas that are used as a spice (saffron) and in homeopathy as a treatment for bleeding and cramps.

Above: Seed capsule of the autumn crocus enclosed by the leaf rosette.

Right: Flowering autumn crocus in September.

'The rose had now withered,
the nightingale flown,
the earnest autumn crocus stood
already in the meadows.'

Ferdinand Freiligrath (1810–1876)

Convallaria majalis L.
LILY-OF-THE-VALLEY

■ *highly toxic, protected* ■
Fall Lily, Meadow Saffron

According to Marianne Beuchert, the pretty, pleasantly scented lily-of-the-valley represents 'love and happiness. Healing for the world. The end of all woes. Purity of the soul. Modesty. Mary's virginity. Eternal rest in Christ.' According to one legend, the flower grew from the tears shed by Mary Magdalene at Christ's tomb. But the lily-of-the-valley has plenty to offer for the beating muscle in our chest as well as for the place where we believe spirit and soul to be: it contains the glycosides convallatoxin and convallarin, both powerful cardiac products that are similar to the foxglove (*Digitalis purpurea*, see page 104) in the way they work. They may only be prescribed by a doctor, though, as the incorrect dosage could be fatal. The dried, pulverized flowers are an excellent snuff, and in fact are added to many commercial products – not something that is normally associated with the gracious, 'innocent' lily-of-the-valley.

■ **Description:** Height to 1 ft (30 cm); leaves dark green, broad and oval, lanceolate, long stalks; flowers white, bell-shaped, nodding, in a one-sided cluster; round red berries; rhizome thin, branched, creeping
■ **Flowering:** May, June
■ **Scent and flavour:** Strong scent to the flower, sweet, drug unscented
■ **Location:** Alluvial forests, hedges, pastures, mountain meadows, gardens
■ **Distribution:** Widespread
■ **Drug:** Herba, Folia, Flores Convallariae
■ **Constituents:** Heart glycoside (convallatoxin, convallarin), essential oils, saponins
■ **Treatments:** For palpitations, weak heart, cramps
■ **Uses:** Pharmaceutical industry, production of snuff, cosmetics and perfume
■ **Homeopathic uses:** See above
■ **What and when to gather:** Leaves, flowers May and June
■ **Lookalikes:** Ramson (*Allium ursinum*, see page 175): leaves in pairs, light green, narrow, not furled, smell of garlic
■ **Other information:** The parts of the plant are collected, dried and stored separately for pharmaceutical products. Only to be taken on prescription.

Far left: Flowering lily-of-the-valley. Warning – the leaves are easily mistaken for those of the edible ramson.

Left: The shiny red berries are also toxic.

Asphodel family
Asphodelaceae

Barbados aloe (Aloe barbadensis), king's spear (Asphodelus) and Jacob's rod (Asphodeline) are the best known of these plants, and really only thrive if cultivated in gardens. This plant plays an important role in the mythology and medicinal history of its home, the Mediterranean. Even Dioscurides described a wide range of medicinal applications for this plant in 1 BC.

Aloe barbadensis Mill.
BARBADOS ALOE

The Barbados aloe comes from Africa. However, it did not begin to make a name for itself as a healing plant until it had been taken to America and the Caribbean. There, and on the Canary Islands, it is grown on plantations and provides the basic ingredient for aloe vera gel which, although it is becoming increasingly popular in the cosmetics industry, is also widely regarded as a 'miracle cure' thanks to its anti-inflammatory properties. Franz Fraschio points out that, thanks to clever advertising, aloe is now widely regarded as something of a 'universal panacea'. 'Comments concerning its efficacy in the treatment of diseases such as cancer and AIDS are most certainly to be treated with concern and scepticism.' Aloe extract, either pure or in combination with other substances, has long been known to be an effective laxative. However, it should not be taken for longer than eight days, and never during pregnancy.

- **Description:** Height to approx. 3 ft 3 in. (1 m); succulent, rosette-shaped leaves, up to 1 ft 8 in. (50 cm) long, 2–2½ in. (6–7 cm) wide, sharp pointed tips and teeth; yellow flowers, three petals in a bunch
- **Flowering:** All year
- **Scent and flavour:** A little like garlic, strong smell; bitter taste, unpleasant
- **Location:** Wild, cultivated, house plant
- **Distribution:** Africa
- **Drug:** Curacao Aloe
- **Constituents:** Aloin, acemannan
- **Treatments:** Internal: for constipation, diabetes, high cholesterol, stimulating the immune system; external: for wounds, burns, skin diseases
- **Uses:** Gel, powder, cosmetics industry
- **Homeopathic uses:** Only Aloe ferox may be used
- **What and when to gather:** Leaves of three- to four-year-old plants, inner layer with clear gel
- **Lookalikes:** Aloe ferox: red-brown flower, lower aloin content
- **Other information:** The fresh gel and thickened leaf gel (Curacao aloe) are mainly used

The Barbados aloe is grown widely in the tropics and subtropics. This picture was taken on Fuerteventura.

Grass family
Poaceae

The stalks of grasses are usually round, hollow, and thickened at the nodules. The leaves are long, narrow, and parallel-veined with a long sheath around the stalk. The unassuming flowers form ears, bunches or panicles. The fruit is a single-seeded achene. Corn differs in various respects and is in a separate category.

Agropyron repens (L.) P. Beauv.
COUCH GRASS

Dog Grass, Twitch Grass, Quick Grass, Quitch

It is well known that there are many plants whose constituents can kill or cure, depending on the dosage and application. Man also has a somewhat ambivalent attitude towards couch grass. On the one hand, the close relative of wheat is a tenacious field and garden weed; on the other, as a healing plant it has helped and even cured many ailments. Its roots form 3 ft 3 in. (1 m), tough, underground runners, and it is these parts, the ones that make it so difficult to keep under control, that contain plenty of carbohydrates, essential oils, vitamins (A and B), mucilage and many other constituents that make it such a valuable healing plant.

Couch grass tea or juice are well-known remedies for kidney and bladder complaints, and for bronchial catarrh. The sweet-tasting rhizomes can even be roasted and used as a coffee substitute. However, it must not be confused with Darnel ryegrass (*Lolium temulentum*), which is toxic.

- **Description:** Height to 5 ft (1.5 m); leaves narrow, green to blue-green, hairs at the top; upright stalks, smooth, bald; flowers four to six, alternating, two-petalled, on a long ear; broad side of the flower faces the axis of the stalk, short-bearded husk; fruit caryopsis, hairy tip; rootstock yellow-white, forms runners; perennial
- **Flowering:** June to August
- **Scent and flavour:** No smell; roots taste sweet to bitter, slimy
- **Location:** Fields, meadows, gardens, trails
- **Distribution:** Common
- **Drug:** Rhizoma Graminis
- **Constituents:** Fibrils, polysaccharides, saponins, carbohydrates, sugar, essential oils, glycosides, chert, iron, vitamins
- **Treatments:** For liver, kidney and bladder complaints, gout, rheumatism, arthritis, tumours, bronchial catarrh, stomach complaints, diarrhoea, purifying the blood
- **Uses:** Tea, decoction, syrup, juice, poultices, coffee substitute, animal feed
- **Homeopathic uses:** Urinary and kidney diseases
- **What and when to gather:** Roots in March and April, September and October
- **Lookalikes:** Darnel ryegrass (*Lolium temulentum*): narrow side of the ears sits against the stalk, toxic; Bermuda grass (*Cynodon dactylon*): violet ears, tip of the stem bushy; other grass varieties (*Agropyron* spec.)
- **Other information:** Recommended daily quantity one to two cups

Inflorescence of the toxic Darney ryegrass

Inflorescence of couch grass.

Avena sativa L.
OATS

Oats

Green oats.

To the botanist, the oat is a grass or, more correctly, a meadow grass. Archaeological findings have shown that it was grown in central Europe 4,500 years ago. Because they are hemapoietic, oatmeal, gruel, grits and groats are ideal for sufferers from gastrointestinal diseases and those who require a special diet. The ground seeds (oat flakes) are extremely popular with children and are a key ingredient in the carefully compiled nutritional plans of many top athletes. An oat bath used to be a popular remedy for the treatment of skin disease, although there is little scientific evidence of its efficacy. The same applies to the use of oat extracts for the treatment of rheumatic disease, as is recommended in homeopathy. Naturopathy uses the freshly harvested flowers as a tea, which is believed to be calming.

- **Description:** Height to 2 ft 8 in. (80 cm); panicle with branches standing proud; small ears ¾–1 in. (2–2.5 cm) long, lanceolate, usually two flowers, hanging, husk smooth, long haired; annual
- **Flowering:** July, August
- **Scent and flavour:** Little smell; floury taste
- **Location:** Fields, ruderal points, wild
- **Distribution:** Grown all over the world
- **Drug:** Fructus, Herba, Stramentum Avenae
- **Constituents:** Starch, sugar, protein, fat, calcium, vanilloside, vitamins, minerals (calcium, magnesium, phosphor)
- **Treatments:** Gastrointestinal diseases, raised cholesterol, age-related problems, impotence, sterility, diabetes, during convalescence, for exhaustion, while growing, straw for skin diseases, formerly also for rheumatic complaints
- **Uses:** Flour, gruel, baths, seeds (seeds rolled into flakes), special dietary and nutritional products, animal food, straw
- **Homeopathic uses:** For sleeplessness, liver problems, skin diseases, rheumatic complaints
- **What and when to gather:** Green flowering plant July and August; seeds August and September, straw August, September
- **Lookalikes:** Other meadow grasses: are not grown in fields
- **Other information:** Oats have been cultivated in different varieties since the Bronze Age. Caution: do not use straw decoctions to treat rheumatism because of the high mineral concentration.

'Oats… are a healthy, pleasant meal for healthy people; it gives them a good humour and a pure and clear understanding, and it gives them a good colour and healthy flesh… But he who suffers from gout and therefore has a split spirit and poor thoughts, so that he suffers from a kind of madness, then his whole body should be dipped in a steam bath of oats cooked in water, and with stones heated in the same water in which the oats were cooked. And he should do that often so that he comes to himself and his health is restored.'

Hildegard of Bingen (1098–1179), Physica

Zea mays L. Off.
CORN

Corn – botanically it is an annual grass – was first brought to Europe by Columbus in the 15th century. Presumably it had been an important cereal for, and cultivated by, the Maya and the Incas for thousands of years. There are now countless different cultivated varieties. In Europe, it is grown mainly as cattle fodder; over-fertilizing often occurs because of its high nitrate content, which in turn has a detrimental effect on flora and fauna.

Naturopathy uses the bushy, flag-like fronds at the top of the female cobs. The tea is diuretic, and is used in the treatment of kidney and bladder diseases. According to Bisset and Wichtl there is as yet no scientific evidence of its alleged efficacy in the treatment of diabetes. Tropical forms contain an alkaloid that is an effective tranquillizer and narcotic. Although corn pollen is relatively large (and therefore not easily inhaled), it occurs in large quantities, which may well cause allergic reactions.

- **Description:** height to 8 ft (2.5 m); leaves 4–5 in. (10–12 cm) wide; stalks pithy; male flowers on the end of a panicle, female in thick cobs, surrounded by many long, brown, silky fronds that turn yellow when ripe; seeds golden, husks bent; bristle-like roots for support, annual
- **Flowering:** July to September
- **Scent and flavour:** Grains sweet, floury
- **Location:** Grown in fields; moist, nutritious soils
- **Distribution:** Home South America, cultivated
- **Drug:** Stigma, Amylum, Oleum Maydis
- **Constituents:** Salicylic acid, fatty oil, essential oils, saponins, carbohydrates, tannins, potassium, vitamins (E, K)
- **Treatments:** For kidney and bladder disease, infections, rheumatic complaints, high cholesterol, overactive thyroid, diabetes, obesity

- **Uses:** Tea (fronds), oil, starch (maize) as powder, flour (polenta), special diets, pharmaceutical industry (binder for pills), cosmetics
- **Homeopathic uses:** See above and skin diseases
- **What and when to gather:** Fronds of the female cobs July and August; seeds, shoots September and October
- **Lookalikes:** None

Female corn flowers with long, silky fronds.

Ripe corn cob.

RANUNCULOIDS

The **Ranunculoids** include ranunculus plants (Ranunculaceae) and poppies (Papaveraceae), two types with numerous varieties, some highly toxic, some – if used correctly – with healing properties, and the barberry family (Berberidaceae), which has edible fruits with a high vitamin content.

There are many different kinds of cultivated peony in various shapes and colours. They are a popular choice for cottage gardens.

Barberry family
Berberidaceae

Most barberry plants are bushes or shrubs that develop berries, the branches of which – such as the various types of berberis – have thorns.

Berberis vulgaris L.
COMMON BARBERRY

■ *mildly toxic* ■
European Barberry, Pepperidge Bush

The barberry is not popular in agriculture as it is a host for wheat rust (*Puccinia graminis*), a serious fungal disease. Accordingly, the shrub has been decimated in many places in response to pressure from farmers. The barberry originally hailed from the Mediterranean (North Africa) and, once it had been introduced, it soon spread to dry, sunny regions throughout central Europe. Hildegard of Bingen mentioned it and warned against the fruits, which are prized today for their high vitamin C content. Only a cream made of barberry buds, wine and powdered mole has her blessing, as a treatment for boils. Later, root and rind extracts were used to produce a tea that stimulated gall and salivary gland activity; Oertel and Bauer also note that barberry tea was useful in the treatment of internal bleeding.

- **Description:** Height to 10 ft (3 m); bush with rod-shaped branches, young rind light red, later grey; long shoots with leaves forming three-part sharp thorns, short shoots with leaf bundles; leaves inverse oval, toothed edge, small flowers, yellow, in hanging bunches; berry bright red, elongated
- **Flowering:** May, June
- **Scent and flavour:** Flowers smell sweet; rind tastes bitter, berries and leaves tart

- **Location:** Bushes, hedges, forest edges, gardens, parks, calciphile
- **Distribution:** Widespread
- **Drug:** Fructus, Radix Berberidis vulgaris
- **Constituents:** Anthocyane, alkaloids (Berberine, Palmatine), essential oils, malic acid, vitamin C, pectin
- **Treatments:** For increasing resistance, treating kidney and bladder disease, liver and gall complaints, varicose veins, loss of appetite
- **Uses:** Tea, juice, jam, vinegar
- **Homeopathic uses:** To treat liver and rheumatic complaints, gout, sciatica
- **What and when to gather:** ripe berries August to October, roots and rind March and April, November
- **Lookalikes:** Mahonia (*Mahonia aquifolium*): blue-grey berries, evergreen leaves, shiny, sinusoidally toothed with thorny tips, usually planted
- **Other information:** Root and rind mildly toxic; warning: not to be taken for urinary infections. Effective in large quantities in the treatment of the Aleppo boil (*Leishmania tropica*)

Flowering barberry.

The perfumed flowers of the mahonia – and the leaves, which are similar to holly leaves (see page 212). The rind of the mahonia is anti-inflammatory.

Left: Tart barberry fruits hang in bunches.

Fumitory family
Fumariaceae and
Poppy family
Papaveraceae

Fumitory and poppy plants, which used to belong to the same family, contain the same amount of alkaloids. Poppy plants contain latex. Their stellar flowers have four petals. The flowers on fumitory plants are zygomorphic; there is no latex.

Corydalis cava (L.)
Schweigg. et Koerte
HOLLOW LARKSPUR

■ *toxic* ■
Hollow Root

Hollow larkspur flowers in March and April in nutrient-rich, slightly moist soils in alluvial and lowland forests in southern and central Germany. Düll and Kutzelnigg call it an 'intelligent flower' because its flowers are rotated by 90 degrees and, as a result, only 'educated' insects are able to find the opening.

The herbaceous perennial flowers either red or white and develops from a walnut-sized corm; the stalk of the older plant becomes hollow and contains toxic alkaloids. Carefully measured, the constituents have a sedative effect and have been added to tranquillizers. According to Schauenberg and Paris, the alkaloid Bulbocapnine is also used in the treatment of Parkinson's disease.

- **Description:** Height to 1 ft (30 cm); ten to twenty flowers on bunch, leaves blue-grey, incised; flowers in terminal bunches, pink to purple, rarely white, zygomorphic with

elongated spur; pod fruit, lots of black seeds with white oil coat (see celandine, page 186 f.); tuber hollow in age; perennial
- **Flowering:** March, April
- **Scent and flavour:** Pleasant smell, numbing
- **Location:** Moist, nutrient-rich mixed deciduous forests, bushes, hedges
- **Distribution:** Common in southern Germany, otherwise rare
- **Drug:** Radix Corydalis
- **Constituents:** Alkaloids (Bulbocapnine)
- **Treatments:** For nervous diseases, Parkinson's disease, intestinal parasites
- **Uses:** Narcotics, pharmaceuticals
- **What and when to gather:** Corm August to October
- **Lookalikes:** Fingered larkspur, pink corydalis (*C. solida*): leaves more deeply incised, round corm, fleshy, rare; orchids (Orchidaceae): parallel-veined leaves
- **Other information:** Take care: toxic due to the alkaloids – only to be taken with medical supervision

Carpets of purple or white larkspur are a frequent sight in beech groves throughout March and April.

Fumaria officinalis L.
FUMITORY

■ *mildly toxic* ■

Common Fumitory, Beggary, Earth-smoke, Wax Dolls

The name 'earth smoke' is easy to explain: seen from a distance, the grey-green leaves look like smoke, and people used to believe that earth smoke developed from the vapours rising from damp fields. Perhaps the same vapours also created the images of future bridegrooms who supposedly revealed themselves to young girls, according to a story told by Friedrich Jantzen, 'through the earth-smoke when they returned from weeding the fields'. The plant also used to be a treatment for skin and gall bladder/liver diseases. Its use for the latter is due to the presence of fumarine, and has been scientifically proven.

Flowering fumitory on the edge of a wheat field.

As yet the only confirmation of its efficacy in the treatment of skin problems is the enthusiastic response from advocates of naturopathy, but it remains unproven by science.

- **Description:** Height to 1 ft 4 in. (40 cm); leaves grey-green, bi-pinnate, narrow pinnates, stalks blue-green, upright or crawling, winding, branched; flowers pink or white, purple tips, multiflorous loose bunch, flower zygomorphic, spur approx. $1/4$ in. (8 mm) long, saccate; fruit spherical, tubercular; root fibrous, yellow-white; annual
- **Flowering:** May to October
- **Scent and flavour:** Almost no smell; taste unpleasant, very bitter, slightly salty
- **Location:** Fields, vineyards, wasteland, waysides, gardens
- **Distribution:** Scattered
- **Drug:** Herba Fumariae
- **Constituents:** Alkaloids (fumarine), bitter principles, resin
- **Treatments:** For loss of appetite, cramps in the gastrointestinal tract, liver and gall bladder complaints, digestive problems, intestinal parasites, haemorrhoids, skin diseases (lichen, scabies), acne
- **Uses:** Tea, compresses
- **Homeopathic uses:** See above
- **What and when to gather:** Flowering plant May to August
- **Lookalikes:** Other fumitories: twining, smooth fruit
- **Other information:** Take care: measure carefully, misuse can cause paralysis of the respiratory organs; ideally use only in teas

Chelidonium majus L.
GREATER CELANDINE

■ *toxic* ■

Garden Celandine, Tetterwort

Celandine contains more than twenty different alkaloids and is highly toxic in large quantities (especially the root). It is known for its antispasmodic effects on gall bladder problems, liver problems and gastrointestinal cramps, but it should only ever be used on medical advice. The yellow-orange latex present throughout the plant is an old natural remedy used to treat warts, and one of the comparatively few external applications of a medicinal herb still widely known and practised today, although there is still no scientific evidence of its efficacy. People who are prone to allergies may react to contact with the latex.

It is interesting how celandine is distributed. The 'appendages' (elaiosomes) on the black seeds contain oil and are much appreciated by ants who help to scatter them. This 'arrangement' obviously works excellently, because the plant is found everywhere – on wasteland, waysides, and the edges of woods and forests, even in cracks in walls and brickwork.

- **Description:** Height to 2 ft 4 in. (70 cm); bottom leaves on long stalks, pinnate leaves, lobate, often notched or saw-toothed, blue-green; stalks and leaves often woolly, standing proud, hairy, branched, thickened at the knots; yellow-orange latex; flowers sulphur-coloured or golden in little-flowering umbels; up to 2 in. (5 cm) long, narrow pod, seeds black with white appendages; strong rootstock, barrel-shaped, red-brown on outside, orange inside; perennial
- **Flowering:** April to September
- **Scent and flavour:** Unpleasantly sharp smell when fresh, none when dried, root 'narcotic'; taste bitter, sharp
- **Location:** Bushes, forest edges, wasteland, paths, gardens; this herb thrives in nitrogen-rich soil
- **Distribution:** Very common
- **Drug:** Herba, Radix Chelidonii
- **Constituents:** Alkaloids (chelidonine, coptisine), essential oils, vitamins
- **Treatments:** For skin diseases (warts, corns, psoriasis), liver and gall bladder problems, yellow fever, gastrointestinal cramps, kidney and bladder infections, as an anaesthetic

- **Uses:** Tea, sitz bath, fresh latex, tincture, pharmaceutical industry, plant protection (e.g. against aphids)
- **Homeopathic uses:** See above, and for pneumonia, rheumatism, menstrual problems
- **What and when to gather:** Young leaves, flowers (not the thick stalks) April to July, root March, September to October
- **Lookalikes:** Akelei (*Aquilegia* spec.): no hairs on leaf stalks, no latex
- **Other information:** Daily dose of one to two cups should not be exceeded; do not allow latex to come into contact with open wounds – it is toxic. Only to be used under medical supervision

Flowering celandine.

Papaver spec.
POPPY

■ *toxic* ■

Papaver rhoeas L.
CORN POPPY

■ *mildly toxic* ■
Copperose, Corn Rose, Cup-puppy, Headwark, Red Poppy

Flowers and ripening seed vessels of the corn poppy.

A field of golden corn under a brilliant blue sky, surrounded by deep-blue cornflowers and red poppies – a typical summer image of bright colours, peace, and tranquillity that will cheer even the weariest heart. By the same token, in 'In Flanders Fields', the poem by the Canadian John McCrae (1872–1918), the red poppy was made the symbol of the lakes of blood shed on the battlefields of Flanders. Like many other meadow 'weeds', the poppy has also been destroyed chemically in many farmed areas; it is, however, often seen as a pioneer plant on roadsides and paths, on rock piles and excavations, in gravel pits and similar places. Unlike the opium poppy, the corn poppy contains no psychoactive substances. Yet it used to be much appreciated as a sedative, painkiller, and an aid to sleep, especially for children,

although there is as yet no scientific confirmation of its efficacy. Dried petals are occasionally added to herbal teas as a 'fining drug.'

- **Description:** Height to 3 ft (90 cm); leaves alternating, lobate, saw-toothed along edge, stalk upright, more or less standing proud and hairy, with latex; flowers usually crimson or scarlet, very thin petals, blue-black stamens, buds and flowers nodding at first, then upright; capsule fruits inverse oval, compartments, pores under the top with striking, star-shaped stigma, very many seeds; annual
- **Flowering:** May to July
- **Scent and flavour:** Almost no smell; latex very bitter
- **Location:** Around fields and meadows, paths, grain fields
- **Distribution:** Widespread, common
- **Drug:** Flores Papaveris rhoeados
- **Constituents:** alkaloids (Rhoeadine not toxic), anthocyane, mucilages, fatty oil
- **Treatments:** For pain, restlessness, disturbed sleep, dry coughs
- **Uses:** Tea, petal sugar, syrup, fining for tea and wine
- **Homeopathic uses:** See above
- **What and when to gather:** Flowers May and June
- **Lookalikes:** None
- **Other information:** Take care: observe daily dose; choose other herbs for babies and small children

Papaver somniferum
OPIUM POPPY

■ *toxic* ■
Garden Poppy, Oil Poppy

The opium poppy is cultivated both as an oil plant and as a decorative plant; it has frosted leaves that encircle the stalk and striking white, violet, or pink flowers with dark spots at the heart.

The opium poppy contains a white, bitter, toxic latex (the 'tear'). This is used to make opium, which is a strong narcotic drug; production and trading are bound to the guidelines of the International Opium Agreement and national narcotics laws. Codeine, which is used in lots of cough mixtures to soothe a dry cough, is made from the root. The black, tasty seeds are not toxic and contain a very precious oil.

Historically, the opium poppy is one of our oldest known healing and cultivated plants. It was probably already used in the stone age. The opium poppy also played an important part in Greek mythology and in religious cult activities. Opium was in great demand as an aphrodisiac. In order to open up the Chinese market to opium from their Indian colony, the British fought the 'Opium War' against China from 1840 to 1842.

- **Description:** Height to 5 ft (1.5 m); leaves slightly split, encircling the stalk, blue-green; upright stalks; large flowers, white, pink, or mauve; capsule, numerous tiny blue-black seeds; root spindle-shaped; annual
- **Flowering:** June to July
- **Location:** Nutrient-rich, highly calciferous soils, gardens
- **Distribution:** Cultivated

- **Drug:** Fructus Papaveris immaturi, Stramentum, Semen, Oleum Papaveris, opium (toxic)
- **Constituents:** Alkaloids in the latex (morphine, codeine, papaverine, narcotine, thebaine), fatty oil in the seeds (including linoleic acid), mucilage, caoutchouc
- **Treatments:** Latex: for severe diarrhoea, severe gastrointestinal pain, respiratory organs, urinary organs and genitalia, musculature, sleep disturbances
- **Uses:** Food industry (seeds, oil), pharmaceutical industry (latex, seeds, oil), paints, soap, animal feed
- **Homeopathic uses:** See above
- **What and when to gather:** Unripe seed capsules without seeds once petals shed; latex from the unripe cut fruits (opium) June and July; seeds, ripe deseeded capsules (poppy straw) September and October
- **Lookalikes:** None
- **Other information:** Take care: narcotic, addictive drug, seeds tranquillizing

Far left: Flowering opium poppy. The mauve 'nectar guide patterns' attract insects to the nectar.

Left: White latex (milky juice) seeps from the scored seed head.

Ranunculus family
Ranunculaceae

The Ranunculus family consists of mainly herbaceous, very attractive perennial plants with alternating split or divided leaves. The flowers are multifarious with cleverly designed, often flower-like honey leaves; the fruits are usually pods or nuts. All varieties contain protoanemonine, which is toxic for humans and animals. Many varieties are also grown in gardens.

Aconitum napellus L.
MONKSHOOD

■ *highly toxic, protected* ■
Venus' Chariot, Wolf's Bane, Monk's Blood, Blue Rocket, Friar's Cap, Aconite

Monkshood not only occurs in the wild, but it is also an extremely popular garden plant because of its magnificent, helmet-shaped, blue-mauve flowers. However, it can safely be assumed that most gardeners do not appreciate just how dangerous this plant is. It is the most toxic flowering plant in Europe, easily on a par with white and green death caps from the mushroom world. Even simple contact with the skin can cause poisoning, and just a fraction of an ounce taken internally is enough to kill a person. Monkshood should never be grown in gardens where small children play.

On the other hand, in line with Paracelsus' principle of *dosis facit venenum* ('the dose makes the poison'), monkshood can, in certain cases, also heal. In homeopathy, high-potency monkshood extracts are used to treat neuralgia (e.g. trigeminus) and severe respiratory diseases such as pneumonia. Under no circumstances should it be left to an amateur to decide whether and how much monkshood should be given; this is something for a qualified doctor.

- **Description:** Height to 5 ft (1.5 m); leaves in five to seven sections, dark green, upright stalks, few branches, helmet-shaped flowers, mauve in tight bunch, stalk of honey leaves arched; pods with winged seeds, thickened rhizome, perennial
- **Flowering:** June to August
- **Scent and flavour:** No smell; taste initially tart, scratchy, then sharp
- **Location:** Alpine meadows, fields, mountain forests to 9,850 ft (3,000 m), gardens
- **Distribution:** Scattered
- **Drug:** Tubera Aconiti
- **Constituents:** Alkaloids (aconitine), flavon-glucosides, protoanemonine
- **Treatments:** Treatment of nerve pain (neuralgia, sciatica), arthritis, rheumatic complaints, fever, pericarditis
- **Uses:** Ready-to-use products, arrow poison
- **Homeopathic uses:** See above, and for pneumonia, headaches, fear and panic

Beautiful but deadly: monkshood.

- **What and when to gather:** Rhizome August and September
- **Lookalikes:** No flowering plants, root with edible turnips
- **Other information:** Just a small amount can be fatal for a person, and even simple contact can cause the first signs of poisoning. Use carefully with children! Only to be taken on medical advice

Adonis vernalis L.
SUMMER ADONIS

■ *toxic, protected* ■

Yellow Pheasant's Eye, Spring Pheasant's Eye, False Hellebore

In Greek mythology, the beautiful Adonis was Aphrodite's lover. A jealous love rival – sources name the gods Hephaistos, Ares or Apollo – changed into a wild boar and killed Adonis. A beautiful flower grew where Aphrodite's tears fell – although presumably it was the red-orange summer adonis (*A. aestivalis*) rather than the spring variety.

Unlike with many other healing plants, it is the haulm of the plant that contains the useful constituents rather than the roots. They are glycosides, which expand the coronary vessels, strengthen a weak heart, and also have a calming effect. The spring adonis is now quite rare in the wild in central and southern Europe and is a protected species in some areas.

- **Description:** Height to 1 ft 8 in. (50 cm); one to three leaves, pinnate, with narrow straight tips; stalk upright; flowers yellow, shiny, 1–2½ in. (3–7 cm) diameter, soft hairs on sepals, single; pod, bundled with hooked beak; rootstock black-brown, strong; perennial
- **Flowering:** April to June
- **Scent and flavour:** No smell
- **Location:** Meadows, sunny hills, pine forests, calciphile
- **Distribution:** Rare, cultivated
- **Drug:** Herba Adonidis vernalis

- **Constituents:** Glycosides (cardenolide), alkaloids (adonidoside, adonitoxine), proto-anemonine, flavon pigment
- **Treatments:** For coronary disease, cardiac insufficiency, epilepsy, rheumatism, pain
- **Uses:** Ready-to-use products, tinctures
- **Homeopathic uses:** Cardiac insufficiency
- **What and when to gather:** Flowering haulm April to June
- **Lookalikes:** Summer adonis (*Adonis aestivalis*): smaller flower, orange-red, straight beak, annual, less toxic, on fields
- **Other information:** Because it is toxic, the haulm must be dried and stored away from other drugs. Only to be used on prescription

The spring adonis is grown in rock gardens. Natural stocks are under strict protection.

Helleborus niger L.
HELLEBORE

■ *highly toxic, protected* ■
Christmas Rose, Snow Rose

It is almost the most wonderful sight to see during mild periods in winter and early spring: mountain meadows full of vast swathes of white- or pink-flowering plants, often right beside the melting snow fields, plants whose occurrence and behaviour seem to contradict all the laws of nature. The hellebore has been known as a healing and toxic plant since antiquity, and is considered 'the most famous medicament in the Greek Materia medica' (Christian Rätsch).

Products obtained from plant roots may only be used for cardiac treatments under medical supervision. Nor is their use in the treatment of specific mental and emotional diseases, as recommended by Hildegard of Bingen and now once more recommended by homeopathy, a matter for medical amateurs. Like the lily-of-the-valley (see page 177), the hellebore is also an ingredient in 'Schneegerber Snuff'.

- **Description:** Height to 1 ft 4 in. (40 cm); evergreen rosette plant; leaves with long stalks, hand-shaped with seven to nine segments, leathery, dark green, glossy; flowers white to pink, five petals, numerous yellow-green honey leaves; bladder fruits, seeds with oil bodies (elaiosomes); rhizome; perennial
- **Flowering:** December to March
- **Scent and flavour:** Pleasant smell
- **Location:** Light mountain forests, gardens, calciphile
- **Distribution:** Rare, cultivated
- **Drug:** Rhizoma Hellebori nigri
- **Constituents:** Alkaloids (Helleborine), proto-anemonine, saponin
- **Treatments:** For strengthening the heart, treating skin abscesses
- **Uses:** Ready-to-use products, sneezing powder
- **Homeopathic uses:** For epilepsy, meningitis, psychoses, severe headaches
- **What and when to gather:** Rhizome
- **Lookalikes:** Stinking hellebore (*H. foetidus*): flowers green, smell unpleasant, stalks with leaves; green hellebore (*H. viridis*): no leaves on stalk, flowers green
- **Other information:** Used in the production of snuff; only to be used as a substitute for digitalis under medical supervision

'He was perfumed like a milliner,
And 'twixt his finger and his thumb he held
A pouncet-box, which ever and anon
He gave his nose, and took't away again;
Who therewith angry, when it next came there,
Took it in snuff; and still he smiled and talked.
And as the soldiers bore dead bodies by,
He called them untaught knaves, unmannerly,
To bring a slovenly unhandsome corse
Betwixt the wind and his nobility.'

William Shakespeare, King Henry IV, Part 1

Flowering Christmas roses against a backdrop of flowering winter heath.

Nigella sativa L.
BLACK CUMIN

Black cumin came originally from the Mediterranean and western Asia, and although found cultivated in spice and herb gardens only in central Europe, it has been present here since the Middle Ages. The peppery black seeds are especially popular in spreads and flavoured soft cheeses, but they are also used in folklore – including as a treatment for high blood pressure and digestive problems, and for problems involving the urogenital tract. According to Schauenberg and Paris, the antispasmodic properties of the constituent Nigellon help to treat whooping cough and bronchitis.

It is related to Damascene (or Turkish) black cumin (*N. damascena*), which is used in the production of a blood-pressure-lowering medication. However, this popular garden plant with the rather unusual flowers is best known as 'love-in-a-mist'.

- **Description:** Height to 1 ft (30 cm); alternating leaves, two- to three-fold, finely pinnate; hairy stalk, branched; perianthal scales light blue, green veined, honey leaves cup-shaped; folliculus rough, glandular; annual
- **Flowering:** May to July
- **Scent and flavour:** Aromatic smell; fruity, peppery taste
- **Location:** Gardens, wild
- **Distribution:** Native to southern Europe, cultivated
- **Drug:** Semen Nigellae sativae
- **Constituents:** Essential oils, saponin, alkaloids (nigellidine, damascenine), protoanemonine, fatty oil
- **Treatments:** For high blood pressure, fever, digestive problems, gall bladder, kidney, and bladder complaints, worms
- **Uses:** Spice, perfume
- **Homeopathic uses:** Stomach problems, yellow fever, liver complaints
- **What and when to gather:** Seeds August and September
- **Lookalikes:** Damascene black cumin: flower white to light blue, surrounded by a slit, fine-leafed green long leaf, used in bread dough, usually as a topping

Above: Genuine black cumin with the typical seed capsule.

Above right: Love-in-a-mist or Nigella: Damascene black cumin.

Paeonia officinalis (L.) emend. Willd.
COMMON PEONY

■ *toxic* ■

The peony grows wild in the southern Alps.

The famous *Hortus Eystettensis*, a magnificently illustrated botanical work dating back to 1713, calls it 'the biggest flesh-coloured rose': the plant that we also know as the Whitsun rose because it opens its large red or white flowers in May/June – that is to say, around Pentecost, or Whitsun. All it has in common with the 'other' rose (see page 244) is the name and a certain superficial similarity – and its old German name of *Gichtrose* ('gout rose') most certainly does not mean that the peony is only used as a treatment for gout in today's sense. The term 'gout' in the past covered a far greater range of diseases, including and especially those with inexplicable, frightening or sudden symptoms such as epilepsy, generally believed to be caused by demons. Until well into the 19th century, people tried to treat these (and many

other) complaints with extracts of peony. Today, the peony is used with far more restraint because of its toxicity, and in homeopathy usually only for abscesses and haemorrhoids. Under no circumstances should pregnant women have anything to do with products made from the peony.

- **Description:** Height to 3 ft 3 in. (1 m); leaves stalked at the base, double tri-pinnated, not stalked on the branch-like trunk; petals up to 3 in. (8 cm) long, spiralled, white, pink, red, very high pollen production; folliculus covered in felty hairs, seeds black, glossy; stronger, yellow-red rootstock with tubers; perennial
- **Flowering:** May, June
- **Scent and flavour:** Flowers scented, root smells unpleasant; slightly sweet taste, then bitter, sharp
- **Location:** Mountain forests, gardens, parks
- **Distribution:** Southern Europe, cultivated
- **Drug:** Flores, Semen, Radix Paeoniae
- **Constituents:** Glycosides (anthocyane), alkaloids, essential oils, sugar, resins, tannins
- **Treatments:** Formerly: for treating diseases of the skin and mucous membranes, haemorrhoids, varicose veins, rheumatic complaints, gout, digestive problems, epilepsy, allergic diseases, menstrual problems
- **Uses:** Filling for aromatic pillows
- **Homeopathic uses:** Against abscesses, gastrointestinal diseases, haemorrhoids
- **What and when to gather:** Side shoots March and April, petals May and June
- **Lookalikes:** None

Pulsatilla vulgaris
COMMON PASQUE FLOWER

■ *toxic, protected* ■

*Pulsatilla, Wind Flower, Meadow Anemone,
Passe Flower, Easter Flower*

The pasque flower plays an important role in homeopathy, where it is more generally known as pulsatilla. *P. pratensis* is prescribed as a 'constitutional treatment' for people who are extremely emotional ('high as a kite – depths of despond'), who are afraid of many things (being alone, darkness), who suffer from self-doubt and indecisiveness, who submit to 'religious melancholy' and whose 'emotions are like an April day' (after W. Boericke).

All pulsatilla varieties are protected and extracts may only be made from cultivated plants.

■ **Description:** Height to 1 ft (30 cm); rosette plant; base leaves with silky hairs, bi- and tri-pinnate, appearing after flowering; young shoots have dense hairs; stalks elongated when fruiting; flowers upright, bell shaped, mauve, untidy hairs on outside, with a wreath of deeply incised top leaves, countless nutlets with a feather-like stalk; deep-rooting, dark brown, thick, branched rhizome; perennial
■ **Flowering:** March to May
■ **Scent and flavour:** No smell; bitingly sharp taste
■ **Location:** Thin grass, pine forests, gardens; this herb likes chalk and warmth
■ **Distribution:** Cultivated
■ **Drug:** Herba Pulsatillae
■ **Constituents:** Saponin, tannins, proto-anemonine, anemonol
■ **Treatment:** Formerly: for gout, pain, cramps, inflammatory skin diseases
■ **Uses:** Compresses
■ **Homeopathic uses:** Important constitutional treatment and for cramps, neuralgias, rheumatism, skin diseases, menstrual problems
■ **What and when to gather:** Whole plant March to May
■ **Lookalikes:** Alpine pulsatilla (*P. alpina*): flowers white or yellow
■ **Other information:** It soon loses its efficacy when dry; highly toxic when fresh. Only to be used under medical supervision

Below: Pulsatilla flowers in March. The long hairs on buds, flowers and stalks offer protection against the cold.

Below right: The slightly odd-looking fruits of the pulsatilla.

Rosidae

ROSIDS

The **Rosids** not only boast a tremendous variety of flower shapes and habits, but also are more important economically than any other. As well as the umbellifer (Apiaceae) and pea families (Fabaceae), the group also includes many important vegetable and spice plants and, under the eponymous order of the rose family (Rosaceae), many fruit varieties.

Whitethorn flowers are not only pretty to look at, but also they are used to make a highly effective tea for the cardiovascular system.

Umbellifer family
Apiaceae (Umbelliferae)

The umbellifer family includes more than fifty genera in central Europe. They are usually herbaceous plants with pinnate, hand-shaped or lobate leaves that are almost always alternating, and often encircle the smooth, angular or grooved stalk with a bulbous sheath. Sometimes the stalk can be bristly, to a greater or lesser degree, and the base may be red. The small, white, red, yellow or green-tinged leaves grow out of semi-circular or circular umbels.

The numerous, tiny, round-to-oval seeds (nutlets), some elongated, some with wings, develop in the two-part ovary and are released when the schizocarp fruit disintegrates. The aromatic, spicy smell and taste of the leaves and roots are typical.

Flowering ground elder in a garden. If intended for consumption, it should be picked before flowering.

The leaves of the ground elder are similar to those of the European black elderberry (see page 111 f.).

Aegopodium podagria L.
GROUND ELDER

Goutweed, Bishop's Weed, Herb Gerard, Snow-in-the-Mountain

Ground elder – who has not seen it, this most tiresome of 'weeds'? Ground elder grows in almost every garden, in shady, moist spots under bushes and trees, and often, to the gardener's disgust, even finds its way into flowerbeds. It is easily recognizable by its long, white rhizomes, which – much to the horror of the gardener – break off easily and thus – much to the delight of the cook – are not eradicable. The plant is rich in vitamin C and, in Roman times, was used to fortify Roman soldiers; in the Middle Ages it was one of the most important vegetable plants. It is unbelievably versatile, and no one who truly knows it would dream of calling it a 'weed'.

Combined with nettles and other wild herbs, cooked like spinach with a little butter (or crème fraîche for fewer calories), even children will enjoy ground elder. Its aromatic, spicy flavour also makes it an ideal seasoning for meat and vegetable dishes or herb soups.

- **Description:** Height 1–3 ft 3 in. (30–100 cm), leaves bi- and tri-pinnate, long stem, often tinged with red at the base, individual leaves oval and pointed, partly asymmetric; stalk hollow, grooved, roots white, long, easy to break; flowers small, white, in a flat umbel made up of numerous flowers.
- **Flowering:** May to July
- **Scent and flavour:** Aromatic, spicy, similar to carrots or parsley
- **Location:** Nutritious, loose loam or clay soils, forest edges under hedgerows, in gardens and parks, river banks, in light mountain forests to over 5,900 ft (1,800 m)
- **Distribution:** Very common, in dense stocks with lots of individual types, ground cover
- **Drug:** Herba Aegopodii podagria
- **Constituents:** Essential oils with as yet undefined constituents, flavonolglycosides, phenol carboxylic acids, ascorbic acid, cumarin, bitter constituents

- **Treatments:** For loss of appetite, purifying the blood, gout, rheumatism, sciatica (kidney and bladder complaints)
- **Uses:** Tea, compresses (for pain), baths (for haemorrhoids), salad, soup, spinach, seasoning, herb punch
- **Homeopathic uses:** For rheumatism, gout, and sciatica
- **What and when to gather:** Slightly under-developed leaves for salads, herb soup March to May, leaves with stalks for tea, compresses, baths, spinach, herb punch, etc. March to September
- **Lookalikes:** Young elder plants (*Sambucus nigra*) have a round stem that often turns woody at the bottom; other umbellifers have differently shaped leaves and grow singly

Angelica archangelica L.
TRUE ANGELICA

Holy Ghost, Wild Parsnip, Wild Celery, Norwegian Angelica

It has long been known that angelica roots stimulate the digestion and the appetite, provide relief from feelings of fullness after a large meal – and taste good too.

True angelica is widespread in plain tracts; wild angelica (*A. sylvestris*) prefers damp, nutritious loam or clay soils that are rich in humus, and grows on wet meadows, along roadsides and river banks, and in alluvial and bog forests. According to legend, it was an archangel (*archangelus*) who first showed mankind how to use angelica. The constituents and uses of true and wild angelica are similar.

- **Description:** Angelica: height 1 ft 8 in.–6 ft 6 in. (0.5–2 m); leaves bi- or tri-pinnate, small leaves oval with spiky tip; bulbous leaf sheath; stalk round, slightly grooved, hollow, often blue-tinged; flowers green-tinged, in large, spherical bundled umbels; seeds have thick grooves; roots 1–3 in. (3–8 cm) thick
- **Flowering:** July to August

- **Scent and flavour:** Aromatic, spicy; roots slightly sweet but also sharp and bitter
- **Location:** Wet, nutritious, sandy clay soils on the banks of major rivers
- **Distribution:** Scattered, occasionally wild
- **Drug:** Folium, Fructus, Semen Angelicae, Radix, Oleum Angelicae fructus
- **Constituents:** Essential oils, resin (pines), furanocumarin (angelicin), cumarin, etc.
- **Treatments:** Leaves for poor digestion, pleurisy; seeds for kidney and rheumatic complaints; roots for loss of appetite, bloating, digestive problems
- **Uses:** Tea, vegetables, candied stems for digestion, liqueur, cosmetics industry as a perfume, mouth wash, compress made of leaves for pleurisy
- **Homeopathic uses:** See above
- **What and when to gather:** Leaves May to July, stalks, seeds from June to July; root of the biennial plant April to May and September to October
- **Lookalikes:** Wild angelica: smaller and slimmer; leaf stalks grooved on top, flowers reddish white, umbel stem with loose hair; thin root; often other umbellifers
- **Other information:** The furanocumarin in the sap may cause an inflammation of the skin if exposed to light, so avoid spending long periods in the sun or in a solarium during treatment. Use with care during pregnancy.

Top: Angelica rootstock.

Above: Wild angelica is smaller than true angelica, but is far more widespread.

Left: Bulbous inflorescence of true angelica.

Carum carvi L.
CARAWAY

True Caraway, Cumin

Umbellifers – well, it's one of those things: even experienced nature-lovers prefer to give them a wide berth – and with good reason. Some varieties can only be reliably defined by the ripe seeds as well as the flower. Carelessness can, in extreme cases, be just as fatal as when mushrooming, because the umbellate poison hemlock (*Conium maculatum*) is deadly. So those who appreciate caraway for its aromatic seeds – and what would a herb salad or sauerkraut be without this spicy little pod, which also helps to prevent bloating? – would do better to acquire their supplies from a shop rather than pick their own. Caraway is also used to make schnapps.

- **Description:** Height to 3 ft 3 in. (1 m), leaves bi- and tri-pinnate with very fine pointed single pinnates, important characteristic: lower leaf pair with the bulbous stem base close to stalks; stalk round, hollow, grooved, little branches at the base; flower small, white or red-tinged, in bundled umbels with eight to fifteen rays of different lengths, spathes either absent or tiny; seed green-tinged, 1/10 in. (2–3 mm) long and wide, blunt five-ribbed, turns brown when dried; root white, flesh thickened like carrot; biennial, flowers and fruits in second year
- **Flowering:** May to June
- **Scent and flavour:** Intensive caraway smell and taste
- **Location:** Nutritious loam or clay soils, rich in humus, fields and meadows
- **Distribution:** Scattered, often in fields, meadows, roadsides, Alps to 5,900 ft (1,800 m)
- **Drug:** Fructus, Oleum Carvi
- **Constituents:** Essential oil (carvone, carveole, limonene), cumarin, also sugar and starch in the root
- **Treatments:** For stimulating the digestion, relief from bloating, feelings of fullness, nervous heart and stomach problems, digestive problems in babies, encouraging lactation
- **Uses:** Tea, spice (bread, cabbage, potatoes), liqueur, schnapps
- **Homeopathic uses:** See above
- **What and when to gather:** Fruits mid-June to end of July, root April to May
- **Lookalikes:** Other umbellifers: expanded leaf sheath without stipule-like paired pinnas, different smell and taste
- **Other information:** Caraway oil may cause liver damage if used inappropriately

Coriandrum sativum L.
CORIANDER

Chinese parsley, Cilantro

Coriander is mentioned in the Bible. Exodus speaks thus of the godly manna that fell from the sky and saved the children of Israel from starving: 'It was white like coriander seed, and its taste was like that of flat cakes made with honey...' The Bible is not a book of herbs, so it is appropriate to point out here that coriander seeds are usually grey to a light golden brown. Coriander has been much appreciated as a herb, especially for bread, vegetables and liqueurs, since ancient times. When farmers still baked their own bread there was much more of it in their gardens than today. It is most likely to be found in traditional monastery gardens. Garden escapees are usually only likely to do well for a long time in areas with the right climate. Coriander loves the warmth of the Mediterranean, where it is one of the main spices. It has never thrived in the wild north of the Alps.

- **Description:** Height 1 ft–2 ft 8 in. (30–80 cm); leaves bi- and tri-pinnate or three-part with straight tips, the unsplit basal leaves die early; stalk round, striped, branches at the top; flowers white or red-tinged, long stalked umbels, outer flowers approx. ¼ in. (7 mm), inner approx. ⅛ in. (3 mm) diameter, seeds spherical to oval, hard, straw-coloured to brown, ⅛–⅕ in. (3–5 mm) diameter; spindle-shaped root, annual
- **Flowering:** June, July
- **Scent and flavour:** Unpleasant smell to the flowering plant, ripe fruits smell pleasantly spicy; taste sweet-sharp
- **Location:** Calciferous soils
- **Distribution:** All over the world, especially around the Mediterranean, often cultivated, cottage gardens
- **Drug:** Fructus, Oleum Coriandri
- **Constituents:** Essential oils, cumarin, triterpene alcohol (coriandrinondiol)
- **Treatments:** Stimulating, inebriating (aphrodisiac), antiseptic, soothes bloating, feelings of fullness, relief for mild cramp-like gastrointestinal problems; oil helps with neuralgia and joint pain
- **Uses:** Essence, spice (bread, meat dishes); cosmetics industry for perfume production, liqueur, schnapps
- **What and when to gather:** Fruits, August to September
- **Lookalikes:** Other umbellifers
- **Other information:** Fresh green parts of the plant may be indigestible

Far left: Flowering coriander in the garden.

Left: The spherical ripe seeds of coriander.

Eryngium campestre L.
FIELD ERYNGO

Eryngo, Sea Holly

Right: Inflorescence of field eryngo, which looks a lot like a thistle.

Below: Sea thistle grows on beaches, but is not a true thistle.

Botany has a special vocabulary with which to describe the many parts of a plant, the peculiarities of their growth and their reproduction, that is not always easy for beginners and amateurs to understand. The terms are easiest to remember with the aid of examples. For instance, 'anemochoric' dispersion is when parts of the plant, especially the seed heads, break free once mature and are scattered by the wind (from the Greek: *ánemos* meaning wind). Many plants are dispersed anemochorically, especially in dry treeless areas with no obstacles for storms or wind, including the field eryngo. 'Tumbleweed' is another, highly appropriate name for it.

Although field eryngo is as prickly as a thistle, and although it and its relatives are called 'thistles' – e.g. maritium, the marine thistle or sea holly – it is an Umbellifer rather than an Asteracea. Mushroom-gatherers in southern and western Europe would do well to search for the tasty king oyster mushroom (*Pleurotus eryngii*) among swathes of field eryngo and sea holly, as it parasitizes the roots of eryngo varieties.

- **Description:** Height to approx. 2 ft (60 cm); leaves long-stalked, coarse, thorny with teeth or sawn, deep spiny, to 8 in. (20 cm) long, white-green with a distinct white-tinged network of veins; stalk thick, flat grooved, light green to almost white, sparse branches and leaves; flowers small, white-tinged, in countless spherical heads, protected by three to eight spiny, long-pointed spathes, sepals spiny, twice as long as the petals
- **Flowering:** July to September
- **Scent and flavour:** Taste initially sweet, then sharp and bitter
- **Location:** On calciferous and humus-rich loam or loess soils, sunny positions, roadsides, chalk-poor lawns
- **Distribution:** Very rare
- **Drug:** Herba (leaves and flowers), Radix Eryngii
- **Constituents:** essential oils, saponine, chlorogenic acid, rosmarinic acid
- **Treatments:** For urinary and bladder complaints, prostate inflammation, bronchial catarrh, root also for skin diseases and regulating milk flow (when weaning)
- **Uses:** Tea, young shoots in salad, vegetables
- **What and when to gather:** Leaves July to August, root spring to summer
- **Lookalikes:** Various thistles (see page 62f.)
- **Other information:** Although sea holly is edible, it is protected, and is found on sandy beaches throughout Europe; the flat-leafed sea holly (*E. planum*) grows from East Germany and south-east Europe as far as the Urals; the root is said to help treat whooping cough.

Foeniculum vulgare Mill.
FENNEL

Fennel has been known as a vegetable, spice, and healing plant since antiquity. Hildegard of Bingen even recommended it as a treatment for melancholia. Its home is the Mediterranean, which is where it is still mainly grown today. It does not occur in the world north of the Alps, where it became known in monastery gardens of the Middle Ages. Fennel tea soothes unsettled stomachs and is even recommended for babies. Fennel honey is also extremely popular and top quality gourmet restaurants occasionally also have fennel pollen on the menu. The exclusive 'spice of angels' is used e.g. in fish dishes and its few producers measure it out in grammes.

- **Description:** Height to 6 ft 6 in. (2 m); stalked, glossy, blue-green, thread-like leaves, leaf sheath very fleshy on the woody base of the stalk, usually 1¼–2½ in. (3–6 cm) long; stalk finely striped, smooth, glossy, branched; tiny yellow flowers in large umbels; seeds dark grey, long ovals, striped, not winged, smooth
- **Flowering:** June to August
- **Scent and flavour:** Aromatic smell; taste strong and spicy, slightly bitter

- **Location:** Mediterranean
- **Distribution:** Cultivated, wild
- **Drug:** Fructus, Oleum Foeniculi
- **Constituents:** Composition varies according to type: essential oils (anethole, fenchone, estragole), limonene, camphene
- **Treatments:** For cramp-like gastrointestinal problems, feelings of fullness, bloating, catarrh of the upper respiratory tracts, traditionally also for eye eczema, conjunctivitis
- **Uses:** Tea, honey, spice, vegetables (own fennel variety), sweets, liqueur, toothpaste, baked goods, bread, cheese, sausages
- **Homeopathic uses:** See above
- **What and when to gather:** Young leaves, roots (annual), seeds September to October
- **Lookalikes:** Dill (*Anethum graveolens*): leaf sheaths max. 1 in. (2 cm) long, seeds lentil-shaped, winged, annual: water fennel (*Oenanthe aquatica*): marsh plant on shallow, still and flowing waters; flowers white, green-brown; stronger effect than fennel, respiratory diseases, digestive complaints
- **Other information:** maximum daily dose approx. ¼ oz (7.5 g)

Far left: Fennel, a yellow-flowering member of the Umbellifer family.

Left: Fennel seeds.

Heracleum sphondylium L.
HOGWEED

Cow Parsnip

Hogweed is one of the most common edible wild herbs in central Europe. It likes soils that are rich in nitrate, which means it will thrive on intensively farmed land. It is extremely versatile in the kitchen and is ideal in pasta dishes (e.g. lasagna), gratins and as a filling for crêpes. The young shoots are the best; older ones should be peeled like rhubarb.

The giant hogweed (*H. mantegassianum*), an immigrant from the Caucasus that has made itself very much at home in ruderal points, gardens, parks and along paths, is to be treated with care. Shoots that take root near schools should be removed as the sap will cause severe burning if it comes into contact with the skin and the skin is then exposed to the sun; seek medical treatment in such instances. This also applies, to a lesser extent, to the common hogweed and many other umbellifers that contain furanocumarin.

- **Description:** Height to 6 ft (1.8 m); dense plant with long, soft gland hairs, very large (to 1 ft 8 in./50 cm) pinnated leaves with lobate, coarsely toothed single pinnates (like a bear's paws); fleshy leaf stalks, base red-mauve, bulbous leaf sheath; strong stalks, angular, hollow, with nodules; small white, rarely green-white flowers in large, shallow double umbels, edge flowers asymmetric; seeds to 1/3 in. (8 mm) long, flat, broad-ovular, winged; biperennial to perennial
- **Flowering:** June to September
- **Scent and flavour:** Highly aromatic, not necessarily pleasant; very spicy taste, quite sweet
- **Location:** Humus, nitrogen-rich moist soils, intensively farmed land, roadsides, light woods and forests, fields of tall forbs
- **Distribution:** Very common, to approx. 8,200 ft (2,500 m)
- **Drug:** Herba, Radix Heraclei
- **Constituents:** Essential oils, furanocumarin, bitter principles, sugar
- **Treatments:** Powdered root for digestive problems, decoction for dysentery, nervous problems, epilepsy
- **Uses:** Powder, tea, vegetable
- **Homeopathic uses:** Digestive and skin problems
- **What and when to gather:** Young leaves and leaf stalks from April to October
- **Lookalikes:** Giant hogweed: height to 10 ft (3 m), introduced as a decorative plant, growing wild; few hairs, leaves to 10 ft (3 m) long, stalks often have dark red stains
- **Other information:** Rabbit food – although allergy-sufferers should take care when picking it because the sap of all heracleum varieties may cause burns if affected skin is then exposed to the sun (known as grass or meadow dermatitis) due to the presence of furanocumarin. So those taking it as part of a phytotherapeutic treatment should avoid spending long periods in the sun or solarium. Use with care during pregnancy

Flowering common hogweed.

Left: Lovage is easy to recognize by its typical broadly lobated leaves.

Right: Broad-leafed sermountain has similar leaves but white flowers.

Levisticum officinale Koch
LOVAGE

Garden Lovage

Lovage is one of the best known and most popular herbs. Although it is a firm fixture in herb gardens everywhere, it rarely grows wild. The name of the plant, which grows to a height of 6 ft 6 in. (2 m), comes from the Latin word *Levisticum*, which in turn is derived from *Liguricum*: it is believed that lovage originally arrived in middle European monastery gardens from Liguria; its true home is believed to be in the Orient.

It was not until the English name 'lovage', and its association with the word 'love', had developed that people began to speculate about its possible uses as an aphrodisiac – an excellent example of the strange ways an old wives' tale can arise. The belief that lovage roots could be used to identify witches goes back even further.

- **Description:** Height to 6 ft 6 in. (2 m); shiny green, smooth, firm, large leaves bi- to tri-pinnate, bushy; thick hollow stalks, small flowers, pale yellow in dense eight- to twenty-headed umbels, with numerous spathes; yellow-brown seeds, five-ribbed; short fleshy rust-coloured rootstock; perennial
- **Flowering:** July to August
- **Scent and flavour:** Spicy smell reminiscent of celery; taste strong and spicy
- **Location:** Humus-rich moist soils
- **Distribution:** Southern Europe, cultivated, often growing wild
- **Drug:** Herba, Fructus, Semen, Radix Levistici
- **Constituents:** Essential oils, furanocumarin, bitter principles, sugar, resin
- **Treatments:** For bloating, digestive and menstrual problems, bronchial catarrh (mucolytic)
- **Homeopathic uses:** See above
- **Uses:** Spice, salad made from cooked roots, liqueur, root decoction added to baths to help with excessive sweating
- **What and when to gather:** Plant end of May, beginning of July, end of August to end of September, roots spring, October
- **Lookalikes:** Broad-leaved sermountain (*Laserpitium latifolium*): hairy rootstock; other umbellifers
- **Other information:** Causes nausea and dizziness if used constantly

Baldmoney is easily recognized by its strongly scented, finely pinnate leaves.

Meum athamanticum Jacq.
BALDMONEY

Mew, Bearwort, Spignel

Baldmoney avoids chalky soils and prefers elevated positions. Compared with other umbellifers, it is quite low-growing; its strongly pinnated, dill-like leaves smell strong and spicy when crushed, which some noses do not perceive as pleasant. Schnapps made of baldmoney really 'cleanses the stomach', even if its flavour does not appeal to everyone. The plant is used in soups and herbed soft cheeses. Overall, this herb is nowhere near as familiar as it was when it was still a highly regarded healing plant. Hildegard of Bingen, for instance,

recommended it as a treatment for gout and yellow fever.

- **Description:** Height to 2 ft (60 cm); leaves finely pinnated like dill (¼–¼ in./2–7 mm long), dark yellow green, smooth, usually basal; stalks finely grooved, hollow; flowers white or yellow-white, outer flowers often wine-red to red-mauve, six to fifteen umbels; seeds approx. ¼ in. (7 mm) long, ⅛ in. (3.5 mm) thick, angular ribs; strong rootstock with thick, fibrous fronds of dead leaf matter
- **Flowering:** May to August
- **Scent and flavour:** Smell strong and spicy; taste very bitter
- **Location:** Chalk and nitrate-poor, humus, stony-loose loam soil, mountain meadows to 7,200 ft (2,200 m)
- **Distribution:** Western and central Europe, quite rare
- **Drug:** Radix Mei athamantici, Radix Foeniculi ursini
- **Constituents:** Essential oils, caffeic acid derivatives
- **Uses:** Digestive problems, weak stomach, menstrual problems
- **Uses:** Herb schnapps, liqueur, tincture
- **Homeopathic uses:** See above
- **What and when to gather:** Root September and October
- **Lookalikes:** No other umbellifer in the mountains has such an intensively spicy flavour or the dill-like pinnated leaves

Pastinaca sativa L. ssp. *sativa*
PARSNIP

Harts-eye, Madnip, Yellow Parsnip

Among umbellifers, which are so difficult to define, there are only a few flowering varieties. One of the few is the parsnip, widespread along sunny paths and in meadows, railway embankments and dry inclines. The parsnip, long known as a healing plant and vegetable, likes a certain amount of lime in the soil and, more recently, its popularity has been boosted in line with the 'organic wave'. Its roots, believed in folk medicine to be antipyretic, can be used like parsley roots. But use with caution – it must be avoided by people with kidney disease, especially dialysis patients. In fact, its potassium content is so high that it could prove fatal to them.

- **Description:** Height to 3 ft 3 in. (1 m); leaves one to two pinnates (two to seven pairs side pinnates), small leaves notched, seated; stalk edgy, grooved or ribbed, with hairs, branched at the top; flowers small, yellow, five- to twenty-spray composite umbels, spathes usually lacking; fruit approx. ⅙ x ⅙ in. (6 x 5 mm), oval, winged; root of ssp. *sativa* fleshy, of ssp. *pratensis* thin and woody
- **Flowering:** July to September
- **Scent and flavour:** Very spicy, sweet, similar to carrot
- **Location:** Loose chalky, nutrient-rich soils, along paths, meadows, dry slopes, cultivated
- **Distribution:** Europe, Asia Minor, scattered
- **Drug:** Herba, Fructus, Semen Pastinacae, Radix Pastinaci
- **Constituents:** Essential oils, cumarin, furanocumarin; root protein, starch, pectin, sugar
- **Treatments:** For blood cleansing, diuretic (dropsy, swollen legs), poor digestion, bloating; root for reducing temperature, lung and stomach problems
- **Uses:** Tea, plant as vegetable, spice, umbels can be stuffed, root vegetable, wine
- **Homeopathic uses:** For delirium
- **What and when to gather:** Young leaves and shoots April to June, umbels July to September, roots autumn
- **Lookalikes:** Hemlock-water dropwort (*Oenanthe crocata*): flowers with spathes, seeds without wings, close to water, poison hemlock (*conium maculatum*): secund spathes, base of stalk with reddish spots, smooth, blue-tinged hoops; unpleasant smell; hedges, fences, walls, toxic
- **Other information:** The root of the wild parsnip can only be used when young and

freshly scraped; because of the furanocumarin levels, the sap may cause inflammation of the skin if it is exposed to light

The yellow-flowering parsnip likes to grow besides roads and paths.

Petroselinum crispum (Mill.) A.W. Hill
CURLY PARSLEY

Parsley used to be held in high esteem as a general tonic and particularly for boosting virility; however, it was also used to induce miscarriage, and the number of women who failed to survive was high. Pregnant women and people with kidney disease should avoid parsley and parsley products (such as oils). Bisset and Wichtl generally advise against the use of parsley products for therapeutic purposes because of the numerous side effects of the constituent apiole.

Curly parsley is highly decorative and very tasty.

- **Description:** Height to 2 ft (60 cm); leaves two- to three-fold tri-pinnate, dark green, matt, edge often curly; stalk angular, grooved, smooth, branched; flowers greeny-yellow to creamy white, long stalks, composite umbel, no sheath, spathes present; seeds not winged; root turnip-shaped; *P. sativum* and *P. hortense ssp. Tuberosum*; biennial
- **Flowering:** June to September
- **Scent and flavour:** Intensive spicy parsley smell and taste
- **Location:** Nutrient-rich humus, loamy or clay soil
- **Distribution:** All over the world, originally presumably Mediterranean, cultivated
- **Drug:** Herba, Oleum, Fructus, Radix Petroselini
- **Constituents:** Essential oils, apiole, flavonoids, vitamins (C, A), carotinoids, chlorophyll, furanocumarin, terpene, seeds: fatty oil, petroselinic acid
- **Treatments:** Diuretic, helping with digestive, bladder, and kidney problems, irritable bladder; root: bloating, menstrual problems
- **Uses:** vegetable, spice, food industry, oil
- **Homeopathic uses:** See above
- **What and when to gather:** Plant February to October; root September and October; seeds August and September
- **Lookalikes:** Dog parsley (*Aethusa cynapium*): underside of leaf shiny, unpleasant smell when rubbed, flowers white, stalk often with wine-red streaks, toxic
- **Other information:** People with an allergy to parsley or apiole should proceed with caution; not to be used in cases of kidney infection; take care if pregnant; oil only to be used in accordance with instructions. If in doubt, seek medical advice

Peucedanum officinale L.
HOG'S FENNEL

■ *protected, toxic* ■

Sow Fennel, Marsh Parsley, Sulphur Wort

Hog's fennel differs from other fennel or wort varieties in that it has slender grass-like leaves. Varieties include mountain parsley *P. oreoselinum*, masterwort, and the parsnip *P. sativum* (pages 206 f.). As its name implies, mountain parsley is a mountain plant that is also occasionally found in lowlands, whereas masterwort *Imperatoria ostruthium* prefers levels above 3,300 ft (1,000 m). The seeds of the *Peucedanum* varieties are lentil shaped with winged edges.

The Latin name *officinalis* or *officinale* (meaning 'of the apothecary') usually indicates that the plant is used in naturopathy. However, hog's fennel is not really collected today any more. Masterwort, by contrast, is still cultivated in places, and especially in Hildegard of Bingen's gardens. The 'patron saint of herbs' from the Rhineland valued it particularly as an antipyretic, and in fact in earlier centuries it was one of the most important healing plants. Some people even ascribed magical powers to it, and believed it offered protection against the plague.

- **Description:** Height to 4 ft (1.2 m); leaves long stalked, grass-like, coarse edges, finely pinnated in threes, cut, pinnates to 3½ in. (9 cm) long; stalks upright, hard, few branches; flowers yellow, buds often hang limp; perennial
- **Flowering:** July, August
- **Scent and flavour:** Intensely spicy, aromatic
- **Location:** Loamy, clay, chalky soils, dry bushes, forest edges
- **Distribution:** rare
- **Drug:** Radix Peucedani officinale, Radix Ostruthii, Radix Oreoselini, Herba Oreoselini
- **Constituents:** Essential oils, cumarin derivatives (e.g. peucedanine), masterwort: imperatorine

- **Treatments:** For catarrh, ague, gout, rheumatism
- **Uses:** Tea, powdered root, bitters
- **Homeopathic uses:** See above
- **What and when to gather:** Roots in autumn
- **Lookalikes:** Hog's fennel: glossy leaves and white flowers, dry meadows and forests; masterwort (emperor's wort): white or reddish flowers
- **Other information:** Masterwort is used as a substitute for angelica (*Angelica archangelica*) in bitters

Hog's fennel is rare and protected.

Above left: Anise seeds.

Above centre: The typical umbel flower of the greater burnet saxifrage.

Above right: Lesser burnet saxifrage: the leaf shape is similar to that of the sanguisorba (see page 248).

Pimpinella major (L.) Huds.
GREATER BURNET SAXIFRAGE

Lesser Burnet, Saxifrage

The greater burnet saxifrage, an umbellifer with unique, nettle-toothed leaves, grows all over the world on chalky soils in meadows and fields. As with the lesser burnet saxifrage (*P. saxifraga*), which prefers drier locations, it is much appreciated in herbal medicine for its high content of essential oils and saponines as a treatment for sore throats and hoarseness. Extracts are also used as bath additives.

The two burnets differ from their close relative the aniseed (*P. anisum*), which is used as a spice plant in the pharmaceuticals industry and for liqueur, and whose origins are still not clear today, in having smooth seeds and stalk tips. On the aniseed, the stalk grows out of a rosette of basal, unsplit leaves. The ripe seeds are distilled to make aniseed essence (*Oleum Anisi*). It also contains some toxins, the effects of which may well be reinforced by contact with the air or light. Pharmacies sell aniseed and aniseed oil, both of which are used in the treatment of bloating and stomach complaints, and to help with coughs and hoarseness (observe dosage).

In folklore, the burnets *Sanguisorba officinalis* and *S. minor* (see page 248), which also belong to the rose family, are often called pimpinelle, and are often sold under that name in plant nurseries and garden centres.

- **Description:** Height to 3 ft 3 in. (1 m); leaves single pinnates, pinnates oval, deep sawn, end leaves often triple lobated, dark green, glossy; stalks angular, hollow; flowers white in double umbels; root spiral-shaped, turns blue in air; perennial
- **Flowering:** June to October
- **Scent and flavour:** Smell strong and spicy; taste spicy at first, then bitingly sharp
- **Location:** Chalky soils, fields, meadows, roadsides, forest edges, to approx. 7,550 ft (2,300 m)
- **Distribution:** Common
- **Drug:** Herba, Radix Pimpinellae
- **Constituents:** Essential oils, cumarin (including furanocumarin, pimpinelline), lactones, saponines, tannin, resins
- **Treatments:** Throat infections, hoarseness (gargle), catarrh, bronchitis, poor digestion, diarrhoea, urinary diseases
- **Uses:** Tea, plant for salad, soup, sauce, herb butter, bath (pimpinelle root)
- **Homeopathic uses:** Temperature, spinal problems

- **What and when to gather:** Young leaves May; roots March to April and September to October
- **Lookalikes:** Lesser burnet saxifrage: leaves oval, deeply sawn; stalks round; great burnet: flowers long and oval, dark red; see page 248; small burnet: smaller, flowers spherical, green, later reddish; see page 248; aniseed: seeds and stalk tips hairy, cultivated in southern Europe
- **Other information:** Sap may cause skin inflammation in contact with light due to the presence of furanocumarin

---

Sanicula europaea L.
SANICLE

European Sanicle, Wood Sanicle

Pretty sanicle grows in shady deciduous forests. It is no longer of any particular value as a healing plant. However, those who study old books of herbs will be amazed to see that our ancestors believed sanicle to be some kind of universal panacea, using it to help wounds heal, treat ulcers and abscesses, and stem internal bleeding. Hildegard of Bingen held it in extremely high esteem. 'Its juice is pleasant and healthy, which is to say beneficial, and it is very good for the poorly stomach and poorly intestines.' According to Lonicerus, sanicle was the 'wound herb of the barber'.

- **Description:** Height to 1 ft 8 in. (50 cm); basal leaves long stalked, evergreen, three to five part, hand-shaped; stalks mostly without leaves, ribbed, smooth; flowers white, often reddish stained, in head-like umbels, sitting in a three- to five-ray bundled umbel, spathes distinct; seeds almost spherical, prickly; rootstock short, black-brown, fibrous; perennial
- **Flowering:** May to June
- **Scent and flavour:** Leaves without smell; bitter taste, astringent
- **Location:** Calciferous, fresh, humus-rich mixed and beech forests, to approx. 4,920 ft (1,500 m)

- **Distribution:** All over the world except Arctic regions and Australia, scattered
- **Drug:** Herba, Radix Saniculae
- **Constituents:** Saponines, essential oils, tannins, bitter constituents, resin
- **Treatments:** Plant for catarrh, cough, stomach, and intestinal bleeding, scurvy, heavy periods, root astringent, formerly for helping wounds heal (no longer recommended)
- **Uses:** Tea, gargle, compresses, washes, bath additive
- **Homeopathic uses:** Wound healing, haemostatic, gastrointestinal diseases, diarrhoea
- **What and when to gather:** Basal leaves before flowering, juice April to May; root September to October

Sanicle in its natural location in a beech forest.

Holly family
Aquifoliaceae

Hollies, usually trees or bushes, have leathery leaves and small, unassuming flowers that produce berries with between one and ten seeds.

Above right: The toxic fruits of the holly.

Above left: The buds and flowers of the holly grow in corymbs on the branches.

Ilex aquifolium L.
HOLLY

■ *protected, toxic* ■
Iles, Cuileann

The holly prefers a mild Atlantic winter climate, where it will grow into a strong tree that can live for up to 300 years. It is easily identified by its dark green, wavy leaves that are protected by sharp spikes on the edges. The coral-coloured berries are poisonous to humans.

Hollies are very popular at Christmas, especially in the UK and the United States, when the branches are used as decoration.

In naturopathy, the holly – which is a native of central Europe – now only plays a secondary role. In the past, the leaves would be gathered in May/June and ground and dried. The dried leaves were used to make a tea that was a popular treatment for gout and bronchitis. The situation is different with the Yerba Mate (*Ilex paraguariensis*) tea bush. This bush, which is a native of South America, gives us the caffeine-rich, stimulating mate or Paraguay tea, which is also known to aid digestion. The annual production in South America is 300,000 tons.

■ **Description:** Bush or tree with many branches, height usually approx. 6 ft 6 in. (2 m), max. 32 ft (10 m); rind smooth, green in winter but not frost resistant; leaves stalked, alternating, extremely variable in shape, wavy, leathery hard, glossy, dark green, leaf edge prickly, thorny; dioecious flowers, small, white, carmine red centre (nectar guide pattern) in corymbs; berries bright red, pea-sized, four to five seeds per berry, toxic
■ **Flowering:** May, June
■ **Scent and flavour:** No smell; leaves taste bitter, slimy
■ **Location:** Underwood in deciduous and beech/pine forests, sensitive to frost
■ **Distribution:** Wine-growing regions, Baltic, Mediterranean, Atlantic regions, planted
■ **Drug:** Folia Ilicis aquifolii
■ **Constituents:** Triterpene, bitter principles (Ilicin), flavonoids; rind yellow dye
■ **Treatments:** For bronchitis, fever, rheumatism, gout, diarrhoea
■ **Uses:** Tea, tincture
■ **Homeopathic uses:** Also for conjunctivitis
■ **What and when to gather:** Leaves May to June
■ **Lookalikes:** Holm oak (*Quercus ilex*): tree, leaves similar

Ivy family
Araliaceae

The original home of the ivy family is in the tropics. The best known exotic members include Korean ginseng (Panax ginseng), which is used as something of a cure-all in convalescence, age-related memory loss and stress situations, and is readily available from pharmacies and drugstores everywhere. The tiny flowers are usually held in umbels; the fruits are generally berries or schizocarp (gap fruit).

Hedera helix L.
IVY

■ *toxic* ■

Algerian Ivy, Canary Ivy, English Ivy, Madeira Ivy

Ivy creeps across the forest or woodland floor, climbs up and around trees and houses, takes over walls and can live for 500 years. Contrary to popular belief, though, it is not a parasitic plant. As is the case with many evergreens, earlier cultures used to believe ivy was a symbol of immortality, which is why it often featured in funeral rites and religious ceremonies. As a tendril that adorned the brow of Dionysus, the Greek god of wine, it is extremely likely that ivy has witnessed more than a little drunken carousing. Ivy is one of the healing plants whose effects are recognized even though its specific action has not yet been decoded. The young leaves are picked in August and September. Ivy tea is a popular remedy for respiratory diseases.

- **Description:** Creeper, climbs to a height of 65 ft (20 m); trunk with numerous winding anchoring roots, lignified; alternating leaves, evergreen, hard, shiny, leathery, three-to five-lobed, no lobes on the flowering sun shoots, oval, pointed tips; flowers green-yellow in scented, hemispheric umbels; fruit blue-black, toxic (ripens March/April)
- **Flowering:** September to November
- **Scent and flavour:** Aromatic smell; bitter taste, sharp
- **Location:** Shade or half shade; climbs up trees, rocks, houses
- **Distribution:** Widespread, common
- **Drug:** Folia Hederae helicis
- **Constituents:** Saponin (hederin), flavonol glycosides (rutin), essential oils
- **Treatments:** For respiratory diseases, spastic bronchitis, cellulitis, skin complaints, chilblains, corns
- **Uses:** Ready-made medical products, cosmetics industry
- **Homeopathic uses:** Thyroid diseases, gastrointestinal tract, liver, gall bladder, pancreas, musculoskeletal system
- **What and when to gather:** Young, fresh leaves August and September
- **Lookalikes:** None
- **Other information:** Berries toxic, watch dose when using ready-made products! Contact may cause an allergic reaction

Ivy flowers in September and is an important source of nectar; the leaves on the shoots are not lobated.

Typical lobated ivy leaves.

Dogwood family
Cornaceae

The dogwood family consists solely of shrubs and bushes (with the exception of the herbaceous Eurasian dwarf dogwood C. suecica L.). The leaves are oval, the veins arched and quite distinct in appearance. The wood is much appreciated e.g. by wood turners for its hardness, and is used to make walking sticks and handles for hammers.

Cornus mas L.
CORNELIAN CHERRY

Cornelian Cherry Dogwood, European Cornel, Cornel Cherry Tree

Unlike the laurel and sweet cherry (see page 243), the cornelian cherry is not a member of the rose family. However, like the blackthorn, or sloe (see page 242), its flowers appear before the leaves. Often, the two shrubs are found in the same hedge; the cornelian cherry appears in early spring and is easy to recognize by its small, yellow leaves, which grow in bushy umbels. In late summer and autumn, the long, bright red hanging fruits are a typical feature. It is not easy to remove the flesh from the large pip, but those who are willing to make the effort will be rewarded with jelly that has a very high vitamin C content. In bygone days, people would roast the seeds inside the pips and use them as a substitute for coffee. Although the yellow dogwood is usually cultivated, its cousin the red dogwood (*C. sanguineus*) often occurs naturally. It produces its flowers after the leaves and has blood-red twigs in winter. If consumed fresh, the black-blue fruits will cause nausea and diarrhoea; cooked, they are safe to use as jelly or fruit juice.

- **Description:** Height to 20 ft (6 m); leaves with short stalks, smooth edges, opposing; small flowers, yellow, in bushy short-stalked umbels at the tips of shoots, before the leaves develop; fruits bright red, shiny, long and oval, approx. ½ in. (1 cm) long, hanging, large pip
- **Flowering:** February to April
- **Scent and flavour:** Delicate smell to the flowers; fruits aromatic, acid, slightly astringent
- **Location:** Dry deciduous forest, cliffs, parks, hedgerows
- **Distribution:** Scattered, often cultivated
- **Drug:** Folia, Fructus Corni
- **Constituents:** Anthocyan glycoside, vitamin C, sugar, tannins
- **Treatments:** For diarrhoea, fever
- **Uses:** Tea, jelly, wine; seeds roasted and used as a substitute for coffee
- **Homeopathic uses:** See above
- **What and when to gather:** Leaves May to June, fruits August to October
- **Lookalikes:** Red dogwood: twigs yellow-green, blood red in autumn and winter; flowers white, appear after the leaves; fruits black-blue

Fruits and leaves of the cornelian cherry.

Flowering cornelian cherry. The delicate yellow flowers appear before the leaves.

Sundew family
Droseraceae

The tiny hairs on the leaves of members of the sundew family secrete a sticky, dew-like substance that attracts and then traps insects. The leaves enfold their quarry and consume the insects to meet their protein requirements.

Drosera rotundifolia L.
ROUND-LEAFED SUNDEW

■ *protected* ■

Common Sundew, Dew Plant, Red Rod, Youthwort

Often, when we hear the term 'carnivorous plants' in our world, dominated as it is by virtual experiences, we imagine vast funnel-like growths, possibly even with hideous grasping arms, somewhere in a distant tropical jungle. But central Europe is also home to a variety of carnivorous plants that help themselves to the nutrients that the soil and air fail to provide them with, or only provide in small quantities, courtesy of the insect world. One such plant is the round-leafed sundew, still widely found in moorland. This tiny plant, with sticky, sparkling hairs on its leaves, grows in rosettes among the sphagnum, but occasionally also in otherwise vegetation-free black moorland soil, and was an important healing herb in bygone centuries. The commercially available drug is made from non-European varieties, such as *D. ramentacea*, which has similar mucolytic benefits and is not a protected species. It is used in particular for a dry cough or whooping cough.

- **Description:** Height to 8 in. (20 cm); leaves with long stalks, round with reddish, sticky, shiny gland hairs; stalks upright, green or reddish; flowers white, ⅙–¼ in. (5–8 mm) large, single-sided cluster; capsule fruit, numerous elongated winged seeds; thin roots; perennial
- **Flowering:** July, August
- **Scent and flavour:** No smell; taste acidic, bitter, astringent
- **Location:** Moors, on turf
- **Distribution:** Common in moors, otherwise rare
- **Drug:** Herba Droserae (Rorellae)
- **Constituents:** Tannins, chinon derivatives (droseron), anthocyane (red), flavonoids
- **Treatments:** For respiratory infections, asthma, whooping cough, hardened arteries, kidney and bladder complaints, liver complaints, traditional treatment for warts, corns
- **Uses:** Tea, tincture
- **Homeopathic uses:** For whooping cough, respiratory infections
- **What and when to gather:** Plant June to September
- **Lookalikes:** Other sundew varieties (*D. spec.*): no round leaves
- **Other information:** Take care: not to be taken by people with low blood pressure or tuberculosis. Long-term use may lead to rheumatic complaints.

Sundew leaf with sticky gland hairs.

Sundew rosettes in peat-bog (Sphagnum), which in the past was used in wars as an absorbent dressing with a low germ count.

Oleaster family
Eleagnaceae

The oleaster family with the eponymous oleaster, or Russian olive (Eleagnus spec.) and sea buckthorn (Hippophae rhamnoides) are bushes or trees that are drought-resistant, usually thorned, with small, nondescript flowers and edible berries. They live in symbiosis with nitrogen-binding Frankia bacteria.

Hippophae rhamnoides L.
SEA BUCKTHORN

Seaberry, Common Sea Buckthorn

Sea buckthorn grows best on sandy soils. Because it is dioecious, it is necessary to plant both male and female bushes if the berries are desired.

The bright orange-red flowers of the sea buckthorn – botanically they are pedicellate – are used to make a juice that is known for its high vitamin C and E content. It is used mainly for convalescents who need energy and for people with a weakened immune system, but also to protect against winter colds.

- **Description:** Height to 20 ft (6 m); bush or tree; leaves alternating, narrow, lanceolate, upper side dark green, underside silver grey to copper red, hairy; branches dark brown, some with thorns; dioecious: male flowers green-white, unassuming in spherical catkins, females tubular, single, short-stalked in bushlets; orange-red, more rarely yellow, berry-like, elongated to spherical stone fruit
- **Flowering:** April, May before the leaves
- **Scent and flavour:** Smell sharp; fruits extremely acidic
- **Location:** Gravel stretches by rivers, rockfall, coastal dunes, along motorways, railway embankments, paths, cultivated

- **Distribution:** Scattered
- **Drug:** Fructus Hippophae rhamnoides
- **Constituents:** Vitamins (vitamin C, E), glycosides, flavonoids, fruit acid, fatty oil
- **Treatments:** During convalescence, for immune weakness, loss of appetite, scurvy, worms
- **Uses:** Juice, syrup, jelly, food industry
- **Homeopathic uses:** See above
- **What and when to gather:** Fruits September, October (cut fully ripe fruits off with scissors)
- **Lookalikes:** Narrow-leafed oleaster (*Eleagnos angustifolia*): leaves broader, branches silvery, fruits sweet, decorative shrub

Ripe sea buckthorn berries in September.

Pea family
Fabaceae

The family owes its colloquial name of 'butterfly plant' to its butterfly-shaped flower with the upward-facing 'flag', the two side 'wings' and the joined petals at the front ('little vessel'). The fruit is either helical like a shell, or a single bursting lobe ('legume'). The pinnas and side leaves that are shaped like thorns on e.g. broom (Ulex), and the symbiosis between the corm with nitrogen-binding bacteria that aids soil fertility, are typical of this family. Important healing herbs include the senna bush (Cassia angustifolia), a native of Africa whose leaves are a well-known laxative, and the tamarind (Tamarindus indica), a native of India whose fruits are used to make a tasty pulp that is also a laxative.

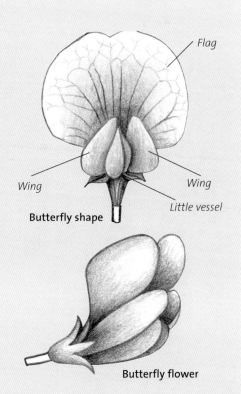

Butterfly shape

Flag

Wing

Wing

Little vessel

Butterfly flower

Anthyllis vulneraria L.
KIDNEY VETCH

Ladies' Fingers, Masmalo

Characteristic of the kidney vetch: the golden-yellow head with white, open calyx.

Kidney vetch grows on calcareous grass in mountains up to 9,850 ft (3,000 m), but it is also widespread in flatter regions; it is much prized as a food plant. The golden-yellow or red-orange flowers are packed tightly inside a head on the end of the stalk. In traditional medicine it was a popular aid in wound healing, although it does not feature in the classic works on naturopathy; the reasons for this are not known. The plant is also used in blood-cleansing teas and laxative teas.

Other clovers, especially the trefoils, are not only important in naturopathy, but also in old customs and traditions. Even today it is still widely believed that finding a four-leafed clover will bring the finder good fortune. Such beliefs often have hundreds and hundreds of years of history. According to Marianne Beuchert, the Celtic druids were the first to believe that a cloverleaf would bring good fortune.

■ **Description:** Height to 1 ft (30 cm); base leaves single, stalk leaves pinnated individually, end leaves enlarged, grey-green;

Licorice (Glycyrrhiza glabra) is used in many recipes as a flavour enhancer, and is also popular as candy; its features are typical of the family: pinnate leaves and butterfly shaped flowers.

Right: Red or meadow clover (Trifolium pratense), well known as animal fodder, will also delight the human palate if used like spinach; it is also popular in naturopathy for the treatment of coughs and skin diseases. In homeopathy, red clover extract is used to treat infections of the parotid gland and bronchitis. Other popular varieties are the warmth-loving medium clover (T. medium) with a spherical head and smooth calyx, and Swedish clover (T. hybridum) with flowers that start out white and later turn pink.

Below left: The flowers of dyer's broom used to be used for dyeing wool yellow; tea made from the plant was used as a diuretic to treat kidney and bladder problems.

Below right: Large flowers – small leaves: in summer, flowering broom is a treat for the eyes.

stalks flat or upright; flowers golden-yellow, often orange or red, approx. ½–¾ in. (1.5 to 2 cm) long, in stalk-end heads, calyx cream, straggly hairs, opens out after flowering, surrounded by three to seven split tall leaves; perennial

- **Flowering:** May to September
- **Scent and flavour:** Slightly aromatic smell; bitter taste
- **Location:** Calcareous grass, railway cuttings, to 9,850 ft (3,000 m)
- **Distribution:** Widespread
- **Drug:** Flores, Herba Anthyllidis vulnerariae
- **Constituents:** Tannins, saponin, flavonoids
- **Treatments:** In traditional medicine for wounds, contusions, coughs, constipation, purifying the blood
- **Uses:** Tea, fresh plant; good food plant
- **Homeopathic uses:** Not known
- **What and when to gather:** Flowering plant May to August
- **Lookalikes:** Other yellow-flowering members of the pea family do not have an open, straggly calyx
- **Other information:** Usually added to tea mixes

Cytisus scoparius (L.) Lk.
BROOM

■ *mildly toxic* ■
Scotch Broom

Broom is difficult to tell from other types of gorse, e.g. *Genista*. It thrives on chalk-poor soils on heathland, but also on roadsides, along railway cuttings and in gardens. A tea mixture with finely chopped young twigs of broom is an effective treatment for heart rhythm problems and low blood pressure, but should not be consumed during pregnancy. Any treatment should only be on medical advice and it is essential that the plant is identified correctly. Too much or confusion with other types of gorse – some of which are highly toxic – could be fatal.

Even the roots and flowers of broom are used in traditional medicine; in fact, the roots would

even be used as food in times of need. A great deal of superstition has also been attached to the true, or supposed, abilities of brooms and its close relatives. It is said that on Walpurgis Night, witches rode on brooms to the Brocken, and in some parts of Bavaria, processions at the Feast of Corpus Christi are scattered with its blossom.

- **Description:** Height to 6 ft 6 in. (2 m); bush, small leaves, lanceolate, three petals, hairy, dropping early; rod-like branches, green, grooved, smooth; large flowers, golden, single or in pairs, smooth calyx; black lobes, hairs on the edge
- **Flowering:** May, June
- **Scent and flavour:** Flowers smell pleasant; taste bitter
- **Location:** Heathland, oak and pine forests, sunny, dry embankments, acid soils
- **Distribution:** Widespread, often planted
- **Drug:** Flores, Herba, Radix Genistae scopariae
- **Constituents:** Alkaloids (spartein, scoparin), flavonoids, glycosides, tannins, bitter principles
- **Treatments:** For cardiac weakness, heart rhythm problems, low blood pressure, kidney and bladder problems, liver disease, edema, rheumatic problems, oxytocic
- **Uses:** In pharmaceutical products and teas, as a dye
- **Homeopathic uses:** See above
- **What and when to gather:** Flowering tips and individual flowers May to July
- **Lookalikes:** German gorse (*Genista germanica*): short shoots with thorns, flowers in 2-in. (5-cm) bunches, hairy lobes; dyer's gorse: stems upright, rod-shaped, flower and lobe smooth
- **Other information:** Take care: only to be used in mixes under medical supervision – dangerously toxic if taken in excess

Melilotus officinalis (L.) Pallas
YELLOW SWEET CLOVER

■ *mildly toxic* ■

Yellow Clover, Field Honey Clover, Melilotis

Sweet clover, or melilot, on an embankment with common yarrow (see page 50).

The soft yellow flowers of the yellow sweet clover give off a delicate, honey-like aroma; this plant is very common along paths and roads, embankments, overgrown gravel pits, and similar areas, and will happily flower into September. Its bitter, acidic flavour is less pleasant.

Yellow sweet clover is one of the healing plants which, as the Swiss doctor and homeopath Martin Furlenmeier writes, was popular in antiquity and in the Middle Ages, was later forgotten, but has recently been rediscovered by homeopathy. It is of particular benefit in treating venous diseases and the associated symptoms, such as persistent itching of the limbs, swelling and a feeling of heaviness in the legs.

Not many healing plants can be used for these symptoms. In their popular book of healing

White sweet clover often grows in the same place as yellow and is used in the same way.

- **Flowering:** June to September
- **Scent and flavour:** Fresh flowers smell of honey, dried ones of hay; sharp taste, bitter
- **Location:** Waysides, embankments, gravel pits, wasteland
- **Distribution:** Widespread to common
- **Drug:** Herba, Flores Meliloti
- **Constituents:** Cumarine, allantoine, flavonoids, mucilage, choline, essential oils, tannins, bitter principles
- **Treatments:** For sleeplessness, cramp, bronchitis, asthma, coughs, venous disease, externally: for headaches, haemorrhoids, badly healing oozing wounds, skin diseases, abscesses, haematoma, sprains
- **Uses:** Tea, compresses, herb pillows, spice; pharmacy (ready-made products) and tobacco industry for flavouring, protection against moths
- **Homeopathic uses:** See above, and for diseases of the central nervous system, headaches, blood clotting problems
- **What and when to gather:** Flowering plant with no woody stalks June to September
- **Lookalikes:** White sweet clover (*M. alba*): higher, flowers white, same uses
- **Other information:** Take care: overdose can cause nausea, dizziness, headaches; internal use only by agreement with a doctor

herbs, Adolf Oertel and Eduard Bauer praise it to the skies: 'Due to its constituents, yellow sweet clover is excellent for treating varicose veins, cramp-like vascular pain in the arms, and acute cramp in the lower leg.' Commission E of the German Ministry of Health, which has analysed the constituents of numerous healing plants, confirms the therapeutic importance of yellow clover extract for the treatment of e.g. bruising and haemorrhoids (see Bisset and Wicht). Any treatment should be given in consultation with a doctor.

- **Description:** Height to 4 ft (1.2 m); leaves alternating, long stems, three pinnates, side leaves inverse ovals, sawn; stalks hollow, grooved, branched; flowers yellow, short stalked in bunches with lots of flowers, hanging to one side; single-seeded lobes, brown, dull, wrinkled; spindle-shaped root; biennial

Ononis spinosa L.
SPINY RESTHARROW

Restharrow

The spiny restharrow likes to grow on dry, stony, sunny waysides and around meadows. The low shrub – its pretty pink flowers are often seen in rock gardens – knows how to look after itself: not only does it have spiky tips that can cause an unpleasant injury, but it is also firmly anchored in the ground by a long hollow root, which makes it very difficult to dig it up. Hence the reference to 'harrow' in its name: it has caused the demise of many of these comb-like tools with pointed metal tips that clean, smooth and separate flax and hemp fibres. The root is of interest to the naturopath. Teas made of the root extract are recommended for the treatment of kidney and bladder problems (e.g. renal gravel). It also used to be a treatment for gout.

- **Description:** Height to 2 ft (60 cm); low shrub with pointed, protruding thorns; leaves single or tri-pinnate, short stalks; stems flat or ascending, branched, reddish, woody at the base; one to three flowers, pink, rarely white; few seeds in the pod; taproot; perennial
- **Flowering:** June to September
- **Scent and flavour:** Weak smell, unpleasant; taste dry, slightly sweet, scratchy
- **Location:** Waysides, thin grass, fields and meadows, calciphile
- **Distribution:** Scattered to common
- **Drug:** Radix Ononidis spinosae
- **Constituents:** Essential oils, flavone glycosides (ononin, ononid), tanning agents, saponin, fatty oil
- **Treatment:** For kidney and bladder disease, stones; rheumatic complaints, gout, skin diseases, purifying blood
- **Uses:** Tea, ready-to-use products, tea blends
- **Homeopathic uses:** See above and for a weak heart
- **What and when to gather:** Roots without fibre March to April and September to October

- **Lookalikes:** Field restharrow (*O. arvensis*): no thorns, stalks glandular-straggly hairs, similar uses
- **Other information:** Take care: watch dosage closely and only use in mixes or ready-to-use products in consultation with a doctor

Flowering restharrow.

Phaseolus vulgaris L.
GARDEN BEAN

■ *highly toxic when raw* ■
French Bean, Common Bean, Haricot Bean,
Flageolet Bean, Kidney Bean

All Phaseolus beans originally originated from Latin America; they have never become natives in colder regions as they are unable to survive the harsh winters. The runner bean was cultivated in its native countries long before the first Europeans arrived. Today the vegetable, which is as healthy as it is tasty, is a firm fixture in gardens and kitchens all over Europe. However, it is important to know that the pods and seeds of all bean varieties contain a protein compound called phasine, which is extremely toxic and can cause severe vomiting and diarrhoea, and colic-like abdominal pains; in extreme cases it can lead to circulatory collapse. The toxin is destroyed by cooking.

It is not such a well-known fact that the bean is a medicinal herb. The pod without the seeds is the part that is of pharmaceutical interest. A tea made from the pods is a diuretic, and it is even believed to have an anti-diabetic effect, although the biochemical mechanisms on which this is based have not yet been fully researched.

The field or horse bean (*Vicia faba*), also known as the broad or fava bean, is only a distant relative of the garden bean. References to 'beans' in old books of herbs and by Hildegard of Bingen usually concern this native plant.

■ **Description:** Height to 13 ft (4 m); left-winding climber; very large leaves, triple pinnated, grooved stalks; flowers usually white, in bunches; smooth pods, elongated; annual
■ **Flowering:** June to September
■ **Scent and flavour:** Some flowers strongly scented, seeds not scented; flavour typically floury
■ **Location:** Often grown in gardens
■ **Distribution:** Native to South America/Mexico
■ **Drug:** Semen, Pericarpum Phaseoli
■ **Constituents:** Protein, toxalbumin (phasine), starch, rubber, fat, amino acids, vitamins, potassium
■ **Treatments:** For kidney and bladder complaints, metabolic disorders, as a boost during convalescence, weak heart and liver, eczema, traditionally for diabetes
■ **Uses:** Tea, gruel, food
■ **Homeopathic uses:** For rheumatic complaints, sciatica, kidney complaints, weak heart
■ **What and when to gather:** Empty pods and seeds July to September
■ **Lookalikes:** Scarlet runner (*P. coccineus*): scarlet flowers; other bean varieties: flowers mauve, yellow, reddish, pods yellow or violet, depending on variety

Garden beans before the harvest.

Trigonella foenum-graecum L.
FENUGREEK

Greek Hay, Buck's Horn Clover

Fenugreek originally came from the Mediterranean and west Asia, and was already being grown in monastery gardens north of the Alps in the early Middle Ages. It is one of the plants which Charles the Great instructed be grown on the royal estates in his *Capitulare de villis vel curtis imperialibus* (dated 812, see page 15), and which Hildegard of Bingen also spoke highly of (she recommended it as a treatment to lower a raised temperature). In India, it has been used in ayurvedic medicine for millennia. In classical Greece, intellectuals enjoyed the strong, spicy seeds roasted in barley oil as a snack – which gave rise to another one of its popular names that is still used today: philosopher's clover.

Today, fenugreek seeds are used mainly as a spice (e.g. in bread) and, because they are highly nutritious, recommended to convalescents and athletes as a source of energy and strength. Little new research has been carried out into its efficacy for the treatment of abscesses, as described in old books of herbs, but it is known to prevent inflammation when used externally.

- **Description:** Height to 1 ft 8 in. (50 cm); leaves tri-pinnate, inverse oval, short stems; stalks soft, upright, lots of leaves; one to two flowers, light yellow to white, situated between the top leaves, calyx furry; pods up to 4 in. (10 cm) long, thin, upright, standing proud, sometimes horn-shaped, long beaked, multi-seeded; annual
- **Flowering:** April to July
- **Scent and flavour:** Unpleasant smell, aromatic; bitter taste, very slimy
- **Location:** Calciphile
- **Distribution:** Grows wild in the Mediterranean, was once widely grown
- **Drug:** Semen Foenugraeci (Trigonellae)
- **Constituents:** Mucilage, proteins, fatty oil, tannins, essential oils, saponin

- **Treatments:** For coughs, constipation, mild diabetes, loss of appetite, thinness, for strength during convalescence, chilblains, inflamed gums, skin diseases (favus)
- **Uses:** Tea mixes, gargle, baths, poultices, roasted as a spice, veterinary medicine and cattle fodder
- **Homeopathic uses:** Metabolic problems
- **What and when to gather:** Ripe seeds August, September
- **Lookalikes:** Other clovers
- **Other information:** Its unpleasant taste can be improved by adding menthol or lemon extract

The unassuming white flower of the fenugreek is situated between the tri-pinnate leaves.

Geranium family
Geraniaceae

The geranium family includes geraniums and stork's bill (erodium). Somewhat confusingly the plants often known as 'geraniums' and grown in pots and in gardens actually belong to the South African variety pelargonium. The scientific names come from the Greek words erodios meaning heron, geranos meaning crane, and pelargos meaning stork, and refer to the beak-like shape of the fruits.

- **Flowering:** April to September
- **Scent and flavour:** Unpleasant smell when crushed; bitter taste
- **Location:** Nutrient-rich, shady locations, gardens, waysides, woods, cliff faces
- **Distribution:** Europe, to 5,900 ft (1,800 m), common
- **Drug:** Herba, Radix Gerani robertiani
- **Constituents:** Essential oils (only in the fresh plant, very volatile), flavonoids, bitter agents (geraniin), ellagic acid, tannins, resin, vitamin C
- **Treatments:** For diarrhoea, traditional remedy for liver and gall bladder complaints; throat infections and laryngitis, kidney and bladder infections, problems with stones, gout, phlebitis, haemorrhoids, haemostatic, healing
- **Uses:** Tea, compresses, gargle; protects against moths
- **Homeopathic uses:** For chronic infections
- **What and when to gather:** Flowering plant May to August
- **Lookalikes:** None

'Geraniums', ever-popular decorations for pots and windows, are properly known as pelargoniums, but are also in the Geraniaceae family.

Geranium robertianum L.
HERB ROBERT

Red Robin, Stinky Bob

The belief in the healing power of Herb Robert is rooted in a centuries-old religious tradition. It was supposedly St Rupert (c. 650–720), the Archbishop of Salzburg, who first recommended it. Not too much importance is attached to its therapeutic advantages, although in the 1940s it was believed to be an excellent remedy for earache. According to Hiller and Melzig, there is some evidence of its benefits, or plausibility, for use in the treatment of diarrhoea.

- **Description:** Height to 1 ft 8 in. (50 cm), leaves bushy, semi-rosette, light green, glossy, three to five lobes; dark red stems, thin, hairs standing proud, knotted, jointed; small flowers, red to lilac, stalked in pairs, stamens with orange-red anthers, red scars on the tip of the long beak; annual

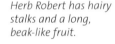

Herb Robert has hairy stalks and a long, beak-like fruit.

Horse chestnut family
Hippocastanaceae

Horse chestnuts which, like the maples (Aceraceae), have now been put with the largely tropical soap tree family (Sapindacea), are deciduous trees with spiny capsule fruits. They have only the spiky shape of the shell in common with the edible or sweet chestnut (see page 166).

Aesculus hippocastanum L.
HORSE CHESTNUT

Conker, Wild Chestnut

The horse chestnut came to central Europe from Turkey in the 16th century, where it soon became a popular choice for parks and alleys; its spiky green fruit husks are of particular appeal to children. It is the only species of its type to be found in central Europe, although there are numerous others in Asia and America. The most frequently planted red-blooded horse chestnut (*A. x carnea*) is a hybrid of the normal horse chestnut and the American Pavie (*A. pavia*).

- **Description:** Height to 100 ft (30 m); tree with a wide, rounded crown, grey-brown bark; opposing leaves, long stalked, five to seven lobes, sawn edges; buds thick, very sticky; flowers white-yellow, red marks, upright panicle on the end of the stalk with lots of flowers; fruit approx. 2½ in. (6 cm) in diameter, green, spherical, soft spines, one to three seeds surrounded by a shiny, red-brown hard shell (chestnut)
- **Flowering:** May, June
- **Scent and flavour:** No smell; flowers and fresh seeds taste bitter

- **Location:** Parks, alleys, gardens
- **Distribution:** Native of India, common
- **Drug:** Folium, Flores, Cortex, Oleum, Semen Hippocastani
- **Constituents:** Saponins (aesculin), tannins, flavonoids (quercetin, rutin), cumarin, bitter principles, sugar, starch, fatty oil, triglycerides
- **Treatments:** For skin diseases, couperose, varicose veins, phlebitis, circulatory problems (night cramps, calf abscesses), edema, haemorrhoids, rheumatic complaints, chilblains, itching, diarrhoea (rind)
- **Uses:** Tea, compresses, tincture, cream, bathings, flour, cosmetics and soap industry, animal food
- **Homeopathic uses:** See above
- **What and when to gather:** Flowers, individually May and June; leaves April and May; ripe seeds October, rind of three- to five-year-old branches March, September to October
- **Lookalikes:** Red-blooded horse chestnut (*A. x carnea*): lower tree, flowers pink to red, fruit smaller, not susceptible to the leaf-mining moth
- **Other information:** Take care: overdose may cause nausea, vomiting, itching and temporary paralysis

Once the bitter principles have been removed, the flour made from the seeds of the horse chestnut is both tasty and nutritious.

Flax family
Linaceae

The members of the flax family are usually plants, more rarely bushes or trees, with five-petalled, stellar flowers and capsule fruits; the alternating leaves are usually split and have no side leaves.

Linum usitatissimum L.
FLAX

Common Flax, Linseed, Flaxseed

Flax is one of the oldest-known cultivated plants. It can be traced back to the time of the Babylonians. It was also widespread throughout central Europe, but was then gradually forgotten – at least in its capacity as a source of textile fibre. It remains important today for its dark, shiny seeds, which are used both by the food and animal food industries ('linseed bread', bird seed) and in medicine. Linseed is a well-known cure for constipation. The fibrils cause the seeds to swell in the intestines, which stimulates their activity.

People with weight problems are advised against consumption of the oil, which is also contained in the seeds: according to Bisset and Wicht, it containts around 470 kcal per 3.5 oz (100 g). However, the oil is not released if the whole, coarsely ground seeds are consumed. Used externally, the seeds, once soaked in hot water, are anti-inflammatory. Our native flora include a number of other flax varieties. Most are extremely rare, and limited to certain regions. The best known is dwarf wild flax (*L. catharticum*).

- **Description:** Height to 4 ft 3 in. (1.3 m); grey-green leaves, three nerves, alternating, linear-lanceolate, pointed, full rimmed; stalks upright, sometimes branched; flowers bound, light blue, approx. 1 in. (3 cm) diameter, long stalks, finely lashed sepals; spherical capsule fruit; shiny seeds, brown, smooth, flat; annual to biennial
- **Flowering:** June to August
- **Scent and flavour:** No smell
- **Location:** Grown in fields, wasteland, embankments, wild
- **Distribution:** Cultivated, otherwise rare
- **Drug:** Semen, Oleum Lini
- **Constituents:** Mucilage, pectin, fatty oil with vitamin F, glycosides (hydrocyanic acid, linamarin), protein
- **Treatments:** Mild laxative, for inflammations, abscesses, boils, suppurating wounds, intestinal parasites
- **Uses:** Cold extract, whole, crushed, coarsely and finely ground seeds, compresses, oil, in baking, bird seed, spinning fibres, dye, linoleum, putty and soap industries
- **Homeopathic uses:** See above and for asthma, urticaria
- **What and when to gather:** Seeds July and August
- **Lookalikes:** Dwarf wild flax (*Linum catharticum*): small, white flowers, on damp meadows, opposing leaves; other flax varieties (*L.* spec.): flowers yellow, reddish or purple, or several together on a stalk

Dwarf wild flax – the delicate white flowers are typical.

Flaxseed capsule and flower.

Evening primrose family

Onagraceae

The evening primrose family includes mainly herbaceous plants that usually have opposing leaves. They have very many seeds that ripen in capsules and a soft comose like the willowherb (Epilobium) or contain large amounts of oil like the evening primrose (Oenothera). The evening primrose is also extremely important in genetic research.

Epilobium parviflorum Schreb.
LESSER WILLOWHERB

Forest clearings and beaches are coloured pink in summer by the candle-like inflorescence of the lesser willowherb (*E. angustifolium*). The lesser willowherb is a well-known healing plant; it is supposed to be highly effective in the treatment of prostate adenoma, and even prostate cancer. Maria Treben (1907–1991) of Austria played an important part in helping willowherb products to fame, and she is widely regarded as the person responsible for redis-covering this otherwise disregarded healing herb. Since then there have been many enthusiastic reports from lay healers testifying to the success of both the lesser and the greater willowherb, and occasionally both (although Maria Treben specifically ascribed no healing powers at all to the lesser). Although Bisset and Wichtl indicated that there is no scientific evidence of its positive effects, internet suppliers of willowherb products claim that it has in fact recently been proven.

- **Description:** Height to 1 ft 8 in. (50 cm); leaves slightly toothed, soft hairs; round stalk, upright, protruding hairs; individual flowers, light pink, to ½ in. (1 cm) long, stigma with four distinct branches; long, thin seed capsule with four lobes
- **Flowering:** July to September
- **Scent and flavour:** No smell; acerbic taste
- **Location:** Alluvial forests, river banks
- **Distribution:** Widespread
- **Drug:** Herba Epilobii
- **Constituents:** Tannins, mucilage, flavonoids
- **Treatments:** For prostate complaints, inflam-mation of the stomach membrane or intestines
- **Uses:** Tea, vegetable
- **Homeopathic uses:** See above and for diarrhoea
- **What and when to gather:** Young shoots and leaves May to September
- **Lookalikes:** Other willowherbs (*Epilobium* spec.): nodding flowers, solid stigma, smooth stalk
- **Other information:** Pleasant-tasting tea made from the flowers

The lesser willowherb has pink, upright flowers.

Oenothera biennis L.
EVENING PRIMROSE

Yellow Nightshadow, Yellow Rapunzel

The evening primrose opens its flowers as night falls. Seed capsules are already developing above the flowers.

The exact definition of our evening primroses is an entire subject in itself, and one that only a few specialized botanists understand. After the first varieties were brought to Europe from America early in the 17th century, they soon spread and interbred. Of the now over forty native varieties and species, the common evening primrose is probably the most widespread. It grows on wasteland and fallow land and amateurs sometimes confuse it with mullein (*Verbascum* spec., see page 115), which grows in similar areas.

The most precious product obtained from the evening primrose is its oil, which is produced from its fine black seeds. Costing somewhere in the region of 50 euros for 1 fl. oz (200 ml), it is one of the most expensive plant oils in the world. It is used mainly in cosmetics and by the wellness industry in skincare products, but is also available as a capsule to offer protection against atherosclerosis. The fleshy roots of the

evening primrose are edible, which is why it used to be grown for food.

The word 'evening' in its name is due to the fact that the flowers open in the evening and close in the morning, when the sun comes up – which explains why they are so popular with moths, and generally fertilized by them.

- **Description:** Height to 5 ft (1.5 m); in the first year: leaf rosette with long, inverse ovoid, hairy leaves; in the second year: hairy, upright stalks with leaves; yellow flowers, ¾ in. (2–3 cm) long, funnel-shaped, stalked in grape-like ears; elongated fruits, four-leafed capsules with numerous seeds; turnip-shaped root, red on the outside, white inside, over 3 ft 3 in. (1 m) long; biennial
- **Flowering:** June to September
- **Scent and flavour:** Flowers smell sweet at night; roots smell of wine and taste like salsify, seeds nutty
- **Location:** Sandy, gravelly waysides, embankments, wasteland, gardens
- **Distribution:** Scattered, spreading
- **Drug:** Herba, Oleum Oenotherae biennis
- **Constituents:** Tannins, fatty oil, flavonoids, gamma linoleic acid, vitamin E
- **Treatments:** For menopause, atherosclerosis, diarrhoea, purifying the blood, skin diseases (neurodermatitis)
- **Uses:** Oil, vegetable (root), cosmetics industry
- **Homeopathic uses:** See above and for diarrhoea
- **What and when to gather:** Roots September and October of the first year, March of the second year, seeds August to October
- **Lookalikes:** Common mullein (*Verbascum* spec., see page 115): leaves with felty woolly hairs

Buckthorn family
Rhamnaceae

The thorns on the members of the buckthorn family are at right angles to the branches and so form a cross. The flowers are tiny; the fruit drupe-like berries.

Frangula alnus Mill.
ALDER BUCKTHORN

■ *toxic* ■

Alder Buckthorn, Aulne Noir, Black Buckthorn, European Alder Buckthorn, Frangula, Glossy Buckthorn, Nerprun Bourdaine

Among our native trees, buckthorn plays a lesser supporting role, which may explain why it is treated as a shrub rather than a tree. Its habitat in and on the periphery of moors is also more 'homely'. That it has nonetheless been used for centuries is due to two unusual characteristics. Its wood was once used in the production of gunpowder, which is why it is also sometimes called powder wood. Also, its unpleasantly scented bark has long been used for healing. The tea brewed from its bark is well-known as a laxative, although it should be stored for at least a year before being used for this purpose. The fresh bark and the fruits of the buckthorn are toxic, and easily mistaken (especially by children) for bilberries (*Vaccinium myrtillus*, see page 147), which often grow close by.

The reason it stimulates the large intestine and is laxative is due to antrachinone, which is also present in Aloe (see page 178), rhubarb (see page 128), and senna leaves (*Cassia angustifolia*, see page 217).

- **Description:** Height to 20 ft (6 m); bush or tree; bark grey-brown with grey-white spiral warts, yellow on inside; alternating leaves, oval, pointed, distinct parallel veins, tapering at the tip; fragile branches, upright, no thorns; yellow-green flowers, in two to ten umbel-like bundles; fruits green at first, then red, turn black when ripe
- **Flowering:** May to September
- **Scent and flavour:** Rind smells unpleasantly rotten when fresh, flowers smell sweet; taste bitter-sweet, slimy, astringent
- **Location:** Forest edges, moors, damp deciduous woods
- **Distribution:** Widespread
- **Drug:** Cortex Frangulae
- **Constituents:** Glycosides (glucofrangulin, anthraol, anthron), tannins, saponin, bitter principles, mucilage
- **Treatments:** For constipation, digestive and gall bladder problems, obesity, skin problems (scabies, lichen)
- **Uses:** Teas, wash
- **Homeopathic uses:** See above, and for haemorrhoids, colic, diarrhoea and rheumatism
- **What and when to gather:** Rind of young, three- to four-year-old branches March to May, berries August to October
- **Lookalikes:** Buckthorn: branches end in thorns, toothed leaves, smaller

Alder buckthorn, which flowers from May to September, is an important habitat for bees.

Rhamnus catharticas
COMMON BUCKTHORN

■ *toxic* ■

Highwaythorn, Waythorn, Hartsthorn, Ramsthorn

Buckthorn lives a quiet, hidden life on waysides and warm hedgerows, preferably on chalky soils. It is also a popular garden plant. The orange-red wood is used for intarsia and other woodwork. The red-backed shrike, a bird that likes to impale its prey on thorns, often builds its nest in buckthorn bushes. Buckthorn berries are highly laxative – so not usually the first choice for normal constipation. Because of its strong action, which can also include nausea and vomiting, some authors, such as Aichele and Schwegler, warn against attempts at self-medicating with buckthorn.

Centuries ago people believed that buckthorn offered protection against witchcraft and magic.

Anyone who mistakes the black berries of the alder buckthorn for elderberries (see page 111) will soon realize their error.

To this end, as Heinrich Marzell reports, people in parts of Bavaria would erect three buckthorn branches outside their house and stables.

- **Description:** Height to 13 ft (4 m); bush or tree; wood orange-red; young rind smooth, fissured when older; branches end in thorns; opposing leaves, round to elliptical, toothed on edges; nondescript flowers, yellow-green, two to eight in bundles on axils; black, pea-sized globular berries with several seeds
- **Flowering:** May to June
- **Scent and flavour:** Fruit smells unpleasant; taste sweet at first, then bitter
- **Location:** Bushes, hedges, light woods and forests
- **Distribution:** Widespread
- **Drug:** Fructus Rhamni catharticae
- **Constituents:** Glycosides (glucofrangulin), bitter principles, saponin, vitamin C
- **Treatments:** For constipation, purifying the blood
- **Uses:** Berries, juice, syrup
- **Homeopathic uses:** Problems with the gastrointestinal tract, rheumatism
- **What and when to gather:** Rind of young, three- to four-year-old branches March to May, berries August to October
- **Lookalikes:** Alder buckthorn (*Frangula alnus*, see page 229): no thorns, smooth-edged leaves
- **Other information:** Take care: not suitable for long-term use. Reduce dosage if cramp-like gastrointestinal complaints occur. Lactating mothers and mothers-to-be should not take products containing buckthorn.

Mistletoe family
Viscaceae

The members of the mistletoe family are dioecious, perennial hemi-parasites that live on trees; they have fork-like branches and slimy-sticky berry-like fruits.

Viscum album L.
MISTLETOE

■ *toxic* ■

European Mistletoe, Common Mistletoe, White-berried Mistletoe, Bird Lime, All-heal, Devil's Fuge

Mistletoe settles in the tops of living trees, flowers in February and keeps its leaves in the autumn. Small wonder, then, that this 'rebel' against many plant laws should have stirred the human imagination as it has. The findings of Pliny (AD 23–79) on the importance of mistletoe to the Celts and the customs and beliefs associated with it, especially with regard to good fortune, are well known.

Mistletoe extract is thought to be important in the treatment of certain cancers. Many adherents of the 'mistletoe therapy' of Rudolf Steiner (1861–1925) swear by it; others are less convinced. Mistletoe tea is most definitely not suitable, because many of the possibly relevant constituents (lectin and viscotoxin) important in cancer treatment are broken down in the gastrointestinal tract. According to Bisset and Wichtl, only injections are to be considered.

- **Description:** Height to 3 ft 3 in. (1 m), age to approx. 70 years; spherical bush; yellow-green leaves, leathery, lanceolate to shovel-like; rind yellow-green, flowers nondescript, white, in few inflorescences at end of branch; berries white to yellow, two seeds; rootstock sinks into the living wood of the host

- **Flowering:** March to May
- **Scent and flavour:** Smell astringent, spicy; taste bitter, sharp
- **Location:** Hemi-parasite on the branches of deciduous trees and conifers
- **Distribution:** Scattered
- **Drug:** Herba Visci albi
- **Constituents:** Saponin, alcaloids, resins, essential oils, choline, acetylcholine, lectin, viscotoxin
- **Treatments:** For high blood pressure, dizziness, poor circulation, atherosclerosis, cramps, epilepsy, bleeding, varicose veins, coughs, asthma, strengthening the immune system, inhibiting tumour growth
- **Uses:** Tea as a cold extract, tea blends, ready-to-use products, injections
- **Homeopathic uses:** See above, and for neuralgia, sciatic problems, diseases of the female reproductive organs
- **What and when to gather:** Leaves and young branches to 1/5 in. (5 mm) thick October to March
- **Lookalikes:** Yellow-berried mistletoe (*Loranthus europaeus*): rind black-grey, yellow berries, on oaks and sweet chestnuts, not wintergreen
- **Other information:** All parts are toxic due to the presence of viscotoxins. Only to be given after medical consultation. Only ever use as cold extract; never brew or boil

In November and December, the fruits of the evergreen mistletoe ripen.

Rose family
Rosaceae

There are many herbs, shrubs, and trees in the large family of the Rosaceae. People have valued their healing powers since ancient times – even though scientific proof of their effects is not (as yet) forthcoming in all cases. Apple tree and sloe, queen of the meadow, woodland strawberry – all belong to this extended family. The generally attractive, hermaphrodite flowers, individual or in panicles, each have (apart from a few exceptions such as erect cinquefoil, see page 240 f.) five petals, sepals and outer sepals. The leaves are entire, dentate, pinnate, lobed and alternate, generally with stipules that may drop off at an early stage. The stems are often woody, and many vines and branches bear prickles or thorns.

Agrimonia eupatoria L.
CHURCHSTEEPLES

Agrimony, Common Agrimony, Creeping Agrimony, Fragrant Agrimony, Cocklebur, Garclive, Sticklewort, Stickwort

Churchsteeples has a healing tradition going back thousands of years. According to Bisset and Wichtl, however, scientific analyses have not produced any proof of the effect postulated by popular medicine on gall bladder problems and a variety of other complaints. The works of the ancients, however, contain some very strange prescriptions. Hildegard of Bingen, for instance, recommends washing the head with an infusion of churchsteeples to treat insanity, and for persons who become 'sick through lust and incontinence' a bath of infused church-steeples, hyssop, ground ivy and menstrual blood, followed by rubbing in an ointment of poultry fat and chicken droppings. It is easy to imagine that such drastic treatment would dampen the enthusiasm of even the worst Lothario. Nevertheless, churchsteeples is still used today in tea blends for the liver and gall bladder and appears at any rate to do no harm. *Agrimony* also forms part of Dr Edward Bach's Flower Remedies, where it is recommended for extrovert, sociable people who desire harmony but who cannot resolve certain inner conflicts and tend to deaden their unhappiness with addictive drugs.

- **Description:** Height up to 3 ft 3 in. (1 m); leaves ovate, dentate, grey on the underside, pinnate with five to nine larger and five to ten smaller leaflets; stems with shaggy hair; petals yellow, scented, in long flower spikes, ten to twenty stamens, two styles, calyx cone-shaped, vertical grooves, no sepals, fruits with hooked spines (burr-like), root thick, short, creeping
- **Flowering:** June to August
- **Scent and flavour:** Scent of fresh herb and root slightly aromatic, unscented when dried; taste savoury to bitter, astringent

Churchsteeples, because of its location and form, is sometimes confused with black mullein, though you can recognize black mullein easily enough by its wrinkled leaves, hairy on the underside and the orange anthers with their violet hairs.

- **Location:** Loamy to sandy, poor soils, waysides, meadows, thin scrub
- **Distribution:** Common, up to 5,250 ft (1,600 m) altitude in Europe
- **Drug:** Herba Agrimonia
- **Constituents:** Bitter principles, tannins (catechin tannins, gallotannins), flavonoids, nicotinic acid amide, silicic acid, choline, essential oils
- **Treatments:** In the past used to treat bedwetting, for inflammations of the kidneys and bladder, incontinence, slight diarrhoea, inflammations of the mouth and pharyngeal area, skin inflammations, diabetes; in folk medicine, for liver and gall bladder complaints and gastrointestinal inflammations
- **Uses:** Tea, gargle, poultices
- **Homeopathic uses:** For bronchitis
- **What and when to gather:** Basal leaves, flowering stem tips and herb June to August
- **Lookalikes:** Black mullein (*Verbascum nigrum*, see page 115)
- **Other information:** In the past the flowers were used for their yellow dye, the herb for tanning (butter, cream cheese, spinach, pesto, oil)

Alchemilla vulgaris L. s. l.
LADY'S MANTLE

Common Lady's mantle, Lion's Foot, Bear's Foot, Dewcup

Lady's mantle in flower.

The finely serrate, pleated leaves of Alchemilla are reminiscent of the mantle worn by Mary in many images of the Madonna. This is the religious and cultural background of a medicinal herb often depicted in paintings of the Virgin Mary. Based on the Doctrine of Signatures (see page 18 f.), lady's mantle, often blended with yarrow (see page 50), was used for all kinds of gynaecological problems, and also for diarrhoea and skin diseases. Herb women and men inspired by religion continue to recommend it. For the 'herb father', Hermann Wagner, lady's mantle therapies were particularly important, as in his opinion abdominal complaints, 'in these times', often occurred even in young girls, 'if they follow unhealthy fashions all too slavishly'.

There is a comparable treatment using Alpine lady's mantle (*A. alpina*) in the form of tea, especially for menstruation and intestinal problems. Careful observers enjoy noting the crystal-clear droplets secreted at the leaf-tips of the Alchemilla plants. Known to botanists as 'guttation droplets', they were used as an early form of natural cosmetic.

Botanically speaking, the Alchemilla are a difficult group. Specialists note 'the shape of the leaves and their degree of division, the profile of the leaf lobes, their indents and dentation', as well as the 'hairs on the leaves, petioles, and stems' (Lippert and Merxmüller).

- **Description:** Height up to 1 ft 8 in. (50 cm); basal leaves dark green, long petioles, palmate, five- to eleven,-lobed, with fan-like folding when young, indented, dentate; stems thin, branching, leaves small, sessile, stem sheathing; flowers yellowish-green in corymbs, no bracts, with outer calyx, four sepals, four short stamens, one style, one nut-like fruit; root dark, very woody due to remains of dead leaves, many-headed
- **Flowering:** May to August
- **Scent and flavour:** Unscented; taste bitter, astringent
- **Location:** Meadows, pasture, banks of streams
- **Distribution:** Common
- **Drug:** Herba, Radix Alchemillae
- **Constituents:** Tannins, flavonoids, resin, saponin
- **Treatments:** For gynaecological problems, leucorrhoea, menstruation problems, diarrhoea, haemorrhages, inflammations of the mouth and pharyngeal region, skin diseases
- **Uses:** Tea, gargle, pressed juice, bath additive; young leaves added to vegetables and salad
- **Homeopathic uses:** Leucorrhoea, chronic diarrhoea
- **What and when to gather:** Flowering root and herb May to August, April to May for vegetables and salad
- **Lookalikes:** Other closely related species of lady's mantle, *Alchemilla* spec.
- **Other information:** Self-pollinating (parthenogenetic)

Crataegus spec.
HAWTHORN

Haw, Hawberry, Hawbush, May, May Tree, Whitethorn

The two *Cratageus* species common in Europe, the oneseed hawthorn and the smooth hawthorn (*C. monogyna Jacq.* and *C. laevigata agg.*) often hybridize and are not easy to distinguish. The oneseed hawthorn, as the common name indicates, has a single style and a fruit with a single stone. Its lobed leaves are more deeply divided. The flower of *C. laevigata* has two styles and forms a more or less ridged false fruit with two seeds. Hawthorn bushes are often found in hedges, gardens and at the edges of woodland, but *Crataegus* is often found as a tree – for instance, as 'red hawthorn' with its red, filled-in flowers – and can live for several hundred years.

Both species have the same medicinal effect. Hawthorn products are used in particular to treat heart and circulatory diseases, but it is essential that the medication is discussed with the doctor supervising treatment. Hawthorn berries have a high vitamin C content and are suitable for making jelly; the young leaves can be added to salads and vegetables.

- **Description:** Height up to 33 ft (10 m), shrub or tree; hard, reddish wood, dark grey, smooth bark, gnarled, many branches, thorns up to 3/4 in. (2 cm) long on the young shoots; leaves with short petioles, three- to five-lobed, serrate, leathery and hard when old; flowers white, in flower-rich panicles; fruits red, firm, oval to spherical, fleshy, seeds hard
- **Scent and flavour:** Scent of flowers unpleasant, musty; flavour slightly bitter, taste of fruit floury, slightly sour, the young leaves nutty
- **Location:** Forest borders, hedges, scrub
- **Distribution:** Widespread

Below left: Smooth hawthorn in flower. The two styles in the centre of the flower are clearly visible.

Below right: Oneseed hawthorn in flower, with its well-defined lobed leaves.

Above: The red fruit of smooth hawthorn can be used in the same way as oneseed hawthorn.

Right: Flowering queen of the meadow on the banks of a ditch.

- **Drug:** Flores, Folia, Fructus Crataegi
- **Constituents:** Flavonoids, essential oils, tannins, vitamin C
- **Treatments:** Heart and circulatory diseases, arrhythmia (also if due to nervous causes), angina pectoris, high blood pressure, insomnia, menopause problems
- **Uses:** Tea, capsules, flower buds and young leaves as salad, fruits as jelly, juice
- **Homeopathic uses:** Heart and circulation problems, heart problems in old age
- **What and when to gather:** Young leaves April to May; flowers with leaves May to June; fruits September
- **Lookalikes:** See above
- **Other information:** The hard wood is very popular with wood turners

Filipendula ulmaria (L.) Maxim.
QUEEN OF THE MEADOW

Meadowsweet, European Meadowsweet, Bridewort, Spirea

Queen of the meadow is a typical inhabitant of damp meadows, the borders of ditches and water meadows. Its stems, up to 6 ft 6 in. (2 m) tall, with their lavish white false umbels, looking like candyfloss from a distance, line the banks of streams and ditches from June to August. Together with other species, they form meadows of tall plants, and in the warm microclimate hosts of minute fungi colonize the stems of last year's plants. Although the plant looks so tempting and has a pleasant scent, the queen of the meadow's other common name – meadowsweet – perhaps has less to do with sweetness than with the use of the leaves and flowers as a flavouring for food and drink. Meadowsweet 'sweetens the mead', is also added to beer and wine, and gives desserts a slightly perfumed touch reminiscent of bitter almonds. The fresh root stock and the rubbed leaves are quite different. The 'scent' resembles that of a dental clinic, and the flavour is like that of cheap chewing gum. This is a very unusual smell and taste experience; the effect on many people is

of something 'artificial' and yet it is derived from a completely natural source.

- **Description:** Height up to 6 ft 6 in. (2 m), leaves petiolate, large, pinnate with five to fifteen leaflets, white underneath, stipules small, serrate; stems tinged with red in the lower parts, sturdy, ridged, branching above; flowers small, numerous, in cream-coloured false umbels; two fruits per flower, spiral like snail shells; root stock sturdy, knotty; perennial
- **Flowering:** June to early September
- **Scent and flavour:** Smell of the leaves and roots reminiscent of the dentist's; flavour of spearmint gum, the flowers have a sweet and bitter almond-like scent
- **Location:** Damp meadows, ditches, tall plant meadows, lowland woodland
- **Distribution:** Common in Europe
- **Drug:** Flores, Herba, Radix Spiraeae ulmariae
- **Constituents:** Essential oils (salicylaldehyde, salicylic acid methylester), flavone glycosides, glycosides (including camphorol glycosides), tannins
- **Treatments:** Colds, kidney and bladder ailments, joint pains, rheumatic complaints, wound healing, stomach complaints, digestive problems, diarrhoea, to prevent cellulitis and adipositas
- **Uses:** Tea, leaves and flowers as an aromatic additive to beer, wine, mead, desserts, vegetables
- **Homeopathic uses:** Fresh root extract is also used for rheumatism and inflammations of the mucous membrane
- **What and when to gather:** Young leaves, shoots and root before flowering March to April; flowers June to July, root also in September to November
- **Lookalikes:** Bride's feathers: in moist ravine and mountain woodland; dioecious
- **Other information:** Do not boil the parts of the plant; the seeds are popular with birds

Aruncus dioicus (Walt.) Fern
BRIDE'S FEATHERS

At a quick glance, it is possible to confuse bride's feathers with queen of the meadow, but the former prefers damp ravine and mountain woodland. It is also used as a healing herb.

- **Description:** Height up to 6 ft 6 in. (2 m), leaves bi- or tri-pinnate with three leaflets, up to 3 ft 3 in. (1 m) long; stems smooth, unbranching, stipules pointed to ovate, doubly serrate; dioecious; male flowers cream-coloured with more than twenty stamens, female white, in densely flowered racemes, individual flowers only $1/14$–$1/8$ in. (2–4 mm) in size, inconspicuous
- **Flowering:** May to July
- **Distribution:** Rare
- **Drug:** Herba Barbae caprae
- **Constituents:** Leaves and stems: glycoside containing hydrocyanic acid; seeds: saponins
- **Treatments:** Digestive tonic, for reducing fever
- **Uses:** Tea
- **Other information:** The only dioecious member of the rose family in central Europe

Bride's feathers in flower.

Fragaria vesca L.
WOODLAND STRAWBERRY

Wood Strawberry, Wild Strawberry

The woodland strawberry will settle in sunny woodland borders and waysides, in clearings, but also in gardens that allow more than an ornamental crew-cut lawn. It is an ancient healing and edible plant with small red berries that have a typical aroma missing from the ordinary commercially grown varieties. The berries are gathered in summer, and older readers may perhaps remember snacking on them on long childhood walks, without their own or their parents' near-hysterical fear of echinoccus tapeworms to spoil the fun. It's less well known that you can make an aromatic tea from strawberry leaves, which in popular medicine is accorded healing qualities, especially for stomach and intestinal complaints. But take care – some people have an allergic reaction to strawberries, for instance, in the form of skin rashes. The woodland strawberry is, of course, taboo for them.

The fruits of *Duchesnea indica*, the Indian strawberry, ripen at the same time or a little later. Originally from Asia, this was introduced as an ornamental plant and now grows wild in many places. The strawberry-like fruits, surrounded by a collar-like arrangement of bracts, taste of nothing at all and are not considered edible.

- **Description:** Height up to 10 in. (25 cm), leaves petiolate, tri-pinnate, ovate, serrate, upper surface glossy green, hairy underneath; stems erect, hairy, few leaves, runners up to 6 ft 6 in. (2 m) in length; flowers small, white, sepals green, yellow nutlets on the outside of the false fruit; perennial
- **Flowering:** May to July
- **Scent and flavour:** Unscented; flavour of the leaves dry to bitter (when old), fruits aromatic, sweet
- **Location:** Nutrient-rich soils, woodland clearings, scrub, woodland borders, waysides, gardens
- **Distribution:** Common
- **Drug:** Folium, Herba, Radix Fragariae
- **Constituents:** Leaves: tannins, salicyclic acid, flavonoids (including rutin, quercetin); fruits: sugar, vitamins (A, B, C), aromatic substances
- **Treatments:** For diarrhoea, sore throats, diseases of the liver, intestinal and urinary tract, rheumatic complaints, menstruation complaints, acne
- **Uses:** Tea, gargle, juice, dessert
- **Homeopathic uses:** Fruits to combat urticaria
- **What and when to gather:** Young leaves and root May to June, fruits June to August
- **Lookalikes:** Hautbois strawberry (*F. moschata*): short runners; green strawberry (*F. viridis*): flowers yellowish-white, fruits spherical, red only at the tip, flavourless, sunny slopes, in gardens, escaped to the wild; strawberryleaf cinquefoil (*Potentilla sterilis*): flowers white, leaves bluish-green, fruits inconspicuous
- **Other information:** Allergic reactions (urticaria) are known; home tea blends made from strawberry, raspberry and blackberry leaves, using only woodland strawberry leaves

Below left: The Indian strawberry escaped to the wild is sometimes mistaken for woodland strawberry, as it flourishes in similar locations.

Below right: Woodland strawberry in flower and fruit.

Geum urbanum L.
HERB BENNET

Wood Avens, Way Bennet, Avens, Clove Root, Colewort

Herb bennet has little yellow-gold flowers with green sepals (take care not to confuse it with the poisonous buttercup species). The pale yellow flowers of purple avens (*Geum rivale*) are pendant and have brownish-red sepals. When you look more closely, though, you can see the similar leaves, showing that the two species are related. They are widespread in Europe and common in some places; purple avens even grows north of the Arctic Circle.

The oil obtained from the rootstock of herb bennet (eugenol) has a slightly clove-like scent, which accounts for the alternative common name of clove root. As with cloves, it has a pain-relieving action and was used above all in dentistry. Leonhart Fuchs writes that 'Herb bennet root seethed and drunk healeth all inner wounds.' But if you follow Hildegard of Bingen, you need to count on risky side effects, because according to that lady, whoever 'takes herb bennet in drink' will 'burn with desire and love'. The comparatively high tannin content means that herb bennet is also used to treat diarrhoea and other digestive upsets. Purple avens has similar effects and is used in the same way, but its tannin content is lower. Its flowers, which taste a little like ceps, can be added to salads.

- **Description:** Height up to 2 ft 8 in. (80 cm), basal eaves petiolate, irregularly odd pinnate, edge serrate, stipules large, palmate, stem-sheathing; stems erect, hairy, branching; petals small, golden yellow, sepals green; fruit: flat, hairy burrs with hooks (former styles) in a small sphere; root thick, reddish
- **Flowering:** May to September
- **Scent and flavour:** Root smells flowery, peppery; taste aromatic, bitter
- **Location:** Damp nitrogen-rich soils, forest borders, scrub, shady gardens

- **Distribution:** Common
- **Drug:** Flores, Herba, Radix Gei urbani, or Caryophyllatae
- **Constituents:** Tannins, essential oils in the root (primarily eugenol), bitter principles
- **Treatments:** For diarrhoea, digestive problems, fever, neuralgia and muscle pain, inflammations of the mucous membrane, toothache, chilblains, haemorrhoids
- **Uses:** Tea, gargle, powder, tincture, in the past liqueur, beer additive, young leaves for salads, root as clove substitute
- **Homeopathic uses:** See above
- **What and when to gather:** Flowering herb May to July, root March to April, September to October
- **Lookalikes:** Tall buttercup (*Ranunculus acer*): yellow, glossy petals, no sepals

The dark reddish sepals give purple avens its name.

Flowering herb bennet, the seed with its hooks in the middle.

Right: The yellow flowers of silverweed cinquefoil form a marked contrast to the silver-white sheen of the leaves.

Facing page, below: Flowering erect cinquefoil with part of the rhizome cut away.

Potentilla anserina L.
SILVERWEED CINQUEFOIL

Silverweed, Common Silverweed, Silverleaf Cinquefoil, Wild Tansy

The yellow flowers of silverweed cinquefoil open in the sunshine, and only then, while the pinnate leaves turn upwards and allow their silvery-white undersides to reflect the sunlight. The plant therefore has the optimum design for its location in open country, by waysides, on slopes, etc. 'Anserina' means 'of geese', and the name derives from the fact that geese like to eat the plant.

- **Description:** Height up to 8 in. (20 cm), plant with leaf rosette and runners up to 20 in. (50 cm) long, creeping, leaves multi-paired, odd pinnate, leaflets elongate, serrate, stipules multi-pinnatisect, undersides silvery white, hairy; stems creeping; flowers with long stems, yellow-gold, c. ¾ in. (2 cm) in diameter; single-seeded nutlet fruit, rhizome branching, short; perennial
- **Flowering:** May to August

- **Scent and flavour:** Unscented; taste bitter, astringent
- **Location:** Nutrient-rich, compressed, dry soils, waysides, paths
- **Distribution:** Very common
- **Drug:** Herba, Rhizoma Anserinae
- **Constituents:** Tannins, flavonoids, bitter principles, vitamin C
- **Treatments:** For gastrointestinal cramps, diarrhoea, inflammations of the gums, poorly healing wounds, menstruation problems
- **Uses:** Tea, gargle, poultices, young leaves and fruit as vegetables
- **Homeopathic uses:** For diarrhoea, gastro-intestinal cramps
- **What and when to gather:** Herb and flowers May to August, roots March to April, September to October

Potentilla erecta (L.) Räuschel
ERECT CINQUEFOIL

Tormentil, Common Tormentil, Bloodroot, Septfoil

Among the three *Potentilla* species listed here, erect cinquefoil has the most extensive medicinal history. The astringent effect, which led to the use of tormentil tincture for oral hygiene and healing wounds and internally for gastrointestinal inflammations, is due to the high tannin content. Father Kneipp recommended it for several treatments, including vomiting blood and jaundice. The drug's effectiveness has been confirmed by scientific research though it is not yet fully explored. Bisset and Wichtl point to anti-allergenic, anti-hypertensive, anti-viral, and immune system stimulating qualities, although their uses in medicine have still to be clarified.

- **Description:** Height up to 1 ft (30 cm), basal leaves with long petioles, pinnate, stipules in threes, lanceolate, sessile; flowers yellow, four petals; rhizome blackish-brown, up to ¾ in. (2 cm) thick, tuberous, turning red when injured; perennial
- **Flowering:** May to September
- **Scent and flavour:** Unscented, flavour of root bitter to savoury, astringent
- **Location:** Poor, acid soils, poor grassland, bogs, heath, open woodland
- **Distribution:** Widespread
- **Drug:** Rhizoma Tormentillae
- **Constituents:** Tannins, phlobaphenes (tormentil red), flavonoids, resins
- **Treatments:** For diarrhoea, strengthening the stomach, staunching blood, inflammation of the gums and mucous membranes, slow-healing wounds, haemorrhoids, chilblains, burns
- **Uses:** Tincture, decoction, gargle
- **Homeopathic uses:** See above
- **What and when to gather:** Rhizome March to April, September to October
- **Lookalikes:** See box
- **Other information:** In high doses the high tannin content can induce vomiting

Potentilla reptans L. CREEPING CINQUEFOIL

The common creeping cinquefoil gets its name because it creeps over the ground with its runners, which can be more than 20 inches (50 cm) long. The plant roots at the nodes, and new leaf rosettes and hairy flower stems, develop.

Creeping cinquefoil, *Potentilla reptans* L., is similar to the other two *Potentilla* species described in its applications and action. It is very common in dry meadows, in gardens, and by waysides. The leaf and flower stems are long, the leaves finger-shaped, roughly serrate, and the flowers are also yellow but have five petals, sepals and outer sepals each.

Flowering blackthorn in a hedgerow.

Prunus spinosa L.
BLACKTHORN

Sloe, Sloethorn

The sight of blossoming woodland borders in very early spring lifts the winter-weary heart. The most that can be seen all around is a little delicate, developing green, but the blackthorn is in radiant white flower – the leaves do not develop until after the blossom. In the country hedges of western Europe and the ancient field hedges of north and north-western Europe, some of which are centuries old, the blackthorn is a frequent plant, and sometimes, together with hawthorn, wild roses and other shrubs, it forms almost impenetrable thickets, providing cover for numerous creatures. Even the red-backed shrike, a bird whose habitat has in many areas been destroyed by modern agriculture, can still find nesting opportunities here.

You won't be putting the fruits, the small, dark blue sloes with their greyish bloom, straight into your mouth after picking them. The bitter, sour, astringent taste is simply not attractive

Right: The sloe fruits with their blue bloom grow on short, thorn-protected shoots.

enough. They don't ripen fully – when they become a little sweeter – until after the first frosts. The berry-eating bird species know it. To get in first before the birds, you can pick the berries before the first frosts and keep them in the freezer until you prepare them. They are good for making liqueurs, purees and jelly, and among other constituents they contain tannins and lots of vitamin C.

In folk medicine, a tea made of blackthorn flowers is considered a mild laxative, while the fruits are used to treat diarrhoea. A tea for the bladder and kidneys is prepared from the leaves, and the bark is supposed to have a fever-reducing action. As is so often the case, symptoms of poisoning may appear after too high a dose.

- **Description:** Height up to 10 ft (3 m); black bark, hairy on lower parts, smooth further along, markedly branching, gnarled, long shoots with long, pointed thorns; leaves small, short petioles, ovate, serrate, narrow, linear stipules; flowers small, snow-white, numerous, short stems; fruit blue-black with bloom, round, with large stone
- **Flowering:** March, April
- **Scent and flavour:** Flowers sweetly scented, taste of bitter almonds; flavour of the fruit very dry, astringent, sourish
- **Location:** Woodland borders, hedges, scrub; this herb likes light and warmth
- **Distribution:** Widespread
- **Drug:** Flores, Folia, Cortex, Fructus Pruni Spinosae
- **Constituents:** Flowers, bark, leaves: glycosides (amygdalin, a hydrocyanic acid derivative), flavones; fruits: tannins, flavonoids, sugar, vitamin C
- **Treatments:** Flowers: laxative (mild), for purifying the blood, rheumatic complaints; leaves: for skin impurities, kidney and bladder ailments; bark: for reducing fever; fruit: for diarrhoea, juice for inflammations in the mouth and pharyngeal area
- **Uses:** Tea, fruit: liqueur, spirits, wine, jelly, gargle
- **What and when to gather:** Flowers March to April, leaves May, green and ripe fruits October to November after first frost (for tip, see above)
- **Lookalikes:** None
- **Other information:** Watch the dose: poisoning is possible if the dose is too high

Prunus avium L. **WILD CHERRY**

The red sweet cherries turn black later and then have a bittersweet, very aromatic flavour. Stones and stems are also used in folk medicine. (Also known as sweet cherry.)

Prunus padus L. **EUROPEAN BIRD CHERRY**

The European bird cherry, with its racemes of intensely scented flowers, often grows in woodland borders and on river banks, as well as in lowland woods.

Other *Prunus* species

Other Prunus *species used not only as wild fruit but also medicinally include the* **wild cherry,** Prunus avium L. *(sweet cherry), the original of our cultivated varieties; the shrub-like* **sour cherry,** P. cerasus L., *with its bitter fruits; the* **European plum,** P. domestica L., *and the* **peach,** P. persica (L.) Batsch, *with its many cultivated varieties; the* **European bird cherry,** P. padus L. *up to 20 ft (6 m) tall, with white, intensively scented racemes of flowers and black, sour to bitter fruit; the* **sweet almond,** P. amygdalus Batsch, *cultivated in Mediterranean countries; and the* **cherry laurel,** P. laurocerasus L., *whose toxic leaves, containing cyanide-like substances, must not be confused with those of the* **sweet bay,** Laurus nobilis *(see page 268).*

Rosa canina L.
DOG ROSE

Briar, Briar Rose, Common Briar, Wild Rose

'No rose without a thorn,' the poets say, as if to claim that 'all that glitters is not gold'. A botanist would frown, hearing the words, because in botanical terms, roses don't have thorns, but prickles. Thorns are part of the wood and firmly fixed to the branch, whereas prickles grow out of the upper layer of the bark and, as is the case with roses, are easily broken off.

Wild roses are not just beautiful flowers; they can be used in many ways. The best-known product is oil of roses, which a 19th-century text describes as follows: 'The true Eastern oil of roses, (known as attar, uttar, or – wrongly – as otto), as is it made in India and Persia, is to other scents and toiletries what the diamond is to jewels. It is the essence of all things fine, exquisite, precious and sumptuous.' The high price is the result of the investment needed – 660–880 pounds (300–400 kg) of petals are needed to make 3¹/₂ fluid ounces (100 ml) of oil of roses. In Europe, the main supplier is the French rose (*Rosa gallica*), which is also considered the ancestor of the many cultivated floribunda, shrub and climbing roses. Recently a programme has begun in Afghanistan to try and persuade poppy growers to change to rose cultivation.

The fruits of the rose, the so-called rose hips, produce those hairy yellowish seeds that in earlier schooldays may have been stuffed down the backs of necks by naughty boys and girls because they tickled so horribly. They can, however, also be used for more sensible purposes and produce, for example, a very tasty jelly. The seeds and the flesh of the fruit are very suitable for use in teas. Rose galls are a growth of cells in which the gall wasp lays its eggs. They contain tannins and are recommended for strengthening the stomach.

■ **Description:** Height up to 16 ft (5 m); branches prickly, overhanging; leaves three to five in number, odd pinnate, orbicular to ovate, edge serrate; flowers with stems, reddish pink to white, anthers yellow, false fruits bright orange-red, oval, smooth, with remains of calyx on top, numerous seeds, ridged, yellowish nutlets with fine hairs

Below left: The flowers of the dog rose...

Below right: ... and the oval rose hips.

- **Flowering:** June to July
- **Scent and flavour:** Flowers often intensely scented, taste sweetish to slightly bitter; fruits sourish, aromatic, seeds a little bitter
- **Location:** Hedges, woodland borders, open woodland, parks, gardens
- **Distribution:** Widespread
- **Drug:** Fructus Rosae; Syn. Semen Cynosbati
- **Constituents:** Fruit: vitamins (primarily vitamin C), sugar, essential oils, gallic acid, vanillin, pectin
- **Treatments:** For strengthening immune defenses against colds, scurvy, seasonal tiredness, tendency to bleed, kidney and bladder disorders (doubtful)
- **Uses:** Tea, fruit puree, jelly, liqueur, wine, punch, rose water
- **What and when to gather:** Leaves April to May, flowers June to July, fruits September to October
- **Lookalikes:** French rose: flowers violet to deep red, prickles straight or curved; rugosa rose (*R. rugosa*): leaves wrinkled, fruits can be more than ³/₄ in. (2 cm) across; other species of rose, only distinguished by specialists using features of the stems and leaves

- **Other information:** Highly recommended as a vitamin C-rich tea for home use

'Roses, shining,
Balsam-scented!
Fluttering, floating,
Secret life giving,
On your winged branches,
Released from your buds,
Hasten to bloom!'

Johann Wolfgang von Goethe (1749–1832)

Below left: The flowers of this vinegar rose are deep violet in colour.

Below right: Fruits (rosehips) of the French rose.

Rubus fruticosus L. s. l. **BLACKBERRY** and *Rubus idaeus* L. **RASPBERRY**

As simple as it is even for those unskilled in botany to tell a blackberry from a red raspberry, it is difficult even for those who have studied botany to determine an individual blackberry or raspberry plant with scientific accuracy. There are more than a hundred species of blackberry with many hybrids, and the raspberry family tree doesn't look much different. However, the ripe, sweet berries are all edible, and if you don't snack on the lot while you're picking them they are very good for making jams, conserves, juices, syrups or liqueurs, or for using to fill a fruit tart.

In naturopathy, blackberry juice is used to treat anemia, although generally 'Folia Rubi fruticosi' – the leaves – are of greater interest, since they contain more vitamin C than the fruits do. They are usually drunk as a fermented tea that can easily hold its own against genuine tea varieties; folk medicine tells us that chewing fresh blackberry leaves can help to treat bleeding gums. As they contain tannin, they can also be used to treat diarrhoea. Since olden times, many curious beliefs have surrounded the tendency of the blackberry tendril to grow in arches and produce new roots at the tips. Crawling under a blackberry arch is believed to heal various illnesses as they are supposed to transfer to the bush, and an old English myth has it that driving bedeviled cattle through blackberry tendrils will free them from bad spells.

The raspberry flowers and ripens earlier than the blackberry. Raspberry syrup is used, among other things, to improve the flavour of cough medicine. However, there is little scientific proof of various traditional uses, such as to treat infections in the mouth and throat, and against skin diseases, although there is no denying that the fresh fruit, which contains plenty of vitamin C, is extremely beneficial.

BLACKBERRY

Bramble

■ **Description:** Height up to 16 ft (5 m) climbing; shrub, part leafless, part leafed in winter, branches overhanging and rooting at the tips; thin, strong, backwards-pointing prickles for climbing on the branches, petioles and the undersides of leaves; leaves three to five in number, elongate-ovate,

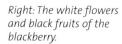

Right: The white flowers and black fruits of the blackberry.

Far right: The European dewberry's fruits have a blue bloom and an acid taste, but are just as edible as those of other Rubus species.

serrate at the edges; flowers white to pale pink, numerous in racemes or panicles on the over-wintered shoot, which dies off after fruiting; aggregate fruit, dark purple to glossy black, with numerous little stone fruits

- **Flowering:** June to August
- **Scent and flavour:** Flowers and leaves unscented; fruit aromatic, sweet to sourish
- **Location:** Nutrient-rich, often lime-poor soils, woodland borders, woodland clearings, forests, hedges
- **Distribution:** Very common
- **Drug:** Folia, Fructus Rubi fruticosi
- **Constituents:** Leaves: tannins, flavonoids, essential oils, vitamin C; fruits: vitamin C, sugar, mucilage, pectin
- **Treatments:** For strengthening immune defences, general strengthening, skin rashes, bleeding of the gums, diarrhoea, fever, regulating menstruation, purifying the blood
- **Uses:** Tea, gargle, jelly, conserves, liqueur, wine, syrup
- **Homeopathic uses:** Young leaves with little hair, treatments see above
- **What and when to gather:** Leaves April to June, fruits August to October
- **Lookalikes:** European dewberry (*R. caesius*): fruited with bluish bloom due to waxy coating, edible; numerous sub-species can only be distinguished by specialists; raspberry (*R. idaeus*): paler green, undersides of leaves whitish, thin, fine prickles, see below

RASPBERRY

- **Description:** Height up to 6 ft 6 in. (2 m); deciduous shrub, rod-like branches first erect, then overhanging, with thin, fine prickles, fruiting in the second year; leaves pinnate, three to seven leaflets, ovate, edge serrate, pale green, undersides of the leaves with whitish hair, leaf veins sometimes have fine prickles; flowers white in loose panicles; red aggregate fruits with numerous small stone fruitlets on the cone-shaped flower head base; sturdy root, forming runners

Left: Ripe raspberries make an inviting snack.

Below: Raspberry vines are less prickly than those of the blackberry. Young leaves make a tasty tea for home use.

- **Flowering:** May to July
- **Scent and flavour:** Leaves when rubbed sweetish, aromatic, astringent; fruits sweet, very aromatic
- **Location:** Nitrogen-rich soils, forest clearings, woodland borders, waysides, scrub
- **Distribution:** Very common
- **Drug:** Folia, Flores, Fructus, Sirupus Rubi idaei
- **Constituents:** Leaves: tannins, flavonoids, essential oils, vitamin C; fruits: vitamin C, fruit acids, sugar, mucilage, pectin, flavonoids, anthocyan glycosides
- **Treatments:** See blackberry; for encouraging labour in childbirth
- **Uses:** Tea, poultices, gargle, flavour corrector in the pharmaceutical industry, jelly, conserves, syrup, liqueur, wine, vinegar
- **What and when to gather:** Leaves April to June, fruits July to August
- **Lookalikes:** Blackberry (*R. fruticosus*): leaves harder, not whitish underneath, coarser prickles, see above
- **Other information:** Good tea for domestic use; pregnant women should only drink the tea when birth is imminent, as the leaves can start labour

Sanguisorba minor Scop.
SMALL BURNET and
Sanguisorba officinalis L.
GREATER BURNET

Official Burnet, Wild Pimpernel

Above right: The dark, wine-red flowers of greater burnet are unmistakable.

Below right: Small burnet in full flower. The leaves of both species can be confused with those of hollowstem burnet saxifrage.

The small and greater burnet are not only closely related but are similarly used in herbal medicine. Both are considered proven remedies for diarrhoea and bleeding (e.g. bleeding of the gums or haemorrhoids). They were also used to treat inflammation. Burnet is also used to season cream cheeses, vegetables and soups.

In the countryside, it is easy to distinguish between both species. Greater burnet, with its tall (up to 4 ft/1.2 m), branching, leafed stems and conspicuous dark wine-red flowers is unmistakable from June to August in moist to wet straw meadows and wetland meadows, and is insect pollinated, as are most members of the rose family. Small burnet prefers drier locations, has inconspicuous greenish flowers, and is pollinated by the wind.

- **Description:** Small burnet: Height up to 2 ft 4 in. (70 cm), leaves odd pinnate (nine to twenty-five), orbicular, ovate, dentate; stems hard, ridged, often with a reddish tinge; individual flowers in small spherical inflorescence, close together, inconspicuous, greenish, later tinged with red; wind pollinated; leaves with long petioles above and brush-shaped large scars below; nutlet fruit; woody root stock
- **Flowering:** May, June
- **Scent and flavour:** Leaves spicy, aromatic, a touch bitter; root salty
- **Location:** Lime-rich soils, waysides, nutrient-poor grassland, dry grassland, likes warmth
- **Distribution:** Scattered
- **Drug:** Herba, Radix Sanguisorbae (minor)
- **Constituents:** Tannins, saponines, essential oils, vitamin C
- **Treatments:** Haemorrhages, wounds, ulcers, bleeding gums, diarrhoea, flatulence, digestive disorders, haemorrhoids

- **Uses:** Tea, culinary (butter, cream cheese, vinegar, wine, soup, vegetable)
- **Homeopathic uses:** See above
- **What and when to gather:** Young leaves May to September; root September to October
- **Lookalikes:** Hollowstem burnet saxifrage (*Pimpinella saxifraga*), carrot family, see page 210
- **Other information:** Often on sale in garden centres instead of hollowstem burnet saxifrage

Sorbus aucuparia L.
EUROPEAN MOUNTAIN ASH

Rowan, Mountain Ash, Quickbeam, Fowler's Service, Witchwood

The ripe red berries of the mountain ash are so bright that it is impossible to overlook them even when leaves colour in the autumn. The splendour is brief, though, because the fruits of this tree attract birds. For humans, they are mildly toxic due to the parasorbic acid they contain. However, the poison disappears when they are cooked, so that the berries can be made into jelly.

The dried leaves are also used, as well as the berries, in herbal medicine. Since the Middle Ages at the latest, the berries have been used as a laxative, but have also been used to treat kidney complaints, rheumatism and gout.

Botanists, anthropologists and etymologists disagree about the names of the tree. 'Mountain ash', it is believed, came about because the tree has leaves that resemble the ash and can grow at relatively high altitudes on thin soil (it is not related to the ash tree). 'Rowan' is thought to derive from the Old Norse name for the tree, 'raun, rogn', though it could also be linked to 'rune' or possibly Gaelic 'rudha-an', 'the red one'. In European folklore, the mountain ash was considered to give protection from evil magic and spirits, hence the alternative English name 'quickbeam' (from the Anglo-Saxon 'cwicbeam', meaning tree of life).

- **Description:** Height up to 50 ft (15 m); bark reddish-brown when young, with white spots, ash grey when older; leaves alternate, petiolate, odd pinnate, pale green; individual leaflets elongate, ovate, sharply serrate; flowers creamy-white in flat, many-flowered corymb at the tip of the shoot; fruits three-chambered, up to ²⁄₅ in. (1 cm) in length, orange-red to coral-red, in pendant bunches
- **Flowering:** May, June

- **Scent and flavour:** Flowers smell unpleasant; berries taste very bitter before the first frost, bitter to sour afterwards
- **Location:** Open mixed deciduous woodland, scrub, parks, streets
- **Distribution:** Common
- **Drug:** Fructus Sorbi aucupariae
- **Constituents:** Tannins, sorbitol, malic acid, vitamin C, provitamin A, sugar, pectin; seeds: hydrocyanic acid glycoside amygdalin
- **Treatments:** For diarrhoea (pureed berries), gentle laxative (pressed juice), treating kidney stones, diabetes, rheumatic complaints, coughs
- **Uses:** Spirit, liqueur, jelly, puree, juice
- **What and when to gather:** Berries August to October (allow to finish ripening in the freezer, as frost sweetens them slightly)
- **Lookalikes:** Ash (*Fraxinus excelsior*): leaves similar, flowers in small bunches, inconspicuous, tree 130 ft (40 m) tall, belongs to olive family
- **Other information:** Fruit when unripe and undried contains parasorbic acid, making it slightly poisonous; the fruits of the Moravian mountain ash (*S. moravia*) taste sweet.

The leaves are 'odd pinnate'. A single end leaflet is added to the paired, opposite leaflet, i.e. the number of individual leaflets is always odd.

Below left: The creamy white corymbs of the mountain ash are similar to elderflowers in appearance.

Below right: In August the shining red berries turn ripe.

PINOPSIDS, CRYPTOGAMAE

Gymnosperms differ from angiosperms in that their seeds are uncovered. Mostly, these species are woody plants with needle-like or scale-like leaves.

The ancient group of spore-bearing plants includes the horsetails (Equisetaceae), club mosses (Lycopodiaceae), and ferns (Pteridophyta). They do not spread by means of seeds but by spores.

With algae, fungi and mosses (Bryophyta), the role of stems and leaves is taken by the thallus, which is not divided into roots, stems and leaves.

Members of the cypress family on the Swabian Alb in Germany; the 'juniper heath' is characteristic of this landscape.

Cypress family
Cupressaceae

Members of the cypress family are shrubs or trees with needle-like or scale-like leaves. The family includes the dioecious juniper (Juniperus), the arborvitae (Thuja), often planted in cemeteries or as a hedge, and also the pillar-shaped cypress (Cupressus), well-known in Mediterranean lands.

Juniperus communis L.
COMMON JUNIPER

■ *protected, mildly poisonous* ■
Juniper

In the Brothers Grimm's collection of fairy tales, *The Juniper Tree* is one of the darkest and most unsettling stories. The juniper plays a central part. The death in childbed of the woman after eating the berries corresponds to the warning in every book of herbal medicine against eating juniper berries in pregnancy. Apart from such warnings, the berries are considered stimulating to the appetite and good for the digestion.

- **Description:** Height up to 33 ft (10 m); shrub or pyramid-shaped tree, can grow up to 1,000 years old; leaves in whorls of three, horizontal to the stem, needle-shaped, hard, pointed, prickly, bluish-grey; branches erect, bark reddish to grey; flowers dioecious: male inconspicuous, yellowish-white, in the leaf axils, female cones greenish, triple scaled on short stems; cones berry-shaped, round, green in the first year, then bluish-grey to blackish-brown, bluish bloom, seeds woody; deep-rooted
- **Flowering:** April to June
- **Scent and flavour:** Scent resinous, spicy; flavour sweetish at first, then spicy, slightly bitter

- **Location:** Heathland, pine forest, dry, sandy or acid, boggy soils
- **Distribution:** Scattered
- **Drug:** Fructus, Lignum, Aetheroleum Junipari
- **Constituents:** Essential oils (pinene, terpinol), bitter principles, tannins, flavonoids, juniperin, inverted sugar
- **Treatments:** For treating gastro-enteric diseases, bronchitis, circulation disorders, bladder complaints, rheumatic complaints, skin diseases, purifying the blood
- **Uses:** Berries, tea, puree, rubbing spirit, oil, inhalation, baths, sauna, culinary seasoning, spirits
- **Homeopathic uses:** See above, and also for diseases of the kidneys and urinary tract
- **What and when to gather:** Ripe black berries September to November, wood from the trunks and thicker branches, young shoots and berry cones May to October
- **Lookalikes:** Savin (*Juniperus sabina*): older leaves scale-shaped, shoots smell unpleasant when rubbed, poisonous; aborvitae (*Thuja orientalis*): when young, has needle shaped leaves, scale-shaped leaves when older, very poisonous due to thujone
- **Other information:** Take care: high doses of juniper berries can lead to irritation of the kidneys accompanied by inflammation; in pregnancy the berries can cause cramp-like pains and bleeding of the womb

The arborvitae contains the essential oil thujone, which has proved fatal to horses. In homeopathy, 'thuja' is an important complex remedy.

The poisonous savin has needles only when young; shown here is a fruiting shoot with scale-shaped leaves.

Left: berries on a juniper shoot with its pointed needles.

Ginkgo family
Ginkgoaceae

The ginkgo is the single remaining survivor of the ginkgo family, which in the past comprised many more species.

Ginkgo biloba L.
MAIDENHAIR TREE

Ginkgo, Fossil Tree, Japanese Silver Apricot

In our aging society, ginkgo products are proving ever more popular – after all, they are supposed, if not to prevent age-related memory loss up to and including dementia, then at least to delay it. As always, when certain plants are praised to high heaven by the media and in advertising campaigns, a certain amount of skepticism is advisable. Ginkgo leaf extracts can't be expected to perform miracles, but they do encourage the circulation of blood in the brain and therefore may contribute to the easing of headaches, dizziness, tinnitus and age-related weakness in brain performance. The knowledge of these treatments, by the way, does not come from traditional Chinese medicine but (as Hans Feist reports) from a group of German researchers who published their findings in the mid-1960s.

In Asia, there are gingko trees presumed to be more than 2,000 years old. The species was not introduced to Europe until 280 years ago.

- **Description:** Height up to 130 ft (40 m); tree pyramid-shaped when young; bark brownish-grey, wood yellowish; 'leaves' with long petioles, fan-shaped, leathery, pale green; dioecious; male flowers in yellowish catkins, 2–2¾ in. (5–7 cm) long; female flowers two to three to each stem, green, small; fruits orange-yellow, cherry-like; seeds hard

- **Flowering:** April
- **Scent and flavour:** Fruit has a rancid smell
- **Location:** Parks, gardens
- **Distribution:** Native to south-east Asia
- **Drug:** Folium, Semen Ginkgo bilobae
- **Constituents:** Glycosides, flavonoids
- **Treatments:** For poor memory, poor circulation of blood in the brain, venous disease, in geriatric medicine, treating dementia, depression, dizziness, tinnitus, in convalescence, for asthma
- **Uses:** Tea, ready-made products
- **Homeopathic uses:** See above, and for tonsillitis, colds, headaches
- **What and when to gather:** Leaves
- **Lookalikes:** None
- **Other information:** Its roasted seeds are considered a delicacy in China

Ginkgos, being very pollution-resistant, are therefore often planted as avenue, garden, and park trees.

Below: The fan-shaped, often split 'leaves' of the ginkgo and the cherry-like fruits, shown here still unripe.

Pine family
Pinaceae

With the exception of the larch, which loses its little bunches of needles in the autumn, the members of the pine family are evergreen conifers, their seeds ripening in erect or pendant cones. The male flower heads are catkin- or cone-shaped

---

Pinus mugo Turra
DWARF MOUNTAIN PINE

■ *protected* ■

Mountain Pine, Mugo Pine, Dwarf Swiss Mountain Pine

The dwarf mountain pine is distinguished by its amazing ability to adapt to the hard conditions in the high mountains. It can withstand frost, storms and many feet of snow. In the Alps, no other tree, apart from low, shrub-like willow species, grows at such high altitudes.

Altogether, the pine family contains a great variety of species, mainly distributed through-out the northern hemisphere. The most common species in central Europe are the Scots pine (*Pinus sylvestris*) and the Austrian pine (*P. nigra*), the Norway spruce (*Picea abies*), the silver fir (*Abies alba*) and the European larch (*Larix decidua*). Thanks to their skin- and circulation-stimulating action, there are plenty of uses for the essential oils and resins of many *Pinus* species. Bath additives are the most established and the most popular. The young shoots of these conifers can even be eaten; they have a high vitamin content.

- **Description:** Height up to 5 ft (1.5 m); evergreen, shrub-like; needles long, paired; branches prostrate, dense; male flower catkins in yellow bunches on young shoots, females in cone-shaped, scaly, sessile cones
- **Flowering:** May, June
- **Scent and flavour:** Characteristic resinous smell
- **Location:** Mountains, high altitude meadows, even above the tree line, high altitude bogs, gardens
- **Distribution:** Scattered
- **Drug:** Oleum Pini (Pumilionis, Sylvestris), Terebinthinae
- **Constituents:** Essential oils (terpene, pinene, terpinol), resins (colophonium), bitter principles, vitamin C
- **Treatments:** For colds, coughs, bronchitis,

Below left: The protected mugo pine grows in the highlands and mountain bogs of the Bavarian Alpine foothills in Germany.

Below right: Scratches are made in Scots pine trunks to obtain resin. Turpentine oil (Oleum Terebinthiae) is produced from the resin.

circulatory disorders, rheumatic and venous diseases, sciatica, muscle ache, in convalescence, for insomnia

- **Uses:** Tea, baths, embrocation (rubbing alcohol), balsam, poultices, inhalation, sauna additives
- **Homeopathic uses:** See above
- **What and when to gather:** Young shoots April to May; branches, twigs, April to June; resin

- **Lookalikes:** Erect trees: Swiss stone pine (*P. cembra*): needles in fives, large cones; Scots pine (*P. sylvestris*): red towards the top of the trunk; Austrian pine (*P. nigra*): trunk greyish-black
- **Other information:** The young needles of pines, larches, spruce and fir can be used in the same way

A COMPARISON: THE MOST IMPORTANT CONIFERS

The long needles of the Scots pine, arranged in pairs.

The needles of the spruce are short and prickly. The fresh shoots in May are pale green.

The flat, soft needles of the silver fir have white stripes on the undersides.

Larch needles grow in bunches. They are soft and are shed in the autumn.

Horsetail family
Equisetaceae

With the various species of the horsetail family, *a distinction is made between sterile and fertile (i.e. spore-bearing) shoots. The stem, usually grooved, is divided into individual sections like 'Lego' bricks and can be pulled apart and pushed together again.*

Equisetum arvense L.
FIELD HORSETAIL

Scouring Grass, Scouring Rush, Western Horsetail, Corn Horsetail

The name 'scouring rush' for field horsetail came about because this plant, which contains silicic acid, was used for cleaning and scouring plates and dishes, particularly those made of pewter. Natural medicine values the field horsetail's diuretic qualities, and its main use is in teas for kidney and bladder complaints, as well as in powdered form for wound healing, gout, rheumatism and ulcers. Apart from the poisonous marsh horsetail, the other species growing in central Europe are also used. In Germany, Sebastian Kneipp was a great believer in horsetail and, because of its strengthening action on the immune system, even recommended it to treat tumours. It should also be mentioned that field horsetail can be used to make an effective broth to strengthen the resistance of garden plants against animal and plant pests.

- **Description:** Height up to 10 inches (25 cm), sterile up to 1 ft 4 in. (40 cm); fertile shoots unbranching, yellowish-brown with cone-shaped sporangia spike at the tip, stem sheaths brown, sterile shoots (from May onwards) green, markedly branched in whorls, ridged, stems hollow, grooved; extensive, perennial network of roots, up to 20 ft (6 m) deep in the soil
- **Flowering:** March to April
- **Scent and flavour:** Scentless and flavourless; crunchy when bitten
- **Location:** Nutrient-rich soils, fields, fallow land, waysides, gardens
- **Distribution:** Very common
- **Drug:** Herba Equiseti
- **Constituents:** Silicic acid, flavonoids, tannins
- **Treatments:** For kidney and bladder ailments, renal gravel, chilblains, heavy bleeding (nose, lungs, stomach), haemorrhoids, heavy menstrual bleeding, mineral salt deficiency
- **Uses:** Tea, baths, poultices, gargle
- **Homeopathic uses:** For kidney and urinary tract inflammations
- **What and when to gather:** Sterile shoots June to September
- **Lookalikes:** Giant horsetail (*E. telmateia*): sterile and fertile shoots much sturdier, up to 6 ft 6 in. (2 m) in height, well-watered sites; marsh horsetail (*E. palustre*): sporangium on the green shoot, poisonous, in wet meadows, marshes
- **Other information:** Daily dose c. ⅕ oz (6 g); overdose can lead to poisoning

The field horsetail appears early in the year on waysides, in gardens and on fallow fields. It looks almost like a small asparagus stalk as it pushes its yellow-brown fertile shoot out of the ground.

Left: the sterile shoot, which does not appear until the summer, is branching and green.

Club-moss family
Lycopodiaceae

Plants of the club-moss family have a branching, creeping shoot from which the erect stems with the sporangia spikes grow upwards. The leaves on the shoot are small and scale-shaped. In some countries, all species are protected; it is permitted to gather the sporangia spikes to collect the spores.

Lycopodium clavatum L.
RUNNING CLUB-MOSS

■ *poisonous, protected* ■
Common Club-moss, Stag's-Horn Club-moss, Running Pine, Running Cedar, Running Ground-Pine, Wolf's Claw

The yellow spore powder, which contains oil and cannot be wetted with water, is used in many ways. Almost impossible to set alight in its compacted condition, it will burn in a glowing fireball if air is blown through it. This effect is used by pyrotechnicians and fire-eaters. Photographers use club-moss spores as flash powder. Club-moss spore dust was also used in the early stages of photocopy technology and in forensic science. The spore powder available on the market today mainly comes from the Himalayas and Russia. In the past, club-moss was a herb used as a kind of cure-all for kidney and bladder ailments. However, the latest research reveals that club-moss teas can no longer be recommended, as the plant contains poisonous alkaloids. There is a particular warning against regular use.

■ **Description:** Height up to 10 in. (25 cm); shoot forking, branched, with dense leaves, evergreen, leaves small, white at the pointed tips, more or less at right angles to the more than 3 ft 3 in. (1 m) long shoot; stem with two to three yellowish-brown sporangia spikes; root forking, branching, rooting at the shoots; perennial
■ **Flowering:** July to August
■ **Scent and flavour:** Unscented, almost tasteless
■ **Location:** Dry coniferous forests, heathland
■ **Distribution:** Scattered, avoids lime
■ **Drug:** Herba, Farina Lycopodii
■ **Constituents:** Herb: poisonous alkaloids (lycopodine, clavatin, clavotoxin), spores: oils, flavonoids
■ **Treatments:** For kidney and bladder ailments, colic, diarrhoea, rheumatism, open, badly healing wounds, eczema, skin diseases
■ **Uses:** Tea, powder, pharmacy (to dust tablets so that they do not stick together), cosmetic (dry shampoo), pyrotechnics, forensic science
■ **Homeopathic uses:** Constitution remedy, in chronic diseases
■ **What and when to gather:** Spores July to September
■ **Lookalikes:** Stiff club-moss (*L. annotinum*): leaf tips not white, single sporangium, short stems, protected; fir club-moss (*Huperzia selago*): sporangia single between leaves
■ **Other information:** The herb contains lycopodine, an alkaloid with a curare-like paralyzing effect. The tea made from the herb must not be boiled!

Top: In the rare, poisonous fir club-moss, the sporangia are situated between the leaves.

Above: Shoots of running club-moss.

Left: In running club-moss, the sporangia are arranged in pairs or in threes on a long, loosely leafed stem.

Polypody family
Polypodiaceae

Ferns are usually perennial plants with leaf fronds, on the undersides of which the spores are formed in so-called 'sori'.

Dryopteris filix mas (L.) Schott
MALE FERN

■ *poisonous* ■

Male Shield Fern, Shield Fern

The young fronds, rolled into spirals like snail shells on their brown scaly stems, will unroll as they develop. On the underside of the frond the kidney-shaped sori (spore containers) will form.

In the high Middle Ages, Hildegard of Bingen considered the fern – fewer species were distinguished in those days – to be a defence against the devil and evil spirits. She also recommended it to treat deafness, failing eyesight, and gout. The fern has a long history of use to rid the intestine of parasites such as roundworms and tapeworms. More recent research has in fact confirmed that the filicic acid contained in the plant has a paralysing effect on lower animals such as tapeworms and liver flukes. However, using fern root extracts as a vermifuge can do more harm than good if they are not given in a professional manner. 'It is necessary to be very careful with the dose of this drug and give it together with a salinic laxative (Na_2So_4) or with castor oil. If combined with alcohol, there is a danger of poisoning' (Schauenberg and Paris).

■ **Description:** Height up to 4 ft (1.2 m); fronds dense, funnel-forming, frond stems sturdy, with light-coloured scales, bi-pinnate, pinnate leaflets rounded, slightly dentate, sori kidney-shaped with a veil on underside, in double rows; sturdy rhizome, brown outside, greenish-yellow inside, perennial

■ **Flowering:** June to September
■ **Scent and flavour:** Scent of the leaves aromatic to musty
■ **Location:** Woodland, scrub, gardens
■ **Distribution:** Common
■ **Drug:** Rhizoma Filicis
■ **Constituents:** Fronds: filicic acid, rhizome; fatty oil, sugar
■ **Treatments:** For removing tapeworms, used externally in folk medicine for aching feet, varicose veins, rheumatism, vermin in bedding
■ **Uses:** Powder, decoction, baths
■ **Homeopathic uses:** Vermifuge, to treat infected wounds
■ **What and when to gather:** Fronds July to October, rhizome September to October
■ **Lookalikes:** Spinulose woodfern (*D. carthusiana*): leaves with thorn-like points; ladyfern (*Athyrium filix-femina*): fronds finer and more delicate
■ **Other information:** Overdoses are poisonous (can lead to blindness and death); only use externally; use ready-made product

Underside of a male fern frond with the veiled sori.

Below: The male fern is a decorative plant often cultivated in gardens.

Polypodium vulgare L.
COMMON POLYPODY

Rock Polypody, Oak Fern, Brake Root

The genus name *Polypodium* means 'many feet', and derives from the fact that the long-stemmed fronds of the common polypody grow out of the creeping rhizome 'like feet'. The rhizome, or root stock, is the part of the plant that has been used as medicine since ancient times. It contains glycyrrhizine, a sweet-tasting constituent, typical also of cultivated liquorice (*Glycyrrhiza glabra*). As medicines are not known for pleasant flavours – they are supposed to do you good, not to taste nice – the sweet polypody root was considered a noble exception and often given to children, whether as a vermifuge or a laxative. Infusions of the dried root produce a lemon-yellow sweet tea, which may be used as a decongestant for colds.

Polypody likes to grow in rocky locations and obtains its nutrients from thin humus that has settled between the rocks. It is also seen on old walls, sometimes even in the crowns of ancient trees. Cultivars available in garden centers are often used in gardens and parks as ground cover in shady areas. The sori, yellow-gold to start with and later turning brown, 'dot' the underside, and are not kidney-shaped like those of the male fern, but rounded.

- **Description:** Height up to 16 ft 4 in. (40 cm); evergreen, fronds with long unscaled stems, with up to thirty leaflets on each side; sori below yellow at first, brown when ripe, round, large (like dots), no veil; creeping fleshy rhizome, densely covered with dry, shiny scales
- **Flowering:** June to September
- **Scent and flavour:** Rhizome: smell unpleasantly sweetish; taste very sweet to bitter
- **Location:** Walls, rocks, tree stumps, oak and birch forests
- **Distribution:** Widespread

- **Drug:** Radix Polypodii
- **Constituents:** Sugar (glycyrrhizine), mucilage, resinous bitter principles, tannins, essential oils
- **Treatments:** For coughs, bronchitis, liver and gall bladder complaints, gout, rheumatism, constipation, intestinal parasites
- **Uses:** Tea
- **What and when to gather:** Rhizome March to April, September to October

Polypody on an old wall. The round yellow sori can be seen on the turned-back frond on the right.

Phaeophytina
BROWN ALGAE

The brown algae, which comprise about 1,500 species, are multi-cellular, usually brown-coloured marine algae. Instead of chlorophyll, the brown-coloured fucoxanthin provides energy by photosynthesis. Alginic acid, alginates and laminarin are of increasing importance in the food and cosmetic industries.

Fucus vesiculosus L.
BLADDERWRACK

Sea Wrack, Cutweed, Kelp, Black Tang

Human beings are only gradually discovering the marine plant world and making use of its benefits. Some species, including bladderwrack, already had their medicinal powers tested in ancient times. Later, it was hoped that the high iodine content of bladderwrack might help with thyroid gland diseases, but this is no longer recommended because of the associated risks. Bisset and Wichtl give a warning about the use of bladderwrack in slimming therapies and curtly refer to its use in 'slimming baths' as 'utter nonsense'. However, we have included bladderwrack in this book as an example to show that, in some cases, traditional folk 'cures'

combined with modern forms of marketing make more promises than they can keep.

Laminaria species – such as sugar kelp (*L. saccharina*) grow on rocks in the tidal zone. They contain, among other constituents, mineral salts and vitamins. Hiller and Melzig report that the 'algae stems, due to their swelling capacity, were used to expand wound channels and body cavities', and are in demand today primarily because of their constituents laminarin and alginic acid, used as 'pharmaceutical and technical aids'.

- **Description:** Length up to 3 ft 3 in. (1 m); thallus yellow to olive-brown, blackish when dry, flat, leathery, forked and branched, edges entire; central rib with air-filled bladders on either side, tips of branches with plump, blister-like reproductive organs; disc for attachment
- **Scent and flavour:** Scent of the sea, salty flavour
- **Location:** On sea coasts, on stones, rocks and wooden structures
- **Distribution:** Northern Atlantic, North Sea, Baltic, cultivated
- **Drug:** Fucus, charred: Aethiops vegetalis
- **Constituents:** Sugar (mannitol), alginic acid, alginate, laminarin, xanthophylls, iodine, potassium, trace elements (bromine)
- **Treatments:** For joint pains, goitre, skin diseases, asthma, adiposity
- **Uses:** Ready-made products, powder for poultices, baths, iodine production, animal fodder, fertilizer
- **Homeopathic uses:** See above and for over-active thyroid glands, goitre
- **What and when to gather:** Whole thallus, all year round
- **Lookalikes:** Toothed wrack (*F. serratus*): edge of thallus serrate
- **Other information:** Take care in cases of over-functioning thyroid gland and allergy to iodine

The thallus of Fucus vesiculosus *with the characteristic bladders along the central rib.*

Lichenes
LICHENS

Lichens are life partnerships, each consisting of an alga and a fungus. The alga supplies energy through photosynthesis, and the fungus provides water. According to the habit of growth, the distinction is made between fruticose (shrub-like), foliose (leafy) and crustose (crust-like) lichens.

Cetraria islandica (L.) Ach.
ISLAND CETRARIA LICHEN

Iceland Moss

'Iceland moss' is not a moss but the name of a lichen of the Parmeliaceae family. It covers large areas of the forests of Scandinavia, together with the reindeer lichen (*Cladonia rangiferina*). It used to be widespread in mountains, heathlands and forests on acid, moist soils, but now, due to air pollutants, particularly dangerous to lichens, it is in danger of extinction. For medicinal purposes the (*Cetraria*) thalli were dried, chopped or powdered and made into teas, often mixed with other herbal extracts. Island cetraria lichen is effective in treating bronchial diseases and, due to its bitter principles, also stimulates the appetite (e.g. in treating anorexia). There are also reports of it being boiled with milk and then given to treat chronic diarrhoea (Boericke). In Lapland, the lichen is used as food after the bitter principles have been removed by boiling. Another lichen used in medicine is lung lichen, which grows on rocks and bark in the Atlantic climate zone, but inland is also threatened with extinction. In some old herbals it is still occasionally found described as 'lungwort', although it is not in any way related to the true lungwort (see page 78).

Left: Island cetraria lichen with its shrub-like thalli.

Below: In lung lichen, the thalli are flat.

- **Description:** Height up to 6 in. (15 cm); thallus shrublike, erect, markedly branched; lobes greenish-grey to dark brown, paler underneath with white spots; flat, ribbon-like to tube-like, small thorny teeth at the edges; fruiting bodies (apothecia), on shorter, broader branches, rare
- **Scent and flavour:** Scent rather fishy; taste, uncooked, very bitter
- **Location:** Sandy heathland, acid-soil woodland, bogs, mountains up to 8,200 ft (2,500 m) and over
- **Distribution:** Widespread and common in northern Europe
- **Drug:** Lichen Islandicus
- **Constituents:** Bitter principles and mucilage, carbohydrates, lichenin, lichenic acid (cetraric acid), vitamins
- **Treatments:** For bronchitis, dry cough, irritation of the mucous membranes in the mouth and pharyngeal region, loss of appetite, diarrhoea, nausea, vomiting, travel sickness, in convalescence
- **Uses:** Tea, tea blends, tincture, ready-made products
- **Homeopathic uses:** For treating bronchitis
- **What and when to gather:** Whole plant, all the year round
- **Lookalikes:** Lung lichen (*Lobaria pulmonaria*): thallus grey-green on the surface, with felted hairs on the underside; other cetrarias
- **Other information:** Do not use if ulcers are present

Angiospermae

OTHER ANGIOSPERMS

In Europe, only a few species represent the mainly tropical families of the calamus (Acoraceae), arum (Araceae), birthwort (Aristolochiaceae) and laurel (Lauraceae). Some of these have been known since ancient times as remedies for gastro-enteric complaints or in gynaecology.

The sagittate leaves of cuckoo pint appear early in the year. The cream-coloured spathe surrounds the flower head, the spadix.

Arum family
Araceae

The arum family is primarily tropical and includes well-known houseplants such as the philodendron and the dieffenbachia, as well as the water arum (Calla palustris), which is sometimes to be found in wetlands. A typical feature is the club-shaped inflorescence, the spadix, often surrounded by a conspicuous bract, the spathe (spatha).

Acorus calamus L.
CALAMUS

■ *protected* ■
Sweet Flag, Sweet Sedge, Sweet Root, Sweet Myrtle, Myrtle Grass

Unless you spot the club-shaped flower head, it is easy to mistake the calamus for iris or bur-reed, both of which thrive in similar locations in the reed belt of lakes and ponds. The fact that iris root has even been sold, with fraudulent intent, as calamus, demonstrates the high market value of calamus root, which sometimes has the aura of a cure-all or miracle drug. This reputation is not justified, but the bitter principles contained in the root do have a stimulating effect on the appetite and can calm a nervous, excessively acid stomach. Calamus root is therefore often added to tea blends appropriate for this purpose. Some of the old 'herb fathers' recommend chewing calamus root as a cure for bleeding gums. The Native American Cree in Canada were also reported to chew the root – although this was for its hallucinogenic qualities. Perfume and incense makers have used the pleasantly scented rootstock since ancient times and, according to Schauenberg and Paris, the root has been used both in Arabia and in Iran as an aphrodisiac.

- **Description:** Height up to 5 ft (1.5 m); leaves parallel veined, about 3 ft 3 in. (1 m) long, sword-shaped, erect, reddish in the lower part; stems ridged on one side, grooved on the other; inflorescence in the middle of the stem, club-shaped, overtopped by a single bract (spathe); individual flowers inconspicuous, yellowish-green, small; rhizome sturdy, branching, creeping, greenish-brown; perennial
- **Flowering:** May to August
- **Scent and flavour:** Scent sweetish, aromatic; flavour bitter, hot
- **Location:** Reed zone, reed beds of ponds, lakes, banks of streams and ditches
- **Distribution:** Scattered, often cultivated and escaped to the wild
- **Drug:** Rhizoma Calami, R. Acori
- **Constituents:** Essential oils (asarone), glycosides (acorine), bitter principles, tannins, mucilage, starch, sugar, cholines
- **Treatments:** For loss of appetite, digestive problems, flatulence, stomach ulcers, rheumatic complaints, inflammation of the gums
- **Uses:** Decoction, tincture, powder, bath additive, beverage production (used to flavour liqueurs, beer, brandies), ginger substitute, mouthwash, insect repellent
- **Homeopathic uses:** For gastro-enteric diseases

The club-shaped flowerhead of calamus.

- **What and when to gather:** Rhizome March and April, September and October
- **Lookalikes:** Iris (*Iris pseudoacorus*): conspicuous flowers, yellow, unscented root; bur-reed (*Sparganium ramosum*): spherical, prickly flowers
- **Other information:** High doses of the fresh root cause vomiting; in long-term use, the possibility of carcinogenic action by the digestive bitters cannot be excluded. Reproduction is solely by division of the root stock, as the seeds do not ripen in our climate.

Arum maculatum L.
CUCKOO PINT

■ *poisonous* ■

Lords-and-Ladies, Adam-and-Eve, Arum, Wake-Robin

In better quality soils in mixed deciduous forest, the cuckoo pint will flower as early as April. The club-shaped spadix is surrounded by a large spathe and looks as if it is stuck in a paper bag. This is, however, a skilful trap to draw insects into the depths of the flower and allow them to escape again after pollination. In August or September, the red berries ripen, clustering densely around the tall fruit stem.

As with many plants with a long medicinal tradition, it is not easy with cuckoo pint to separate the actual effect from the legends that have grown up around it. The phallic shape of its flowerhead probably led to its reputation as the 'plant of love' – but whether cuckoo pint roots or leaves in a woman's shoe do indeed make the wearer irresistible would have to be tested in each individual case! It is a fact that the plant, the whole of which is toxic, can only be used uncooked in homeopathic dilution, as is recommended, for example, to treat diseases of the respiratory tract. When cooked, the poison is destroyed, which is why the rhizomes, rich in starch, were in the past roasted and eaten.

- **Description:** Tuberous geophyte; height up to 2 ft (60 cm); leaves with long petioles, broadly sagittate, sturdy, dark green, glossy, sometimes spotted with red or black; inflorescence club-shaped (spadix), surrounded by a cream-coloured bract or spathe (*spatha*), flowers inconspicuous, male flowers above, female below; berries dense, bright orange-red, root tuberous
- **Flowering:** April, May
- **Scent and flavour:** Scent of the flowers carrion-like; berries taste sweetish, leaves sourish, burning hot
- **Location:** Lowland forest, deciduous woodland, hedges, scrub; this herb likes lime
- **Distribution:** Common
- **Drug:** Tubera, Radix Ari
- **Constituents:** Aroin (toxic effect on the central nervous system), starch, saponines, calcium oxalate
- **Treatments:** Chronic gastro-enteric disease, bronchitis
- **Uses:** Tincture, powder, when roasted, a starch-rich food
- **Homeopathic uses:** For treating diseases of the respiratory tract
- **What and when to gather:** Roots March to May
- **Lookalikes:** None
- **Other information:** Highly poisonous; use only in consultation with a doctor

Fruit of the cuckoo pint. They are sometimes confused with those of lily of the valley (see page 177) – both are poisonous.

The cuckoo pint flower is a 'kettle trap' for pollinating insects.

Birthwort family
Aristolochiaceae

The birthwort family, too, has most of its species in the tropics, where the genus Aristolochia comprises about 350 species. Apart from scattered escapes of birthwort into the wild, gardeners also know the pipevine (A. macrophylla), which can be used to make green arbors. A native species is European wild ginger (Asarum europaeum).

Aristolochia clematis L.
BIRTHWORT

■ *poisonous* ■
Clematitide, Smearwort

This is an ancient healing plant, native to the Mediterranean region. Furlenmeier (as late as 1978) ascribed greater healing powers to it than to arnica (see page 53) or marigold (see page 59) in healing wounds and treating various kinds of inflammation, and also accords it great importance in gynaecology. Yet in recent years its reputation has suffered. According to some specialists, animals given regular doses of aristolochic acid developed tumours and changes to genetic material, which is why consumers are advised not to use products containing this agent. Unless there are further developments, therefore, birthwort is now more of a 'historical' medicinal plant. The botanical genus name, by the way, is derived from Greek, *Aristolochia*, meaning the 'best birth'. The name tells us that the plant was used very early on to speed up contractions and for abortions.

The flower consists of a bulging, kettle-like structure, a tube and a waxy, smooth lip. Insects slide off the tongue-shaped lip and down the pipe, where downward-pointing bristles prevent their escape. After pollination of the stigma the bristles dry up and the 'prisoners' are free once more.

- **Description:** Height up to 2 ft 8 in. (80 cm); leaves with long petioles, large, cordate; stems erect; sulphur-yellow flowers act as kettle traps (pitfall-trap flowers), in scorpioid cymes of two to eight flowers (winding); six-compartmented, green, fleshy capsule fruits; geophyte, rhizome; perennial
- **Flowering:** May, June
- **Scent and flavour:** Scent fruit-like; flavour peppery
- **Location:** Nutrient-rich woodland borders, vineyards, fences, likes warmth
- **Distribution:** Mediterranean countries, monastery herb gardens, rare
- **Drug:** Herba Clematitis
- **Constituents:** Essential oils, aristolochic acids, bitter principles, tannins
- **Treatments:** In the past: for healing wounds, encouraging labour, abortifact, for menopausal problems, rheumatism
- **Homeopathic uses:** To treat menstrual problems
- **What and when to gather:** Flowering herb, rhizome May and June
- **Lookalikes:** None

Birthwort in flower.

Asarum europaeum L.
ASARABACCA

■ *poisonous* ■

European Ginger Root, Hazelwort, European Snakeroot, Wild Nard

Asarabacca flowers early in the year, when all the world rejoices in the reawakening of nature and delights in the sight of anemones, primroses and many other colourful spring flowers. Even though the plant is widespread, most walkers overlook it. But European asarabacca has no need of spectacular colours to draw attention to itself. Its dark purple-brown flowers hide themselves close to the ground under leaves that look a little like ivy and are self-pollinating. The seeds have appendages rich in nutrients and oil, and are distributed by ants.

The root of asarabacca has a bitter and bitingly hot taste – horrible enough to be used in folk medicine as an emetic. In powdered form it is added to snuff mixtures. Asarabacca extracts are also given for bronchial asthma and other respiratory tract diseases, although they are rarely used today. It is interesting to see that asarabacca is recommended in old herbals for memory problems and in homeopathy for nervous exhaustion. Both cases seem to indicate an as yet unexploited potential, which ought to be researched by modern methods.

- **Description:** Height up to 6 in. (15 cm); stems short, prostrate, hairy; paired leaves with long petioles, winter-hardy, dark green, reniform, leathery, glossy; the dark purple, foxglove-like flowers grow where the leaves fork, close to the ground; capsule fruit with numerous seeds; rhizome brown, creeping, widely branched; perennial
- **Flowering:** April, May
- **Scent and flavour:** Root has an aromatic scent, camphor or valerian-like; taste peppery to biting hot, bitter
- **Location:** Mixed deciduous woodland with lime soils, waysides; this herb likes shade

- **Distribution:** Regionally common
- **Drug:** Rhizoma, Radix Asari
- **Constituents:** Essential oils (asarone), flavonoids
- **Treatments:** Emetic, for bronchospasm, bronchial asthma, alcoholism, stimulates urge to sneeze
- **Uses:** Standardized ready-made products; veterinary medicine
- **Homeopathic uses:** For nausea, diarrhoea, nervous exhaustion, irritation of the mucus membranes (snuff)
- **What and when to gather:** Leaves July and August; rhizome and roots August and September
- **Lookalikes:** Hepatica (*Hepatica nobilis*): leaves triple-lobed
- **Other information:** Used in snuff blends, e.g. Schneeberger blend

Top: Hidden flowers, very early in the year; asarabacca.

Above: Flowering hepatica is easy to recognize. However, the leaves are sometimes confused with the unlobed leaves of asarabacca.

Laurel family
Lauraceae

The laurel family mainly consists of tropical and semi-tropical species with leathery, evergreen leaves and small flowers. The fruits, either berries or drupes, have only a single seed. There are at least 2,000 species worldwide, but the sweet bay (Laurus nobilis) is its only representative in Europe. Among its relatives are sassafras (L. sassafras), the camphor tree (L. camphora) and the cinnamon tree (L. cinnamonum).

Left: Sweet bay in flower.

Laurus nobilis L.
SWEET BAY

There are few plants in mythology and custom as loaded with 'positive' connotations as the sweet bay or laurel. In ancient times, the *poeta laureatus* was the prize-winning poet crowned with the laurel wreath, and the baccalaureate examination, still used in some countries, and the title 'baccalaureus' (laurel berry) also derives from winning the 'laurels'. The evergreen tree, widespread in Mediterranean countries, was dedicated to the god Apollo in ancient Greece and for the biblical King David it was a symbol of wealth.

Various spices, salves and aromatics were and are obtained from the scented leaves, sweet bay oil, and other parts of the tree. Sweet bay is a constituent of some anti-rheumatic ointments and a tea made from fresh leaves calms the stomach. The sweet bay or bay laurel is no relation to the cherry laurel (see page 243), a member of the rose family.

- **Description:** Height up to 50 ft (15 m), shrub or tree; leaves alternate, short petioles, broadly lanceolate to ovate, leathery-hard, glossy green above, edge crimped, evergreen; branches stiff, erect, bark smooth, grey; flowers dioecious, off-white, small, in bushy umbels; berries dark brown to black, oval
- **Flowering:** April, May
- **Scent and flavour:** Scent of leaves and flowers aromatic; taste of leaves, spicy, aromatic, fruit peppery
- **Location:** Damp ravine woodland, in gardens or as a container plant; this herb is not frost-hardy
- **Distribution:** Native to the Mediterranean region, in Ireland, central western Germany (Rhineland-Palatinate)
- **Drug:** Folia, Fructus, Oleum Lauri
- **Constituents:** Essential oils (cineol, laurin), bitter principles, tannins; fatty oil (berries)
- **Treatments:** For digestive problems, externally for rheumatic complaints, disinfectant
- **Uses:** Tea, spice, embrocation, salve (oil), cosmetic industry
- **Homeopathic uses:** See above
- **What and when to gather:** Leaves without petioles June to August; fruit October, November
- **Look-alikes:** Cherry laurel (*Prunus laurocerasus*): flowers white in many-flowered racemes, fruits purple-black, spherical, whole plant poisonous
- **Other information:** In veterinary medicine, the viscous green oil is also used as a treatment to remove insects, e.g. rubbed into the skin of horses

Above: The flowers of cherry laurel are in upright racemes.

Duckweed family
Lemnaceae

The duckweed family is distributed all over the world. The plants are perennial floating aquatic plants that bloom only rarely and then have extremely small flowers. Propagation is generally asexual (vegetative).

Lemna minor L.
COMMON DUCKWEED

Lesser Duckweed, Duck's Meat

Common duckweed can spread explosively in the warm season and cover the surface of a pond within a few days. While waterfowl and fish initially profit from the excess of food on offer, the resulting oxygen deficit may within a short time lead to the 'point of no return' for the water, with all the typical negative consequences (death of fish, etc.). The plants should be removed regularly from garden ponds.

The healing powers of duckweed were used by doctors in ancient and medieval times. Dioscurides recommended duckweed poultices to treat inflammations. Hildegard of Bingen wrote that duckweed would 'reduce the useless fluids within a man'. According to Adamus Lonicerus, duckweed helped to treat 'St Anthony's Fire' (ergotism), which as we know today is caused by grain affected by the parasitic fungus ergot (*Claviceps purpurea*). In more recent times, such past treatments have been forgotten, but we have now discovered that duckweed can contain large quantities of radium, bromine, and iodine. It is still uncertain whether and to what extent this will lead to new medical opportunities.

- **Description:** 0.08–0.11 in. (2–3 mm) in diameter, floating leaves green, leaf-like, flat, orbicular to ovate; flowers small, inconspicuous; each floating section has one root
- **Flowering:** May, June
- **Scent and flavour:** Unscented, neutral in flavour
- **Location:** Nutrient-rich ponds, slow-flowing water
- **Distribution:** Common
- **Drug:** Lemna minor
- **Constituents:** Flavonoids, iodine, bromine, radium
- **Treatments:** In the past used for inflammations of the mucous membranes, rheumatic complaints
- **Uses:** Fresh
- **Homeopathic uses:** For chronic colds, nasal polyps, asthma
- **What and when to gather:** Whole fresh plant
- **Lookalikes:** Swollen duckweed (*L. gibba*): leaves bladder-like, white on the underside; common duckmeat (*Spirodela polyrhiza*): each floating leaf with a bunch of roots

Thousands of water plants form a green 'skin' on a pond.

Healing with herbs

On the following pages you will find a description of the most common complaints and diseases, together with an overview of herbs that can help to ease the symptoms and speed up recovery. Tables, recipes for tried and tested tea blends, and bath additives, as well as tips for preparing the above, will make it easy for you to find your way.

With any illness that lasts for a longer stretch of time, you should go to the doctor. Children should be treated by a doctor after three days at the latest.

The use of teas in treatment must be discussed with a doctor, particularly in cases of heart and circulatory disease, kidney ailments and during pregnancy.

Herbs for many ailments

Medicinal herbs should always be taken and used (see page 46 ff.) in consultation with the doctor supervising the treatment. The herbs may interact with prescribed medicines, intensifying, weakening or neutralizing the action of the drugs, and may in extreme cases be dangerous to life. The famous caution included in pharmaceutical advertising applies: 'For risks and side effects, ask your doctor or pharmacist.'

The dose given is intended for an adult weighing about 155 pounds (70 kg). The dose is reduced proportionally for children, as follows:

Age in years	Quantity
From 2–5	1/4
From 6–10	1/3
From 11–14	1/2
From 15–18	2/3

Overview:
Action, time of day, frequency of dose, quantity of dose, preparation (for tea)

Action	Time of day	Frequency	Quantity, preparation (Tea)
Diuretic	Not relevant	Several times a day	One cup on each occasion
Stimulate the appetite Improve digestion Stimulate the gall bladder Strengthen the stomach	15 to 30 minutes before meals	Three times a day	Small cup or glass (3½ fl. oz/100 ml)
Stimulate the metabolism Lower blood pressure Prevent hardening of the arteries For gynaecological problems	Before meals	Sips over the course of the day	Several cups (maximum 17 fl. oz to 25 fl. oz/½ to ¾ l)
Laxative, to regulate bowel movements	Evenings or on an empty stomach in the mornings	Once a day	One small cup (3½ fl. oz/100 ml), hot tea
To ease pain, binding, to treat flatulence	Not relevant	As required, once a day	Sipped in small quantities (c. 3½ fl. oz/100 ml)
Anti-rheumatic	Evenings	As required	Warm, may be sugared
Sedative, for sleep	Evenings	As required	One cup, hot, may be sweetened
Expectorant	Evenings	Once a day	One cup, hot and sweetened
Sudorific	In bed	Several times a day	Hot as possible, sweetened
To treat parasitic worms	Before going to bed and on an empty stomach in the mornings	Twice a day	Unsweetened

RESPIRATORY TRACT
Throat, nose, bronchial tubes, lungs

Flu and colds
Colds (rhinitis)
Inflammation of the sinuses (sinusitis)
The following can form part of a cold or flu-like viral infection: colds, coughs, inflammations of the throat and of the pharyngeal area. Many well-known home remedies, such as teas, inhalations, gargles, steam inhalations, wraps and poultices are used. The common cold is distinguished by increased nasal secretions, sneezing, light coughing and soreness in the throat. Apart from teas and tea blends, footbaths are helpful remedies. Afterwards, brush dry and generally strengthen the immune system, for example, with coneflower (*Echinacea*) or kidney-leafed pelargonium products. Cold symptoms may, however, also be caused by external irritants such as cold air, chemicals, or pollen (pollen allergy, hay fever, *pollinosis*; see below). In *sinusitis* there is an inflammation, caused by viruses or bacteria, of the sinus cavities; this is often combined with headache and, in the case of the maxillary sinuses above the jaw, with toothache.

Tips:
■ Sudorific teas (to provoke sweating) such as elderberry or linden blossom tea (one to two cups, drunk as hot as possible in bed) or hot elderberry juice will strengthen the body's own immune defenses.
■ **For fever:** Queen of the meadow, calamus and bogbean, cold wet wraps around the calves or a mixture of powdered oak, white willow and poplar bark.
■ **For coughs, dry coughs:** Teas and tea blends, pastilles, syrup using marshmallow, narrow-leaf plantain, ivy, thyme, sage, coltsfoot, sundew, anise burnet saxifrage, etc.

Sore throats, inflammation of the pharyngeal region and tonsils
Laryngitis, Angina
A slight soreness in the throat, hoarseness, a feeling of dryness and the urge to clear one's throat or swallow, often at the start of a cold, all indicate an inflammation of the pharyngeal region caused by viruses. Enlarged and reddened tonsils, combined with difficulties in swallowing, swollen lymph glands, headache, and fever are symptoms of tonsillitis, caused by bacteria, viruses, or fungi.

> *A doctor must be consulted for viral influenza with fever that lasts for several days and for children's illnesses accompanied by fever. Linden flower and elder tea may not be drunk if the temperature is very high.*

Bronchitis
The most frequent disease of the respiratory tract is bronchitis. Damage to the mucous membranes of the respiratory tract, whether caused by viruses, bacteria, nicotine or dust, causes coughing with mucous expectoration, often with pain behind the breastbone, sometimes with fever. The disease may also become chronic. Tea, inhalations, hot poultices, and wet wraps of the chest or the torso, footbaths and sunbathing, together with a change of air, can bring relief.

> *Because of the danger of contagion, a doctor must be consulted for inflammations of the throat.*

Bronchial asthma *Asthma bronchiale*
In bronchial asthma, a narrowing of the airways causes shortness of breath, together with often severe coughing attacks. The catalysts can be inhaled allergens (e.g. animal hair, pollen), physical exertion, or psychological factors, leading to cramps of the bronchial muscles, causing the mucous membranes to swell or creating an increase in secretions. Often, the relaxing effect of chest compresses, rubbing in of eucalyptus and pine oil, calming teas (for instance St John's wort) or ready-made products with extract of pestilence wort will help.

Sage – here dried – can be used for sore throats, among other treatments.

➤ What medicinal plant for what symptoms?
An aid to selection

Respiratory tract / Disease	Important medicinal plants				
	Marshmallow *Althaea officinalis* ➤ page 150	Sundew *Drosera rotundifolia* ➤ page 215	Fennel *Foeniculum vulgare* ➤ page 203	Ivy *Hedera helix* ➤ page 213	Chamomile *Chamomilla recutita* ➤ page 60
Influenza infections, fever			X	X	
Colds			X		X
Sinusitis					
Tonsillitis	X				
Cough, dry cough	X	X		X	X
Bronchitis	X	X	X	X	
Asthma		X		X	
Uses, notes	Tea, tea blends	Drops, juice	Tea, honey; syrup also suitable for children	Drops, tablets, suppositories	Tea, drops, oil; allergy possible

RECIPES

Tried and tested tea blends

Basic tea recipe:
Unless otherwise instructed, use one teaspoon of dried herbs per cup, pour boiling water over them and let the tea infuse for 5–10 minutes

For bronchitis
Tea blends:
One part each of the following herbs: anise, liquorice root, narrowleaf plantain, fennel, coltsfoot
or: *Mullein, liquorice root, marshmallow root, marshmallow herb, coltsfoot*
or: *Lungwort, arnica flowers, St John's wort, thyme, marshmallow root*
Preparation: *Use one teaspoon per cup, pour over boiling water, allow to infuse for 5–10 minutes, strain, sweeten with honey or brown sugar, drink hot two to three times a day*

For influenza, bronchitis
Mallow flowers, marshmallow root, fennel, coltsfoot leaves, island cetraria lichen, liquorice root, coltsfoot leaves, elder flowers, cowslip flowers, gypsyweed
Preparation: *Place herbs in water 6–12 hours before use (e.g. the evening before) at room temperature, bring the extract to the boil, strain, sweeten if required*

For colds:
One part each elder flowers, cowslip flowers, coltsfoot, yarrow

Preparation: *Use one teaspoon per cup, pour over boiling water, allow to infuse for 5–10 minutes, strain, sweeten with honey or brown sugar, drink hot two to three times a day*

For coughs:
Four parts marshmallow root, three parts liquorice, one part mullein, one part mallow, one part field poppy flowers, one part anise
Preparation: *Use one teaspoon per cup, pour over boiling water, allow to infuse for 5–10 minutes, strain, sweeten with honey or brown sugar, drink hot two to three times a day*

Anise *Pimpinella anisum* ➤ page 210	Pine *Pinus* ➤ page 254	Narrowleaf *Plantago lanceolata* ➤ page 105	Cowslip *Primula* ➤ page 153f	Elder *Sambucus nigra* ➤ page 111	Thyme *Thymus vulgaris* ➤ page 99	Linden *Tilia* ➤ page 157	Coltsfoot *Tussilago farfara* ➤ page 74
✗		✗	✗	✗		✗	
✗	✗		✗	✗		✗	
			✗				
	✗						
✗	✗	✗		✗	✗	✗	✗
✗	✗	✗	✗	✗	✗		✗
	✗				✗		
Tea, essential oil	Ointment, oil, tea	Tea, juice, drops, syrup; allergies are possible	Tea blends, juice, drops	Tea, juice, gargle	Tea, juice, drops, bath, syrup, also for children	Tea	Tea, allergies possible

Decongestant cough and catarrh tea
(Dr Haas-Basel's recipe)
One part each of common gypsyweed, ground ivy, dandelion
Two parts anise, thyme, nettle, fennel, coltsfoot, linden flowers, mallow, sage, mullein
Three parts marshmallow root, narrowleaf plantain, violet leaves and flowers, prostrate knotweed, lungwort
Preparation: *Use one teaspoon per cup, pour over boiling water, allow to infuse for 5–10 minutes, strain, sweeten with honey or brown sugar, drink hot two to three times a day*

For fever:
One part each marigold, St John's wort, linden flowers, elder flowers, bogbean, queen of the meadow
Preparation: *Place one teaspoon per cup in cold water, bring to the boil, allow to infuse for 10 minutes*

For sore throats and pharyngeal inflammations
Gargle solution:
Gargle hourly with a tea made from:one part each chamomile, sage
or: *one part each chamomile, prostrate knotweed*
or: *a dilute solution of arnica tincture*

or: *with oak bark*
or: *five parts of mallow, three parts narrowleaf plantain, two parts chamomile*
Throat poultices: *Soaked in an infusion of horsetail or chamomile*

For inhalation:
Preparation:*To a pot of steaming water, add 5–10 drops eucalyptus, dwarf mountain pine, peppermint, thyme or chamomile oil; then place a towel or blanket over your head and, mouth open, breathe the steam in as deeply as possible. Do this for 10 minutes.*

DIGESTIVE TRACT AND METABOLISM
Stomach, intestine, liver, gall bladder

Dandelion root is rich in bitter principles.

Numerous ailments and diseases of the digestive tract, together with symptoms of an affluent lifestyle such as excess weight, gout and diabetes II, can be eased by herbal medicine. Healing herbs such as chamomile, peppermint, and caraway are important aids, as are plants that contain bitter principles, known to us from monastery liqueurs and digestive bitters, such as gentian, angelica and bearwort.

Inflammations of the mouth and pharyngeal areas
Stomatitis
Inflammations of the inside of the mouth may accompany infectious diseases but also occur in periodontosis, gum problems, fungal infections and allergies. They often take the form of painful swelling, coated tongue and bad breath. Gargles are recommended to support the doctor's treatment (see table and recipes page 293).

Diseases of the stomach and intestine
Colitis, gastritis, ulcus
The stomach and digestive tract of many adults, and also of many children, is often sensitive in its reactions to certain foods, psychological problems, or external stimuli such as rocking motions. Such irritation is expressed in heartburn, nausea, vomiting, and/or diarrhoea. Heartburn is not a separate illness, but a symptom occurring in many diseases (e.g. too much or too little stomach acid, inflammation of the esophagus, peptic ulcers, gall bladder disease). Heartburn, like an upset stomach, is often caused by too much high-calorie food, sweet foods, alcohol or nicotine. In heartburn, there is a backflow of some of the acid stomach contents into the oesophagus.

Tips:
- Change to foodstuffs low in fat and protein and with little acid (avoid coffee, alcohol, sweet foods) and avoid nicotine
- Take several small meals spread throughout the day
- Place a hot water bottle on the stomach
- Herbal teas (gentian, wormwood, centaury, chamomile, peppermint, balm, calamus)

With an upset stomach accompanied by heartburn and feelings of pressure and bloating in the upper abdomen there may be additional causes; psychological factors such as stress at work or in private life. Loss of appetite and problems with digestion are the consequences.

Tips:
- For loss of appetite and 'weak stomach', drink the following teas for 4–6 weeks in rotation: juniper berries, angelica root, hops, bogbean, gentian root, centaury. Drink half a cup of these teas daily, in small sips, 15 minutes before the main meal.
- With the gentian species of yellow gentian, centaury and bogbean, the daily dose must not be exceeded

Nausea and vomiting can be caused by infectious diseases, medicines, and anaesthetics, but more common reasons are foods that are hard to digest, past their best or poisonous, misuse of alcohol, travel sickness (e.g. rocking motions) or psychological reasons.

Tips:
- The stomach nerves are usually calmed very quickly by a lump of sugar drizzled with 10–15 drops of spirit of sweet balm or tincture of valerian, 5–8 drops of lavender oil or peppermint oil (take care with extracts that contain alcohol).
- If nausea and vomiting continue for a longer time, ready-made products or teas will help, but in all cases a doctor should be consulted.

Inflammation of the stomach membranes (gastritis), ulcers (ulcus)

In gastritis, there are inflammation-related changes to the mucous membranes lining the stomach, caused by alcohol, medicines or infectious disease. The distinction is made between acute gastritis, combined with pain in the upper stomach area and widespread chronic gastritis. In many patients, evidence of the bacterium *Helicobacter pylori* has been found.

> *In cases of poisoning – e.g. by fungi or berries – contact your emergency hospital department or clinic and a doctor immediately.*

Tips:
- In acute gastritis, a diet with porridge and thin oatmeal gruel will help, as will weak peppermint or chamomile tea and one teaspoon of oil of St John's wort on an empty stomach in the morning.
- In many cases, chronic gastritis will over time develop into a peptic or duodenal ulcer. Typical symptoms are pain in the right upper stomach area and pain on an empty stomach.

> *An old healer's saying:*
> *'Health lies in the gut.'*

Tips:
- For gastritis, take flax seeds, one tablespoon two to three times a day with plenty of fluids, chew well
- Alternate the following teas, two to three times a day, a cup of each before meals with a little milk: liquorice, fennel, calamus, balm, peppermint, coltsfoot, silverweed cinquefoil, sanicle, narrowleaf plantain, or chamomile
- Or one cup of marshmallow root tea one to two times a day (place one teaspoon per cup in cold water for 6–12 hours, heat to drinking temperature)

Diseases of the large intestine

Diarrhoea
Constipation

There are many different causes for the two most frequent symptoms of disease of the large intestine – namely diarrhoea and constipation. Diarrhoea can be caused not only by infections, medicines, allergies, parasites, hyperfunction of the thyroid gland and stress, but also by diseases affecting the stomach or small intestine. Counteracting diarrhoea is one of medicine's most difficult problems; discovering the causes and finding out the right anti-diarrhoea remedy is like a case for a detective.

Tips:
- With diarrhoea, it is essential to replace the fluids and minerals lost
- Drink two to three cups of tea a day, one of the following varieties, with a pinch of salt in each cup: lady's mantle, silverweed cinquefoil, prostrate knotweed, dried bilberries, unsweetened black tea
- Or chew dried bilberries, 15–20 berries several times a day (they taste good)
- Or take powdered erect cinquefoil (tormentil) several times a day, stirred into gruel, apple puree or tea
- Or mixed with oak bark
- Or make a warm poultice of boiled mashed flax seeds

The causes of constipation may include lack of exercise and poor nutrition (food too rich in sugar and protein, too low in fibre), but there may, on the other hand, be damage to the wall of the intestine (e.g. by tumours), deformities, inflammations in the anal area and haemorrhoids.

Tips:
Change your diet:
- No chocolate
- No white flour products
- No sugar
- More exercise
- Take one tablespoon flax seeds (whole or coarse-ground) with plenty of fluid, chew well
- Alternate one cup of the following teas, generally in the evenings, if the constipation persists mornings and evenings: glossy buckthorn bark and berries, senna leaves and pods, calamus, aloe, silver thistle, chicory
- Ready-made tea blends

The flowers and fruits of Alexandrian senna (Cassia angustifolia) provide an important laxative. The shrub belongs to the pea family.

Laxatives should only be taken in an emergency. As with all medicines, taking laxatives over a long period of time leads to habituation. As a consequence, the muscles of the intestine become weaker, meaning that laxatives soon become essential, the dose needs to be increased, or ever-stronger medicines need to be taken.

Liver and gall bladder ailments
Hepatitis, colitis
Disease of the liver, which may occur after infection, with heart disease or metabolic disorders (such as diabetes), in pregnancy or after poisoning, is often first diagnosed by disordered function of the gall bladder. Fatty liver, a disease of affluence caused by too much rich food and considerable over-indulgence in alcohol, can develop into cirrhosis of the liver. In cirrhosis of the liver, the most important remedy is the blessed milkthistle, followed by celandine (prepared fresh). A diet rich in protein and vitamins, together with absolute abstinence from alcohol, forms part of a successful therapy.

Gallstones, and the gall bladder inflammations that can follow them, are widespread diseases. Women are more often affected than men. Gallstones can make themselves known by severe cramp-like pains in the upper stomach area, but are usually linked to less characteristic complaints. Apart from taking care to ensure regular digestion, a strict low-fat diet, avoiding foodstuffs that are hard to digest (beans, peas), alcohol, coffee and hot spices, the condition is helped by warmth, herbal teas or pressed juices, which you can prepare yourself or buy from your pharmacist, drugstore or health food store.

Tips:
For gall bladder ailments:
- Low-fat diet
- Herbal teas, one cup two to three times a day
- Take flax seeds with liquid, twice a day; chew well

- One to two tablespoons of pressed juice of radish, yarrow, and/or dandelion
- Warmth

Overweight *Adipositas*

If normal weight for a person is exceeded by more than 10 per cent, this is called clinical overweight. The cause is consuming too many calories for one's needs, and often psychological problems or constipation also result. High blood pressure, shortness of breath, joint problems, oedema in the ankles and eventually diabetes may also result.

A good support for a diet is a tea blend, which should be drunk two to three times a day for 4–6 weeks. Once a week, you could also have a juice day. On this day, drink 2 pints (1 l) of apple or grape juice spread over the course of the day. The effect of seaweed such as bladderwrack, which is contained in many cosmetic products, against excess fat, is disputed.

Gout *Arthritis urica*

With gout, a metabolic disorder, the insoluble crystals of uric acid are deposited in the joints, particularly in the big toes, in the tissues and in the kidneys. There, it may cause reddening, swelling, and severe pain.

Tips:

- Change your diet to purine-free foods (no offal, no legumes, little meat and alcohol)
- **Herbal teas:** one cup three times a day of bishop's goutweed, birch leaves, nettles, goldenrod, or other uric acid-eliminating or diuretic and sudorific herbs
- Rub in tincture of arnica or oil of St John's wort
- Foot baths or poultices of horsetail

Diabetes

Diabetes mellitus

Diabetes is a metabolic disorder that accompanies a lack of insulin production and, if left untreated, will cause serious symptoms of disease, ranging from problems with wound

healing to disordered functioning of the kidneys right up to coma. It is particularly important to keep to a diet. Treating less serious forms of diabetes with teas needs to be discussed with a doctor.

Tips:

- Keep to the diet.
- Drink tea made from bean pods, bilberries, burdock and centaury. One cup of tea two to three times a day is recommended. Alternate the varieties regularly.
- Add sicklefruit fenugreek seeds to stewed fruit.
- Oat straw as an infusion: boil 3½ oz (100 g) chopped oat straw for 30 minutes in 6 pints (3 l) of water; use for wet wraps or add to bath water.

*Candyleaf (*Stevia rebaudiana) *has leaves that can sweeten ten to fifteen times as intensively as cane sugar and may be used as a sugar substitute. (In some countries,* Stevia *is not approved as a food.)*

➤ *What medicinal plant for what symptoms?*
An aid to selection

Digestive tract and metabolism	Important medicinal plants				
	Yarrow *Achillea millefolium* ➤ page 50	Garlic *Allium sativum* ➤ page 174	Caraway *Carum carvi* ➤ page 200	Gentian *Gentiana lutea* ➤ page 80	Flax *Linum usitatissimum* ➤ page 226
Disease					
Heartburn, upset stomach				✗	
Loss of appetite		✗		✗	
Stomach and digestive disorders	✗		✗	✗	
Nausea, vomiting					
Gastritis					
Stomach and duodenal ulcer					
Diarrhoea		✗			
Constipation					✗
Liver disease					
Fatty liver		✗			
Gall bladder disease					✗
Gout					
Uses, notes	Tea, juice Allergies possible	Oil, capsules, pills, tablets; lowers cholesterol	Tea, oil: allergies possible	Tea, tea blends, digestive bitters	Flax seeds, whole or coarse-ground

RECIPES

For heartburn, upset stomach
Half to one cup gentian, wormwood or centaury herbal tea

Preparation: *Use one teaspoon per cup, pour over boiling water, drink slowly in small sips mornings on an empty stomach or ½ hour before meals*

For upset stomach and digestion, stomach ache
Tea: *one part each of yarrow, angelica, valerian, fennel, caraway, peppermint, chamomile, silverweed*

cinquefoil, sweet balm, anise **or:** *one part each of anise and fennel or the above herbs individually, alternated regularly*

	Chamomile *Chamomilla recutita* ➤ page 60	Peppermint *Mentha* ➤ page 92	Erect cinquefoil *Potentilla erecta* ➤ page 240f	Blessed milkthistle *Silybum marianum* ➤ page 62	Dandelion *Taraxacum officinalis* ➤ page 73	Sicklefruit fenugreek *Trigonella foenum-graecum* ➤ page 223	Nettle *Urtica dioica* ➤ page 170	Whortle berry *Vaccinium myrtillus* ➤ page 147
	x	x						
					x	x		
	x	x						
	x	x						
	x							
	x							
			x					x
					x	x		
				x				
				x	x			
					x			
							x	
	Oil, oil drops: allergies possible	Tea, oil; take care with babies	Powder, capsules, teas	Tablets, capsules, pills	Juice, tincture, tea; encourages gall flow	Seeds, powder: lowers cholesterol	Tea, juice, capsules, drops	Dried berries

One cup of tea, two to three times a day, with or after meals, unsweetened. Drink in sips (if required, sweeten with liquorice root)

or: *Anise boiled in milk*
or: *Tincture of balm or valerian drops (10–15 drops on a lump of sugar)*

For gout
One part queen of the meadow, one part yarrow, two parts nettle, one part willow bark, one part birch leaves, one part goldenrod

Preparation: *Put one to two teaspoons per cup in water, boil for 3 minutes, allow to infuse and drink in sips over the course of the day (two to three cups per day)*

HEART AND CIRCULATION

> *Herbs must only be used in consultation with the doctor supervising the treatment.*

Angina pectoris

Sudden severe pains in the chest, often radiating outwards to the left shoulder and upper arm, combined with a feeling of tightness and panic, are termed angina pectoris. They may be caused by physical exertion, excitement, cold or over-rich meals. Angina pectoris indicates disease of coronary blood vessels and as a possible precursor of a heart attack, it is a warning that must be taken very seriously.

Hardening of the arteries *Arteriosclerosis* Circulatory disorders

Arteriosclerosis is the most common change that occurs in the arteries, either by hardening or thickening, at first through deposits of fat and later of calcium. A blood clot (thrombus) may form in the narrowed blood vessel and the surrounding tissue is no longer supplied with oxygenated blood and nutrients; eventually it dies off. Risk factors include, for example, high blood pressure, being overweight, too high a cholesterol level, smoking, lack of exercise, diabetes; symptoms are forgetfulness, pain in the legs, impotence. Disease of the coronary vessels eventually leads to a heart attack or stroke.

Tips:
- Remove risk factors
- Kneipp therapies
- Mistletoe, hawthorn, and/or yarrow tea two to three times a day
- Mistletoe, hawthorn, or garlic drops two to three times a day, 1–2 drops each time, garlic, ginkgo, also as ready-made products
- Check the package information and the different quantities of active constituents for each manufacturer

Heart insufficiency, weak heart
Myocardial insufficiency

The causes of heart insufficiency, which manifests itself in shortness of breath, rapid heartbeat, and edema among other symptoms caused by the poor supply of oxygen, may be due to congenital heart defects and infections, but nowadays are often the consequences of chronic stress, high blood pressure and the misuse of alcohol and medication.

Tips:
- 10–20 hawthorn drops a day, alternating week by week with mistletoe drops
- Hawthorn tea (one cup a day)
- One cup of yarrow tea, with a maximum of 2–3 drops of arnica added, mornings on an empty stomach

Heart rhythm disturbance, palpitations
Atrioventricular arrhythmia

The term arrhythmia is used for a heartbeat faster than 80 beats a minute or one slower than 60 beats a minute, or when the pulse is irregular (palpitations, irregular heartbeat, up to life-endangering ventricular fibrillation). The causes may include psychological and other stress, electrolyte balance disorders (e.g. in diseases of the thyroid gland and kidneys) or heart muscle disease. A doctor will often prescribe digitalis-based medicines, which must be taken exactly according to the prescription.

> *Before starting any therapy, it is vital to establish the causes!*

Tips:
- For stress-related arrhythmia, take valerian drops, maximum twice a day
- Drink tea made from chamomile, balm, hawthorn, hops in the evening, valerian, one cup two to three times a day
- Take hawthorn in juice, drops, or elixir form

High blood pressure *Hypertonia*

High blood pressure almost always takes its course without symptoms. Nonetheless, it damages the blood vessels, leads to them becoming narrowed or blocked, and may in the end lead to a heart attack or stroke. It can be caused by diseases of the kidneys or the thyroid gland, but usually the causes are lack of exercise, excess weight, stress, too much salt in the diet, nicotine, coffee, and alcohol. (Blood pressure depends on age: the normal range for an adult is around the systolic/diastolic value 140/90 mmHg.)

Garlic, buckwheat and mistletoe have the effect of reducing blood pressure. The doctor can prescribe ready-prepared products with lily of the valley or pheasant's eye but, because these can be toxic, the dose must be adhered to strictly.

Low blood pressure *Hypotension*
Fainting *Syncope*

Low blood pressure (for adults, systolic/ diastolic values below 100/60 mmHg) is not life-threatening, but symptoms such as tiredness, lack of drive, poor concentration, headaches, and dizziness, plus the tendency to faint, are unpleasant.

Tips:
- Kneipp water therapies
- One cup of tea made from yarrow, broom, or rosemary, with 2–3 drops (no more!) of tincture of arnica, on an empty stomach
- Bath with rosemary or broom infusion added
- Rubbing in oil of St John's wort or tincture of rosemary, mistletoe drops

Venous disease
Venous inflammation *Thrombophlebitis*

Varicose veins
Varicose veins are knotty, often serpentine swellings of the veins, affecting primarily the veins in the calves and often considered merely a cosmetic problem. Often, as a consequence of standing at work, pregnancy or excess weight, swelling of the legs, a feeling of heaviness and cramps in the calves at night can result.

Tips:
- Kneipp water therapies, swimming, walking, sitting, or lying with legs raised
- Compression bandages
- Weight reduction
- Regulated digestion
- Rubbing in American witch hazel, ginkgo, sweetclover (ready-made products)

Haemorrhoids (piles)
Haemorrhoids are knot-like swellings of the blood vessels in the lower rectum and anus. They may be internal or external. Symptoms are itching, bleeding and painful bowel motions. Regular, soft bowel motions are important.

Tips:
- One cup buckthorn tea in the evenings
- Alternate chicory, cranesbill, dandelion, or chamomile tea for about 4 weeks, two to three times a day
- Take hip baths for 2 weeks, alternating chamomile flowers and/or oak bark. After a break of 1–2 weeks, you can repeat the process

> *No water pressure massage, no mechanical vibrations. Surface venous inflammation can – for instance, if the patient is confined to bed – develop potentially fatal complications.*

Superficial venous inflammation caused by varicose veins can lead to localized signs of inflammation such as reddening, soreness and heat.

Tips:
- Sleep with legs raised at night
- Plenty of exercise during the day
- Twice a day, alternate one cup of yarrow or chamomile tea, for a maximum of 4 weeks; apply cool, moist poultices with chamomile, arnica or coneflower (*Echinacea*)
- Bean pod tea can help with venous inflammations caused by diabetes

Horse chestnut extracts can be helpful in treating venous inflammation.

➤ *What medicinal plant for what symptoms?*
An aid to selection

Heart and circulation	Important medicinal plants				
Disease	Yarrow *Achillea millefolium* ➤ page 50	Horse chestnut *Aesculus hippocastanus* ➤ page 225	Garlic *Allium sativum* ➤ page 174	Arnica *Arnika montana* ➤ page 53	Hawthorn *Crataegus* ➤ page 235
Angina pectoris					✕
Hardening of the arteries	✕		✕		✕
Heart insufficiency, weak heart	✕			✕	✕
Arrhythmia					✕
High blood pressure			✕		
Low blood pressure	✕			✕	
Venous disease		✕	✕		
Haemorrhoids					
Uses, notes	Tea, allergies possible	Ointment, capsules, pills; watch aescin content	Oil, capsules, pills, tablets; lowers cholesterol	Ointment, tincture, allergies possible	Tea, pills, capsules, drops

RECIPES

Tried and tested tea blends
Basic tea recipe
Unless otherwise instructed, use one teaspoon of dried herbs per cup, pour boiling water over them and let the tea infuse for 5–10 minutes

For low blood pressure
Rosemary tea
or:
Baths, poultices
Preparation
Infusion: Boil up 1¾ oz (50 g) per 2 pints (1 l) of wine or water and add to the bath water

Spirits of rosemary:
Preparation: *Soak 1½–2 oz (45–60 g) of rosemary leaves in 1 pint (½ l) of spirits of wine for 4–6 days to extract. Filter and apply externally*

Rosemary wine:
3½ oz (100 g) fresh chopped rosemary twigs with flowers and leaves
2 pints (1 l) white wine
Preparation: *Pour white wine over the rosemary, leave for 3 days to extract, drink one small spirits measure three to four times a day*

For hardening of the arteries
In consultation with your doctor one part hawthorn flowers one part lavender flowers one part mistletoe

one part yellow spring bedstraw one part rosemary one part sweet balm one part goldenrod one part crushed juniper berries one part birch leaves one part centaury

Preparation: *Place one to two teaspoons per cup in cold water, bring to the boil, allow to infuse and drink in sips throughout the day (can also be drunk cold); if required, sweeten with honey*

Ginkgo *Ginkgo biloba* ➤ page 253	Hops *Humulus lupulus* ➤ page 164	Chamomile *Chamomilla recutita* ➤ page 60	Sweet clover *Melilotus officinalis* ➤ page 217f	Pine *Pinus sylvestris* ➤ page 254	Rosemary *Rosmarinus officinalis* ➤ page 95	Valerian *Valeriana officinalis* ➤ page 118	Mistletoe *Viscum album* ➤ page 231
✕							✕
							✕
	✕	✕				✕	
✕							✕
					✕		✕
✕		✕	✕	✕			
		✕		✕			
Drops, tablets, allergies possible	Tea, capsules, pills	Tea, drops, oil: allergies possible	Tea, drops, tablets	Ointment, oil, bath	Bath, tea, ointment, tablets	Tea, drops, pills, tablets	Tea

For weak heart, heart insufficiency
*In consultation with your doctor
one part rosemary
one part sweet balm
one part arnica flowers
one part hawthorn berries, crushed
one part mallow
one part valerian*
Preparation: *Place one teaspoon per cup in cold water, bring to the boil, allow to infuse and drink in sips (can also be drunk cold) during the day (two to three cups a day); may be sweetened with honey if required*

For venous inflammation, varicose veins, and haemorrhoids
*one part marigold
one part mistletoe
one part arnica flowers
one part mullein flowers
one part aloe
one part yarrow
one part St John's wort*
Preparation: *Place two teaspoons per cup in cold water, bring to the boil, allow to infuse, and drink in sips (can also be drunk cold) in the course of the day (two to three cups a day)*

For painful haemorrhoids
Warm hip bath with an infusion of chamomile flowers and oat straw

UROGENITAL TRACT
Kidneys, bladder, urinary tract

Right: The beneficial action of field horsetail (scouring rush) is primarily felt in hip baths and steam baths.

It is important with all kidney diseases to keep the kidneys and bladder well irrigated by drinking plenty of water (4–6 pints/2–3 l per day). Untreated disorders in the functioning of the kidneys can lead to a gradual poisoning of the organism.

Burning pain when passing water, the urge to pass water frequently, pressure within the bladder, dribbling and incontinence are all symptoms of a bladder inflammation, which may be caused by bacteria, viruses, chemical, or mechanical irritants. Kidney and bladder stones occur in 1–2 per cent of the population and mostly consist of calcium oxalate. Colicky pain can result if the stones begin to migrate. Hot poultices, hip baths and warm herb pillows with chamomile or hot flax seed paste have a calming and pain-relieving effect, and can limit inflammation. Rest, plenty of fluids, and a lot of warmth will support the healing process. As a preventative measure, you could also try and stop the formation of stones by avoiding foods too rich in fats and protein and those that contain calcium oxalate (e.g. tea, rhubarb, sorrel).

Tips:
- Drink plenty of fluids to support urine production and flow and to help prevent kidney gravel and stones
- Drink tea or tea blends of birch leaves, nettles, goldenrod with bearberry leaves: drink three to four cups in sips throughout the day (morning, midday, afternoon, and in the evening no less than 1–2 hours before going to bed, otherwise the strongly diuretic tea will disturb your night's rest)
- Hip baths with horsetail
- Warm poultices with horsetail, oat straw or hot flax seed
- Warm herb pillow with chamomile
- Plenty of rest

'Purifying the blood'
The herbs that in folk tradition are named as 'purifying the blood' have a diuretic and sudorific effect, and therefore can increase kidney and bladder activity, improve circulation, stimulate the activity of the intestines, help you lose weight, gain a better complexion, and thereby generally increase well-being.

The best detoxification and cleansing programme can be carried out in spring with soups, sauces, blanched vegetables, salads and juices made from watercress, nettles, dandelion, yarrow and daisies. Use young, fresh parts of the plants. You can support this by drinking teas of herbs with a diuretic or sudorific and laxative action such as nettle, birch, daisy, dandelion, parsley, goldenrod, restharrow and bearberry. This is drunk as a 'house tea blend' in spring and autumn for about 4–6 weeks, two to three cups a day. Teas made from only one herb should be changed weekly.

Enlarged prostate *Prostate adenoma*
Problems in passing water due to a benign enlargement of the prostate gland is a widespread complaint among men over 50. It cannot be healed by herbal medicines but the symptoms can be eased.

Suitable aids are preparations and teas made from, for example, nettle root and smallflower hairy willowherb. Pumpkin seeds are also a tried and tested remedy.

GYNAECOLOGY

Many plants will help with women's problems, whether these are menstruation disorders or ailments during pregnancy, after childbirth or during the menopause. Sometimes the name alone is an indication of such uses (for instance, birthwort, lady's mantle). The herbs primarily have a pain-relieving, cramp-easing, sedative, relaxing and antiseptic action.

Menstruation disorders

A disturbed female cycle may have organic, hormonal or psychological causes. Menstrual period pains can occur as back or abdominal pain or headaches, and are often linked with nausea, vomiting, diarrhoea, a feeling of tension in the breast and mood swings.

Tips:

- **For heavy periods** Mistletoe drops: 10–15 drops two to three times a day
- **For cramps** Chamomile or yarrow tea (internally)
- **To counteract mood swings** St John's wort tea

Pregnancy

For the first three months of pregnancy, the expectant mother should only take medicinal herbs in consultation with her doctor. External applications – such as peppermint or lavender oil for headaches – and chamomile after child-birth are allowed.

Menopause disorders

Complaints during the menopause and climacterium (the time leading up to the menopause) include hot flushes, dizziness, outbreaks of perspiration, arrhythmia, mood swings, osteoporosis and increased choles-terol values. They can be eased by the use of herbs.

Tips:

- Drink prepared blends of tea (e.g. nettle, chamomile, lady's mantle, rosemary, wormwood, liquorice)

- Drink two to three cups throughout the day (you can easily take the tea to work in a thermos flask)
- In the mornings, drink one to two cups of yarrow or horsetail tea or
- Take one tablespoon yarrow or horsetail juice (diluted in water)

For hot flashes and outbreaks of perspiration

- Washes with infusion of sage (½ oz/15 g to 2 pints/1 l of boiling water, allow to infuse for half an hour)
- Sage tea (one cup in the evenings, drunk slowly and in sips, before going to bed; allow to infuse only briefly)
- To combat slight or medium depression and insomnia, take St John's wort tea or ready-made products
- Pamper yourself and treat yourself to a bath: horsetail, yarrow and mistletoe ease cramps, rosemary is stimulating (it also makes a good rub), lady's mantle and hops are calming, chamomile stops inflammation and valerian helps induce sleep

Leucorrhoea, secretions, fluor

If unpleasant-smelling, discoloured vaginal secretions continue for a longer period of time, a doctor must be consulted and the cause established.

Tips:

- Douches with chamomile, deadnettle, lady's mantle or horsetail mornings and evenings for 3–4 weeks
- One cup chamomile, lady's mantle, yarrow or deadnettle tea twice a day

Rosemary can bring back your joie de vivre.

➤ *What medicinal plant for what symptoms?*
An aid to selection

Disease	Important medicinal plants				
Urogenital tract & Gynaecology	Yarrow *Achillea millefolium* ➤ page 50	Bearberry *Arctostaphylos uva-ursi* ➤ page 146	Birch *Betula* ➤ page 162	Willowherb *Epilobium* ➤ page 227	Horsetail *Equisetum arvense* ➤ page 256
Bladder and urinary tract inflammation		✗	✗		✗
Bladder and kidney stones		✗	✗		✗
Enlarged prostate				✗	
'Purifying the blood'	✗		✗		✗
Menstruation disorders	✗				✗
Pregnancy complaints					✗
Menopause	✗				✗
Outbreaks of sweating					
Leucorrhoea	✗				✗
Uses, notes	Juice, tea for period pains; allergies possible	Tea blends, pills; diuretic	Tea, juice, pills	Tea	Tea, juice, pills, capsules, tablets

RECIPES

For bladder and urinary tract infections

Tea blend 1:
one part bearberry leaves
one part bean pods
one part quackgrass root
one part horsetail

or tea blend 2:
Diuretic tea, according to Dr Walser:
one part rose hips
one part nettle
one part parsley root
one part blackthorn flowers and young leaves

Or tea blend 3:
one part chamomile
one part birch leaves
one part juniper berries
one part centaury
Preparation: *one teaspoon per cup, pour on boiling water, leave to infuse for 10 minutes, drink one cup each morning and evening*

Tea blend for incontinence:
four parts narrowleaf plantain
three parts erect cinquefoil
two parts horsetail

Preparation: *one teaspoon per cup, pour on boiling water, leave to infuse for 20 minutes, take three tablespoonfuls three times a day*

	St John's wort	Chamomile	Peppermint	Spiny restharrow	Sage	Goldenrod	Lady's mantle	Nettle
	Hypericum maculatum	*Chamomilla recutita*	*Mentha*	*Ononis spinosa*	*Salvia officinalis*	*Solidago virgaurea*	*Alchemilla vulgaris*	*Urtica dioica*
	➤ page 149	➤ page 60	➤ page 92	➤ page 221	➤ page 96	➤ page 71	➤ page 232	➤ page 170
				X		X		X
		X		X		X		X
								X *root*
		X				X		X
	X	X	X *(period pains)*					
		X	X				X	
	X		X		X		X	X
					X			
		X					X	
	Tea, capsules, pills for mood swings; avoid sunlight	Tea, drops, oil; allergies possible	Tea, oil, also for headaches	Tea blends, tablets	Tea, baths, oil, especially for excessive sweating	Tea, tincture, tablets, capsules	Tea, tea blends	Tea, juice, drops, capsules

Women's tea
one part deadnettle flowers
one part lady's mantle
one part St John's wort
one part marigold flowers
one part rosemary
one part blackthorn flowers
Preparation: *Place two teaspoonfuls per cup in cold water, bring to the boil, leave to infuse, and drink in sips (can also be drunk cold) throughout the day (two to three cups a day)*

For pregnancy complaints
To counteract nausea and vomiting
one part mint
one part chamomile

Preparation: *Use one teaspoonful per cup, pour on boiling water, leave to infuse for 10 minutes*

For bladder inflammations, menopause disorders, leucorrhoea
Hip bath or douche with horsetail

Preparation: *Briefly (4 minutes) boil one teaspoonful per cup* **or** *Bath: Boil 1–2 handfuls of horsetail in 4 pints (2 l) water and add to the bath water*

SKIN, EYES

The skin, the body's largest organ, covers and protects the whole organism. It regulates hydration and temperature, protects from radiation and penetration by harmful bacteria, and is equipped with numerous sensory receptors for warmth, pain, and touch. Herbs in the form of salves, creams, oils, and poultices to treat inflammation, scarring, burns, frostbite, acne, psoriasis and neurodermitis are part of traditional herbal medicine.

Wound healing

The most common form of first aid, for children as well as adults, is probably the treatment of small injuries to the skin. Healing will proceed at a different pace depending on the position, extent, and contamination of the wound and depending on the layers of skin affected. The formation of pus and metabolic diseases such as diabetes can delay the healing process. Medicinal herbs with an anti-inflammatory effect are used (e.g. chamomile, marigold), as are those with an astringent (burnet, yarrow, horsetail), antibacterial (narrowleaf plantain, marigold, arnica) and anti-viral action (marigold, coneflower, erect cinquefoil) or with a combination of these effects (narrowleaf plantain, common daisy, deadnettle).

Tips:

- For **insect bites**, cuts, and grazes, crush plantain leaves and place these on the bite or on the wound
- For **swellings**, e.g. following bites or stings, apply poultices with tincture of arnica

For first-degree burns (sunburn), scalds and skin irritations, poultices with oil of St John's wort, marigold, poplar or plantain can help. After using oil of St John's wort, you will have to avoid sunbathing or using artificial sunbeds because of its photosensitizing effect. If larger areas of skin are affected or the burns are second to third degree, treatment must be carried out by a doctor.

Baths or poultices with horse chestnut or oak bark are used to treat chilblains and frostbite.

Rashes, acne, psoriasis
Eczema, psoriasis, pityriasis
Eczema, acne and psoriasis can have different causes: fungi, bacteria, viruses, allergies to foods, medicines or detergents, or psychological problems.

In skin diseases such as neurodermitis, applying borage or mullein oil has proved helpful; in clinical studies, American witch hazel and common balm have even proved effective in treating herpes. The treatment of boils (small, often nodular, pus-filled, and painful inflammations of, for example, sebaceous glands) on the face should be left to a doctor, because of the danger of complications (septicemia, meningitis).

Pansy and white deadnettle, taken internally or externally, help treat eczema and cradle cap. Drink the tea regularly for 4 weeks, alternating it with walnut leaf tea. Poultices and packs of freshly infused horsetail and oat straw also support healing.

Eye inflammations, *Conjunctivitis*
Take care: Eye inflammations require an immediate specialist examination, and home cures can only be used after consultation with a doctor. Conjunctivitis may be due not only to drafts, smoke, gases, and foreign bodies, but also to dangerous bacteria. If treatment does not bring quick results, you must see an eye specialist in order to avoid damage to your eyesight or even blindness.

Tips:
- Eye washes (an eye bath can be of practical help here)
- Dabbing the eye with or making lukewarm compresses of cotton wool soaked in eyebright, chamomile, fennel or narrowleaf plantain

- For conjunctivitis, the application should be repeated every 2–3 hours. The tea must be made fresh each time and filtered through a clean cloth to avoid contamination (remains of tea, bacteria)

Nosebleeds *Epistaxis*

Nosebleeds may be caused by damage to a blood vessel by a foreign body (e.g. a toy) or picking the nose, or the consequence of an accident (blows, chemical irritation). However, it may also point to a fracture at the base of the skull or infectious disease (typhus).

If nosebleeds are frequent, the cause must be established, as they may be disguising more serious diseases such as circulatory disorders (high blood pressure, arteriosclerosis) or vitamin deficiency diseases.

Tips:

- Raise the patient's upper body, place a cold cloth on the back of the neck
- Have the patient draw in a cold (if required, iced) infusion through the nostrils
- Teas made from shepherd's purse, oak bark, erect cinquefoil, or horsetail (for oak bark and horsetail, one teaspoonful per cup, boil for 5 minutes) or
- Introduce a swab of cotton wool soaked in shepherd's purse infusion into the bleeding nostril

Excessive perspiration, night sweats

Hyperhidrosis

Sweating is essential to regulate body temperature in heavy physical work or great heat. Excessive sweating and night sweats may have several causes. The symptoms often occur in stress situations and during the menopause (see page 287), but can also be symptoms of liver damage due to alcohol misuse and thyroid disease, acute infectious disease or weakness of the immune system, including (for example) in acute leukaemia, tuberculosis and AIDS.

Tips:

- Washes with infusions of sage (½ oz/15 g per quart /1 l of water, allow to infuse for 30 minutes); sage tea, allow to infuse only briefly; sip one cup slowly in the evenings before going to bed
- Two to three cups of horsetail or prostrate knotweed tea; drink mainly during the day because of the diuretic effect

Marigolds encourage wound healing.

➤ *What medicinal plant for what symptoms?*
An aid to selection

Skin and eyes	Important medicinal plants				
Disease	Arnica *Arnica montana* ➤ page 53f	Borage *Borago officinalis* ➤ page 76	Marigold *Calendula officinalis* ➤ page 59	Horsetail *Equisetum arvense* ➤ page 256	American witch hazel *Hamamelis virginiana* ➤ page 165
Wounds, inflammation	✗	✗	✗	✗	✗
Insect bites and stings	✗				
Burns	✗		✗		
Neurodermitis		✗		✗	
Acne				✗	✗
Herpes				✗	✗
Eye inflammations					
Nosebleeds				✗	
Sweating				✗	
Uses, notes	Salve, tincture; allergies possible	Oil, capsules, cream	Salve, tincture, tea, gargle solution; allergies possible	Tea, juice, pills, capsules, tablets	Baths, poultices, salve, tincture

RECIPES

Tried and tested tea blends
Basic tea recipe:
Unless otherwise instructed, use one teaspoonful of dried herbs per cup, pour boiling water over them, and let the tea infuse for 5–10 minutes

For badly healing wounds:
Poultices soaked in a tea made from:
one part white deadnettle
one part churchsteeples

two parts witch hazel
or: one part pansy
one part walnut leaves
Preparation: *Use one teaspoonful per cup, pour on boiling water, allow to infuse for 10 minutes*
or: Walnut
Preparation: *Two handfuls of walnut leaves to 2 quarts (2 l) of water, boil for 15 minutes*

For insect stings and bites, burns
Poultices with the juice of crushed plantain leaves or a poultice soaked in plantain infusion: place one to two teaspoonfuls per cup in cold water, bring to the boil, strain

For skin diseases
Poultices, wet wraps, baths
three parts pansy
three parts American witch hazel (Hamamelis)

two parts churchsteeples
two parts white deadnettle
Preparation: *One handful to 2 quarts (2 l) boiling water, allow to infuse for 15 minutes*
or: Witch hazel
Preparation: *Six tablespoons to 1 pint (500 ml) of boiling water, allow to infuse for 15 minutes*
or: Horsetail
Preparation: *Use one teaspoonful per cup, allow to boil briefly (4 minutes)*

	St John's wort *Hypericum maculatum* ➤ page 149	White deadnettle *Lamium album* ➤ page 88	Chamomile *Chamomilla recutita* ➤ page 60	Common balm *Melissa offcinalis* ➤ page 91	Evening primrose *Oenothera biennis* ➤ page 228	Narrowleaf *Plantago lanceolata* ➤ page 105	Poplar *Populus nigra* ➤ page 155	Sage *Salvia officinalis* ➤ page 96
	X	X	X			X		
						X		
	X		X			X	X	
		X			X			
		X		X	X			
				X				
			X			X		
								X
	Tea, oil; avoid sunlight	Tea, baths, poultices	Tea, drops, oil; allergies possible	Tea, tincture, oil, cream	Oil capsules	Tea; allergies possible	Baths, poultices, ointment	Tea, baths, oil

or: *Freshly infused herb (one to two handfuls to 2 quarts (2 l) of water)*

For eye inflammations
Compresses with eyebright
Preparation:
Decoction: pour 1 pint (½ l) of boiling water over one tablespoon of herb, filter through a clean cloth, place compresses on the eyes overnight

To support treatment internally:
Tea; sip one cup over the course of the day

For perspiration, attacks of sweating
Sage: Infusion for washes, ½ oz (15 g) to 1 quart (1 l) simmering water, infuse for 30 minutes

For inflammations of the mouth Gargle:
Oak: bark cut into small pieces Boil one teaspoonful per cup for 5 minutes
or: *Bilberry: bring two teaspoonfuls of dried berries to the boil, allow to infuse for 10 minutes*
or: *Marigold: use one teaspoonful per cup, pour on hot water, allow to infuse for 10 minutes*

or: *Sage: use one to two teaspoonfuls per cup, pour on boiling water, allow to infuse*
or: *Erect cinquefoil: use one teaspoonful per cup, pour on hot water, allow to infuse; or use tincture*

MUSCULOSKELETAL SYSTEM

Ailments of the musculoskeletal system may occur in the bones, joints, and musculature as acute injuries (bruises, contusions, haematomas, tenosynovitis, fractures), but can also include chronic or inflammatory diseases. For blunt injuries, natural plant therapy can help to reduce pain, cool and prevent inflammation, using poultices, salves or gels.

Chronic and often very painful joint diseases, such as rheumatoid arthritis and osteoarthritis, cannot be cured by natural medicines, but the symptoms can be eased. Reducing the synthetic chemical medication for rheumatism lessens the strain on the body.

The ailments of old age can also be eased with carefully selected herbal therapies.

Muscle pains

Insufficient preparation (warm-up) before sporting activities, poor condition, or over-tiring are often causes of muscle injury such as pulled muscles, sprains or sore muscles. If muscle cramp is more frequent, this may be hiding a serious disease. Sudden, intense 'shooting' pains in the lumbar area of the spine are known as lumbago.

Tips:
- Rub with mint oil or oil of St John's wort
- Compresses with horseradish or mustard powder
- Relaxing and analgesic baths, e.g. with dwarf mountain pine, common balm or oregano

Blunt injuries (hematomas, contusions, bruises, etc.)

After a blunt injury causing a bruise or contusion, the parts of the body affected are treated with compresses. For tenosynovitis, bursitis and tennis elbow, treatment comprises rest and treatment with comfrey and horse chestnut.

Tips:
- Poultice soaked in infusion of arnica flowers, St John's wort or comfrey
- Or with tincture of arnica or comfrey
- Or with walnut leaves

Rheumatic complaints *Rheumatoid arthritis*

The term 'rheumatism' covers numerous causes and symptoms, and herbal medicine has a corresponding number of plant species and recipes to help ease the pain. A distinction is made between soft tissue rheumatism affecting muscles, tendons and ligaments, and arthritis, where the symptoms are inflamed and painful joints and bones. The easing effect of the herbs relies on the one hand on diuretic constituents (birch, nettle, restharrow, ruptureweed, elder, juniper, bean pods, goldenrod) and on the other on analgesic and antispasmodic substances (queen of the meadow, yarrow, common balm).

Arnica flowers: the 'raw materials' for tincture and ointment.

Tips:

- One to two cups of tea two to three times a day. You should change the individual varieties or the ready-made blends (see above) regularly
- Pain-relieving poultices and baths with horsetail, dwarf mountain pine, horse chestnut, oat straw, or
- Massage with oil of St John's wort or spirit of balm (Melissengeist)

Osteoarthritis (degenerative arthritis)

Osteoarthritis, a symptom of wear on the joints in age, makes itself known through sensations of tension and stiffness in the joints affected (primarily hip or knee joints) and increasing pain. Medication that stimulates the circulatory system and also healing herbs such as mistletoe, horse chestnut and arnica can be used, in the form of poultices, packs, embrocations and heat treatment. There are also ready-prepared products available using goldenrod, ash bark, poplar bark and poplar leaves.

➤ *What medicinal plant for what symptoms?*
An aid to selection

Musculoskeletal system	Important medicinal plants				
	Horse chestnut *Aesculus hippocastanus* ➤ page 225	Arnica *Arnika montana* ➤ page 53	St John's wort *Hypericum maculatum* ➤ page 149	Common balm *Melissa officinalis* ➤ page 91	Mint *Mentha* ➤ page 92
Disease					
Muscle pains			✗		✗
Lumbago			✗		✗
Blunt injuries	✗	✗			
Tenosynovitis	✗				
Soft tissue rheumatism				✗	✗
Rheumatoid arthritis		✗		✗	
Osteoarthritis	✗	✗		✗	
Uses, notes	Poultices, tincture, salves, baths; take careful note of aescin content	Ointment, tincture; allergies possible	Oil: avoid sunlight	Baths, cream, embrocation	Oil

RECIPES

Tried and tested tea blends
Basic tea recipe
Unless otherwise instructed, use one teaspoonful of dried herbs per cup, pour boiling water over them, and let the tea infuse for 5–10 minutes

For muscle pain, lumbago
St John's wort; massage with oil
Mustard poultices:
Preparation: *Stir mustard powder into a paste with some warm water, apply, allow to work for a maximum of 10–15 minutes, wash off using plenty of water*

For blunt injuries
Poultices with arnica and other comfrey roots
Preparation: *Pour 1 quart (1 l) boiling water over two teaspoonfuls of arnica flowers*
or: Use two to three tablespoons tincture of arnica for 1 quart (1 l) of water (take care: if the skin reddens severely, reduce the dose. Use externally only, and not if open wounds are present)
or: Decoction of comfrey: one tablespoon for 1 pint (1/2 l) of water, boil for 15 minutes
or: Tincture of comfrey dissolved in water or as a paste or poultice

Preparation:
Paste: two parts fresh roots, finely grated
or: Salve: add fresh, finely chopped comfrey root to melting pork lard, press out any liquid (will keep in the fridge for about a year – external use only)
or: Poultice: add two parts fresh root, one part fresh silverweed to one part melting pork fat, press out any liquid
or: one part walnut leaves one part fumitory one handful to 2 quarts (2 l) of water, boil for 15 minutes

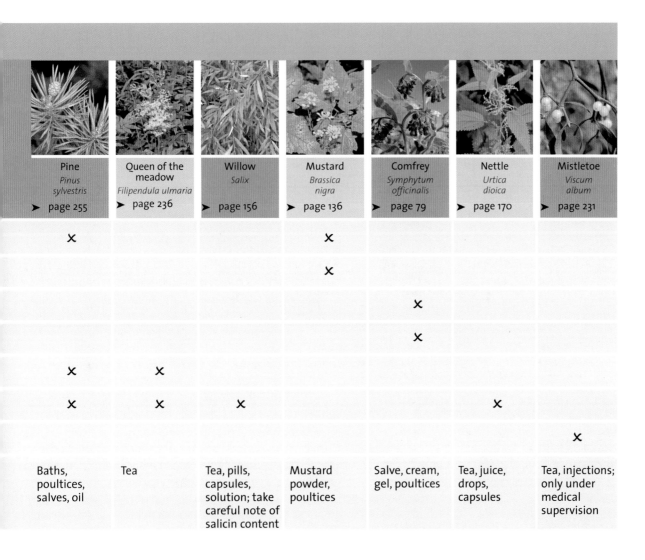

	Pine *Pinus sylvestris* ➤ page 255	Queen of the meadow *Filipendula ulmaria* ➤ page 236	Willow *Salix* ➤ page 156	Mustard *Brassica nigra* ➤ page 136	Comfrey *Symphytum officinalis* ➤ page 79	Nettle *Urtica dioica* ➤ page 170	Mistletoe *Viscum album* ➤ page 231
	✗			✗			
				✗			
					✗		
					✗		
	✗	✗					
	✗	✗	✗			✗	
							✗
	Baths, poultices, salves, oil	Tea	Tea, pills, capsules, solution; take careful note of salicin content	Mustard powder, poultices	Salve, cream, gel, poultices	Tea, juice, drops, capsules	Tea, injections; only under medical supervision

For soft tissue rheumatism
Pine, dwarf mountain pine:
Bath: Place 18–35 oz (500 g–1 kg) pine needles and shoots into c. 5 quarts (5 l) of water, bring to the boil slowly, allow to infuse for 5–10 minutes, strain, and add to the bath water

For osteoarthritis
Horse chestnut:
Massage with tincture
or: *Warm poultice of chopped, soft-boiled, peeled chestnuts*
or: *Bath: decoction made from 2¼ lbs. (1 kg) chopped boiled chestnuts per bathtub*

For arthritis

For sore muscles and rheumatic complaints
Hay bath:
The hay – long-stalked hay from hill farmers is best – needs to be soaked for 30 minutes before the bath. The water is then added to the bath.
'Real hay bath' – a variation
Add about 4½ lbs (2 kg) of hay to 7 quarts (7 l) of warm water and allow to infuse for at least 30 minutes.
Spread half the hay onto a waterproof sheet of foil, lie down on it and spread the other half over your body. Covered in the foil and wrapped in a blanket, the hay's scented active constituent parts can now develop their beneficial relaxing effect. The constituents (such as cumarin) are primarily contained in sweet vernal grass (Anthoxanthum odoratum) and clover (Trifolium). The body gently overheats, leading to strong perspiration and an antispasmodic and spasmolytic effect.
Take care if you suffer from heart or circulatory disease.
After a hay bath, do not sunbathe or use sunbeds

or: *Poultices and baths:*
Oat straw
Preparation: *Infusion: boil 3½ oz (100 g) chopped oat straw in 3 quarts (3 l) of water for 30 minutes; use for wet wraps, or add to bath water*

NERVOUS SYSTEM

Neurological disorders may affect the brain, memory, speech, senses, muscles and the musculoskeletal system, and range from relatively harmless headaches to life-threatening strokes.

Headache
Migraine *(chronic)*

Headaches (tension headaches) may be caused by tense muscles, overtiredness, psychological problems, alcohol, nicotine, lack of fluids, etc. Migraine, with its attacks of pain that often affect only one side of the head, and which is also linked to vomiting, nausea and sensitivity to light and noise, can last for several days.

The 'leaves' of the ginkgo tree. The uses of ginkgo products include preventive treatment for strokes and age-related memory loss.

Tips:
Antispasmodic, calming, relaxing:
- Valerian drops or spirit of balm (Melissengeist) on a lump of sugar
- Forehead compresses with common balm (spirit of balm) or mint (menthol)
- One cup several times a day of a tea blend of, for example, valerian, common balm, silverweed, primrose, mint, chamomile, or the individual herbs drunk alternately

Neuralgia

Nerve pain occurs in the area of the nerve affected (e.g. trigeminal neuralgia in the area of the largest of the cranial nerves, sciatica in the lower back area).

Steam baths with chamomile or mint to the affected regions, daily at first and then every two days, have an antispasmodic, anti-inflammatory, and analgesic effect. To help treat the neuralgia, drink a cup of chamomile, common balm or speedwell tea in the morning and in the evening for 4 weeks, alternating the different teas daily.

Stroke *Apoplexy*

Strokes can be caused either by bleeding from a ruptured blood vessel in the brain or by a clot in a blood vessel that interrupts the blood supply to the brain. Herbal medicine can only help to treat causes such as high blood pressure, high cholesterol levels and hardening of the arteries (see page 282). To help prevent lasting damage after a stroke, the sufferer must be taken to hospital immediately. Substances that improve circulation include garlic and ginkgo products.

Depression, nervous anxiety, fear, sleep disorders

Probably just about every human being is familiar with pessimism, melancholy, low self-esteem, fear of almost insoluble tasks and nervous anxiety. Remedies that calm and brighten the mood, such as valerian, hops or St John's wort can help with everyday problems. Sleep disorders may be caused by anxiety,

stress or anger, but may also be due to depression, illness, pain, medication or alcohol or coffee consumption.

Tips:
- One cup of chamomile or balm tea, mornings and evenings, for 4 weeks, alternating the teas
- St John's wort, valerian, and hop pills or capsules (no more than two a day of each) or
- Valerian drops (10–15 drops on a lump of sugar or dissolved in a glass of water) or spirit of balm (Melissengeist) (take care, contains alcohol)
- Exercise in the fresh air

- Relaxing bath with lavender, sweet balm, rose petals
- To treat nervous insomnia: one cup of St John's wort tea in the evenings, half an hour before going to bed

> Serious psychological illnesses, which may also display the above symptoms, require medical treatment, and the herbs may be used to support treatment in consultation with the doctor.

Migraine is a widespread complaint – and it does not only affect women.

➤ *What medicinal plant for what symptoms?*
An aid to selection

Important medicinal plants					
Nervous system	Garlic *Allium sativum* ➤ page 174	Ginkgo *Ginkgo biloba* ➤ page 253	Hops *Humulus lupulus* ➤ page 164	Lavender *Lavandula angustifolia* ➤ page 89	St John's wort *Hypericum maculatum* ➤ page 149
Disease					
Headache, migraine		X			
Neuralgia					
Stroke (prophylactic)	X	X			
Sleep disorders			X	X	X
Sweating					
Depression			X		X
Nervous anxiety			X	X	X
Fear				X	X
Uses, notes	Oil, capsules, pills, tablets	Drops, tablets; allergies possible	Tea, capsules, pills	Tea, baths, oil	Tea, capsules, pills; avoid sunlight

RECIPES

For headache, migraine
one part valerian, one part common balm, one part silver-weed, one part primrose, one part mint, one part chamomile
Preparation: *Use one teaspoon-ful per cup, pour over boiling water, infuse for 10 minutes*

For insomnia
one part valerian, one part hops
or: *three parts common balm, one part valerian, one part hops*

Preparation: *Use one teaspoonful per cup, pour over boiling water, allow to infuse for 10 minutes, drink in the evenings half an hour before going to bed*

For depression
St John's wort, one cup mornings and evenings

For anxiety
one cup chamomile or common balm tea, mornings and

evenings, for 4 weeks, alternating the teas
or: *Valerian root: boil one teaspoonful per cup vigorously. Infuse for 5 minutes, strain*
or: *Cold extraction*
or: *10–15 drops on a lump of sugar*
or: *Hops: use three to four teaspoonfuls, infuse for 10–15 minutes (one cup before bed)*
or: *one teaspoonful per cup several times a day*

For headaches, migraine
one part St John's wort, one part hop flowers, one part lavender flowers, one part common balm, one part valerian, one part cloves, one part angelica root, one part chamomile, one part bitter orange blossom (or orange blossoms), one part oregano
Preparation: *Place two teaspoonfuls per cup in cold water, bring to the boil and allow to infuse. Drink in sips*

Common balm *Melissa officinalis* ▶ page 91	Mint *Mentha* ▶ page 92	Pine *Pinus sylvestris* ▶ page 254	Willow *Salix* ▶ page 156	Sage *Salvia officinalis* ▶ page 96	Valerian *Valeriana officinalis* ▶ page 118	Oregano *Origanum vulgare* ▶ page 94
✕	✕	✕	✕		✕	✕
✕	✕	✕				✕
✕		✕			✕	
				✕		
		✕				
✕		✕			✕	
✕	✕					
Tea, tincture, oil, cream, gel	Tea, oil, also for headaches	Baths, tea, ointment, oil	Pills, capsules, solution, tea; take careful note of salicin content	Tea baths, oil; internal and external use	Tea, baths, drops, pills, tablets	Tea, baths, poultices

(can also be drunk cold) during the course of the day (two to three cups per day)

For anxiety, insomnia
Lavender oil: 5–8 drops, twice a day on a lump of sugar or in water
Lavender tea: pour boiling water over one teaspoonful per cup
Bath: pour boiling water over one handful of lavender flowers and infuse for about 15 minutes.

Add to warm bath water. After the bath, care for your skin with warmed bath oil.

Flower bath with orange, rose, or lavender flowers:
Pour 2 quarts (2 l) of boiling water over two to three handfuls of orange, rose, or lavender flowers, allow to infuse and pour the infusion into the warm bath water. If you sprinkle a few rose petals on top of the bath

water and add 1–3 drops of orange or 2–5 drops of rose oil, you can enjoy the wonderful scent and relax with classical music and a glass of dry white wine
Take care: *Orange oil may cause allergies. Do not go sunbathing or use a sunbed after a flower bath*

Bath with lavender flowers and blackberry leaves
Pour boiling water over 3½ oz (100 g) of lavender flowers and the same amount of blackberry leaves, allow to infuse for about 25 minutes, then add the infusion to warm bath water. For an especially soft skin, add one cup of honey and one teaspoonful of bath oil to the herbal infusion

> *What medicinal plant for what symptoms? An aid to selection*

IMMUNE SYSTEM, POOR CONSTITUTION

Increased susceptibility to infections is a sign of a weakened immune system. The causes range from weakening of the body through stress, sleep deficit, lack of vitamins, nutrition, or minerals, or the side effects of medication or radiotherapy to metabolic diseases such as diabetes or illnesses such as AIDS or forms of cancer.

Products prepared from coneflower, Cape pelargonium (also known as umckaloabo), and vitamin C-rich remedies such as seaberry juice or rosehip tea are recommended to strengthen the immune system and also to help ward off flu and colds. Allergic reactions – for example, against animal hairs or pollen – and auto-immune diseases such as rheumatoid arthritis are disorders of the immune system. In cases of gluten allergy, buckwheat has many dietary uses as a grain substitute. When the immune system is weakened by cancer, mistletoe products are used as a complementary therapy.

Convalescence, age-related weakening of the constitution, exhaustion

If the constitution is weakened, whether through illness, psychological or physical strain, or increasing age, herbs can help. Relaxing baths with lavender and/or pine are recommended in convalescence, as are strengthening remedies. If the illness was linked to considerable loss of weight, a diet with oat or buckwheat porridge (served, for instance, with rosehip jam) will help build up the body. If the heart is weakened, hawthorn (see page 235) can help. If memory is becoming poor, ginkgo products, taken over a period of time, have proved to be successful. The diet should have plenty of variety, be rich in vitamins, fibre and protein but low in fat.

Vitamin-rich fruits such as rosehips can help with a weakened immune system and susceptibility to infections.

Immune system Poor constitution
Disease
Weakened immune system
Susceptibility to infection
Allergy
Exhaustion, stress
Poor constitution
Convalescence
Dementia, Alzheimer's
Uses, notes

RECIPE

For weakened immune system, susceptibility to infections, stress, in convalescence

Oat or buckwheat porridge with two to three tablespoons of seaberry juice (either fresh juice or syrup) **or:** *With rosehip jam*
Rosehip infusion: one tablespoon of seeds or whole fruit per cup, boil for 5 minutes
(the fresh seeds are slightly laxative, the dried ones a little astringent)

Pine, dwarf mountain pine:
Bath: place 18–35 oz (500 g–1 kg) pine needles and shoots into c. 5 quarts (5 l) of water, bring to the boil slowly, allow to infuse for 5–10 minutes, strain and add to the bath water

Important healing plants

Oats *Avena sativa* ➤ page 180	Hawthorn *Crataegus* ➤ page 229	Coneflower *Echinacea* ➤ page 66	Buckwheat *Fagopyrum esculentum* ➤ page 126	Ginkgo *Ginkgo biloba* ➤ page 259	Mistletoe *Viscum album* ➤ page 229	Seaberry *Hippophae rhamnoides* ➤ page 216	Rosehip *Rosa* ➤ page 244f
					X	X	X
		X				X	X
		X	X *for gluten allergy*				
				X		X	X
	X		X		X	X	
X			X			X	X
				X	X		
Porridge	Tea, pills, capsules, drops	Drops; allergies possible	Porridge, gruel	Drops, tablets; allergies possible	Tea, injections; only under medical supervision	Juice, syrup, puree, jam	Tea, jam

For stress, exhaustion, tiredness, depression
Bath:
Pour boiling water over
one to two handfuls of
rose petals
one handful of lavender flowers
one handful of mint leaves
and allow to infuse for about
15 minutes. Add 10–15 drops of
lavender or lemon oil and pour
the scented essence into the
warm bath water.
After bathing, care for your skin
with warmed bath oil

For stress, exhaustion:
Alcohol-free drinks:
Herb punch
(April to September)
Juice of 1 lemon

1 quart (1 l) natural cloudy apple juice

For the herb bunch:
10 stalks bishop's goutweed
2 stalks ground ivy
2 stalks common balm
2 stalks mint (optional)
Bind the herbs into a bunch with
string, pour apple juice over the
bunch, add the juice of a lemon
and leave in the fridge, covered,
for 24 hours. Dilute 1:1 with
mineral water and drink chilled.

or: Filipendula *punch*
(Queen of the meadow summer punch)
5–10 queen of the meadow flowerheads in full bloom
2 stalks common balm

Juice of 1 lemon
1 quart (1 l) naturally cloudy apple juice

Pour the apple juice over the
flowers, add the juice of a lemon,
and leave in the fridge, covered,
for 24 hours. Dilute 1:1 with
mineral water and drink chilled.

CHILDREN'S ILLNESSES

Children suffer particularly frequently from colds, stomach aches, flatulence, infections of the urinary tract, rashes, injuries, insomnia, anxiety, headaches and travel sickness.

Infectious diseases such as measles, scarlet fever, chickenpox, mumps, rubella, etc. should always be treated by a doctor. Herbs can, however, help to alleviate the accompanying symptoms. Please take note of the advice on page 272 as to dosage. Ready-made products, which often contain alcohol (used for extraction), should be given to children only in exceptional cases or only be used externally (e.g. spirit of balm).

The teas, often refused by children because of the unaccustomed or unpleasant flavour, are best sweetened with honey.

Colds, influenza, runny nose, middle ear infections

Children, especially those of nursery and school age, are particularly susceptible to colds and related diseases. This means that strengthening the immune system by exercise in the open air, a varied diet rich in vitamins and additionally supported by various preparations (such as coneflower) is of the foremost importance.

With influenza, about 90 per cent of cases do not require antibiotics. Elder or linden flower tea (or both, blended), drunk as hot as possible

---

Remember: *A feverish child needs to stay in bed. Keep up the fluid levels by giving plenty of water, very dilute fruit juice and teas.*

Take care: *Chamomile can cause allergies. Never leave small children in the bath or let them inhale steam without supervision (due to danger of scalding). It is essential to consult a doctor in cases of viral influenza or fever that lasts for several days.*

---

in bed, is a good old home cure, as is hot elder-berry juice. A less well-known fever-reducing, pain-easing and anti-inflammatory remedy is queen of the meadow tea.

Tips:
To fight a cold, use:
- Decongestant and anti-inflammatory teas that also reduce coughing (see page 274), gargles (see page 275 – but not for children younger than three)
- Steam baths (e.g. with dwarf mountain pine or pine)
- Inhalation (e.g. with chamomile)
- Poultices (e.g. for the throat or – to reduce inflammation – the calves)

Middle ear infections are caused by streptococcus, staphylococcus or pneumococcus bacteria. They often accompany colds and can be very painful and cause fever. The mucous membranes of the Eustachian tube (it joins the nose and mouth areas to the ear) swell and its secretions can no longer drain. The consequences can range from a ruptured eardrum to deafness and meningitis – which means the disease must be treated by a doctor!

Thyme and the old home remedy of onion juice – the essential oils have a warming effect and reduce inflammation – can ease the condition (see below).

Stomach ache, trapped wind, diarrhoea (see also page 276 ff.)

Children often suffer from stomach pains. The causes range from trapped wind, particularly prevalent in babies and toddlers, to too much snacking and indigestible foods, to psychological problems and anxieties, and to bacterial or viral infections.

Nausea and vomiting often accompany stomach pains. If the pains are cramp-like, mint tea, possibly blended with chamomile (but beware of allergies), can help. Diarrhoea in small children can be potentially fatal due to the high loss of fluids.

With diarrhoea, it is important to compensate for the loss of fluids. Do not offer children solid food until the symptoms have gone and start with a bland diet low in fibre based on porridge and rusks. In cases of severe attacks of vomiting and recurrent diarrhoea the doctor must be consulted.

Tips:
To combat diarrhoea:
- A grated apple
- Tea made from dried bilberries
- For older children, dried bilberries, well chewed
- Powdered erect cinquefoil, stirred into apple puree, accompanied by black unsweetened tea
- A pinch of salt in drinks will compensate for the loss of minerals

Even babies and toddlers can have trapped wind and stomach pains eased by a bottle of fennel and caraway or chamomile tea, sweetened if required with fennel honey. A hot waterbottle also helps and a loving abdominal massage – always moving the hand clockwise – will be good for little children and larger ones.

Constipation is relatively rare in children. It can be treated with crushed flax seeds mixed into food. Adjusting the diet to include more fibre will also help, as will more exercise, mild enemas, or Epsom salts, Glauber's salts or Karlsbad salts (dissolved in a glass of water).

Inflammations of the urinary tract and bedwetting (see also page 286)
Girls are particularly prone to inflammations of the urinary tract due to their shorter urethra. The treatment is the same as for adults: warmth, plenty of fluids (tea, water) and treatment by a doctor.

For children who wet the bed, loving attention and emotional care are very important. These

children need love, emotional warmth and joy; they need to be helped to lose their fear. Yarrow and St John's wort tea are also helpful, but the latter can only be given during the day (one cup in the morning and in the afternoon) to very small children because of the calming, sedative effect. For older patients, capsules of St John's wort or juice are more effective (the concentration of active ingredients varies from one producer to another).

Rashes, cradle cap, neurodermitis, inflammations, burns (see also page 290)
Cradle cap in infants takes the form of yellowish-red, seeping, subsequently crusted scales on the head, chest and genitalia. It is best treated as part of a daily hygiene routine with

The juicy fruits of the elder can be used in many ways, e.g. for juice, puree and jelly.

Beware of allergic reactions to treatments (often recommended) with chamomile and marigold.
In impetigo (impetigo contagios), little blisters form which then burst and develop honey-yellow crusts. The high danger of contagion means that this disease must be treated by a doctor.

Exercise in the fresh air and in the countryside – whether playing sports or games or, as here, helping to harvest flax seeds – will help prevent many diseases.

emollient and moisturizing care products. Cradle cap, also known as atopic eczema, atopic dermatitis or *Neurodermitis atopica*, may persist and lead to unpleasant skin changes on the face and at the joints up until adulthood, and is often combined with an excruciating itch, hay fever and bronchial asthma. Poultices using pansy, white deadnettle and American witch hazel, and applying mullein or borage oil, will help the itching. Clinical trials have shown that mullein arrests the process of inflammation and can also be used to treat neurodermitis and herpes. Diets – with gluten-free foods such as buckwheat (see page 126) – are often necessary, and these should be discussed with the doctor supervising treatment.

Eye inflammations (see also page 290)

Conjunctivitis may be caused by drafts, dust, salt, chlorinated water, and pollen and animal hair allergies, as well as viruses or bacteria. Its symptoms are burning, reddened and itching eyes, watering eyes, a yellowish secretion and sensitivity to light.

Compresses with eyebright ease the symptoms.

If the symptoms persist for more than 48 hours, please consult an opthalmologist or a paediatrician.
*Take care: in diseases such as rubella or measles a doctor **must** be consulted. The consequences of no treatment or the wrong treatment may even extend to blindness.*

Teething

It is often very painful for infants when milk teeth start poking their way out of the gums. Anti-inflammatory and analgesic plants can help here, such as chamomile, geum (cloveroot), or marshmallow or 'violet' root. As well as roots to chew, chilled teething rings, painting the gums with tincture of chamomile, cold chamomile or sage tea can help. Older children can also use chamomile or sage gargles (see page 275).

Nosebleeds (see also page 291)

These are often caused by injury to the blood vessels – for example, by toys, blows or simply picking the nose.

Cuts, bruises, sprains, insect bites and stings (see also page 294)

Grazes, cuts, bruises, sprains, insect bites and stings are so common where children are concerned that it is important to be prepared to give first aid quickly anywhere and at any time. Among the first aid plants that grow in every meadow are the plantain species, just as helpful in treating insect bites as they are small bleeding cuts or the rash resulting from contact

with nettles. Daisies, sorrel and dock are also widespread. Marigold, oregano and coneflower have a wound-cleansing action, and marigold, American witch hazel and chamomile ointments have a healing effect. Poultices soaked either in a tea infusion or tincture (e.g. arnica flowers, St John's wort, silverweed, comfrey) can help, as can comfrey salve or oil of St John's wort.

Beware of allergies to asterids such as chamomile or arnica.

Nausea, vomiting, travel sickness, sleep disorders, anxiety, headaches

Even schoolchildren can suffer from typical stress symptoms such as nausea, sleep disorders, anxiety, fear and headaches, whether because they are under strain, surrounded by too many stimuli or suffer from family problems, poor diet, lack of exercise or misuse of alcohol and drugs.

Tip:
For nausea, vomiting, travel sickness:
- 1 sugar cube drizzled with tincture of lavender, common balm, mint or valerian

If nausea and vomiting persist for a long period of time, common balm tea or a tea blend will help, but a doctor must then definitely be consulted.

For occasional headaches, insomnia, anxiety, and fear, calming, relaxing and antispasmodic remedies such as St John's wort, common balm, lavender, valerian, or mint will help, whether in the form of teas, tincture, oil or baths. It is better to avoid products containing alcohol, such as spirit of balm (Melissengeist).

If the symptoms occur more frequently, the causes need to be established with medical help.

➤ *What medicinal plant for what symptoms?*
An aid to selection

| Children's illnesses | Important medicinal plants | | | | |
Disease	Yarrow *Achillea millefolium* ➤ page 50	Arnica *Arnica montana* ➤ page 53	Marigold *Calendula officinalis* ➤ page 59	Caraway *Carum carvi* ➤ page 200	Chamomile *Chamomilla recutita* ➤ page 60
Colds, susceptibility to infection					X
Middle ear infection					
Stomach ache, trapped wind	X			X	X
Nausea, vomiting, travel sickness					
Bedwetting	X				
Skin inflammations	X	X	X		X
Insect bites and stings		X			
Burns			X		X
Eye inflammations					X
Cuts, bruises, sprains	X	X	X		X
Headaches					
Sleep disorders, fear, anxiety					
Uses, notes	Tea, juice; allergies possible	Ointment, tincture; allergies possible	Ointment, tincture, poultices	Tea, oil; allergies possible	Tea, drops, oil; allergies possible

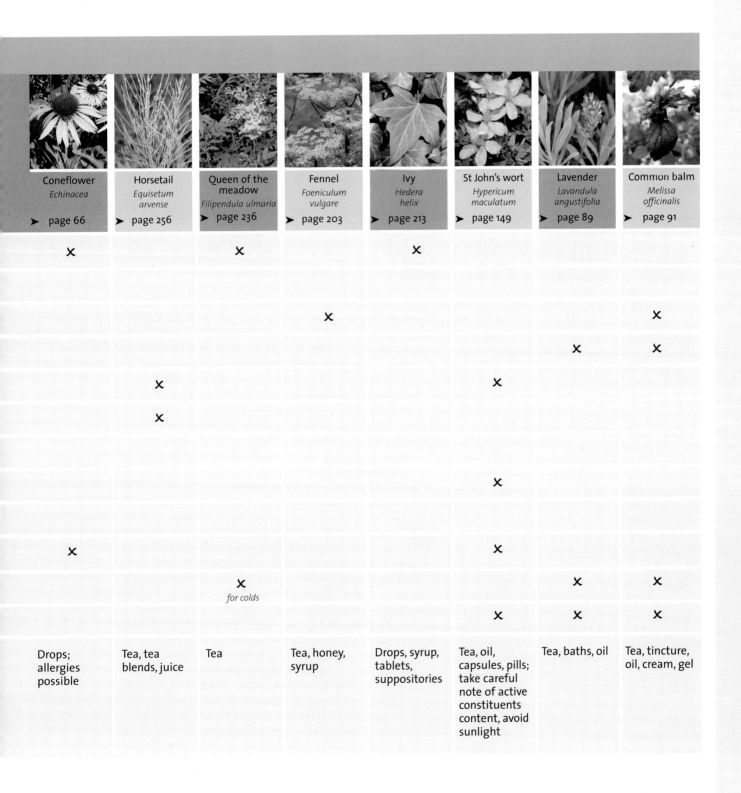

	Coneflower *Echinacea* ➤ page 66	Horsetail *Equisetum arvense* ➤ page 256	Queen of the meadow *Filipendula ulmaria* ➤ page 236	Fennel *Foeniculum vulgare* ➤ page 203	Ivy *Hedera helix* ➤ page 213	St John's wort *Hypericum maculatum* ➤ page 149	Lavender *Lavandula angustifolia* ➤ page 89	Common balm *Melissa officinalis* ➤ page 91
	✗		✗		✗			
				✗				✗
							✗	✗
		✗				✗		
		✗						
						✗		
	✗					✗		
			✗ *for colds*				✗	✗
						✗	✗	✗
	Drops; allergies possible	Tea, tea blends, juice	Tea	Tea, honey, syrup	Drops, syrup, tablets, suppositories	Tea, oil, capsules, pills; take careful note of active constituents content, avoid sunlight	Tea, baths, oil	Tea, tincture, oil, cream, gel

Continued on page 310

➤ *What medicinal plant for what symptoms?*
An aid to selection

Children's illnesses	Important medicinal plants (continued from page 309)				
Disease	Mint *Mentha* ➤ page 92	Anise *Pimpinella anisum* ➤ page 210	Narrowleaf plantain *Plantago lanceolata* ➤ page 105	Sage *Salvia officinalis* ➤ page 96	Elder *Sambucus nigra* ➤ page 111
Colds, susceptibility to infection		✗	✗	✗	✗
Middle ear infection					
Stomach ache, trapped wind	✗				
Nausea, vomiting, travel sickness	✗				
Bedwetting					
Skin inflammations			✗		
Insect bites and stings			✗		
Burns			✗		
Eye inflammations			✗		
Cuts, bruises, sprains			✗		
Headache	✗				
Sleep disorders, fear, anxiety					
Uses, notes	Oil for headaches; take care with babies and small children	Tea, essential oil	Tea, juice, drops, syrup; allergies possible	Tea, baths, sweets	Tea, juice, gargle

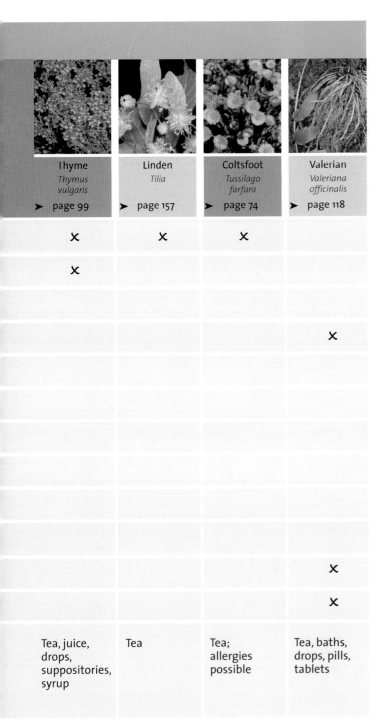

Thyme *Thymus vulgaris* ➤ page 99	Linden *Tilia* ➤ page 157	Coltsfoot *Tussilago farfara* ➤ page 74	Valerian *Valeriana officinalis* ➤ page 118
✗	✗	✗	
✗			
			✗
			✗
			✗
Tea, juice, drops, suppositories, syrup	Tea	Tea; allergies possible	Tea, baths, drops, pills, tablets

RECIPES

For stomach ache, trapped wind
Tea blend
one part each of anise, caraway, coriander, fennel, angelica root
or:
one part each of anise, fennel, coriander, caraway
or:
one part mint or fennel
one part caraway (crushed seeds)

For bedwetting
Tea blend:
four parts narrowleaf plantain
three parts erect cinquefoil
two parts horsetail
Preparation: *Pour boiling water over one teaspoonful per cup, allow to infuse for 20 minutes, take three tablespoons three times a day*
or:
St John's wort: for small children, one cup of tea in the morning and afternoon; for school-age children, pills or capsules

For sleep disorders, anxiety, colds
Pine, dwarf mountain pine bath
Preparation: *Place 18–35 oz (500 g–1 kg) pine needles and shoots in 5 quarts (5 l) of water, bring to the boil slowly, allow to infuse for 5–10 minutes, strain, and add to the bath water (only from 3 years onwards)*

For diarrhoea
Erect cinquefoil: stir a small pinch into apple puree or grated apple and give over the course of the day

For teething children
Marshmallow or 'violet' root to chew

For burns, bruises, sprains
St John's wort; apply oil
or: *Plantain: poultice with the juice of crushed plantain leaves*
or: *Poultice with plantain leaves*
Preparation: *Place one to two teaspoonfuls per cup in cold water, bring to the boil, strain*

To calm, for sleep disorders, anxiety, stomach ache, travel sickness
Common balm: alcohol-free solution, 10–15 drops on a lump of sugar

For middle ear infection
Onion: wrap a finely chopped onion in a muslin bag (or a diaper), warm over steam and place on the ear

Contents

Bibliography

Bach, Edward & Judy Ramsell Howard (Random House: 2005) – *The Essential Writings of Dr. Edward Bach: The Twelve Healers and Other Remedies and Heal Thyself.*

Balch, Phyllis A. (Avery: 2002) – *Prescription for Herbal Healing: An Easy-to-Use A–Z Reference to Hundreds of Common Disorders and Their Herbal Remedies.*

Balch, Phyllis A. (Avery: 2006) – *Prescription for Nutritional Healing, 4th edn: A Practical A-to-Z Reference to Drug-Free Remedies Using Vitamins, Minerals, Herbs & Food Supplements.*

Bisset, Norman Grainger & Max Wichtl (Duetscher Apotheker Verlag: 1997) – *Herbal Drugs and Phyto-pharmaceuticals: Handbook for Practice on a Scientific Basis.*

Boericke, William (Kessinger Publishing: 2004) – *A Compend of the Principles of Homeopathy As Taught by Hahnemann and Verified by a Century of Clinical Application.*

Boericke, William & Oscar E. Boericke (South Asia Books: 2003) – *Pocket Manual of Homeopathic Materia Medica.*

Brill, Steve (Harper Paperbacks: 1994) – *Identifying and Harvesting Edible and Medicinal Plants in Wild (and Not So Wild) Places.*

Burckhardt, Jacob (Dover Publications: 2002) – *History of Greek Culture.*

Burckhardt, Jacob (St Martin's Griffin: 1999) – *The Greeks and Greek Civilization.*

Chevallier, Andrew (Dorling Kindersley: 2000) – *Encyclopedia of Herbal Medicine: The Definitive Home Reference Guide to 550 Key Herbs with All Their Uses As Remedies for Common Ailments.*

Couplan, François (McGraw Hill: 1998) – *The Encyclopedia of Edible Plants of North America.*

Crow, Tis Mal (Book Publishing Company: 2000) – *Native Plants, Native Healing.*

Dahl, Jürgen (Timber Press: 2004) – *The Curious Gardener.*

Dobat, Klaus & Werner Dressendorfer (Taschen: 2001) – *Leonhart Fuchs: The New Herbal of 1543.*

Duke, James A. (Rodale Books: 1999) – *The Green Pharmacy: New Discoveries in Herbal Remedies for Common Diseases and Conditions from the World's Foremost Authority on Healing Herbs.*

Duke, James A. & Steven Foster (Houghton Mifflin: 1999) – *A Field Guide to Medicinal Plants and Herbs of Eastern and Central North America* (Peterson Field Guides).

Earleywine, Mitch (Oxford University Press, USA: 2005) – *Understanding Marijuana: A New Look at the Scientific Evidence.*

Farmer-Knowles, Helen (Gaia: 2007) – *The Garden Healer: Natural Remedies from Flowers, Herbs and Trees.*

Gillman, Jeff (Timber Press: 2006) – *The Truth about Garden Remedies: What Works, What Doesn't and Why.*

Gladstar, Rosemary (Storey Publishing: 2001) – *Family Herbal: A Guide to Living Life with Energy, Health and Vitality.*

Green, James (Crossing Press: 2000) – *The Herbal Medicine Maker's Handbook: A Home Manual.*

Green, James (Crossing Press: 2007) – *The Male Herbal: Health Care for Men and Boys.*

Hahnemann, Samuel; ed. Richard Hughes (B. Jain Publishers: 2003) – *Materia Medica Pura.*

Hanson, Bryan (Haworth Press: 2005) – *Understanding Medicinal Plants: Their Chemistry and Therapeutic Action.*

Heatherley, Ana Nez (The Lyons Press: 1998) – *Healing Plants.*

Heiser, Charles B. (Timber Press: 2003) – *Weeds in My Garden: Observations on Some Misunderstood Plants.*

Hoffmann, David (Healing Arts Press: 2003) – *Medical Herbalism: The Science Principles and Practices of Herbal Medicine.*

Homer (Penguin Classics: 2006) – *The Odyssey.*

Johnson, Hugh (Crescent: 1990) – *Hugh Johnson's Encyclopedia of Trees.*

Jones, Susan Smith (Hay House: 2007) – *The Healing Power of Nature Foods.*

Lewin, Louis (Park Street Press: 1998) – *Phantastica: A Classic Survey on the Use and Abuse of Mind-Altering Plants.*

Longe, Jacqueline (ed.) (Thomson Gale: 2004) – *Gale Encyclopedia of Alternative Medicine.*

Mabey, Richard (Fireside: 1998) – *The New Age Herbalist: How to Use Herbs for Healing, Nutrition, Body Care and Relaxation.*

Mars, Brigitte (Basic Health Publications: 2007) – *The Desktop Guide to Herbal Medicine.*

Moldenke, Harold N. & Alma L. Moldenke (Kegan Paul International: 2002) – *Plants of the Bible* (Kegan Paul Library of Religion & Mysticism).

Mowrey, Daniel (McGraw Hill: 1986) – *Scientific Validation of Herbal Medicine.*

Murray, Michael T. & Joseph Pizzorno (Three Rivers Press: 1997) – *Encyclopedia of Natural Medicine*, revised 2nd edn.

Murray, Michael T. (Gramercy: 2004) – *The Healing Power of Herbs: The Enlightened Person's Guide to the Wonder of Medicinal Plants.*

Pengelly, Andrew (CABI Publishing: 2004) – *The Constituents of Medicinal Plants: An Introduction to the Chemistry and Therapeutics of Herbal Medicine.*

Plaitakis, Andreas & Roger C. Duvoisin (1983) – *Homer's moly identified as Galanthus nivalis L. Physiologic antidote to stramonium poisoning.* Clinical Neuropharmacology 6: 1–5.

Rätsch, Christian (Park Street Press: 2005) – *The Encyclopedia of Psychoactive Plants: Ethnopharmacology and Its Applications.*

Roth, Lutz (John Wiley & Sons Ltd: 1995) – *Roth Collection of Natural Products Data: Concise Descriptions and Spectra.*

Rudd, Carol (Element Books: 1998) – *Flower Essences: An Illustrated Guide.*

Rudd, Carol (Element Books: 2000) – *The Complete Illustrated Guide to Flower Remedies.*

Schauenberg, Paul & Ferdinand Paris (Lutterworth Press: 2001) – *Complete Guide to Medicinal Plants.*

Scheffer, Mechthild (Healing Arts Press: 2001) – *The Encyclopedia of Bach Flower Therapy.*

Schultes, Richard Evans, Albert Hofmann & Christian Rätsch (Healing Arts Press: 2001) – *Plants of the Gods: Their Sacred, Healing and Hallucinogenic Powers.*

Seamon, David & Arthur Zajonc (eds) (State University of New York Press: 1998) – *Goethe's Way of Science: A Phenomenology of Nature.*

Steiner, Rudolf (Steiner Books: 2000) – *Nature's Open Secret: Introduction to Goethe's Scientific Writings.*

Sumner, Judith (Timber Press, 2000) – *The Natural History of Medicinal Plants.*

Sumner, Judith (Timber Press: 2004) – *American Household Botany: A History of Useful Plants, 1620–1900.*

Tierra, Michael (Pocket: 1998) – *The Way of Herbs.*

Tillman, Jon, Kevin Hudson, Susan Holden & Dan Wolf (Astrolog Publishing House: 2003) – *The Ultimate Guide to Health from Nature: Vitamins, Minerals, Herbal Remedies, Bach Flower Remedies, and Aromatherapy Essential Oils.*

Van Wyk, Ben-Erik & Michael Wink (Timber Press: 2004) – *Medicinal Plants of the World.*

Von Bingen, Hildegard (Beacon Press: 2002) – *Hildegard's Healing Plants: From Her Medieval Classic Physica.*

Wardwell, Joyce A. (Storey Publishing: 1998) – *The Herbal Home Remedy Book: Simple Recipes for Tinctures, Teas, Salves, Tonics and Syrups.*

Williams, Jude (Llewellyn Publications: 2002) – *Jude's Herbal Home Remedies: Natural Health, Beauty & Home-Care Secrets.*

Wood, Matthew (North Atlantic Books: 1997) – *The Book of Herbal Wisdom: Using Plants as Medicines.*

Zhu, Yi-Zhun, Benny K. H. Tan, Boon-huat Bay & Chang-Hong Liu (eds) (World Scientific Publishing Company: 2007) – *Natural Products: Essential Resources for Human Survival.*

Ailments and medical complaints by keyword

Latin index

English index

Picture credits

All photos from Botanik-Bildarchiv Laux, Biberach, except:

Corbis: 10 Christel Gerstenberg, 11 Corbis (t.), Corbis Sygma (b.), 12 Charles & Josette Lenars (t.), 13 Archivo Iconografico, S.A., 17 Bettmann, 18 Krause, Johansen / Archivo Iconografico, S.A. (t.), 19 Stapleton Collection, 20 Stapleton Collection (l.), Michael Nicholson (r.), 21 Bettmann, 23 Stephanie Maze (l.), Bettmann (r.), 24 Tony Wharton; Frank Lane Picture Agency, 25 Bob Krist (t.), Kelly-Mooney Photography (b.), 26 Archivo Iconografico, S.A. (l.), Chris Hellier (r.), 27 Jodi Hilton, 33 Andrew Brookes, 37 Ford Smith, 38 David Aubrey (l.), Klaus Hackenberg/zefa (r.), 270/71 Trinette Reed/zefa, 294 Steve Prezant, 299 Ute Kaiser/zefa

Getty Images: 12 Hulton Archive (m.), 16 Hulton Archive (l.), Kean Collection (r.)

Hecker: 260 (Fucus vesiculosus, Laminaria spec.)

Dr. Ute Künkele: 15 (b.), 18, 22, 62 (t.), 66, 69, 80, 84 (t.), 91 (l.), 113 (t.), 115, 140, 150, 164 (b.), 165 (t.), 174 (t.r.) , 174 (b.l.), 175 (b.), 216, 224 (b.), 238 (l.), 253 (t.), 256 (t.), 279, 280 (allium sativum), 281 (silybum marianum), 284 (allium sativum), 286, 293 (melissa officinalis), 296 (melissa officinalis), 300 (allium sativum), 301 (melissa officinalis), 303 (echinacea angustifolia), 303 (echinacea angustifolia, hippophae), 309 (echinacea angustifolia, melissa officinalis)

Till R. Lohmeyer: 70 (t.), 78, 88 (t.), 100 (t.), 113 (t.), 119 (t.), 155 (m.), 156, 171 (r.), 204 (l.), 257 (m.), 297 (salix alba)

t = top
b = bottom
m = middle
l = left
r = right

Acknowledgements

This book would not exist if several lovely fellow human beings had not selflessly supported us in our work. Wolfgang Lohmeyer (Taching am See), Christel Rost (Tittmoning) and Ursula Weiß (Altenmarkt) helped us with the research and editing. Sincere thanks are given to them.

Copyright © 2007 Parragon Books Ltd
Queen Street House
4 Queen Street
Bath BA1 1HE, UK

Production: ditter.projektagentur GmbH
Project coordination: Michael Ditter
Design, layout and composition: Sabine Vonderstein
Lithography: Klaussner Medien Service GmbH
Designers: Kim Caspary, Dennis Kreibich
English edition produced by: Cambridge Publishing Management Ltd
Translation: Susan James and Mo Croasdale
Editing: Juliet Mozley
Proofreading: Penny Isaac

ISBN: 978-1-4054-9549-3

Printed in China